Texas Reporter, Texas Radical

The Writings of Journalist Dick J. Reavis

"There has never been a Texas journalist like Dick Reavis. His self-described 'lack of refinement' has reliably guided him to stories about every sort of outcast, from revolutionaries to the criminally insane to the doomed members of an apocalyptic cult. He writes about these people with matter of fact empathy, from deep inside their worlds, never judging, never sentimentalizing or showboating. This book is an important record of a unique and courageous voice."

—STEPHEN HARRIGAN, *NEW YORK TIMES* BESTSELLING AUTHOR
BIG WONDERFUL THING &
THE LEOPARD IS LOOSE

"Dick Reavis's career in journalism has spanned decades and covered some of the most consequential social movements in modern history, both in Texas and across the nation. His most keen observations, his most thoughtful analysis, and his most hard-hitting investigations are collected in this remarkable volume."

—ELADIO B. BOBADILLA, PHD, ASSISTANT PROFESSOR OF HISTORY
ABC NEWS EXPERT ON U.S. LATINX AND
IMMIGRATION POLITICS

"My friend Dick Reavis has the soul of a poet. Everything he has written is a work of literary merit, as this fine collection of his political writing demonstrates. There's an urgency to his work that makes it compelling. Plus he's been a first-hand witness to (and at times a participant in) significant radical drama. Therefore these accounts have historic value. *Texas Reporter, Texas Radical* is a first-rate work by a first-rate writer."

—W.K. (KIP) STRATTON, AUTHOR OF *THE WILD BUNCH,*
LOS ANGELES TIMES BESTSELLER

"Dick J. Reavis, who survived a head-on collision while on his motorcycle, is one of the toughest writers Texas has ever produced. He's also one of the best. This treasury of his fearless, sharp-eyed reporting brings previously marginalized people roaring to life."

—STEVEN L. DAVIS, WITTLIFF COLLECTIONS CURATOR
PAST PRESIDENT, TEXAS INSTITUTE OF LETTERS

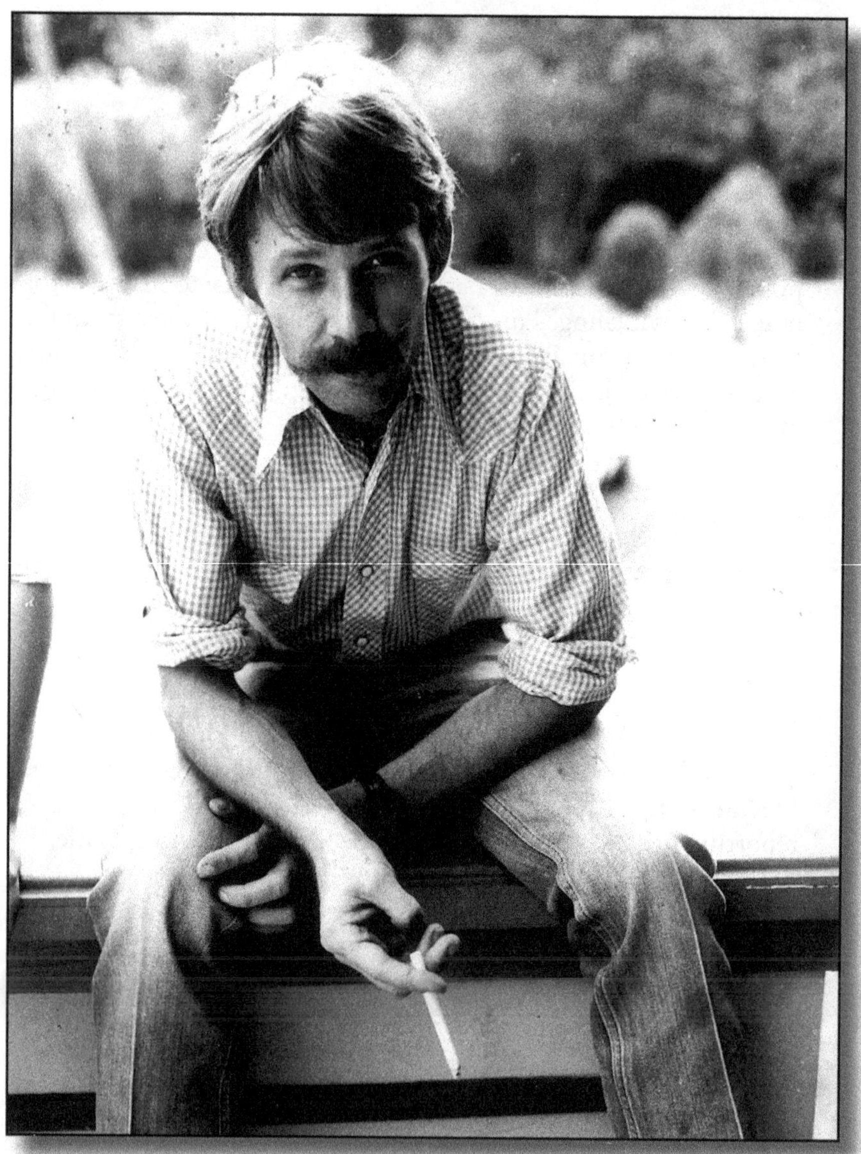

Dick J. Reavis in Galveston circa 1981. Photographer: Janice Rubin. Image courtesy of the Wittliff Collections

Texas Reporter Texas Radical

The Writings of Journalist

Dick J. Reavis

Compiled and Introduced by
Michael Demson

★trp
Texas Review Press
Huntsville, Texas
www.texasreviewpress.org

Copyright © 2022 Michael Demson and Dick J Reavis
All Rights Reserved
Library of Congress Cataloging-in-Publication Data
Names: Reavis, Dick J., author. |
Demson, Michael, ed., writer of introduction
Title: Texas reporter, Texas radical : the writings of American journalist, Dick Reavis / Collected and Introduced by Michael Demson.
Description: First edition. | Huntsville, Texas : Texas Review Press, [2022]
Includes bibliographical references and index.
Identifiers: LCCN 2021058203 (print) | LCCN 2021058204 (ebook)
ISBN 9781680032260 (paperback) | ISBN 9781680032277 (ebook)
Subjects: LCSH: Texas–Miscellanea. | Texas–Politics and government–20th century. | Texas–Politics and government–21st century. | Texas–Social conditions–20th century. | Texas–Social conditions–21st century. | Texas–Emigration and immigration–Political aspects. | Reavis, Dick J. Journalists–Texas–Biography. | Civil rights workers–Texas–Biography.
Classification: LCC F386.5 .R43 2022 (print) | LCC F386.5 (ebook)
DDC 976.4/064–dc23/eng/20220222
LC record available at https://lccn.loc.gov/2021058203
LC ebook record available at https://lccn.loc.gov/2021058204
FIRST EDITION
Front cover photo: Will Van Overbeek
Printed and bound in the United States of America

★trp

The University Press of SHSU
Huntsville, Texas 77341
texasreviewpress.org

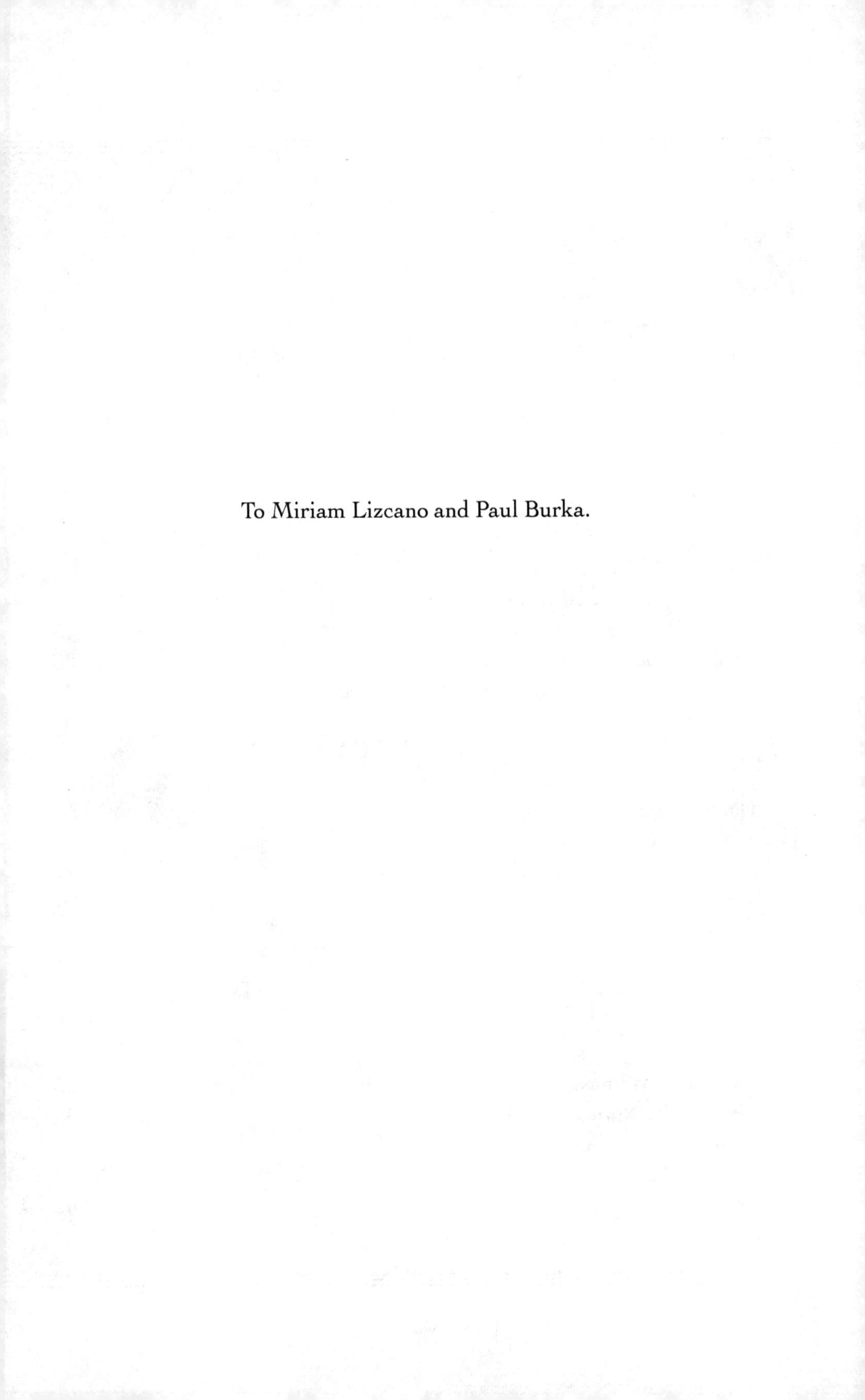

To Miriam Lizcano and Paul Burka.

Contents

The 1990s

The 2000s

The 2010s

List of Illustrations

Introduction: Doing Reavis Justice

by Michael Demson

Writing about Texas, Oklahoma, Mexico, and Texan-Mexican relations for over four decades, Dick J. Reavis (his father, Everett Richard Reavis was also a writer known as Dick Reavis) is one of the most poignant political voices of Texas. Not as a politician—though his writings are infused with politics—but as a candid, unsentimental, probing reporter and nonfiction writer, the kind of journalist this country urgently needs today. At a time when the United States of America has become so polarized in its politics, when everything has become politicized, when the once-esteemed practice of journalism has been sorely re-branded "the media," when news reports are now assumed to be so biased they are either in favor of a cause or perpetrators of "fake news"—it is vital that we return to reading writers who have set a precedent or doing justice to the truth, who found a way (in their own beleaguered times) to listen to, and report on, and be read by, people on all sides of these ever-deepening sociopolitical divides. What better place to find this just and fiercely independent voice than in a controversial borderland like Texas?—where the word "radical" has always been a milder pejorative—for left *and* right, red *and* blue—for those crazy neighbors down the road, bless their hearts. Dick J. Reavis was this sort of radical reporter—the Texas kind.

Author of well over a hundred articles, Reavis also worked as a features author, staff writer, and editor across the state of Texas. He wrote for the *San Antonio Express-News, Fort Worth Star-Telegram, Dallas Observer, Texas Observer, San Antonio Light,* and *Texas Monthly.* He published book-length investigations into Mexican political culture, the harsh realities that face illegal immigrants in Texas, the Waco siege of the Branch Davidians in 1993, and the plights of day-laborers, as well as memoirs of his life as a civil rights activist. Late in his career he accepted a faculty position as Professor of Journalism at North Carolina State University, but he has retired now, and as always, he returned to Texas.

Throughout his award-winning career, Reavis consistently wrote about the lives of everyday Texans, always challenging prevailing political assumptions. It was precisely this commitment that prompted him to investigate the federal government's siege of the Branch Davidians in 1993 outside of Waco, Texas, when all other reporters had left. *The Ashes of Waco: An Investigation* (Simon & Schuster, 1995; Syracuse UP, 1998) shook the nation after its publication and Reavis was called before a House committee in Washington, D.C. to review what occurred during the siege. If at first this book stirred confusion and controversy, it has nonetheless become the prevailing account of what transpired.

In part, the controversy over *The Ashes of Waco* was a result of its commitment to both good reporting and good journalism, its objectivity yet humanity. But even more, what came into question were Reavis's own commitments, and the complicated (and perhaps uncommon) stance Reavis took in the book.

As an experienced reporter, Reavis practiced strict adherence to collecting evidence, to reading and interpreting the records and details of the event, and to reporting the facts he found, even when these facts made powerful people and entities look bad.

As an experienced journalist at the peak of his powers, Reavis was committed to avoiding stereotypes—caricatures that painted people too simply: evil or good, deserving or undeserving of justice—instead his writing revealed their human complexity. The powerful scenes and background stories Reavis deployed in his writing humanized his subjects, evoking compassion from readers who perhaps had been headset on hating. In other words, Reavis's refusal to polarize and politicize the situation and people involved, and instead to humanize them, was the problem.

Political spokespersons and media personalities on both the left and right of American politics read Reavis as a radical, a fanatic for the opposition. In response he was blacklisted by publishing houses and news outlets. Thus in part, the controversy was also about society's misreading or reluctance to admit complexity, our preference for the "easy-read," for things to be black or white, our prejudice against gray areas, our hesitance to admit that real life situations are complicated. And, Reavis would argue, our societal fear of *conversion:* the fear of our own human susceptibility to be swayed by others. Many in society have come to believe it's safer to shun, silence, purposefully misread, hate, and even obliterate those who (we fear) might convert us. Reavis's seeming lack of fear, his openness to entering the Branch Davidian compound, to letting the people he interviewed speak about their beliefs, backgrounds, and experiences, including their views of the violent incident, and his decision to publish these interviews, confused some readers. Wasn't he afraid of being converted? Was he already a convert?

Those on the far right who claimed Reavis as one of their own, as an anti-government, gun-rights celebrity—touted interview clips from news stories and documentaries in which he denounced the FBI and ATF for their treatment of the Branch Davidians, or cited his memorably recalcitrant testimony during the 1995 Congressional hearings.

And yet those on the far left who did their research found that Reavis had always been a committed labor- and civil-rights activist, a self-identified lefty socialist. He was a unionist, a Wobbly, a Community (Communist) Party member, a self-proclaimed Maoist, and a member of the Students for a Democratic Society. He had been sentenced to six months (he served three weeks) for civil rights agitation in Alabama, and lived in the mountains of Mexico with agrarian guerrillas.

In time, however, Reavis's findings were accepted as the mainstream assessment of the events as they occurred, and Reavis's unconventional and humane approach to journalism proved to be admirable, as well as just. The Emmy-Award-winning, and Academy-Award-nominated, 1997 documentary, *Waco: The Rules of Engagement*, which adopted most of Reavis's theses, did much to canonize Reavis's book and to reclaim his good name.

This collection of Reavis's work strives to put *The Ashes of Waco* into the context of the greater body of his writings, which addressed such diverse and still relevant topics as: the Civil Rights Movement; the Wobblies; Mexican guerrillas; sex workers and their clientele; hospice nurses; Texas biker gangs; death-row inmates; the struggles of urban day laborers and of undocumented immigrants; the activities of the Klan; and the activities of fringe political and religious groups, to identify but a few.

It is the aim of this collection to do Reavis' work justice. And to offer its generous spirit to a new generation of readers and young journalists already life-weary from too much "isolated-at-home" screen time. To bring into focus Reavis's commitment to diverse voices, his commitment to all forms of social justice, and most importantly, his commitment to a fair and just journalism, *Texas Reporter, Texas Radical* offers the collected works of this critical, contemporary, Texas writer.

"The truth will out," or so the saying goes. But these days the truth seems more complicated than ever. To find anything like it, a new generation of young writers and journalists will need to turn their backs on mainstream's admiration of the "Easy Read" and set their own sights on the kind of challenging off-road adventure Reavis always pursued in his accounts of real life—the difficult real lives of the real people of his times. Even in his *Fodor's Guide to Texas* (1994; 1997; 2004), we encounter an author who appreciates the struggles of Texans, Mexicans, mainstream people, and those who live in the shadows of the mainstream.

The Making of a Storyteller: Family Tradition / Texas Tradition

Dick Johnson Reavis was born in 1945 in America's first co-operative hospital in Elk City, Oklahoma, on old Route 66, not far from the Texas panhandle.[1] The hospital had been founded fourteen years before by the Lebanese physician and socialist, Michael Abraham Shadid, who also had the backing of the Oklahoma Farmers' Union, which became a necessity when the Beckham County Medical Society, the Oklahoma Board of Medical Examiners, and the American Medical Association sought to have Shadid's license revoked, all lining up, one after another, to oppose his mission to bring socialized medicine to the sorely under-served local farmers and migrant community. With the support of the union, Shadid ultimately prevailed; his patient-owned hospital was established, and at the time of Reavis's birth it served the entire southwest region of the state.[2] Perhaps it is not entirely coincidental that today Reavis is a member of the Democratic Socialists of America, and that he continues to support Medicare for All.

Reavis's family had lived in this Oklahoma-Texas region for decades, mostly in the contested border counties claimed by Texas until 1896 (U.S. vs. Texas: Judicial Decree). The area was then decreed to be part of the Oklahoma Territory, which opened it to the 1898 "Land Grab." Oklahoma wouldn't receive statehood until 1907. Reavis knew his maternal grandparents into adulthood. Their influence on him can be hypothesized from their hardscrabble persistence, and the example such family stories must have set for his own aspirations.

His maternal grandfather, Clyde L. Johnson, had begun life as a farmer. For a spell he became a hardware dealer in Granite, until the Depression closed down everything. Then he went back to farming in Greer county with his wife, Mona. His daughter Kathleen, Reavis's mother, was born in 1918 on her father's farm, about a dozen miles from Lone Wolf, up the North Fork of the Red River, once the Texas side of the dividing line between Oklahoma and Texas. But Clyde would not be satisfied with the simple life of a farmer; soon thereafter he enrolled in college to become a teacher. He taught first in Lone Wolf and ultimately in nearby Carter, where he went on to become the superintendent of schools, also serving in a profession new to the world—ever since Henry Ford's iron horse rolled into town—as a driver's education instructor. During the Second World War, Reavis's mother enrolled in Southwestern State College of Diversified Occupations, now Southwestern Oklahoma State University, where she met Reavis's father. They were married in Willow, Oklahoma, but when her husband was shipped off to war she returned to her people, taking a teaching position in Retrop, a crossroads near Lone Wolf.

Lone Wolf was founded in 1901 after the opening of the Kiowa-Comanche-Apache Reservation, and then settled mostly by Romanian immigrants, reporting a population of 307. It had hardly grown by the mid-1940s when Reavis was born, and even as recently as the 2010 Census the population was listed as 438. A small agricultural town on the train line surrounded by wheat and cotton fields, Lone Wolf has never won much national attention. The man for whom the town was named, however, was notorious in his day. Kiowa Chief Guipago, or "Lone Wolf" (1843–1879), was renowned across south Oklahoma and north Texas. Reavis's mother told stories about having encountered Lone Wolf on more than one occasion, though it seems probable that it was his adopted son she met, "Lone Wolf the Younger" or Maymaydate, another warrior and prominent political figure in the region, who unlike "Lone Wolf the Elder" was still alive until 1923.

Guipago fought alongside Satanta, the last of the Kiowa's great War Chiefs, in countless territorial skirmishes, traveled all the way to Washington to negotiate with U.S. President Ulysses S. Grant for Satanta's release after his arrest in Texas, raided cattle north of Dallas with Satanta upon his release, and died as a result of his eventual incarceration in the Texas state prison system, just as Satanta did.[3] Satanta was imprisoned in the infamous Walls Unit, located in Huntsville, Texas, and in 1878 he allegedly committed suicide by plunging headfirst from a window. The U.S. Army sent Guipago and his raiders to Fort Marion in Florida to be incarcerated in its dungeon. When he contracted malaria in the dank conditions, they sent him back to his tribe where he died, a year after Satanta's death.

Such were the stories of the lands upon which Reavis spent his childhood.

Reavis's paternal grandfather, Everett Peyton Reavis, had been a Linotype operator at a daily newspaper in Shelbyville, Tennessee. After he married the printshop foreman's daughter, Mabel Gregory, he moved with her to Oklahoma, carting around a printing press on his truck, traveling from town to town in hopes of becoming a small-town editor and publisher—to not much avail. He died before Reavis was born, and Reavis's grandmother died when he was very young.

Dick's father, Everett Richard Reavis, attended college before the Second World War at Panhandle A&M, where he became editor of the school newspaper. In 1945, when Dick was born, his father was serving in Guam and the Philippines as a B-29 navigator. He stayed on in the Reserves until the 1950s, retiring a Major. When he returned from the war, Reavis's father went to Oklahoma State, where he returned to newspaper work, again editing the university's paper. Having served overseas with African Americans, he had little patience for segregation, and at the university he had some involvement with the Communist Party, though the Oklahoma Legislature had crafted a loyalty oath for all state employees. Not only was it an oath to defend the U.S. and Oklahoma Constitutions, but also employees had to swear that they were not, nor had been in the past five years, members of the Communist Party.[4] Reavis's father packed up the family and moved across the border to Texas, traveling from small town to small town, trying to become a small-town newspaper publisher, much as his father had before him.

Education, Social Justice, and Other Influences

Starting in the second grade, Dick worked paper routes until the age of twelve when he was put to work in the print shops of his father's newspapers, gaining respect for the hands-on production and design skills that print-workers needed to produce a newspaper, an important parts of publishing that many reporters or writers never grasp. He would draw upon these experiences the rest of his life.

By the eleventh grade, 1962–63, Dick had begun to participate in the Civil Rights Movement. His father had settled the family (for the moment) in Littlefield, Texas, a cotton town of about 5,000 people named after the Confederate-officer-turned-Texas-rancher, George Washington Littlefield, where Reavis and a friend from Littlefield High School campaigned to integrate a restaurant in town. His commitment to the Civil Rights Movement intensified in the ensuing years as he moved around the south and southwest, variously pursing an institutional college education as well as his passion for grassroots social justice work. In the fall semesters of 1963 and '64, he attended Texas Tech College in Lubbock, Texas, where he worked in the college print shop. He declined to print racist fraternity lyrics—instead, he joined the local chapter of the NAACP. In the summer of 1964, he moved on to the University of Arizona in Tuscon, and then Panhandle A&M College in Goodwell, Oklahoma during the spring of 1965. That summer he went to Alabama with the Southern Christian Leadership Conference (SCLC), and in the fall of 1965 he started at the University of Texas in Austin, where he joined the University of Texas Chapter of the Students for a Democratic Society (SDS).

In the summers of 1965 and 1966, Reavis lived in Demopolis, Alabama, where he joined the Demopolis Youth Organization, an educational initiative run by SCLC. He worked to register voters and organize boycotts. By March 28, 1966, the FBI had begun to follow his activities, opening a counterintelligence program file that would grow to be hundreds of pages in length.[5] In 2001, Reavis published a memoir of these summers and his experiences, *If White Kids Die: Memoirs of a Civil Rights Movement Volunteer*, extracts of which are included in this collection.

Reavis returned to Austin, completing his undergraduate degree in Philosophy in 1968 and became a regular contributor to *The Rag*, Austin's radical underground newspaper. During their fiftieth-year anniversary celebration (in 2018), founders of *The Rag* described its reporting in the late 1960s as driven by "rebellious political content." While Paul Buhle, the renowned cultural historian of the American Left, fondly reminisces: "*The Rag* covered a radical student movement, a growing antiwar movement, civil rights and [B]lack liberation, police repression, Chicano labor insurgencies, and gay liberation, forging important, long-lasting alliances. *The Rag* staff also wrote about rock 'n roll, the drug culture, arts and literature, the sexual revolution, and even food . . . and it was all seasoned with a heavy dose of Texas Humor."[6]

As much as Reavis investigated and reported on these various movements, he was also often caught up in them. The first article in this collection is one that Reavis wrote in 1967 for *The Rag* about his commitment to labor unions. In "The IWW: One Big Union: The Relevance of Anarchism," Reavis wrote about social and political issues he would continue to explore in later decades. For *The Rag,* he writes as an impassioned activist. In later articles, such as "Unionbusters" (*Texas Monthly,* June 1986), also included in this collection, he is twenty years older, more nuanced, and able to explore labor agitation from various perspectives with a confidence only long-term commitment to a movement can give.

By 1974, he had decided upon journalism as a career; he took a job at *Moore County News,* the paper owned by his father in Dumas, Texas. However, Reavis was already too much a man-of-the-world to be satisfied with smalltown life for long. Having experienced the underground Austin scene, having traveled the south, participating in radical social movements, Reavis soon found Dumas stifling; in 1977 he returned to the University of Texas at Austin, this time as a graduate student in Philosophy. Still freelancing, he had an article picked up by the *Texas Observer*:

"The Kickapoo: A Hut is Not a Home" (included in this collection)—launching him for the first time into magazine-writing. As he recounts in a previously unpublished "Autobiographical Sketch" (also included in this collection), the *Observer* article caught the attention of *Texas Monthly,* which published some more of his freelance reporting that year, but then Bill Broyles, editor of *Texas Monthly,* offered him the chance to write a feature. "The Smoldering Fire," a piece about Mexican guerrillas, was published in the *Monthly's* March 1978 issue.

That same year, Reavis published *Without Documents* (Condor Publishing Company, 1978), a book-length report on the realities that illegal immigrants from Latin America face in the United States. For it, Reavis had interviewed Mario Cantú in 1977, a San Antonio restaurateur and Chicano activist who was deeply involved in revolutionary activity in Mexico. He pursued that lead in 1978. In an unpublished memoir for *Texas Monthly*, Reavis discloses: "I knew something more about Mario, too, something nearly secret. He was buying guns and sending money to a guerrilla outfit in Mexico led by a Maoist peasant, Florencio "Güero" Medrano. I proposed to Broyles that I go to Mexico to write about those rebels and their patron. He liked the idea. I told him that I'd ask Cantú to authorize the trip and went to San Antonio to discuss the prospect."[7]

An agrarian guerrilla, Medrano led efforts in Oaxaca to seize lands from ranchers— Cantú was funding and sending him arms—in 1978, Cantú brought him Reavis.

Medrano did not live to see 1980, but Cantú became a lifelong friend. In 2018, Reavis contributed declassified FBI files on Cantú to the Mario Cantú Papers held in the Nettie Lee Bensen Latin American Collections at the University of Texas at Austin.

Reavis among *campesinos*, somewhere in Oaxara, 1977.
Photographer: Ramón Tianguis Pérez. Courtesy of Wittliff Collections.

From 1978 on, Reavis took a wide variety of assignments, delivering award-winning articles. He wrote his first "Reporter Column" for *Texas Monthly* during the summer of 1977, working as a freelancer until January 1979, when he was listed as contributing editor. He was first listed as an associate editor—a salaried position—in May 1981. He remained in that position until mid-1990.

One of his early assignments for *Texas Monthly* was to explore the world of Texas biker gangs. Even though he had not been a motorcyclist before, Reavis bought a Harley in order to ride with the Bandidos Motorcycle Club. He became an enthusiast; however on October 15, 1978, he was near-fatally hit by a drunk driver. His passion nonetheless continued unabated, and a flurry of writings and photographs from this time attest to it—here in this volume represented by his article "Never Love a Bandido" from *Texas Monthly*, May 1979.

More and more Reavis's approach and style set him apart from the other young journalists of his time, who were professing a different version of their generation's "new" journalism. For though Reavis's early writing coincided with the New Journalism movement of the 1960s and 1970s, and though he was clearly developing a style of journalism at *Texas Monthly* that shared much in common with the best of his New Journalist contemporaries, his distance—geographically, socially, economically and in important ways philosophically—from the movement's inner circle helped him avoid being caught up in the movement's worst features.

New Journalism emerged in the rebellious 1960s and '70s. Appearing in nationally regarded U.S. magazines (eg. *Esquire, Harpers, New York, Rolling Stone*), and channeled through the hip literary voices of its college-educated, often ivy-league, wealthy or upper-middle-class *creative writers*—as opposed to traditionally trained journalists or newspaper reporters who'd fought their way up through the ranks—New Journalism, like the generation that inspired it, was driven by its rebellion against the conventions and expectations required of serious journalists as well as novelists at the time. Tom Wolfe, Truman Capote, and Gay Talese are widely credited with initiating the movement, though it came to encompass many other well-known authors, such as Joan Didion, Norman Mailer, and Hunter S. Thompson. Most New Journalists quickly turned from writing journal articles to publishing book-length works. Known for their edgy subject matter (some critics claimed "trendy") and a narrative style of writing, (some critics claimed "too subjective" or "rambling") many within the New Journalists' inner circle are classified today as creative nonfiction writers more than reporters, and are credited with redefining nonfiction as a genre.

However, in his numerous lectures given over the decades following the movement, Tom Wolfe explains that his connection with journalism was formative and essential to his purposes at the time. A Yale graduate, jaded by academia and bored with bourgeois society and the literary world's restrictions, Wolfe became fascinated with the practices of small-time reporters, a life he had mostly read about in books: conducting on-foot investigations, logging notepads full of details and dates; the reporter's total immersion in the situation, pursuing leads down dark alleyways or through prison gates for face-to-face interviews. New Journalism was an attempt to combine "low-brow" newspaper reporting techniques with the "high-brow" literary, narrative conventions traditionally reserved for short stories and fiction, including: character development; situational exposition and dialogue; interviewee's thoughts (like main character's thoughts in fiction) presented as first-person narration; shifts of point-of-view; and plotted, sequential scenes. The techniques made for powerful reading experiences that transported the reader into the situation described, that seemed to feel more real or gritty or physical. And, as Wolfe has repeatedly claimed, *better* than the contemporary fiction of the time, because it was "all true." New Journalism proved to be capable of conveying deep emotion, evoking compassion, swaying opinions, and even ideological conversion. On the other hand, New Journalists were sometimes criticized for stretching the truth, fudging the facts, substituting stereotypes for observation, or letting their own flamboyant personalities overtake the voices and real situations of their subjects.

In a 2022 conversation with Reavis about the influence that New Journalism had (or didn't have) on his writing style, he recounted to me that in the early 1980s he had spent a day in Dallas with other contributors to *Texas Monthly,* all of whom were being filmed for a *Texas Monthly* television advertisement. A reporter among the onlookers, purportedly writing an article for a national journal about *Texas Monthly*, quizzed then-editor Greg Curtis, asking, "But, what does *Texas Monthly* do?" and Curtis said that several of the reporters, including Reavis, were doing New Journalism. However, Reavis admitted, "Later, I had to ask somebody what New Journalism was." In that same 2022 conversation with me, Reavis asserted that it was John Silas Reed, American journalist and communist activist—best remembered for his 1919 book *Ten Days that Shook the World,* about the October Revolution in Petrograd, Russia—who was the first practitioner of New Journalism.

Reavis resisted the trend, but he was also a man of his times. In his best pieces, unlike the New Journalism writers and Thompson's gonzo journalism to follow, Reavis quieted his personal voice to allow those of others to be heard—a strength most critics approved, but also a factor that played a roll in *The Ashes of Waco's* misreading. In his 1st-person works his voice may sound down-to-earth and easy, but even here his research is always startling in its depth, and his arguments are always carefully crafted and nuanced assessments of multifaceted social conflicts. His narratives, built in accumulated layers of complexity, turn unexpectedly while remaining forthright and honest in tone. He seems to delight in the paradoxes and contradictions inherent in every human conflict, while avoiding caricature, exaggeration, or satire. He is never condescending in tone. While he often picks subjects that others would avoid or dismiss as inconsequential—day laborers, sex workers, immigrants, criminals, fanatics—he eschews that which would prompt laughter at, or contempt of, his subjects. Once immersed in his stories, the suffering and humanity of the people Reavis profiles emerges; yes, he often writes about people outside the mainstream, but he places them squarely in their life situations, letting them explain their actions and motivations—as well as those forces they feel pressing upon their lives—in their own voices, often even letting them use their own humble and colloquial, or offensive and even violently misogynistic and racist words.

"Klan on the Ropes," included in this collection, is an example of the extremes to which Reavis was willing to go to allow interviewees their own voices. At the start of the 1980s Reavis was briefly hired by Rod Davis, then-editor of the *Texas Observer,* under the title Associate Editor. "All the full-time writers got that title;" Reavis claims today, "but since the *Observer's* early days, in the 1950s, it had always published 'polite liberal articles.'" Davis undoubtedly hoped Reavis's fresh journalistic approach would shake up the *Observers'* readership. Reavis accepted the position. At the time, Davis was at odds with the co-founder and owner-publisher, Ronnie Dugger. If Dugger was wary of Davis's left-leaning political views,

Reavis, Kreuz Market, circa 1981-1982. Photographer unknown. Image courtesy of the Wittliff Collections.

he was infuriated by Davis's decision to hire Reavis who, Dugger had been warned, was a political radical. Two pieces Reavis wrote for the *Observer* are included in this collection: "Unreliable Witness" from the July 25, 1980 issue, and "Klan on the Ropes" from the September 19, 1980 issue—one of the most risky articles Reavis had penned to date. "Klan" pushes Reavis's journalistic commitment to allow interviewees to speak for themselves to the limits of most editor's allowance, both then (in the 1980s) and today.

But be they white Christian Nationalists, or militant Mexican Socialists, Reavis refuses to reduce either to stereotypes or caricatures, offering instead his analysis of the ideological coherence, or supposed coherence, that produces their zealotry. To that end, most people in Reavis's stories are not geniuses, but representatives of a group of people who have adopted, and sometimes adapted, repressed, unpopular neglected, or marginalized ideologies. Even as he immerses himself in the language spoken by people who are bigoted and misogynistic, reading Reavis's articles collectively reveals the tremendous range and conflict of ideological perspectives active across all strata of American life; his writings demonstrate his commitment to fight against the hegemonic force of the mainstream that would reduce all to convention, a commitment that got him into some trouble.

Whether it was a direct result of Reavis's *Observer* articles or not, Dugger decided that both Rod Davis and Reavis were out, and the rupture within the *Texas Observer* drew national attention. *The Washington Post,* taking both sides at once, described the *Observer* as "one of the noble experiments in American Journalism, an underfunded, understaffed biweekly that has been a beacon for endangered liberals in Texas, and the scourge of a state legislature that has more often than not acted with cavalier disregard for the citizenry."[8]

In a recent email response to an earlier draft of this introduction, Reavis contradicted the mainstream depiction of the event, which he felt to be inaccurate on a number of counts; in his usual unbiased and humorous manner he writes,

> Davis and I did not "leave" the *Texas Observer*. Ronnie Dugger fired us both. He left a letter in the office telling us we were fired and we both left that day. The *Texas Observer* was liberal,

> always. Dugger's letter came with a statement that the *Texas Observer* was devoted to "peaceful and incremental" change. That was why he fired us. Plus Rod had refused to endorse a Presidential candidate in 1980, though when he hired me I didn't know as much. The word I got after my firing was that a certain, un-named, *Austin-American -Statesman,* political writer told him I was a Maoist, and Dugger believed him. I had been—ten years earlier—but that's beside the point. I had never met Dugger when Rod hired me, and didn't meet Dugger until a few years later.

It would be several years before Reavis would write for the *Observer* again. However, as his creative momentum continued to build, the 1980s were just as productive for Reavis as the late 1970s. Undaunted by his critics, he continued to pursue the important, controversial stories and taboo subjects avoided by the mainstream press.

According to the Wittliff Collection's overview of the Dick J. Reavis Papers, he published thirty-seven features for *Texas Monthly* over twelve years, in addition to publishing in other venues. In "Town Without Pity" which originally appeared in the May 1980 issue of *Texas Monthly,* Reavis explored, through numerous quickly shifting perspectives, the experiences of those who "visit," and those who live in, one of the many Mexican brothel districts existing along the Texas border since at least the early 1900s. Such communities, microcosms with their own rules, continue to reveal systemic and economic exploitation that perpetuates—through highly codified binary enactments of gender and desire—sexist, economic, racist, and nationalist interactions and aggressions. Today, Reavis's stance, in this 1980 article, is strangely prescient of the explosive debates among American feminists later in that decade over multiple issues concerning sexual activity and sexuality. The "Feminist Sex Wars" introduced ideas and language—through competing leftist vs. liberal and right-wing-radical ideologies—into the American vernacular years later in the mid-80s and 90s. Terms such as, "Pro-Sex," "sex-positive," "sex worker," and "anti-censorship," which focused on women's socioeconomic realities (leftist feminists) vs. condemnation of prostitution as "disempowering to women," (liberal and right-wing feminists) focused on increased "police-powers" and legislated "morality bans," all were unavailable or undiscussed concepts prior to feminists' coining.

However, Reavis, by his own admission, was not in 1980—is not today—and never has been interested in journalistic stories that promote a singular politicized or moralistic point of view, always wary of the tendency for ideas such as "political correctness" and "cancel culture" to be co-opted for accusations flung both right and left. Instead, "Town Without Pity" stands out as an example of Reavis's closest flirtation with New Journalism's most controversial literary techniques, his own presence as narrator and interviewer almost conflated with his Texas-boy characters, it reads almost like confessional or social-realist fiction, as the story of particular characters in a particular time and place, where Reavis's use of close third-person narration, sprinkled with free-indirect speech, allows the idiomatic qualities of his characters' words to tell the story—engaging, complicating, and forestalling the easy judgments his more polarized American readers might be tempted to make.

In the mid-1980s Reavis grew restless; using the itch to his advantage he embarked on a "National Tour of Texas," for *Texas Monthly*. Driving 103,000 miles in a Chevrolet Suburban—over every highway and farm-to-market road across the state—he wrote a series of fourteen articles in 1987, documenting his travels in a daily log book that he had stamped at post offices across the state, charting his travels on maps, and amassing a large collection of photographs and Texas postcards, all of which can be viewed at the Wittliff Collections online exhibition, *The National Tour of Texas: The Ultimate Texas Roadtrip*, which includes the *Texas Monthly* articles.[9]

When he concluded the tour, Reavis moved to Mexico for a year to work on what would become, *Conversations With Moctezuma: Ancient Shadows over Modern Life in Mexico* (William Morrow & Co., 1990), an account of some of the political realities that have plagued Mexicans for generations that Reavis wrote in 1st-person, a narrative technique he'd used periodically from the start of his career in both his memoir writing and articles, which in this case had the extra advantage of foregrounding (or making visible) his "I" subject-positioning as a not-Mexican in conversation with Mexican subjects who speak for themselves.

By the time he got back to the states Reavis no longer felt in step with *Texas Monthly*. He resigned—as always, following his convictions—picking up work alternately in Mexico and Texas as a correspondent in Monterrey (Mex.) for the *San Antonio Light*, and as a reporter for the *Dallas Observer*, shifting back and forth across the border, as if waiting for the next turn in his career

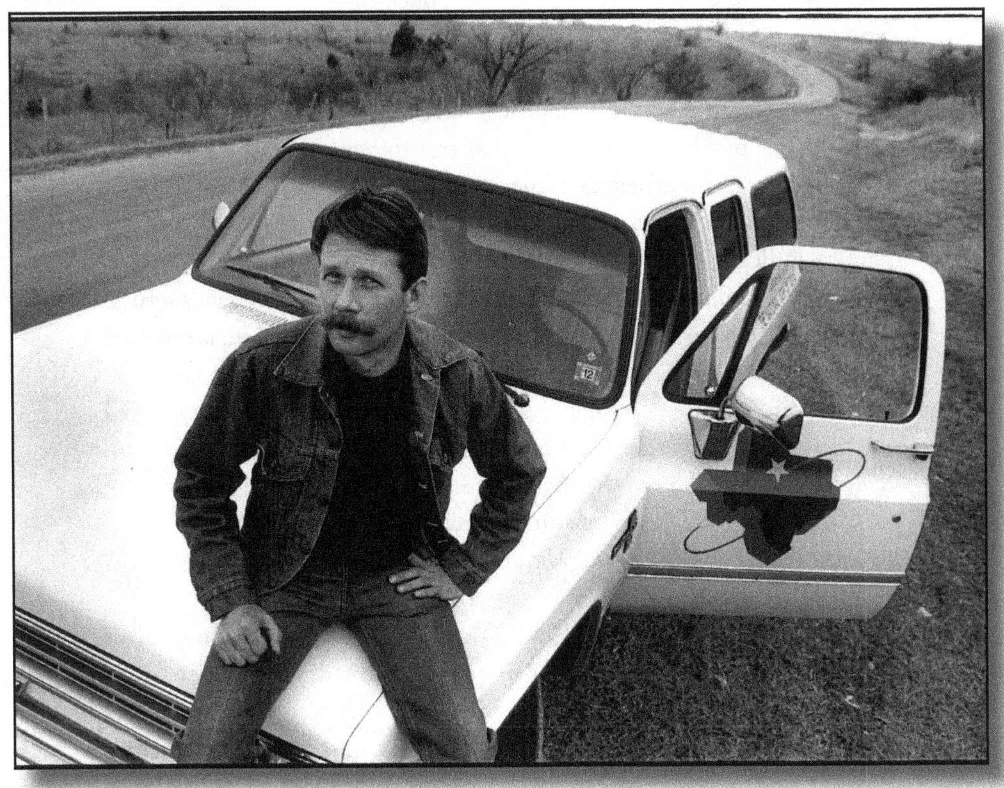

Reavis on his *National Tour of Texas*, Farm-to-Market Route 973, December 1986. Photographer: Will Van Overbeek. Image courtesy of the Wittliff Collections.

REASSESSING *THE ASHES OF WACO: AN INVESTIGATION*

The historical events that unfolded in 1993 at Mt. Carmel outside of Waco, Texas are now well-known: the failed raid by the Bureau of Alcohol, Tobacco, Fire Arms, and Explosives (ATF) on the Branch Davidian compound, during which four agents and six Davidians were killed;

the ensuing 51-day standoff, during which the FBI joined the ATF and then assumed command of the siege; and finally, the FBI's decision to force the residents out on April 19, resulting in the loss of seventy-two lives—including the life of David Koresh, the charismatic leader of the community—in a fire that consumed the entire compound. Waco has become the go-to example of the incommensurate and retaliatory violence with which the U.S. government and its police enforcement agencies can (and often do) reply to citizens or communities who refuse to comply.

Today, the government's violent response is the most searingly memorable feature of the Waco siege, even when weighed against the physical and psychological abuses that transpired in the compound. In 1993, however, the expected, American (mainstream, moderate, left *or* right) journalistic stance when reporting on potentially violent, armed, political radicals was to whitewash the government's actual violence and to demonize the Branch Davidian religious group members. Reavis's refusal to do so, his choice to let the facts, the record, and the individuals involved speak for themselves, ran contrary to the growing sentiment in the U.S., that the truth should be simple, and that only the facts that already served the bias of the consumer need be reported—a sentiment that was soon to become a demand met by social media's supply—that news reporting should be modified to fit consumers' particular polarized views.

As Reavis's 1995 book, *The Ashes of Waco: An Investigation*, has established, the historical events on and leading up to April 19 prove enduringly difficult to reconcile with any cultural and political narratives about life in America that profess simple truth, freedom or justice for its citizenry. The two chapters included here in "Selections from *The Ashes of Waco: An Investigation*," clarify two of Reavis' most significant themes and, at the same time, two of the most significant threats Reavis's book posed to American readers.

The first excerpt offers Koresh's rhetoric to the reader openly, bucking the irrational societal fear that a mere examination of radical ideas might cause a mass conversion of the reading public to Branch Davidian beliefs.

Reavis's research placed Koresh's rise to leadership in the context of his early rivalry with George Rodin, another leader at Mt. Carmel, revealing Koresh to be a member of a community with a complex theology stretching back for the better part of a century, not simply a monstrous cult leader.

The second excerpt carefully reviews the records of the authorities, the interviewees' responses, and the testimony of individuals on both sides of the compound walls, all of which called into question (and in fact, utterly contradicted) government accounts of what transpired, providing evidence that no other reporter in Texas, or in the nation, had dared to investigate or put in writing for assessment by the public.

Thus, *The Ashes of Waco* defies two unwritten taboos: 1) it introduces Americans to the people of Mt.Carmel as religious citizens with families, not as weaponized monsters—dispelling the bogeyman under the bed, the deep societal fear American's have of those who seem ideologically different, as well as the irrational fear of conversion to such ideas, and 2) it defies the U.S. government's accounts of what happened, raising questions for the reader about America's professed freedoms and liberties as well as wider questions about what any citizen's odds might be for receiving fair justice during times when the political pendulum has shifted away from one's party or beliefs.

The ensuing controversy and confusion over Reavis's stance as a result of his seeming openness to Branch Davidian viewpoints brought his journalistic methods and even his personal character into question. His methods of investigating, interviewing, reporting, and researching, along with his writing style, which throughout his career had often included an honest portrayal of his own culpability as a well-meaning, yet faulty, human immersed in a situation, had long included an understanding of the culpability of all humans in the inadvertent maintenance of the very systemic forces we hope to oppose. In this collection of his work, we see the ways Reavis's resistance to social injustice and his courage to hear out the "opposition," respecting, or at least allowing, differences of opinion, thought, and expression, could be co-opted by those with views counter to his own—those with racist, sexist, oppressive, and violent agendas. However, above all, we see his commitment to his readers, his courageous constant trust—never more evident than in his understated style, its refusal to sell the reader short, to "put the dots closer together," to proselytize, to provide political-correctness for the mere sake of avoiding "cancellation"—trusting that, given the facts, the context, and the interviewees' words, straight from the horse's mouth, his readers can, and will, sort the complications out for themselves.

AFTER *THE ASHES*

Exactly two years after the April 19, 1993 siege of the Branch Davidians' compound, on the second anniversary of the conflagration that ended the conflict outside Waco, Timothy McVey and Terry Nichols bombed the Alfred P. Murrah Building in Oklahoma City. McVey, who had driven down to witness the siege of Mt. Carmel in '93, would claim that the Oklahoma bombing in '95—which killed 168 people and injured more than 680 others—was his response to what happened in Texas.

Still embroiled in the controversy over *The Ashes of Waco's* political stance, it would have been understandable if Reavis had let his fear of further misreadings—the probable assumptions of "guilt by association" with the Oklahoma City right-wing radicals—keep him from addressing McVey's claim. But true to form, Reavis began a correspondence with the incarcerated McVey in 1997, now committed to uncovering the full ideological underpinnings that McVey might attribute to his choice to initiate such devastating violence.

Reavis wasn't adverse to interviewing people in prisons; in 1983, for example, he had been the only reporter to whom the convicted killer Charles Brooks Jr., also known as Shareef Ahmad Abdul-Rahim, had granted an interview while he was awaiting execution in the Ellis Unit in Huntsville, Texas.[10] McVey, however, was wary of Reavis and remained silent about his ideological network—he recommended instead that Reavis interview a fellow inmate, Ted Kaczynski, "The Unabomber," whose writings he'd heard were intriguing. Reavis did not follow up on this suggestion and soon abandoned his correspondence with McVey,[11] again returning to the wide array of projects and human issues he'd been exploring for years.

In 1998 Reavis returned to school earning an MA in English from the University of Texas, Arlington, and in 2004 he joined the English faculty at North Carolina State University in Raleigh, continuing to publish articles and books into the turn of the millennium.

In 2001 Reavis published, with University of North Texas Press, a memoir recollecting his participation in the Black Civil Rights Movement of the late 1960s, a selection of which appears at the beginning of this collection with Reavis's autobiographical writings, rather than in chronological order. The title, *If White Kids Die,* plays upon Stokley

Carmichael's conviction that white allies had to be involved in the movement, in part because white deaths would get a different kind of media attention—for while Black Lives *should* Matter as much as white lives, historically, this has never been validated in the U.S.

Here, Reavis's radical activism and his memoir do the kind of white-ally work that has become the basis of modern diversity training: taking responsibility for and holding difficult conversations within white communities about race and racism, be they regional or national, social or institutional. Reavis's approach in his 2001 memoir was not to erase or whitewash his characters' racialized and sexist language. Here his character's, and his own, former blasé use of the term "Negro"—which was still used in both white and Black mainstream American society in the 1960s—a word we rarely encounter in print today because of its now-recognized connotations and references to slavery and racist ideologies—is a startling reminder to today's reader of the power of language—words do matter. As Reavis looks back at his own and his fellow white activists' youthful selves in this memoir, he takes responsibility for their mistakes, employing that same wry wit he used throughout his career, poking fun at himself, while also honoring and voicing their struggle to understand both their privilege and Black activists' need to build a movement that empowered Black leadership.

In his most recent writing, as in his memoir, Reavis is not only concerned with the past, but also with the intersections between today's current issues. His 2010 book *Catching Out: The Secret World of Day Laborers* (Simon & Schuster), for which he immersed himself in a wide variety of physically demanding manual labor jobs, is both a series of profiles of day laborers he met and a reflection upon aging, race, class, economic, and gender issues involved in the day laborer's plight. Still fearless, and always a master of understated humor, especially when the subject is himself, Reavis's fiery spirit of defiance and hope continually resurface through even his most serious pieces.

Reavis resides today in Dallas, Texas, where he continues to write.

Endnotes

1 See Michael Abraham Shadid's *A Doctor for the People: The Autobiography of the Founder of America's First Co-operative Hospital* (Elk City, OK: Vanguard Press, 1939), and *Crusading Doctor: My Fight for Cooperative Medicine* (Boston: Meador Publishing Company, 1956).

2 David Peters, "Red Scare Comes to Orange County," *State: The Official Magazine of Oklahoma State University,* May 1, 2018. https://news.okstate.edu/magazines/state-magazine/articles/2018/spring/loyal-and-true.html.

3 J. Lee Jones Jr., *Red Raiders Retaliate: The Story of Lone Wolf* (Seagraves, TX: Pioneer, 1980); Mildred P. Mayhall, The Kiowas (Norman: University of Oklahoma Press, 1962; 2d ed. 1971); Pauline D. and R. L. Robertson, *Cowman's Country: Fifty Frontier Ranches in the Texas Panhandle, 1876–1887* (Amarillo: Paramount, 1981).

4&5 Reavis filed a Freedom of Information Request to see this file, a copy of which now resides in the Dick J. Reavis Papers at the Wittliff Collections.

6 Thorne Dreyer, Alice Embree, and Richard Coxdale, "About the Book," *Celebrating The Rag: Austin's Iconic Underground Newspaper,* edited by Thorne Dreyer, Alice Embree, and Richard Coxdale (Austin: New Journalism Press, 2021). See also Paul Buhle's "*The Rag* in Radical History: An Outsider's View," in *Celebrating The Rag,* pp. 14–15. Reavis's essay from *The Rag* included in this collection was also reprinted in *Celebrating the Rag,* and I thank Alice Embree for granting permission to reprint it here.\

7 A copy of the "TM memoir" is held in the Dick J. Reavis Papers at the Wittliff Collections.

8 Susan Duffer argues that the split between Dugger and Davis was political,

and Davis had become "extremely disillusioned by the wave of conservatism sweeping the country [and] couldn't hide his disaffection."
See Dan Balz, "Lone Star Lament: *The Observer* Bids for Survival," *The Washington Post,* February 21, 1981.
See also "Paper Tiger: *The Texas Observer* Is Down, But Don't Count It Out," *Texas Monthly,* April 1981, p. 112.

9 *The National Tour of Texas: The Ultimate Texas Roadtrip,* curated by Steve Davis of the Wittliff Collections, can be accessed at https://exhibits.library.txstate.edu/thewittliffcollections/exhibits/show/the-national-tour-of-texas.

10 See Reavis's "Charlie Brooks' Last Words," *Texas Monthly,* February 1983, vol. 11, no. 2, pp. 100–101.

11 All of the Reavis-McVey correspondence is held in the Dick J. Reavis Papers in the Wittliff Collections at Texas State University.

Acknowledgments

First and foremost, I want to thank Dick, who has been generous in his correspondence with me for years. Modest about his achievements, generous in giving of his time, sharp in his observations, and brilliantly funny, Dick always surprises in conversation. I am humbled by the range, probity, and depth of his writings, and I am enriched by having had the opportunity not only to immerse myself in them but also to talk with their author.

I want to thank J. Bruce Fuller, Peter J Carlisle, and Charlie Tobin at Texas Review Press, who have been unwavering in their enthusiasm and support for this project from the start. I am indebted to Michelina Oliveri, my graduate research assistant, for her help in my initial survey of Dick's writings, as well as to my colleague, Lisa Tremaine, for her early encouragement. Trent Shotwell, the Special Collections Librarian, spent hours exploring with me and my students the Waco Siege Collection held in the Newton Gresham Library at Sam Houston State University. Lee Miller and her staff at the Center for Community Engagement at Sam Houston State University, Deanna Briones, Community Event Coordinator for the College of Humanities and Social Sciences, Rhoda Owens and Sarie Fuller, administrative assistants to the Department of English at Sam Houston State University, provided much appreciated administrative support.

Dick J. Reavis retained the copyrights to all of his writings after their initial print run, but I want to thank all of the editors, publishers, authors, and photographers who have graciously encouraged me to republish Dick's writings in this collection. I want to thank Alice Embree from the New Journalism Project, who has known Dick since their college years, Alice R. Pfeiffer, Director of Syracuse University Press, Ron Chrisman, Director of University of North Texas Press, Russell Roe, Managing Editor of Texas Parks & Wildlife magazine, Jamie Maloney, Senior Marketing and Media Sales Manager at Mother Jones. For the images, I want to thank Janice

Rubin, Miriam Lizcano (Reavis's wife), John Avant, Ramón Tianguis Pérez, Chris Wahlberg, and Will van Overbeek.

My research was supported by a Teaching Innovation Grant, awarded by the Professional and Academic Center for Excellence at Sam Houston State University, which enabled me to take students to Mount Carmel and Waco, Texas. I am also indebted to Eric Lupfer and Humanities Texas for a mini-grant that enabled me to bring Dick to Huntsville on the twenty-sixth anniversary of the siege of the Branch Davidians. The Wittliff Collections at Texas State University, to which Dick donated his papers, provided research funds—Lead Archivist Katie Salzmann deserves special thanks as she helped me navigate researching in the archive during the pandemic. Dr. Jacob Blevins, Chair of the English Department and the College of Humanities and Social Sciences at Sam Houston State University, also generously supported my research and the development of this book.

Finally, I dedicate my work on this collection to my wife, Audrey Murfin, who accompanied me on my first trip to Mount Carmel—the moment when I first conceived of this project—and who has supported me throughout its development.

Texas Reporter, Texas Radical

The Writings of

Journalist

Dick J. Reavis

He has chosen to walk down a trail strewn with legal, moral, historical and religious issues as prickly as cactus.

—Dick J. Reavis's description of restaurant owner and transnational agitator, Mario Cantú, but also an apt description of Reavis himself.

Autobiographical Writings

Reavis and his VW Beetle (which, 44 years later, he is still driving). Photographer: Miriam Lizcano.
Image courtesy of Dick Reavis, circa 1990.

As a supplement to his report, "Mexican Border: U.S. Reports Lead to Improved Mine Safety in Unregulated Pocitos," in *Investigative Reporters & Editors Journal* (IRE), March/April (2003): 22, Reavis included the following notice, which captures the wit and down-to-earth, intrepid personality of its author.

Have Beetle, Will Travel

The problem that San Antonio-based reporters most frequently encounter in covering news in northern Mexico is not language—many of us are bilingual—but transportation. It's not easy to introduce an American-registered vehicle into Mexico.

The *San Antonio Express-News* provides its photographers with Jeep Cherokees, and when reporters travel with photographers the Jeeps are the vehicles of choice: they're roomy, they're equipped with security trunks to protect photo gear, and they're tough enough for Mexico's rural roads.

But the Jeeps are leased, and one cannot take a leased vehicle into Mexico without authorization from the leasing company. It, in turn, requires an OK from its insurer, which prefers to issue Mexico authorizations on a six-month basis. Having a car that's ready to pass through Mexican customs is a constant nightmare of paperwork.

As a fallback, reporters and photographers take their own cars into Mexico, buying insurance at a daily rate from border-city agencies. The arrangement isn't perfect; the *Express,* like most American companies, reimburses personal vehicle use at 36 cents a mile. Gasoline in Mexico costs about twice as much as in the U.S.

During our series on *pocitos,* paperwork was pending for Gerry Lara's Jeep on several days when we needed to make a trip. On one trip, it was damaged by a hit-and-run driver, sidelining it for weeks. On another, for security reasons, we didn't want to take his Jeep because it's emblazoned with the newspaper's logo. The solution was that on about a third of our dozen journeys to the region Lara had to put up with my personal car, a 1974 Beetle. It's not air-conditioned or comfortable, but it's sturdy, and in Mexico it's anonymous—and even for fill-ups south of the Rio Grande, it doesn't leave me broke at the pump.

Reavis, reporting for the *Daily World,* with Angela Davis and others circa 1972–73, at the Black International Longshoremen's Association's Hall, a few months after Davis had been acquitted of murder charges stemming from a Marin County Courthouse shootout in 1970. Photographer unknown. Image courtesy of Wittliff Collections.

In 2001, Reavis published If White Kids Die a memoir of his early engagement with the Civil Rights Movement. In the first excerpt included here Reavis gives his reasons for joining—without his parents' consent—the movement in 1965. In the second excerpt, which picks up later that summer—after Reavis had worked for months in Demopolis, AL with SCLCs and locals, after he was harassed by police, jailed by a judge, released, and sent, with another white "rebel," to SCOPE's Director, Hosea L. Williams for relocation. Here, Reavis recollects his struggle to understand the extent of systemic racism, how to combat it, the role white participants in the movement might play, and how they might support Black activists.

Selections from *If White Kids Die*

A white teenager from Texas leaves college in 1965 to help transform the South.

FROM CHAPTER 1

I got into the Southern civil rights movement, I believe, thanks to the mistake of a mailing room clerk. During the spring of 1965, I was a student at a small Oklahoma school, Panhandle A&M College, a place known for its rodeo team and the motto inscribed on the marker at its entrance, "Progress Thru Education."

I had gone there because, during my first three semesters in college, I had done poorly at a state university in my home state of Texas.

One afternoon I stepped into the Panhandle student union cafeteria to grab a glass of iced tea, and if I recall rightly, to lay eyes on Annette, a Black co-ed whom I was secretly dating. She worked at the Union in the afternoons.

Lying on the table where I took a seat was a brochure; its purpose was to recruit students for summer civil rights duty in the Deep South.

It wasn't supposed to be there. Panhandle wasn't the place for it. Reed College, it was not. Its students, mostly whites from farming towns, many of whom came to college to study agriculture, weren't those that civil rights organizations were making an effort to court.

The summer of 1964 had been "Freedom Summer" for a few campuses. The most militant civil rights group, SNCC, the misnamed Student Non-Violent Co-ordinating Committee, had drawn some 500, mostly white students from Ivy League and prestige liberal universities to help its integration efforts in Mississippi. White Boston Congressman Barney Frank, [today known as the first member of Congress to come out as gay, and an outspoken advocate of same-sex marriage] was 24 then, and one of the Harvard boys who went South for the SNCC (pronounced "SNICK") crusade.

SNCC's purpose in organizing the whites was unknown to me at the time. In 1964, an up-and-coming leader named Stokely Carmichael [who later changed his name to Kwame Ture] had told a group of prospective volunteers in New York that SNCC wanted to be sure that if Blacks were killed on Movement duty, whites would die with them. The demise of kids from the nation's Harvards and Yales, he said, would attract press attention to the brutalities of Jim Crow. That wasn't the only reason that SNCC wanted whites, perhaps, but what Carmichael said was absolutely prophetic, even if it wasn't popular. A few weeks after his speech, three students were murdered by Ku Kluxers in Philadelphia, Mississippi: Michael Schwerner, 24, a white Congress of Racial Equality (CORE) staffer, Brooklynite and student of both Cornell and Columbia; Andrew Goodman, 20, another white New Yorker and Freedom Summer volunteer recruited from Queens College; and James Chaney, 21, a Black Mississippi plasterer and CORE member. The press and most of the nation were scandalized.

In March 1965, Mrs. Viola Liuzzo, a white Detroit housewife, had been murdered during the Selma campaign, while working with Dr. Martin Luther King Jr.'s Southern Christian Leadership Conference (SCLC). Again the press, and with it most of the nation, was enraged. Her death confirmed that whites were useful as martyrs, even if they didn't have Ivy League credentials. Perhaps the bulletin I found at Panhandle was mailed to all colleges, thanks to her martyrdom, but I doubt that the Movement had the resources to make a blanket appeal.

That afternoon at Panhandle, understanding nothing of all the controversy about the participation of whites, I assumed that we were needed simply because the Movement wanted to build their internal brotherhood. I decided to go South as soon as I'd scanned the brochure. I believe my motivation had less to do with dating Annette than with something else: I was a Young Democrat, foolish enough to believe Party leaders who said that citizenship, not race or class, was the subject matter of American politics.

I knew, of course, that there was a small chance that I might get killed, but the prospect wasn't particularly dispelling; as an ROTC student, I also knew that there was a war in Vietnam. In those days, a lot of young men grew up thinking that risking death in the name of a cause was an inevitable passage into adulthood.

Nor did I think—even for a minute—that I was going into an environment that was in any way foreign to me. Texas was segregated; Oklahoma, too. Colleges and some high schools had been integrated, but Annette Owens and I saw each other secretly because appearing together in public wasn't safe.

The brochure set forth terms for work with several organizations. All of them promised to lodge their volunteers with Black Movement families, but SNCC planned to select only a handful of volunteers, and could not pay stipends. SCLC wanted to recruit hundreds of summer workers, and offered a stipend of $12.50 a week. The money that SCLC (called "SLICK" by SNCC rivals) promised wasn't much, but I had no resources and expected none. Immediately I wrote a letter asking the group to count me into its summer program, called SCOPE, for Summer Community Organizing and Political Education. SCOPE's purpose was to organize people to demand the vote; and in order to help overcome the literacy tests that were imposed on prospective voters, SCOPE organized volunteers to teach the basic lessons of civics texts.

I didn't know it, and I'm not sure that anybody was aware, but SCOPE represented a dramatic shift in the character of the civil rights movement. Always before, at least until the passage of the Civil Rights Act of 1964, the Movement had in many ways pleaded—though sometimes in militant ways—for whites to accept Blacks. The shift towards political organizing meant that the Movement would henceforth demand, not the seat next to whites in a diner, but, the seat on which the whites were sitting—it was a struggle to take from whites the seats of power and patronage. Since white people already occupied almost all of the political positions in the South, and there was little room for expansion—a city can have only one mayor, a county, only one sheriff—the Movement was not asking for acceptance, tolerance, or love—it was demanding power.

When a movement sets out to capture political power it soon finds that power and prosperity are links in the same chain, and while people vote on paper at the ballot box, people also cast votes at the cash register with every purchase they make. If people are to be represented politically, they will soon demand that their economic ballots buy representation too. Boycotts and a struggle for Black employment across the economic spectrum were a natural extension of the logic of political enfranchisement. After the enactment of the Civil Rights Act of 1964, the Movement wasn't asking anybody for acceptance, it became a movement for power and economic position.

My decision to go South was made without the consultation of anybody, and without the consent of my parents. I soon went to inform them. They had recently moved to Dumas, a refining and wheat-and-sugar-beet town at the northern tip of Texas. I dreaded the business of explaining myself to them because—though few adolescents truly know their parents (knowing would mean admitting a sameness)—I knew that they would be opposed.

It wasn't that they were exactly racists. Things weren't as simple as that. My mother is a folkloric American character, a Dust Bowl Okie who has never left her upbringing. Profoundly instinctive and sly, she's a shrewd player at dominoes and bridge. Her ideology is that of the First (Southern) Baptist Church, no matter what the town. First Baptist Churches in the South are composed of farmers, foremen, and small businessmen; the economically marginal usually belong to more passionate congregations. First Baptists, in those days before the abortion debate, were sure that God was in His heaven and that all was right with the world. Therefore, they rarely railed against anything but alcohol. My mother's attitude towards me going South, I knew, would have nothing to do with the right or wrongness of politics or power for Black people. She would object, I was sure, for the same reason many Black women her age might, because in the near-perfect world in which we lived, white people weren't supposed to take up residence on the Black side of town.

Dad, I figured, would be a much tougher case because of his testy temperament. He had come from the same dusty red plains that had produced my mother. His father had been a ne'er-do-well printer and sometime-publisher of weeklies, and Dad faced no better prospects until he'd become a flyboy officer during World War II. He'd come away from the War with enough savings to buy into a prospering, smalltown Texas newspaper, and our lives since had been a series of shifts to acquire new pinches of capital. In high school, when I had dated Angela Calzada, a Mexican American, he'd been upset, not because she was bronze-skinned, but because I was hanging out with the daughter of a gas station manager. He thought that the Reavis name had come a long way up from the Dust Bowl, and worried—ensuing years have shown that he worried with some justification—that I would carry it back to poverty.

The Dumas place where my parents lived was a typical split-level tract house of the Sixties: central air conditioning, sheetrock walls, two-car garage, a cedar fence surrounding the backyard. Its kitchen sat on the back side of the upper level, a counter facing over into the living room. One night, after supper, sitting there at the bar, I announced what I intended to do.

My father called me into the living room, while my mother watched from the kitchen sink. Dad sat on a couch; I sat in an armchair facing him. His initial approach was one of indirect reasoning.

"The demonstrations of the Negroes," he said, "are flawed on two scores. Many of their actions are illegal, and breaking the law isn't justified so long as the legislative process is open, even if only to whites." The demonstrators had also demanded 'Freedom Now!' "But immediate change is an infantile idea. History doesn't work that way," he declared.

"What do you want them to do, wait another hundred years?" I asked him.

His grimace said that I was being impudent. He grappled for words, exasperated.

My mother broke in, still drying dishes."I know what it is, Dick J.," she intoned. "At Panhandle, don't you have a Negro girlfriend? Is that what it is?"

Because I knew her opinions, I lied.

"But doggone it," Dad sputtered. "Don't you see what they plan to do with you? The only reason that this Dr. King wants you down there is so that you'll get killed, like those three boys in Mississippi."

I shrugged.

"Don't you see," he continued. "If white kids die, then this Dr. King will get more publicity."

He had hit a nail on the head, and I couldn't get around it by lying. I considered the point.

"Dad," I said after a while, "if we live in a country where nobody pays attention when Negroes die, then I guess that's the way it has to be. Somebody has to pay the price."

He didn't act as if I'd said anything noble, and I suppose that he was right; nobility is a characteristic of the mature, who have conflicting motives for everything. Logical consistency, on the other hand, is the ideal of academics and college students, whose best role is to demand that the rest of us be rational.

Mother came in from the kitchen and sat down beside him. Then Dad really explained.

He had bought two quarreling and unprofitable newspapers in Dumas, both of them badly in the red, and was in the process of merging them. One had been a free circulation or "throwaway," the other a five-day-a-week daily with little circulation.

Within weeks, a new competitor sprang up from the ranks of those who had formerly produced the "throwaway." This crimped Dad's plans, and at the moment that I came home to make my announcement, he was struggling for his business life.

To establish the combined newspaper, he needed an expanded circulation, and I was the key to that; in high school I'd sold subscriptions and managed newsstand distribution in two different towns. Dad wanted me to do the same during that summer in Dumas. If his new newspaper failed, the family failed, and the family included not only the three of us, but my elementary-age brothers as well. A part of the family's future was in my hands. I couldn't turn my back, he said.

Not for a minute did I consider his plea. I didn't know enough to imagine the import of what he was saying. I didn't know how a mortgage works—or that our house was mortgaged—and it didn't worry me that in order to make the newspaper deal Dad had borrowed money. As far as I was concerned, my parents were relatively rich and secure white folks putting up the usual resistance to reform. My attitude was entirely just, and even sagacious from the point of view of the world into which I was entering, and indeed, just as I expected, my parents prospered without my help. But from the point of view of the world that I was leaving, I had repudiated my debt to my kinship group.

By the time that discussion ended, I knew better than to ask permission to take my car South; I didn't pay for insuring it, and couldn't pay. A few days later my parents drove me to board a train for Atlanta. As the train pulled in Dad handed me a twenty-dollar bill. I didn't know how to respond. It was as if he was for me and against me at the same time.

FROM CHAPTER 5

"They tell me you two boys are rebels," Hosea bellowed.

He wasn't being cute, or joking . . . *rebels!*

"Well, I wonder, should I take you over to the SNCC House?"

Gandy and I shot glances at each other. Didn't Hosea Williams know that SNCC was no longer accepting whites?

"Are they here?"—Williams said, looking out his office's doorway—"why, sure they are!" He waved to two, suit-clad men, "ya'll come in here, I want to introduce you." The two preachers came in. Pat and I introduced ourselves. We all took seats in Hosea's office.

Then turning to Gandy and me Hosea said, "Now, I'm sending you boys to Liberty County, Georgia, with these gentlemen. You guys do what they say, and don't get in trouble. I don't want to hear anything bad about you."

And that was it. No hearing, no questions, no chance to defend myself. In a minute's time Gandy and I had picked up our things and loaded them into the trunk of the late model sedan that belonged to one of the preachers.

On the outskirts of Atlanta, the preachers stopped at an integrated chain restaurant and bought supper. While we were waiting to be served one of them told us a little about Liberty, a county that lies just west of Savannah. There were no big towns in Liberty. Its farms belonged mostly to Blacks, and Blacks were an overwhelming majority, more than eighty percent of the population, he explained.

"About eighty years ago, malaria hit Liberty County and wiped out all of the whites," the preacher said. "What this means to you is that there are no light-skinned Blacks in Liberty County. We expect it to stay that way," he said.

About 10 p.m. the two preachers dropped Pat and me at the rear entrance of a big, wooden, two-story building. They didn't tell us where we were. The two of us entered the rear door of the place, which opened to a large meeting room. We exited that room and came into a big, sparsely furnished foyer, and beyond it, into a cavernous dining room. We found an institutional kitchen at the rear of the dining room. Then we went outdoors into the yard, and peered in the darkness. We couldn't see the profiles of any other buildings, nor any lights of town, only pine trees. It was as if we were on a great estate.

Pat looked back at the building.

"My God, Georgian columns!" he exclaimed.

It was true. The hotel-like building that we'd come out of looked like an antebellum mansion.

Perplexed, we went back indoors and up a staircase. A dozen dormitory-style bedrooms were on the second floor. We turned on light after light, looking for some clue to our whereabouts. Finally, Pat ran across a bulletin.

"Ah, Dorchester Institute!" he said, greatly relieved.

Dorchester was a school where SCLC conducted citizenship training classes. Its purpose was to school cadres from across the South in civic topics and literacy-teaching techniques, so that they could prepare their townsmen to face voter registration exams.

Pat went downstairs, hungry. In the kitchen we found utensils, cooking oil and a package of frozen potatoes. Pat put the potatoes on the stove to fry, then began rummaging around, exploring. I followed him, step by step. In the dining room we found a jukebox. With a screwdriver or a knife from the kitchen, Pat pried open its money chamber and took the coins for himself. Then, as we ate, he began to explain how he'd wound up with me.

He'd been called into Americus, Georgia, about 150 miles west, a couple of months before. Americus was at the moment SCLC's hot spot. Staff were being pulled in from everywhere.

In Americus he'd taken up with a Black girlfriend. When other staffers raised objections, he'd refused to quit seeing her. He was thinking about getting married, he said.

We had been sent to Liberty, he told me, "because we won't get in trouble here. Liberty County is what is called a 'low-tension' area. There's nothing doing here. This is a place where they send people that they're not sure about, people with psychological problems, SCOPEs whose parents are worried, things like that."

I was stung. I told him about our troubles in Demopolis, and said that I wanted to go back.

"If you go back, you'll get fired," he warned.

I kept talking, telling him everything that I knew about Demopolis, trying to convince him that I should go back.

"Well, what you don't like is SCLC," he said. Then he explained. "You see, SCLC has a strategy. 'Local failure, national success,' that's what SNCC, and sometimes some of us, call it. What that means is that SCLC goes into a place, gets the existing leadership to back its plan, and then creates a crisis that will bring in TV and the press. When they do that, see, it puts pressure on the politicians up in Washington to pass the kind of bills that we need."

I was at last learning the basics, but I didn't like what I heard.

"Dr. King comes in," he said, "at the point of the crisis, to bring it to a head or to dramatize it. He doesn't stay there afterwards, he doesn't go there beforehand. That's not his role."

"Now, the trouble with the strategy," he continued, "is that it's just what it says, 'local failure, national success.' People lose their jobs, get evicted, things like that. They're left with cases pending in the courts. We do what we can, but we can't stay around forever, you know. The purpose of the strategy is to create a national atmosphere. We can't be 'married to the community,' as they say."

I was somewhere between tears and rage.

"It's like Selma now," he said. "If you go back there now, you'll find that a lot of people are disgusted with the Movement. They'll feel like they've been left holding the bag. They'll say, 'Where is Dr. King now? He's run out on us,' because they don't understand. We come around—the national office does—with all sorts of community programs afterwards, like the Community Center at Selma, trying to patch things up, but really, there's not a lot that we can do until things get better in Congress. The battle has to be won nationally, not on the local level."

"Demopolis," he concluded, "is one of those places, maybe like

Americus, that we tried to develop into a national crisis. But you can't always do it. Locally or nationally, conditions aren't always right."

I protested that Demopolis still had potential, and that, even more important, the crackers there deserved to be broken. The town hadn't been integrated, everything was in bad shape, a fight had to be made.

"Well, then," he said, "Hosea was right about you. You ought to be in SNCC. Of course, you're white, so you can't be."

"SNCC," he explained, "they do get married to the community. They go in and spend two years—two years is what they're saying that you've got to stay in a town now—building up a leadership, from the beer joints and union halls, places like that. They think that the old preacher-style leaders are too conservative, and for what SNCC wants to do, they are. SNCC says that you've got to turn the whole society around, from the bottom side up. It's a radical idea. It takes time to do that."

Then he told me that the confrontation at Selma had essentially been SNCC's work. "They'd been there for two years, and to hear them tell it, Dr. King came in just at the last moment, stole the show away from them. They're bitter about it," he said.

I told Pat that I felt married to Demopolis and that I wanted to leave Liberty County.

"If I were you, I'd stick around a few days. See what they're doing here, if they're doing anything," he said with a chuckle.

The next morning we located a SCOPE, a male student from Pennsylvania who had a two-bedroom house to himself. The guy was a terrible housekeeper, but his house sat along a highway. Dorchester was isolated, so Pat and I moved in with the guy. That night I attended a mass meeting with him. The meeting was held in a country church. The locals were discussing the formation of a credit union. It wasn't a bad idea, I thought—but SCOPE could organize credit unions in Philadelphia's ghetto. One came to the South, I thought, to join a fight.

The following morning I told Pat that I was going to catch the bus into Atlanta when it passed along the highway.

"Tell me if you go," he said. "I'll have to call headquarters and they'll fire you."

"But I was thinking of taking my case to Hosea, to tell him what's going on in Demopolis," I whined.

"It won't work," he said. "You've got yourself crossways with some of the local leadership. That's not your job. Your job is to work for them. Hosea probably won't even give you a hearing."

"Well, if that's true," I told him, "then what I'm going to do when I get to Atlanta is catch a bus for Demopolis. I'll get back and get the locals to explain."

"Just let me know," he repeated. "I have to make the call."

About noon, the bus came by. I got on. Pat's call had unforeseen consequences. When I got back to Mrs. Frost's place, she said that my parents had been calling. I got on the phone and, to my surprise, learned that they were relieved that I'd only been fired. SCOPE's office had called, they said, to advise them that I had left Liberty County and that SCLC would no longer be responsible for anything I did. Their caller professed not to know why I'd left Liberty, or where I was headed.

My parents had thought that they knew where I was heading and they didn't like the conclusions that they'd drawn. During the few days that I'd spent at home before leaving for Atlanta, a letter had come for me. Its return address bore the initials, RAO, for Ruth Annette Owens, my girlfriend. My mother had remembered those initials. A week or two later, another letter came, this one from the University of Texas. Its return address was that of the Division of Married Student Housing. I'd written the Division when Annette and I had been dating. Alarmed, my parents had asked a friend in the Panhandle administration to match the initials with a student's name. Only one name had turned up. My parents decided that I'd left SCLC to marry a Black woman, a prospect that pleased them no more than the idea that, at the age of nineteen, I was thinking of marriage.

I soon visited a couple of the members of the Civic Club to explain that I'd been fired. They got together, called a mass meeting from which I was excluded, and discussed the affair. Henry Jr. didn't attend the meeting, which made two decisions: that the commercial boycott should be resumed and that SCLC should stand by me. The meeting drew up a petition that, over the next couple of weeks, between 150 and 200 people signed. It asked SCLC to reinstate me as a SCOPE.

To revive the boycott, Mrs. Frost called a new round of mass meetings at a small church on Ash Street. She could not match Henry's oratory and the crowds were half their former size. But good news pushed the boycott on. Within two weeks, a grocery store near the color line hired its first

Black cashier. She was afterwards afraid to attend the mass meetings—afraid that she'd lose her job—but she sent a word of thanks, sufficient to persuade us that the store should be exempted from the boycott. Nearly overnight, it filled with Black customers. Then she sent word again, asking that Black customers not segregate themselves in the line that led up to her cash register. It gave her more work than one checker could handle, her messenger said.

One afternoon a big package was delivered to Mrs. Frost's house. Inside was a roller-type mimeograph machine with tubes of ink—the state of the art in those days. Linda Brown had gone back to New York after the stillborn march, and the machine was a gift from the tenants in her Harlem apartment building. Because Johnny Ray no longer seemed willing to participate in DYC [Demopolis Youth Committee] affairs, those who were still active regrouped under a new name, the Demopolis Youth Organization. They put the machine to work churning out leaflets about the boycott. The Movement wasn't as healthy, in numerical terms, as it had been when the summer had opened. But it was moving again.

I was in bad shape, however. I was without even so much as a promise of a stipend from SCLC and was soon reduced to credit at one of the ghetto's little grocery stores owned by a man who called himself a minister. I'd go and charge a loaf of bread and a jar of peanut butter. I got by on that diet, but it quickly got old.

I was also in Arkansas's shoes, but lacking his courage; if I were arrested, no organization was pledged to go my bail. The only felicitous note in life was that Collier was back in town, at Mrs. Frost's house with me.

Collier's salary was twenty dollars a week, but he was low on money, too. We'd at first been able to buy cans of food at the ghetto's corner stores, and from time to time, had been invited for after-church meals, but only on Sundays. One afternoon Collier, as if he'd discovered gravity, told me, "I know what we'll do!"

We took up door-to-door begging. Collier took his guitar. We'd pick a house whose inhabitants we knew. He'd knock on the door, and before anyone answered, shout, "Food! Food!" strumming on his guitar. We were never turned away, although quite often, people would tell us to come back at suppertime—or on Sunday.

The tactic worried me, however. We could have been arrested for vagrancy, had the police only known.

There were other problems at the Frost house that, as time went by, began to undermine my resolve. I wasn't adapted to the poor man's life. Bathing was difficult. We used the chicken house that sat in the backyard, as the Frosts did. One of its two rooms was covered with wire mesh; chickens lived in that room. The other room was enclosed. It was the bathhouse. Our procedure was to heat up a pan of water on the stove—Mrs. Frost allowed us to use the stove for that—carry the pan out to the bathhouse, pour its contents into a ceramic-clad large steel bowl, and take a sponge bath. The hot water didn't help much, though. Demopolis was a cauldron in summer, and in the enclosed bathhouse, one sweated as much as one washed. I came away clammy, clothes sticking to my body. Ruth clothed herself in a cotton dress, and bathed while wearing it, coming out, always, in a state similar to mine.

Shaving was difficult, too. Heating water was a hassle, and I had no mirror. After a few trials, I bought a can of depilatory powder, a sulfur-smelling chemical that locals used to avoid razor bumps. I'd mix the power with water until it formed a paste, spread it across my face with a flat stick, and wait while the chemical burned. The process left my neck and jaws red and tender, though it did remove facial hair. Being clean-shaven required preparation and fortitude.

I was lonely, too. Though I envied the apparent indifference to women that I'd noted in Collier and Arkansas, I couldn't muster it. A shapely sixteen-year-old nicknamed T-Tot lived in the neighborhood, a block away. Every afternoon, about the time that I could be expected to return from canvassing, she'd come to our block and put a chair beneath a tree on the other side of the street from Mrs. Frost's house, then watch for my return. After a few days of this, I asked someone why. "She has a crush on you," I was told. The next day I stopped by to say hello to her, just to see if the rumor was true. She invited me to her place, where only her grandmother lived, she said. I declined—for about a week. Then one night, knowing better in a hundred ways, I knocked on T-Tot's door. Within ten minutes we were kissing on the front porch of her house. I heard a rumble or a banging inside, then saw T-Tot's grandmother in the living room coming towards us, an ax in hand. She shouted something about "that white man," and I took to my heels. T-Tot survived our brush with her grandmother, and never sat waiting for me again.

Despite such discomforts and misadventures, in brief moments I was at peace. While walking through the corn patch between the back door and the outhouse, or when sitting on the back step at night, looking at the stars through the pines, or when watching a quiet rain through an open front door, I'd sometimes asked myself just what we were struggling to gain. Demopolis had a tranquil side when only its rustic setting was in view. One time I mentioned these feelings to Collier. It wouldn't spoil nature, he said, for Mrs. Lena to have an air conditioner or two. It was easy to feel that he was right.

Perhaps a week or ten days after I'd told my parents that I was back in Demopolis, a letter came in the mail to Mrs. Frost's house. It was from my father, the first that he'd sent. Inside was a check made out for $15, and marked, "For a steak dinner." Dad didn't have any idea what life in the ghetto was like. There was no place where a steak dinner could be had. A small restaurant on Ash served fried chicken as its top-of-the-line menu item, but on the occasions when I'd been there, my budget had allowed me only a pig ear sandwich. The check enabled me to repay the grocer and start a new peanut butter tab.

About this time a hearing was held downtown. Officers of a committee of the United States Civil Rights Commission came to Demopolis to hear complaints from across the region. This was the event towards which field staffer Jerry—who had been in and out of Demopolis, sometimes staying at the Frost place—had been working all summer. Ruth Levin came back from Linden to attend, and Charlie and I decided to drop by.

The hearing was staged in a banquet room on the second floor of the Demopolis Inn, which faced the town square in the commercial district. The Inn—I'd never been within a block of it before—turned out to be an old but well-maintained hotel, whose bellman and waiter I knew; he was one of the men from the Brickyard. On our way Charlie and I saw a crowd of whites gathered around the plate glass windows of a drug store. The drug store also faced the square, on the same block as the hotel. Charlie and I went into the drugstore to see what was causing the commotion outside.

Ruth Levin and James Orange, an oversized staffer from a nearby county, and perhaps two or three other staffers—all Black—were sitting at a lunch counter, chatting nervously. The drug store's personnel had refused to serve the group. Its members had decided to sit-in. A couple of stools were vacant and somebody in the group invited us to join. I don't recall what Charlie did, but I looked back towards the plate glass windows. Some of the onlookers had the look of hoodlums or Klansmen, the two types being the same. I asked myself if I wanted to risk a beating or arrest for the sake of integrating a drug store, and unlike the brave Freedom Fighters who'd come before me—I decided not to. I said so-long to the group and went towards the hotel, a little bit ashamed.

I didn't understand much of the testimony that the sharecroppers and farmers gave at the Commission hearing, but during a break somebody introduced me to a reporter. He was from the *Southern Courier,* a weekly that volunteers from the *Harvard Crimson* operated that summer. The *Courier* carried Movement news, stories about arrests and boycotts and legislation and the like. The reporter, whose name I don't recall, was white, fairly tall but frail, wearing a sport coat, a dress shirt, and a tie. The conference resumed as we were shaking hands, and a few minutes later, he got up. Through one of the room's open windows, I saw him go onto the town square.

"The Klan types!" I thought to myself.

I got up and followed his steps. The square was a grassy place, crisscrossed by sidewalks that converged in its center where a statue to the Confederate Dead stood. A telephone booth stood on one side of the square, within a stone's throw of the drugstore. The reporter was making a call from the booth. I scurried over and posted myself in front of it, eyes alert to trouble. I was going to protect him.

Years later, I decided that they'd probably come because they saw me, not him, but come they did, a group of toughs, probably the same ones that I'd seen at the drugstore. They had parked a car at the edge of the square and came walking. Whether there were four, five, or six of them, I don't recall, but pretty soon they were standing in front of me. They were guys in their twenties, all of them stout with thick limbs but not tall. It was clear that I couldn't win any tiff with them, so I folded my arms and didn't answer their taunts of "n***-lover" this and "n***-lover" that. My celluloid SCLC button—I wore it still—was pinned on the breast of my shirt. One of them tugged on it. Then they began pushing on me. The next thing I knew, I was lying on the sidewalk, knocked down by blows to the neck and face. They kicked my rib cage, kidneys, legs. Then I saw feet flying and heard car doors slamming. I got up, dusted myself, and glanced at the telephone booth. It was empty.

I was enraged. Here I'd come to protect this Harvard boy—and had he done anything to help me? I stormed over to the banquet hall, saw the reporter sitting there, and—before I could accost him—heard the meeting's public address system say, "Would you like to testify?" Everybody's eyes turned on me. I stopped. The chairman, who was white, like all the members of the committee, again said, "Would you like to testify?" I looked around. Everybody was still staring at me. "Who me?" I asked. The men on the committee nodded. I turned towards the chairman, "About what?" "About what just happened to you," the chairman said, beckoning me to a table. I took the seat he indicated, in front of a microphone. The half-dozen men on the committee asked if I knew the men who had assaulted me, if I knew why they'd assaulted me, and if I'd informed the police. "About what?" I asked, incredulous. "To report the assault," one of the committeemen said. "The police wouldn't do anything about it," I told them. I was astounded: the committee was having me testify about the basic facts of life.

When the hearing adjourned, I collared the reporter and asked why he'd abandoned me. "You don't understand," he said in a lecturing tone, "As a journalist my role is different from yours."

In the years since, I have become a journalist myself, and it is my daily prayer that I shall never find myself in the company of colleagues like him.

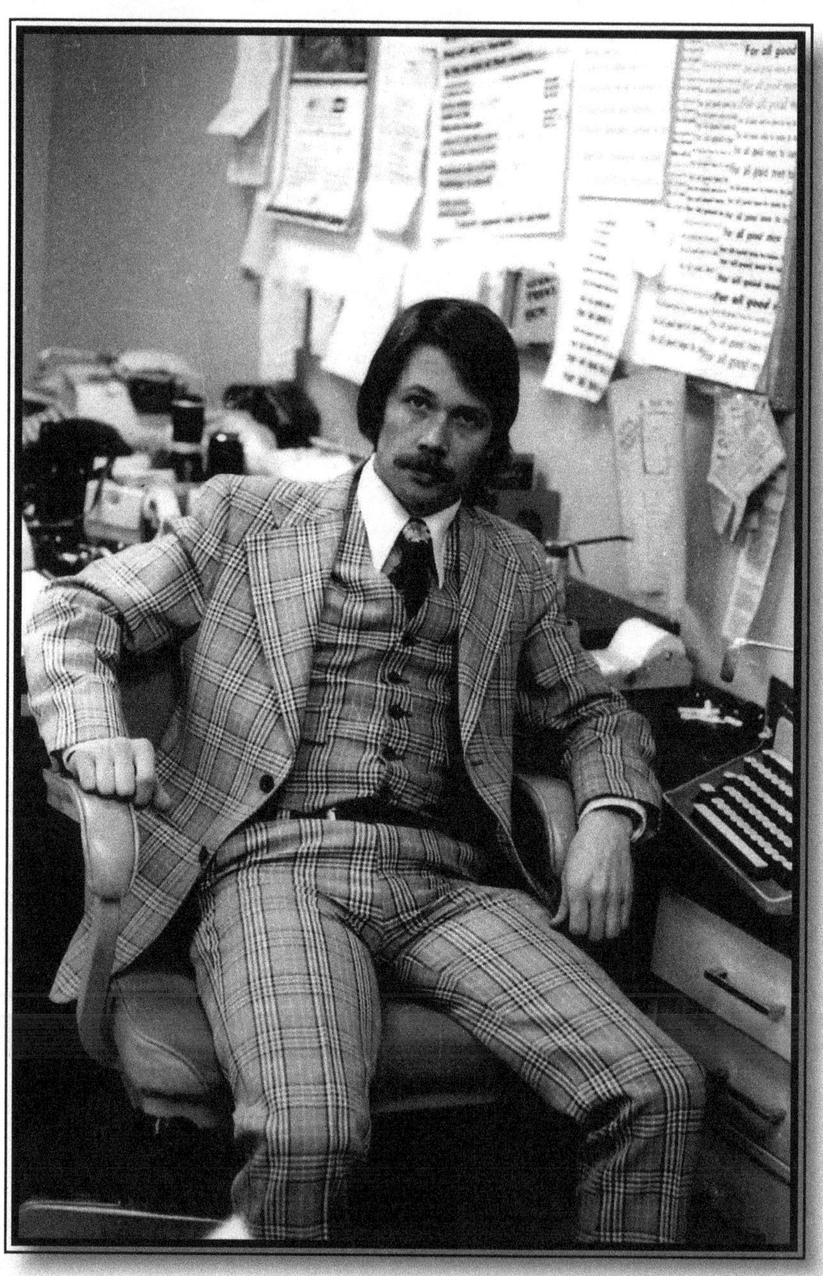

Reavis, reporter for *Moore County News,* Dumas, Texas, 1974. Photographer: Gardner Collins. Image courtesy of Wittliff Collections.

In this 2020 sketch Reavis reflects upon his decision to put aside the political activism of his youth, and become a reporter in 1974. Though resigned to changes in the national political culture, he continued to be committed to Leftist causes and demonstrations, even into his later years. A master of concision even in complex introspection, he encapsulates the history of American left-wing politics since 1955, utilizing the signature down-to-earth voice he developed throughout his lifetime of writing; its deceptive simplicity belies the deep, self-effacing pathos, humor, and humility it paints through its quick, deft strokes. A copy of the manuscript is held in the Dick J. Reavis Papers of the Wittliff Collections, Albert B. Alkek Library, Texas State University.

An Autobiographical Sketch

I came into journalism only because the Revolution failed.

Between 1955 and 1975, a generation of young Americans passed into and out of left-wing activism, and I was one of them.

I never got over our defeat.

During its first ten years, our Movement, as the New Left called it, won enough victories to engender faith, hope and belief in the American political system: if the citizenry demanded justice long enough, and forcefully enough, it could change the nation, most activists believed.

But its last ten years, those of my agitator's career, taught a different lesson. Despite our perpetual efforts, and despite widespread public doubt, nothing could end the Vietnam war.

Most of us were disheartened by the time the Seventies came. One by one, we decided that there was little point in continuing our crusades.

The decision to retreat or surrender came sooner for some than others, and was easier for some than for others. I was one of the others. As with everything, I temporized for months before coming to any resolve.

The turning point for me was Richard Nixon's 1972 defeat of the Democratic peace candidate (!), George McGovern.

I was 26 years old. It had been seven years since my first arrest, for civil rights activity in Alabama, and I'd spent most of the interval on picket lines.

The tumult of the Sixties had driven the Movement's most dedicated volunteers to the fringes of the economy, and to the ends of ideology as well. I had gone from being a Kennedy liberal to calling myself a "revolutionary socialist." Like most of my peers, I probably would have forgotten our critique of capitalism had McGovern been elected, or had Nixon brought the troops home. We'd have felt vindicated, worthy, and, as the phrase of yahoos puts it, "proud to be Americans."

But it had always been clear to me that wearing flag pins wouldn't bring peace, or honor, and Nixon's reelection made it clear that protest wouldn't end the war, either. No process of democracy was capable of doing that, most of us concluded. The political system didn't work; that was plain. The mainstream parties were bought, and the working class—which a lot of us had hoped would rise against all of this—worshipped its bosses.

I was at the time heavily influenced by two Marxist-Leninist publications, the *Daily World*, organ of the Communist Party, to which I belonged, and *Workers Vanguard*, the biweekly of the Spartacist League, a Trotskyist outfit. Their discrepancies over the '72 election were especially wide, and had forced me to assess my circumstances wholly outside of the dogmas that were my guide.

The World had reported McGovern's defeat with a banner headline that read something like, "Nixon Wins, But Voters Not Moving Right." I had already begun to suspect that the chief vice of the Communist Party, having nothing to do with the usual charges, was simply optimism. The Nixon headline confirmed that for me.

The headline in the Spartacist paper—"Oh, Shit!"—was not fit for distribution to the masses, and, as an activist, that irritated me. But the paper's analysis was more troubling yet. The editors said that Nixon's victory showed that the nation was continuing a "right-wing drift" that had begun in 1968. Setbacks and defeats lay ahead for the Left, the *Vanguard* said. I didn't like it, but its argument seemed to square with what all of us were seeing in daily life. By 1972, the protest movement of the Sixties had begun to fade away.

It took me months to face the implications.

I had to figure out how to best make use of my life during a downturn, and to do that, I needed to know how long it might last. What little I knew of history was my guide.

The American Left made gains during the Teens, in crusades led by the Socialist Party and the Industrial Workers of the World. But the momentum was turned back by World War I and the Palmer Raids. The Communist Party rose to influence during the Depression and World War II, only to see its ranks decimated, more than 90 percent, by the McCarthyism of the late Forties and early Fifties. The Left's third wave of popularity had peaked in mid-1968. The "drift" that the Spartacists discerned was in many ways a reaction to the bubble of its passing success.

The pattern seemed to be one of 20-to-25-year swings of a pendulum. History doesn't run in such mechanical cycles, I knew: but I also knew that nothing, including the glory of American Free Enterprise, lasts forever. In 1972–73, I found it perfectly reasonable to assume that if the Right began its ascent in '68, the Left would be back on its feet again, give or take a couple of years, about 1988.

Once I worked out a timetable for the drift, I had to figure out what to do while it lasted.

Over the years, I had come to know the stories of a handful of McCarthyism's survivors. Some of the tales were doleful.

A former accountant in New Orleans had fled Louisiana when he was indicted for Party membership, and thereafter, under the slogan, "No A, No Pay, That's Moe's Way," he made a living by writing term papers for Austin fraternity boys.

I couldn't bear to think of that.

I had known a carpenter who, when expelled from his union for Party membership, solicited wooden shipping crates from dock workers, built houses from them—and had become a landlord.

I had no manual skills.

Friends told me that many college-educated Party members in New York, who had worked mostly in garment factories or on construction crews trying to organize the working class, had turned to selling insurance.

I didn't see anything impossible or immoral in that.

Instead, what I saw was that these insurance agents had played by the rules that capitalism imposed, had survived and even prospered, despite their pasts and the repressive times. Not a few of them, though they didn't give up their middle-class identities and occupations, had been reinvigorated by the movements of the Sixties.

Their example was good enough for me, I decided. But insurance was a game that I knew nothing about.

I can't say that I always wanted to be a writer, but I can't deny it, either. I had grown up in small-town newspaper shops, because managing them was my father's trade. Reporting had never been of interest to me. The reporters that I had known were tie-strung, and I thought, as pale, pompous and pretentious as preacher men.

But I often stood in drugstores and leafed through *Argosy, Saga* and *True.* These weren't like today's men's magazines; they weren't about fads or nudes. Their writers told of climbing mountains and finding ancient ruins and crossing the high seas.

I had entertained fantasies of a life of adventure before I joined the Movement. While it lasted, it was adventure enough for me.

Thanks to the opportunities that it provided, to a degree, I had learned to write, progressing from 50-word leaflets telling people where to vote, to 1000-word news bulletins for the *Daily World,* which gave me my first press card. I was as skilled as most of the kids who today work in the alternative, indy, or 'zine press.

After Nixon's reelection I realized that journalism was my best ticket into a career. My decision had nothing to with politics. The historical record was pretty clear; newspapers were a part of the System. The mainstream press had tried to be neutral towards slavery and segregation, the New Deal and the war in Vietnam. Yet during a half-dozen conflicts, dating at least to the Spanish-American War, our dailies reported war news in the way that sportswriters, whose partisanship is assumed, report stories about the home team. And the home team, during every strike or labor action that I knew about, had been the publisher's team, the team of business interests.

I figured that, like the insurance agents of New York, I'd have to live a life of quiet desperation—until about 1988.

Journalism wasn't dreary, as things turned out. Among other things, it encouraged me to complete the education that I had so badly neglected in youth. I became conversant in Mexican history, culture, and political affairs, studied Baptist doctrine and factions, spent weeks and months learning the history of penology. I untangled the theology of David Koresh, and figured out the economics of coal. In time I enrolled in graduate school where I studied the art of writing itself.

But journalism's best feature, as far as I was concerned, was that from time to time it gave me a way to indulge my taste for adventure. I hung out with hoboes and winos, took undercover jobs, traveled with a carnival, rode with a motorcycle gang, all for pay. I even found a set of Maya pyramids whose location, archaeologists had told me, had been lost.

Not only did I have fun, notebook in hand, but as a financial matter, I didn't, as we say, do half bad. Over a period of 30 years I took salaried jobs for eight publications, freelanced to two dozen others, and along the way, wrote five books, editing and translating two more.

But 1988 came, and instead of the resurrection of the Left, the world soon witnessed the collapse of the Soviet Union. Nobody that I knew had ever thought it any paragon of socialist values, but we knew that its very existence lent plausibility to our proposals. After the Fall, those of us who still quoted Marx came to be viewed as mere cranks.

By the late Nineties, I was afraid that all hope was lost. If the Red insurance agents of the Fifties had waited ten or fifteen years for a breath of fresh air, I'd been underwater for nearly twice as long.

On trial as a defendant in 1956, Fidel Castro had made a famous speech, "History Will Absolve Me."

"He got his verb wrong," I told my friends. "He should have said, 'History will dissolve me.'"

But in 2003, all of that changed. When George W. Bush unleashed the war in Iraq, he shook a nation from a slumber of thirty years, and even the Left stood up from its grave. At the time, I was working at the *San Antonio Express-News*, wincing as its editors strewed headlines, like flowers for a crusading prince on horseback, in Bush's path. Because I made no secret of my proclivities and outrage, my editors warned me to stay away from protests. I ignored them. I also ignored unspoken instructions to write stories that would promote the war. When my hand was called, I glowered and sneered.

I am now an assistant professor of journalism in the department of English at North Carolina State University. Writing and reporting are technical, not Movement skills, and I try to teach them without agitating for the Left. But when there's a demonstration, I show up, like the faded Reds who outlived McCarthy, with apologies to no one. I send money to causes and candidates, and do other things forbidden to members of the press. I now take part in the supposedly sacred rituals of American life, exercising the rights of citizenship! If one sets one's goals high enough, that can be an adventure. No one yet knows how or when the debate over the war on Iraq will end.

To land a teaching job, I had to abandon my Texas homeland, and perhaps, paid journalism as well. "You're leaving the trade!" a fellow writer exclaimed when I informed him of my plans.

A bit taken aback, I again had to think for awhile. Maybe he's right, I concluded. Journalism, for me, was a good career—between two imperial wars.

Reavis in his "Lenin cap" at a Vietnam protest in 1967. Photographer: John Avant. Courtesy of John Avant.

Before he became a professional journalist Reavis was involved in newspaper production through his father's press, later writing for school newspapers. When he moved to the University of Texas at Austin to pursue an undergraduate degree in philosophy, he began writing for a new, underground weekly—*The Rag* (1966–77)—which would become a legendary counterculture paper, and a significant political force in Austin. This article originally appeared in *The Rag,* vol. 1, no. 19, March 20, 1967.

The IWW: One Big Union and the Relevance of Anarchism

Six months ago I didn't know what the IWW was—and now I am one! It all began last September, when Mike Davis came to town and began extolling the glories of anarchism. The first time I sat in jail I decided that the state was an evil, but until Mike came I was unaware that this country had ever seen an organization which was even sympathetic to statelessness. Mike explained to me the anarchist traditions of the Wobblies, and I followed him up with reading.

Among other things, Mike was an IWW delegate, and he sold several fellow agitators into the One Big Union. But I was hesitant to join, for fear that the feds would pull out my fingernails the moment I did, since the IWW is on the Attorney General's list. But by the time Mike left Austin, he had persuaded me not only to join, but to take up recruiting myself. Thus far I've signed up about 10 like-minded troublemakers (including National SDS vice president Carl Davidson) and haven't lost a fingernail yet.

The Industrial Workers of the World, an old revolutionary syndicalist union, was known in its time for wit, songs, free speech fights and "quickie strikes." The IWW's reputation for militancy caused the capitalist press to nickname its members the "I Won't Work" or "International Wonder Workers," but IWW's themselves preferred to be called "Wobblies" or "Fellow Workers." (To this day it is customary in correspondence for Wobs to address one another as "Fellow Worker.")

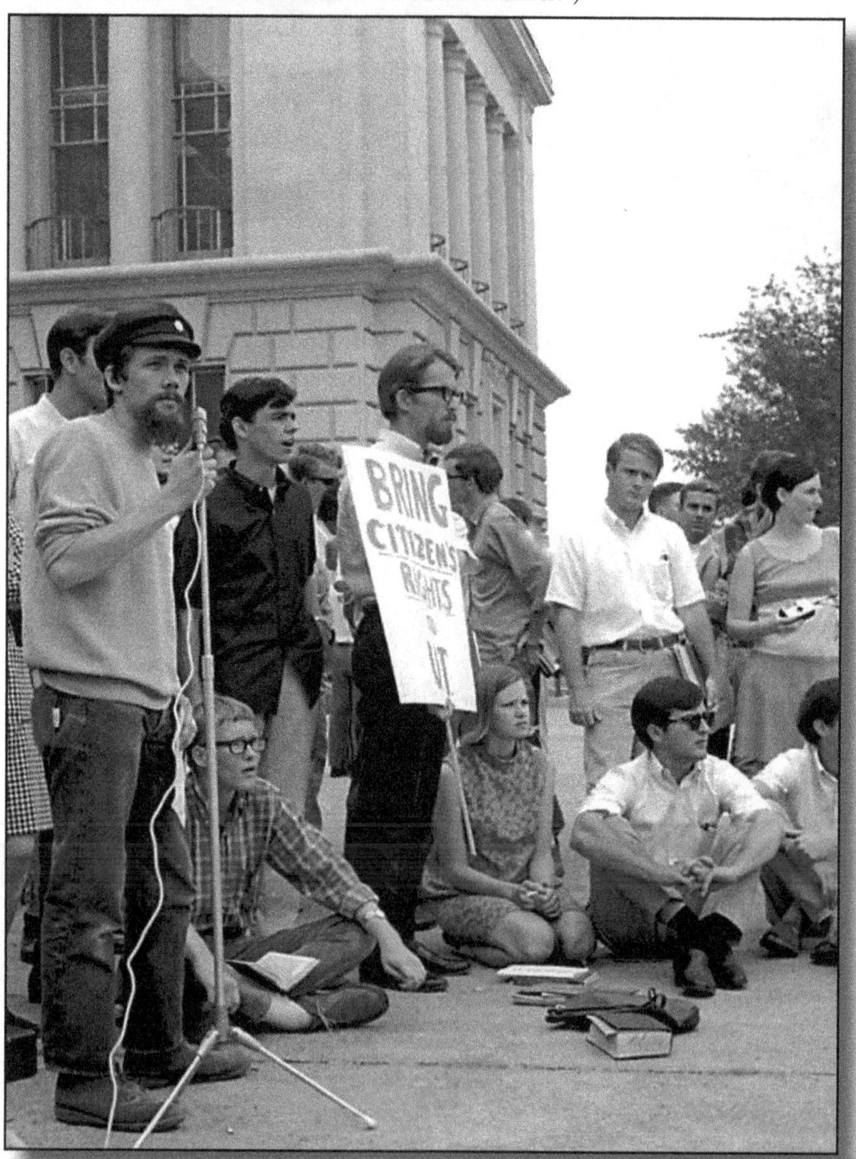

Reavis at the mic, 1967. Photographer; John Avant. Courtesy of John Avant.

Among the Union's founders was Lucy Parsons, widow of the Haymarket martyr Albert Parsons (whose anarchistic soul, incidentally, was reared here in Austin!). Before the union was forced into its decline, it could count among its ranks such figures as Jack London, Elizabeth Gurley Flynn, and "Big Bill" Haywood.

The Wobs would have no truck with cops, politicians, and priests. Joe Hill's parody, "The Preacher and the Slave," sung to the tune of "In the Sweet Bye and Bye," is probably the best known of their anti-clerical polemics:

> Long-haired preachers come out every night,
> Try to tell you what's wrong and what's right,
> But when asked how 'bout something to eat
> They will answer with voices so sweet:
>
> CHORUS:
> You will eat bye and bye,
> In the glorious land above the sky;
> Work and pray, live on hay,
> You'll get pie in the sky when you die.

Teddy Roosevelt once denounced the IWW as an organization of "undesirable citizens" (the following week, thousands marched in Chicago, wearing buttons that said, "I Am An Undesirable Citizen") and the Wobs, many of whom were disenfranchised immigrants, respected him about as much.

In their heyday, the Wobs planned to organize all the workers into their One Big Union, then go on one big strike—for worker ownership of the means of production. With such plans, they had little need for the help that puny politicians could give!

The general strike ideology was a nonviolent one but this was obscured by the bosses' newspapers. Ultimately, the character of the One Big Union was entirely defamed, and this was one of the factors that must be reckoned as a cause of the decline of the old IWW.

There's an old and common joke told about the "I Won't Work," who also refused to do military service during World War I. (The Wobs felt that only the bosses could profit from such a conflict. And they were probably right. Bob Dylan says he can't figure out why that war was fought.) According to the story, an intemperate judge summoned the

Wob to the bench, and queried, "Do you believe in the overthrow of the government by force or violence?" To which, after some hesitation, our Wob replied, "by violence!"

IWW art, March 20, 1967. Courtesy of *The Rag*.

The story is representative of those now told about the Wobs, who since 1917 have been everywhere pictured as bomb-throwing anarchists of the Haymarket variety. However, such stories seem to have little or no basis in truth. For although the Wobs talked a lot about sabotage, (which had a series of meanings for them) nobody was ever convicted for the explosive sort. Normally, "sabotage" for the IWW took on the form of "striking on the job," of sit-downs and slow-downs; the IWW did not advocate bomb-throwing because it intended to take over the factories—and therefore had an interest in their preservation.

While the Wobs were oft-slandered, there are some seemingly reliable tales around. The Catholic pacifist and anarchist Ammon Hennacy (himself once a Wob) claims to have talked to a Fellow-Worker from Texas named Will. According to *The Book of Ammon,* Will was brought before a judge for non-registration with the Selective Service and asked why he did not want to join the war in Europe. Will retorted with, "Why don't you go yourself you son of a bitch?"

The judge was startled, and threatened to find Will in contempt of court. Will replied that contempt was all he had for courts, and was promptly grabbed by two cops. He raised these two off the floor, one in each hand, and knocked their heads together. Finally, Will the Wob was sentenced to twenty years in Leavenworth, where he behaved in the same manner. For his antics (which included multiple threats on the lives of his poor guards) he was sent, ultimately, to the "headdoctor" as Will called him.

Among other things, the shrink asked why Will would not reform himself. Will claimed it would ruin him for the "outside." The shrink was so confounded by the ex-oilworker that he had Will catalogued as a "natural born anarchist" and immediately released from prison, since with Will among the prisoners, there could be no semblance of cell house discipline.

Before the War, the infant Union (founded in 1905) reached its peak of 150,000 members, and thereafter declined due to government repression and passage of criminal syndicalism laws on the state level. Two other factors, perpetual scabbing by the milder pro-capitalist AFL, and the changing nature of the working class, might also be added to the list of the IWW's troubles. Nevertheless, the One Big Union saw revivals in the '20s and '30s, especially among unemployed agricultural workers. But the days of 1911 (when the Wobs organized an integrated timber workers' union in Louisiana) were never to return.

The Taft-Hartley Act and the red scares of the late '40s took the Wobs out of the unionizing business for good; its leaders refused to sign the loyalty path required by the Act, and when in 1950 the IWW was added to the Attorney General's list of "subversive" organizations, the last shop disaffiliated.

To this day, however, the IWW maintains an organization of sorts. Its national office (2422 N. Halstead, Chicago) still published the *Industrial Worker,* and the Union also produces a monthly in Finnish. IWW propaganda, dating back to the "teens" has also been published. Wobs have seen a growing membership among students, some of whom join to avoid the draft. Berkeley, New York, and Chicago all boast organizations of young Wobs, and the older members still get together in Seattle, Chicago, Houston, Duluth, and Yakima.

Among the accomplishments of the more youthful bunch is the Chicago-produced *Rebel Worker,* a sporadic journal of witty anarchist and surrealist thought. The *Rebel Worker* is known for advocating that the Beatles are revolutionary, for urging teenagers to drop out of high school, and for never letting its readers know whether to take it seriously or not.

At this point, I don't think anybody can predict whether or not the IWW will be revived full-blown. We could dry up any day. Then again, there's a suit in court that promises to take us off the God Almighty List; we could have a chance then. A prominent Houston lawyer told me that the IWW was a "dead horse" a long time ago, and advised me that serious New Leftists should instead rejuvenate the (God-awful liberal) Socialist Party.

Only a week before, a CPUSA agitator was brought to laughter at finding me "fooling around with an antique union." (All our comrades on the right, then, seem united in pessimism.) But even if they're right, even if the revival does not come, I still think there are reasons why one should call himself a Wob. In *Howl,* Ginsberg says he's "sentimental" about the Wobs. Well, so am I. Stronger movements have been founded on less than that.

The 1970s

Having returned to the University of Texas at Austin to pursue a graduate degree in philosophy, Reavis seized an opportunity to introduce himself to a guest speaker on campus, an editor at the *Texas Observer*. Reavis contributed to the *Observer* throughout his career as an investigative journalist. This was his first feature. Unpacking racist stereoptypes that perpetuate misunderstanding and authorize hate crimes, this article offers an early example of Reavis's commitment to letting all sides speak, while still sticking to his anti-racist convictions by giving the Kickapoo the last word (*Texas Observer,* June 3, 1977).

The Kickapoo: A Hut Is Not a Home

For most Texans, Kickapoo is a word associated only with the tribe of half-drunken, half-crazed savages cartooned in the Li'l Abner comic strip. In Eagle Pass, where honest-to-goodness Kickapoo live, Al Capp's indictment of the tribe seems validated by nearly everyone white because, without trying, the Kickapoo have collided with community values here.

The 700 Kickapoo who seasonally encamp at Eagle Pass are migrant farm workers, homebased in Nacimiento, Coahuila, about 150 miles south of the Rio Grande. Each spring, the tribe comes to town to bargain with labor contractors for harvest jobs in fields as far north as Wyoming. In the fall, the Kickapoo travel through Eagle Pass on their way home to take part in religious ceremonies.

Poverty and Beliefs

The Kickapoo at Eagle Pass are descendants of a people firmly established in what is now Wisconsin before George Washington was born. Uprooted by tribal war and bloody encounters with white settlers, the Kickapoo migrated first to Illinois, then to Missouri, then Kansas, and finally Oklahoma, where several hundred tribesmen live today. But Kickapoo chieftains say their elders were denied religious freedom in Oklahoma and that, around the time of the Texas Revolution, some Kickapoo found their way to northern Mexico. Today, most Kickapoo are based in the mountains of Coahuila state.

The Kickapoo grate on the white Eagle Pass citizenry because their poverty and religious beliefs fly in the face of property relations. Landowners regard the Kickapoo as squatters looking for a stake. Too poor to pay rent, the tribe has been evicted from a dozen uncultivated tracts along the Rio Grande. Now they have found a refuge—though not a haven by any means—on federal property underneath the international, bridge. Some 150 Kickapoo are camped there today, in cardboard huts lacking water, sanitation facilities, and electricity.

"We have asked for a water line to be put here, with a single faucet and a meter. But nobody is willing to do it," notes George Whitewater, Kickapoo chief.

Ranchers regard the Kickapoo as poachers. Tribal religious teaching equates hunting leases with usury, and more than once Kickapoo have been chased off area ranches for taking deer out of season and on the sly. Deer have ceremonial importance for the Kickapoo, whose own hunting preserve on the reservation at Nacimiento has been regularly violated by American sportsmen.

"We used to have enough deer of our own, down at Nacimiento. But now we have a hard time keeping hunters out, and we have to pick up deer and skins wherever we can. Sometimes we find hides in the Eagle Pass city dump," says Whitewater.

Golfers at the Fort Duncan Club say that the Kickapoo are a hazard: an overdrive on the fourth hole will land a ball squarely in the cardboard Kickapoo village, underneath the bridge.

On top of the bridge, the Kickapoo present immigration officers with something of a dilemma. By law, the Kickapoo are neither Mexican nor American citizens, though they enjoy dual residency status; by century-old tradition, tribe members may cross the Rio Grande at will, without inspection or visas. Yet the Kickapoo must carry immigration papers stamped with the designation "parolee."

"The federal government has tried to act as if we weren't American citizens, but I don't see how that's possible. We were in the United States before both the Bureau of Indian Affairs and the Immigration Service were established," Whitewater says.

Merchants in Eagle Pass say the Kickapoo are only a source of small change in an economy where peso devaluation has taken a big slice out of retail trade volume.

Even welfare workers gripe about the Kickapoo. The tribe holds that the deity does not want their language committed to writing, and so most Kickapoo shy away from public schools on both sides of the border. Only a handful speak English, and the Kickapoo's command of Spanish is negligible. Their language does not distinguish sons from nephews—a point of importance to welfare administrators—and the tribe is religiously casual about the documents that make bureaucracies click.

A STAGING GROUND

The Kickapoo have been coming to Eagle Pass for nearly a century—originally to pick up annuity checks on lands they owned in Oklahoma—and they don't plan to abandon the custom. Instead they have now asked for legislation that would give them a secure staging ground on the Rio Grande floodplain.

A measure to empower the Texas Indian Commission to apply federal money to the needs of the Kickapoo passed the state Senate in early May, under the sponsorship of Sen. Ron Clower (D-Garland). The bill's House backer, Rep. Susan McBee (D-Del Rio), won its approval in subcommittee; final passage is expected before the legislative session ends (and as the *Observer* goes to press).

"WHITE MAN'S GOD"

Jim Brown, city manager for Eagle Pass and a partisan of the Kickapoo, foresees more tranquil times for the tribe once federal funds are tapped.

"The Kickapoo haven't gotten state funds of any kind and won't even if the Clower-McBee bill is passed. But the state would be able to get them federal money, with which we hope to buy them land and eventually set up health services of some kind. People in Eagle Pass have tried to ignore the Kickapoo, but the present situation is a mark against the whole community," Brown says.

"Our religion tells us that God put the earth here for all human beings. The earth is not the property of anyone, not in God's eyes. But the white man says he owns the earth, and now he wants to be our landlord," Whitewater declares.

"The Kickapoo believe in God. But the white man's god is money, and that's why we are careful about adopting the ways of white men. If we become what you are, then we are lost."

By the late 1970s, Reavis was working with national joutrnals. Mother Jones, a progressive magazine founded in 1976, and named after the infamous Irish-American trade union activist, Mary Harris Jones, sent Reavis into the mountains of southern Mexico. As one of his earliest articles on Mexican politics, "At War in the Mexican Jungle" lays the groundwork for much of his subsequent writings [for example, see "The Smoldering Fire"] about the social conflicts within Mexico and across the Mexico-Texas border. This article first appeared in Mother *Jones,* May 1978.

At War in the Mexican Jungle

Mario does not measure up to our expectations of a revolutionist. He is owner and boss of a San Antonio restaurant that employs 30 waiters and grosses a million dollars a year. He is a gourmet and a patron of private clubs. A short, light-skinned man with the accent of northern Mexico, Cantú smiles often; his voice is gentle and good humored. Though he frequently donates to and speaks for Chicano causes, he lives in a neighborhood that is both Anglo and impeccably petty bourgeoisie.

Cantú doesn't satisfy the standards of this neighbors, either. His sole experience with higher education was as an inmate in the federal prison system. Released on parole in 1970, his rehabilitation was short lived; now he is on probation, this time for "shielding" undocumented aliens. Cantú is wanted in Mexico on gun-running charges, and he has proclaimed his affiliation with a secret organization of peasant revolutionaries whose fundraising activities include kidnapping. Many Chicano leaders in Texas who once respected Cantú now shun him because of his insistence on implementing his own unpopular theory: that until Mexico dispels yanqui influence the way Cuba did, Chicanos will not win in their struggle against discrimination in the United States. The theory is a novel one, but it is contradicted, in at least one instance, by the continuing struggles of Chinese Americans. Yet, Cantú insists with questionable relevance, whoever heard of prejudice against Miami's Cubans?

Whatever its merits, the Cantú thesis is probably the first Mexican-American liberation strategy to locate the Chicano future in an international matrix. Because of that, Cantú believes that events in the United States will be deeply affected by the outcome of some events in Mexico that few North Americans know about: the scattered, but growing, bloody armed warfare going on in the villages scattered across Mexico's southern mountains.

THE HIDDEN WAR

Cantú styles himself after Ricardo Flores Magón, the anarchist prophet who coined the cry of Mexico's last revolution—"Land and Liberty!"—and who inspired its first strike movement. Magón, who organized in San Antonio at the beginning of his American exile in 1904, died in Leavenworth prison while serving out a sedition sentence. His latter-day disciple has not created a slogan for the Mexican masses; but if he did, it might be "Land and Liberty and Oil!"

Today Mexico is a country reaching for a promise and heading for a crisis. The promise is the untapped petroleum reserves that could make Mexico a power of significant rank within two decades. But the nationalized oil industry is dependent on foreign financing and a foreign market for its expansion. Mexicans both inside and outside the government charge that the International Monetary Fund and other international lending agencies are subservient to the interests of industrialized, oil-consuming nations. They fear that Mexico will be forced to cut export prices in exchange for new loans. That demand has already been made by the U.S. State Department, which in January offered to arrange sales of Mexican natural gas—at a price 16 percent below the world market. Thus far, the Mexican government has balked at price cuts. But with a foreign debt of $30 billion—the largest of any nation its size—Mexico is in no position to bargain. The promise of petroleum wealth is for the moment beyond reach.

Meanwhile, Mexico's domestic economy is swamped by a rising population for whom there are no jobs. Today, the country has more than 64 million inhabitants and one of the fastest population growth rates in the world. The population is expected to double over the next 20 years, and the job market is already overwhelmed. Unemployment and underemployment today affect an estimated 50 percent of the work force, and millions of Mexican laborers have fled to El Norte in search of survival. Massive deportations from the U.S., advocated by some Carter spokespeople—as a threat to force petroleum prices down, the Mexicans say—could plunge Mexico into irreversible despair.

Mexico's ruling political party, Partido Revolucionario Institucional (PRI), is staggering to maintain its equilibrium. Chiefly through skillful manipulation of patronage, the PRI built an electoral machine capable of producing a majority in almost every Mexican precinct, rural or urban; indeed, the PRI has won every major election in modern history. The costs of its victories have been an inflated bureaucracy and national debt. To avoid bankruptcy, the current government has called a halt to most public-works programs. The result is that patronage runs thin, while international conflicts thicken. Weakened cohesion gave the PRI's leftists an aperture for forcing the legalization of opposition socialist parties last fall. For the first time in more than 30 years, the PRI faces the prospect of electoral challenges. If the insurgent parties show strength, many of the PRI's laborites and intellectuals—traditionally its links to the people—will jump ship.

Faith in the PRI and its government has collapsed in the countryside where change has been awaited longest and implemented least. The government has sought to alleviate peasant discontent and privation (family cash-incomes of peasants still average less than $100 per year) by the creation of *ejidos*, collectively owned farms that are self-governing villages as well. Residents of ejido villages, *ejidatarios*, are granted plots of land by their townspeople but may not sell, rent, or lease their tracts. Even though existing ejidos usually lack financing and modern technology, they are nevertheless popular. The peasants' chief complaint is that agrarian reform has proceeded too slowly: 60 years have passed since the end of the revolution that promised land to the tiller, and only half the country's arable acreage is in the hands of ejidatarios and small farmers. Large landowners have the rest.

Armed guards, or *pistoleros*, often protect these large land-holdings from angry, land-hungry peasants. Sometimes landowners will loan or rent pistoleros to one another, thus pitting peasants against miniature private armies that can move about from one threatened big farm to another.

1,000 Deaths

From the state of Sonora, at the top of the nation, to Chiapas at its base, peasants and large landholders are at war over land rights. Property-less peasants occupy the tracts of estate owners, the ranchers, and marijuana growers who themselves frequently encroach upon ejidos. In the north, peasant land invaders are generally unarmed and usually are turned back by bullets from pistoleros. But in the south, where jungle-covered hillsides provide a geographical advantage, the Partido Proletario de México (PPM) and kindred groups are arming the peasantry to defend its turf and to reach out for more. Last year more than 300 land invasions and nearly 1,000 associated deaths were estimated in Mexico. Mario Cantú, who is a leader in the American wing of the PPM, sees this peasant insurgency as the harbinger of a civil war that will redeem Mexico from foreign dependence and underdevelopment. Oil-rich and anti-imperialist, Mexico will then be able to bargain with clout, conferring its prestige on the Chicano movement in the U.S.

Revolutionary visions, however, are not hard currency with journalists anymore. To show evidence that the peasant movement exists, and to disseminate his prophecies, Cantú has twice arranged my passage into remote villages where discontent is armed.

On my first trip last summer, I saw both the florid physical beauty of southern Mexico and the poverty of its peasantry. The hardships of peasant life are many and obstinate: palm huts and adobe villages with no sanitary facilities whatever, no electricity or mail service; towns in which the only water source is a shallow creek and the chief agricultural implement is the machete; towns with children whose bellies are swelling with parasites. Constitutional liberties in the remote areas of states like Oaxaca are a fantasy: pistolero white guards have ruled in the the mountains since the days of Porfirio Díaz, 80 years ago, when Indians were deprived of their communal lands. The poverty of southern peasants knows no parallel in Mexico, and I was surprised, not that they had organized, but that they had organized so well. In the villages I visited, even the mayors were members of the PPM.

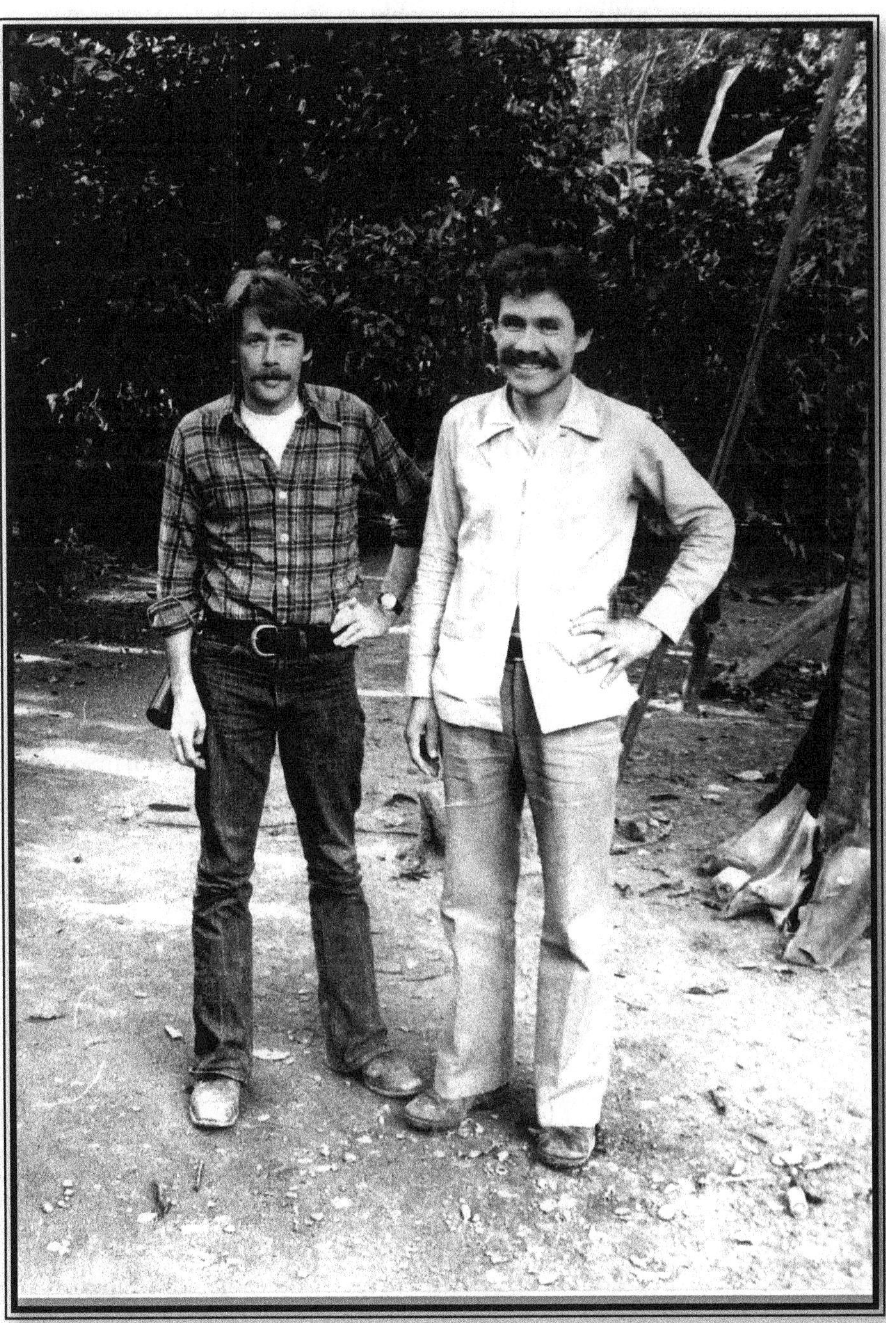

Reavis and Florencio "Güero" Medrano Mederos, a guerrilla organizer and chief figure in the Partido Proletario Unido de America (PPUA), somewhere in Oaxara, 1977. Photographer: Mario Cantú. Image courtesy of the Wittliff Collections.

On this trip I am to see the legendary Florencio Medrano Mederos, or "Güero," the PPM's commander. (His nickname means "blond" or "fair-skinned," and by extension it is a term of endearment.) No reporter—Mexican or American—has been granted an interview with him since 1974, when Medrano formed his clandestine party. Now Mario Cantú has not only arranged an interview with Güero but has also promised me a chance to take photographs for *Mother Jones.* Güero may soon become Latin America's next guerilla hero—or martyr—and I am anxious to see him before some violent destiny intervenes. But before I reach his hiding place, I am brought face to face with the bloodshed that has now become commonplace in Mexico's rugged backcountry.

THE UNDERGROUND MAKES CONTACT AT LAST

This trip, like the first, has been characterized by delay. Early one morning I call Cantú in San Antonio to complain that I had been waiting a week in Mexico City and no one from the revolutionary movement had come to see me. He assures me that within five minutes a courier will telephone my hotel. The five minutes pass; then more than five hours pass, and still I have no message from the rebels.

No; there is a knock on the door. The courier is here. He tells me his name is Ernesto, but I already have learned not to believe the names anybody in the Underground gives. He is a thin and extremely delicate young man, about 25, who speaks in a squeaky voice more appropriate to an adolescent girl. His frail bone structure gives an impression of refinement: slender lips and narrow, arching nose, the thin hands of a pianist or jewelry craftsman. But his skin is a deep brown and his accent is unmistakably peasant, rural and southern; he tells me that he is originally from the countryside around Jalapa, in the state of Veracruz. Ernesto wears a flowery nylon shirt and tan twill slacks. Nothing about him suggests an affinity for violence.

I am not surprised when Ernesto tells me that I shall have to wait—he does not say how long—before he guides me into the hills where Güero is holed up. We agree that he will call in three days.

Ernesto does not call until the evening of the appointed day. His message is short: be ready to leave in half an hour. When he shows up to meet me, he is not alone. Standing on the curb outside, baggage in hand, is Mario Cantú. He is nervous as he greets me, for there is a warrant out for him in Mexico, issued at Monterrey on allegations of sedition and arms trafficking. Cantú had planned for me to be up in the hills by the time he crossed the border into Mexico. But arrangements went askew, and now the three of us will travel together.

On our way to the bus terminal, we stop at a drugstore to find a remedy for my intermittent "turista." Ernesto counsels against the nostrum proffered me and orders the pharmacist to bring a bottle of Zetaquin instead. Then he reads the contents listed on the label and pronounces it satisfactory. Ernesto, I realize, is the guerrilla known in the Underground as "El Médico," a former university student who is now in charge of the PPM's program to eradicate intestinal parasites in the villages it controls—and a man who, from time to time, pulls bullets out of wounded peasants.

By noon Thursday, our bus has reached Coyontla, a market town in the state of Oaxaca. Cantú and I take hotel rooms. The tension we are already feeling grows as El Médico departs for an unspoken destination in the surrounding hills. He comes back the next day with another guide, who takes Cantú away with him. El Médico and I have to wait until the following Thursday before we make the last leg of our journey to join them in the village where the PPM's leader, Florencio "Güero" Medrano Mederos, is in hiding.

A Death In The Jungle

Finally, El Médico and I set out Thursday morning for the backcountry. When our bus drops us at the roadside, a thin, red-faced man comes up and signals for us to follow. As we walk with him down the road he tells me who he is. Don Pedro, now in his 60s, was once an elementary school teacher, now retired to farming on the ejido that employed him. His age, long residence, and status as an educated man have made him widely known in the cranny of the mountains. What is not known beyond the boundaries of Ejido Estribu is that for three years he has been a local leader for the PPM.

Don Pedro has gray hair and is hatless, which is rare in these parts. A laughing, good-natured man, he talks as we walk along about the parasites in the local water and the cures he uses for them, and about his work as a schoolteacher. There is no government school here, so the ejido simply took up a collection and hired him.

He also talks about the mounting tension in this area between the ejidatarios and the three or four big local landowners. Nine months earlier, one landowner took over a tract of uncultivated ejido land and began to grow marijuana on it. (Poorer peasants rarely grow marijuana in Mexico because the government sends in helicopters to defoliate their fields. The soldiers leave the big landowners alone.) In retaliation, ejido peasants have been killing and eating the big landlords' cattle. Feelings are running high. Pistoleros have ambushed and killed two peasants in the last year.

Suddenly a pickup stops a few yards in front of us, halting our discourse. Three pistoleros are inside, each dressed norteño-style, like Dodge City cowboys. The Driver steps down and, from inside the cab, one of the others hands out an M-16, which the driver trains on us. Neither El Médico nor Don Pedro looks aside. "Listen, old man, I want to know where that boy Domingo went to. We think he may know something about those cattle you people stole," the cowboy says menacingly. Don Pedro keeps walking but hollers back, "Domingo ran away with that whore you call your mother. Ask her where he is."

Normally, those are fighting words in rural Mexico. But today machista insults passed between peasants and pistoleros are subject to strategic considerations. The pistolero does not shoot us, probably because it is broad daylight, perhaps because my backpack—the badge of an outsider—confers an immunity on us. The pistolero tells us we are animals undeserving of his courtesy, then remounts his pickup and drives past in a cloud of grit.

The road in front of us slopes at a river that must be crossed by dugout. When we get there, we see that the pistoleros have gone before us; their pickup is parked at the riverbank. A ten-year-old boy is in charge of the dugout; he, too, is involved with the PPM. Don Pedro has left his rifle with the boy, who brings it out of a hiding place in the jungle. Once across the river, Don Pedro proceeds up the trail with the bolt of his carbine cocked, for we are afraid the pistoleros are lying in wait.

The jungles of Oaxaca are no less dense than those of the Orient. Vines crisscross the foliage above, moss hangs down, and underfoot the ground is soft with moisture. Overgrowth sometimes reduces visibility to as little as three meters. Don Pedro goes in front, with me behind, and El Médico about five meters to my rear, carrying my pack. We come upon a dip in the trail and Don Pedro scurries down.

Suddenly someone shouts *"Alto!"* Don Pedro stops. I am about three feet behind and above him on the steep trail. Through the leaves I see, on the other side of the dip, a torso hidden in the foliage. Then I make out the face of a pistolero, cowboy hat pushed back on his forehead. Images flash through my head: being turned over to the police, torture, death. I have money sewn into the lining of my boot, and I imagine handing it over to them to buy back our lives.

Don Pedro points his rifle forward from chest level, and instantly I know what will happen. I spin around and start to run. Don Pedro edges back toward me and then—crack!—he fires. Crack! Crack! I am running back toward El Médico, who is lying on the ground. I run past him and trip, throwing my hands out to break the impact. He grabs my cuff. Dat-dat-dat-da-dat-dat. An automatic weapon is speaking, probably the M-16. Poof-pow, poof-pow, poof-pow, there are pistols as well. We hear a trampling in the undergrowth.

El Médico, who has peeled off the backpack without rising from the ground, leaps up and springs past me. I chase behind, following him toward the river. He darts sharply to the right and, on hands and knees, crawls into the virgin jungle. I follow his lead and seconds later lie down, panting, beside him. We wait with our heads buried in crossed arms for nearly 15 minutes. Everything is silent now. "The bastards probably ran the other way. They're hiding too," El Médico ventures.

He instructs me to stay where I am until he comes back, or until dark. Then he crawls out to the trail again. I cannot see him as he creeps back to the dip, but I hear the undergrowth crack under his steps. When he returns, Don Pedro's M-1 is slung across his shoulder. Without a word, he holds it out for my inspection. Only four shots are gone from its banana clip. In the seconds when Don Pedro fired those shots, he could have discharged a dozen bullets or more with an M-16. The costs of archaic arms are obvious. El Médico says that a dozen slugs hit the old man. The one through his forehead killed him.

To El Medico this killing is one in a series; he is almost matter-of-fact. His evaluation of the death is cruelly scientific. "The village will want revenge, I know. But Don Pedro shouldn't have fired without taking cover. We've lost him because our people are too confident once they have guns."

REVENGE

We leave the body on the trail. We must get to the village, but the trail we had been following is clearly too dangerous. The pistoleros are still nearby. I have almost forgotten that my goal is to meet and interview Güero. The death of Don Pedro has, for now, obliterated all else.

We go back to the river, which the pistoleros must cross to get to their pickup. El Médico tells the boat boy to let them pass, and to inform the village as soon as they are gone. The boy leads us upriver for more than a quarter mile, pointing out a second trail to the ejido. El Médico pulls back the bolt on the M-1, and we advance.

The trail winds around farmland outlying the village. By the time we arrive, Don Pedro's body has been retrieved. Women crowd around the widow's palm hut; barefoot girls go in and out. The men are assembled in the open hut, which serves as city hall, and they are discussing revenge. Cantú is there; on the edge of the gathering he has already pieced together what happened and makes no gesture to greet us. In the middle of the hut, on the bench where town officials sit, is an older man wearing a palm sombrero, two younger peasants at his side. Güero is nowhere around. Cantú tells me that he left the ejido yesterday for a village in the state of Veracruz.

M-1s and old Mausers stick up in the midst of the gathering like fence posts in a field of new corn. Everyone has already agreed that vengeance must be taken tonight if possible, before the pistoleros flee with their belongings. The mayor, Don Rogelio, will lead a raid on the house near the highway where the pistoleros live, taking the two young peasants as lieutenants and a dozen armed men for firepower. The raiding party will leave at dusk.

Planning stops when the widow comes in, led by her daughter. Her shriveled frame convulses as she moans, tears rolling down dark sun-beaten cheeks. Her daughter holds her up as she strains to state her case. Her language is Chinanteca, which I do not understand. El Médico tells me that she wants Güero to lead the attack, as an honor to her dead husband. Apparently, the sentiment is that Don Pedro would have wanted it that way.

The men do not want to show disrespect—most have removed their hats—but they do not want to wait, either. It is Don Rogelio, seated on the bench, who speaks the first words, in Spanish, to the assembly. "It would be fitting for El Comandante Güero to be here, but that cannot be. The bastards will be gone by morning, and we must move quickly."

Everyone nods. No show of hands is taken, however; the old man is bearing full responsibility for the decision. He speaks to the widow in Chinanteca, and she wails again. Several men crowd around to help the daughter usher her off. She flails her arms and shrieks as they lead her down the street.

The assembly breaks up. Don Roglelio will not grant my request to witness the ambush. El Médico, Cantú, and I are all outsiders, he says, and it would be best if we left immediately. Don Rogelio gives us a guide and a gun—an old lever-action Remington—and bids us good-by. When we cross the river, the pistoleros pickup is still there.

That evening, all three pistoleros are shot and killed as they drive their truck back home.

Meeting Güero

Two days later, we come into a village that is prosperous by ejido standards. Whitewashed adobe houses with palm roofs face onto a village green. There is electricity here, although no running water and no telephones. Next to the municipal hut stands a red International Harvester tractor, bought with funds donated by the PPM. Behind the home of the local storekeeper, in an orange grove, we find Güero sitting in a hand-hewn chair, talking to comrades from the state of Michoacán.

Members of the PPM deny that if Güero were killed, the movement would go under. They like to say that he is a political and military strategist only, that he is replaceable and that charisma has little to do with his stature. But they are wrong. When I return to the U.S. with my taped conversation with Güero, the first comment my wife, Marta, makes on hearing it is: *"Qué voz tan varonil!"* "What a masculine voice!" Military caution and sensitivity to peasant needs have built the PPM, but Güero's personal magnetism is an essential ingredient.

Güero stands out among peasants. He is light-skinned and has blue eyes to match, both rare traits among southern farmworkers. Keeping the Army off his trail has meant keeping on the move in regions with few bus and rail connections. Consequently, Güero has developed the strength and grace of a Sherpa and the alertness of a hunted species. When Güero walks through a village, his wife and child follow behind, as is peasant custom. But when he sits down, he can expound knowledgably about Mexican history and politics, Marxist theory, or armaments. He speaks the sing-song dialectic of the unlettered, and his grammar is often faulty. His diction is distinctively rustic: Güero says "pior" instead of "peor," "pos" instead of "pues." When he talks, his hands dart about this body like butterflies around a sunflower.

My first questions are autobiographical. I translate them as Güero answered, grammar intact:

"I am born in 1945 in a little town, Limón Grande, inside the state of Guerrero. My parents are peasants without land. My family was big and always struggled until the death against the exploitation of landlords. Several times we were repressed, and the majority of my forefathers were killed off by the pistoleros and the Army. . . . When I more or less was old enough to go to school, I remember one time when my mother sent me, for a few days only, because on the third day, they expelled me for not having a uniform or the proper shoes. After that, I could never go back to school."

When Güero reached adolescence, he went to work on estates around Limón Grande and joined the struggle for land rights. After a confrontation with the pistoleros, he fled to Mexico City.

"In the Federal District I have to face up to not knowing how to read. Several times on leaving out for where my relatives sent me to buy tortillas, I could not find my way back, because all the houses looked alike to me, and I couldn't read the street signs. Well, I moved away from there because I couldn't find work, because everybody asked me for a primary school certificate or a diploma from at least fourth grade. I worked awhile pushing a little cart around La Merced market, and then I moved on to Cuernavaca."

There he joined a company of traveling handicrafts hawkers. While on tour with them, a group of Maoist students befriended Güero. "They gave me precisely a set of the works of Mao, but to tell the truth, I was just learning to read, and it was very hard. So I went to their discussion groups, where I could learn more by just listening," Güero says. In 1969, his mentors took him to China, and he came back convinced that he could lead the peasantry in revolt. His first effort was the founding of a squatters' camp of some 30,000 on the outskirts of Cuernavaca.

Soldiers marched on the shantytown in 1974 and killed Güero's younger brother in a shoot-out. Along with the surviving leadership of the encampment, Güero retreated to the hills where the PPM, then called the Partido Proletario de América, was formed. The group's more militant members joined ranks with Lucio Cabañas, a guerrilla leader whose operations were centered in the state of Guerrero. Cabañas, captured and executed later that year, was already losing in skirmishes that were becoming increasingly defensive.

"Our forces had been converted into bands of errant guerrillas, with almost no political base," Güero told me. "I went to discuss this with Cabañas, and he agreed that we were rapidly failing. But unfortunately, the repression was already so heavy that it was too late to change tactics. So I told him that I was taking my people out, and he consented to let us leave." Güero led his armed band, about 45 men, to the state of Michoacán, where they began training peasants for armed land-seizures. Their movement has now spread into pockets of Oaxaca, Morelos, Veracruz, and back into Guerrero, where Cabañas failed. Thus the PPM is not a guerrilla military movement fighting troops, as were the Cuban and Chinese revolutionaries, but rather a movement for arming peasants to fight landlords. The PPM is now planning a land invasion that will involve some 10,000 to 20,000 peasants. If it succeeds, the next step—several years in the future—will be declaration of a "liberated zone" over much of southern Mexico's mountains.

A Mexican Vietnam?

Güero and his American attaché, Cantú, believe that, as the peasant rebellion raises its head, U.S. military penetration into Mexico will increase. Members of the PPM who were imprisoned in Cuernavaca last summer told me that they were interrogated by translators for English-speaking men, and a similar report comes from Ramón Chacón, a Texan who was jailed in Monterrey on arms charges. The Pentagon denies that Green Berets or other Army personnel are doing counterinsurgency work in Mexico. The CIA refuses to comment. Güero says that helicopters the U.S. gave Mexico for policing the drug traffic have instead been used for spotting peasant arms-training camps. PPM organizers claim that within months they will be able to hold the Mexican Army at bay in the remote regions of the south—but not if the Army gets American technical backing or troop support. "We want to send a message to your countrymen," Güero tells me. "We want to ask them to protest imperialist military involvement here, like they did for Vietnam. We especially look to the Chicanos, our brothers by blood. As long as Mexico is on her knees, they cannot really rise up."

Taking his cue from Güero, Cantú outlines the task he sees for Chicano activists. "In 1968, when the Mexican students were massacred at Tlatelolco, thousands of Parisians went to the streets to protest. But there was not one demonstration in the U.S. Today, Amnesty International says there are more than 200 political prisoners missing in the state of Guerrero alone, but again, there is no protest in the U.S. The Chicano movement has been muzzled." Cantú charges that important Chicano leaders have made a pact of silence with the Mexican government and the ruling political party, the PRI. He particularly accuses Reies Tijerina of New Mexico and José Angel Gutiérrez, chair of the Texas Raza Unida Party. Both men have recently met with Mexico's President José Lopez Portillo, and also were hosted by his predecessor, Luis Echeverría. (Gutiérrez has on another occasion told me that he believes it is "irresponsible, untimely and inappropriate" to talk, as Cantú does, about revolution in Mexico.)

The pounding Güero and Cantú give both American and Mexican leaders runs at a clip faster than I can absorb. But in their explanations, I detect that profound sense of national outrage that has always motivated Mexico's rebels—and even its reactionaries. It was the hated dictator Díaz, after all, who said that Mexico's chief problem was that it was so far from God and so close to the United States. That same viewpoint, laced with socialist rhetoric and armed with archaic yanqui rifles, is at the heart of the PPM's peasant movement.

. . . Or A Mexican Chile?

But patriotic sentiment, prophecy, and peasant support do not a revolution make. American sympathy, if it emerges, cannot add the missing ingredient. Mexico cannot be the scene of a successful revolt so long as its cities, where half the population lives, are outside the revolutionary current. The PPM is isolated in the hills. Other socialist parties are rapidly growing in urban Mexico, but among them there are no competent groups dedicated to armed insurgency. Neither is there any revolutionary agitation worthy of mention inside the ranks of soldiers, who are largely of peasant origins. The PPM's leaders are gambling on the hope that economic conditions will produce revolutionary organization in the cities—before the government makes an all-out effort to flatten the movement in the countryside.

If there is any hope for socialism in Mexico within the next three decades, it lies in accommodation of the urban electoral movement with the armed movement in the countryside, the only movement the peasants fully trust. But unity is far off. City dwellers as a group deplore violence, and peasants as a group have no use for politicians—even those who call themselves socialists. Both ballot and bullet socialists in Mexico seem to deny any chance of linking their movements together.

Yet the leaders of both movements say that any uprising that fails or any election that is close could become the pretext for a military coup. Mexico is no more immune to junta rule than was Chile. In Mexico, as in Chile, rival leftist factions may once again teach us that we can be neither socialists nor revolutionaries from our graves.

This article, which appeared in *Texas Monthly,* March 1978, should be read in conjunction with Reavis's travels into the southern mountains of Mexico, discussed in the preceding article, "At War in the Mexican Jungle." Crossing cultural, economic, and linguistic borders, Reavis does not attempt to nullify them as arbitrary, but to present the rifts that define political geography.

The Smoldering Fire

It is a typical Saturday night in Mario's Restaurant on the fringe of San Antonio's West Side. Beyond the crowded foyer, mariachis gather around a group of anniversary celebrants. Virtually unnoticed in the restaurant's hubbub, two men at a table in the corner sit staring at out-folded newspapers. One man, the larger of the two, is a convicted gunrunner who has spent time in prisons on both sides of the border. But the other smaller man is clearly the one in charge. He is Mario Cantú, convicted felon, radical Chicano leader, accused arms smuggler, and the proprietor of Mario's Restaurant. They are plotting a new Mexican revolution.

Mexican political intrigue is nothing new to San Antonio. Cantú styles himself after Ricardo Flores Magón, the radical prophet of Mexico's last revolution. Driven into exile in 1904, Magón came to San Antonio to publish his newspaper *Regeneración*. It was in San Antonio that Francisco Madero penned the Plan of San Luis Potosí, the program for the 1910 Revolution. In the fall of 1910, from the old Hutchins Hotel, Madero and his cohorts plotted their rebellion. From San Antonio they sent arms and dollars to comrades across the border. After Madero became president, his rivals regrouped against him—again in San Antonio—for a futile uprising.

Today Mario Cantú hopes to follow in their footsteps as the spokesman for a clandestine revolutionary party operating in southern Mexico.

I have known Cantú for about six months. It has taken me this long to persuade him that I can be trusted to go into the mountains to report on guerrillas who are trying to organize peasant revolts. As I make my way past the rows of tables to join Cantú and his *compañero,* Cantú rises to welcome me warmly. For a few minutes we make polite conversation. Then he gives me the name of a modest hotel in a residential section of Mexico City. I am to go there, take a room, and wait. The underground will contact me and lead me south to revolutionary strongholds in Oaxaca. Cantú does not say how or when and I do not ask; in these circles, inessential questions raise suspicions. I bid the men adiós.

The city of Oaxaca lies in a warm semitropical valley surrounded by the summits of the rugged Sierra Madre del Sur. It is one of Mexico's jewels, a mixture of Indian and modern Mexico, famous for pink arcades and black pottery. But away from this principal city of southern Mexico and from the Pan American Highway linking it with Mexico City, modern Mexico is nowhere to be seen. Draw a circle around the city of Oaxaca, perhaps fifteen miles in diameter, and outside that circle the federal presence is almost undetectable. In those mountains, which reach 11,000 feet, are villages with no paved roads, no schools, no telephone lines, no railroads, no mail service, and no electricity, villages where Zapotec and Mixtec Indians scrape out an existence. Beans, tortillas, rice, and chiles make up their diet, and in that remote backcountry, peasants live in thatched palm huts with dirt floors and take their water from shallow creeks. The jungle—Oaxaca is well south of the Tropic of Cancer—is the universal sanitary facility, outhouses being unknown. Malaria is a constant menace, and the mortality rate in the state of Oaxaca is the second highest of Mexico's 32 districts. Only two states have lower literacy rates; none has a lower proportion of dwellings (18.7 percent) with running water. Nowhere in Mexico do more people speak local Indian dialects instead of Spanish.

Peasant unrest in these mountains goes back as far as Santa Anna. The two great political figures who dominated Mexico for the latter half of the nineteenth century came out of the Oaxacan mountains: the Indian lawyer Benito Juárez and his successor, the mestizo general Porfirio Díaz. Juárez set out to break the stranglehold of the clergy on the Mexican agricultural system by forcing the Church to sell its immense land holdings, but it was Díaz who left a legacy that still casts its shadow on modern Mexico. During one 11-year period of his 34-year reign, Díaz gave away 134,500,000 acres of public land—about a fourth of the entire area of Mexico—to friends and influence-buyers. He broke up the Indian *ejidos,* the farms and villages owned collectively by the tribes, and sold them off. So successful was Díaz in reshaping Mexico that at the onset of the Mexican Revolution of 1910, less than 10 percent of the Indians' communities owned any land, and big estate operators held 96.6 percent of the nation's cultivated acreage.

Ever since the new government established itself half a century ago, it has struggled with the problem of land reform. It has tried to reestablish the ejidos, and more than half of the land that was in large haciendas in 1910 has been delivered to small farmers and *ejidatarios.* Yet the economic picture in the countryside doesn't seem much better than it did in Díaz' time. Most peasants still work on ranches and large estates. Their medium of exchange is the crops they raise; cash income is often less than $75 a year. There are simply too many campesinos for the available land: even if all remaining large holdings were split up, barely one in fifteen of Mexico's landless peasants could get standard-sized tracts to plow.

Mexico's economic woes continue to thwart the government's efforts to deal with its agrarian crisis. Its huge foreign debt is the largest in the world; its birthrate, the highest of any nation its size; its staggering rate of persons out of work or marginally employed, now 45 percent. Consequently, idle campesinos, frustrated by government inaction, have begun seizing property owned by ranchers and corporations. Last year there were more than 300 land invasions, and in the ensuing violence, over 200 peasants and estate guards were killed in the state of Oaxaca alone. To organize and arm peasants for this virtual land war, revolutionary groups like the *Partido Proletario Unido de América* (United Proletarian Party of America) have organized in the mountains. The PPUA (called POO-ah by its members) is the party of Mario Cantú, and its guerrillas will take me deep into the mountains of Oaxaca, where few government officials, civil or military, ever go.

The PPUA is a small, secret, and illegal organization. Unlike many leftist revolutionary cabals, it has little interest in political theory. Since it keeps no membership roster, estimating its size is difficult and requires several standards of participation. If the PPUA is regarded as an organization of professional revolutionaries, then there are perhaps not more than a hundred members. But leaders of ejidos in five states—Oaxaca, Michoacan, Guerrero, Veracruz and Morelos—have joined the PPUA, and the ejidatarios support the party's activity as if they belonged. Peasant leaders who have read the party's program and accepted the goal of revolution probably number less than five hundred, but their local following numbers in the thousands.

The PPUA is widely known in Mexico for a 1974 kidnapping that was sensationalized in the Mexican press. The target, American millionaire Tom Davis, was not in his Cuernavaca mansion when the PPUA paid its visit; instead raiders carried off his Mexican wife. She was released 77 days later, after Davis paid a $40,000 ransom and signed over a tract of farmland near Cuernavaca to leftist Bishop Méndez Arceo, who, on instruction from the PPUA, split it into plots for distribution to landless peasants.

Unlike Mexico's urban terrorists, PPUA leaders do not believe that detonating bombs in public plazas will provoke mass action. The party has an elaborate timetable for revolution, including the seizure of a large area of mountainous countryside that can serve as a base for conventional battles beyond its boundaries. However, military preparations are no more the PPUA's forte than kidnappings. The party's more sensational actions, like the Davis abduction, have not gone smoothly, and the archaic arms it provides supporters are no match for the automatic weapons the army wields. The PPUA's strength and any future it has lie in the leadership's ability to weld peasants together for small goals with short-term payoffs. With tractors financed by PPUA money, peasants in several ejidos are increasing their productivity. With vintage rifles supplied by the PPUA, they are taking over new acreage and defending themselves, not from federates but from *pistoleros*, the private armies of cattle, lumber and marijuana operators. It is as much like a wild-West range war as a guerrilla uprising. The chief figure behind the PPUA is known to police as Florencio Medrano Mederos; in the mountains of Oaxaca he is known to the people as Güero.

Güero: El Comandante

Ten days pass before the courier contacts me at my Mexico City hotel, and he takes me not to the peasant south, but to an industrial suburb of the city. He leads me into a junkyard and up to an adobe apartment at the rear. A man in his middle thirties, muscular and unmistakably *güero*—"light-skinned"—rises to embrace me. Unlike most of the people I will meet, Güero has few Indian features. He has clear, deep-set blue eyes and curly, sandy hair cut short. "So you are the cousin whom Mario has sent," he cries out, as if overjoyed by my presence. I am not related to Mario, of course, but to Güero everyone the revolution touches becomes part of his clan.

Güero came down from the hills just this morning and rented the apartment on arrival. Pasteboard suitcases, still packed, are scattered around the room. A pile of floor sweepings rests in a corner beside a broom, and the smell of dust laces the air. In the center stands a single chair and an unvarnished table stacked high with wrinkled paper bags and fresh tortillas. Along one wall is a narrow cot where we sit down side by side. We are not alone in the room: there are three young men who act as guards. They glance repeatedly at the doorway, looking for soldiers or police, but if the authorities learn Güero is here, they will come in such numbers that the bodyguards will be useless. Near the table an Indian woman bends over her infant daughter. She is about thirty, less than five feet tall, with attractive dark spots on the crests of her cheekbones. Her name is Silvia, and she is Güero's wife.

Güero tells me that our meeting was delayed because several days earlier an army search party marched on the ejido where he is headquartered. Forewarned, he and his aides retreated further up on the jungle-covered mountainsides, where only peasants and outlaws go. He did not come down until spotters told him that the troops had abandoned the region.

Güero wears laced boots that reach up to his calves, and the cuffs of his tan khaki pants are stuffed into the tops. Although he is only five feet, six inches, his athletic build makes him seem taller. Every movement reveals fine muscle tone. He is clean-shaven and, if his pink shirt were not soiled by the grime of mountain trails, he might easily be mistaken for a high-school gym coach. I have been told he has bleeding ulcers in need of treatment, but nothing in his manner betrays illness of any sort. I ask about the ailment. "Well, I've had that problem for a few months, and I guess it's getting worse. But we'll straighten it out in the next few days," Güero says, as though he were talking about plumbing repairs.

He politely refuses my request to photograph him. Police pictures show a man with a moustache, but Güero says he trimmed it off last night to avoid detection in the city. He is not too concerned about giving authorities a new view of him for their dossiers; instead, he doesn't want his picture taken because his new look doesn't compliment him.

Admirers compare Güero to Che Guevara, and indeed his boyish soccer-star appearance is reminiscent of Che's Mexican period, just before he embarked with Fidel for the invasion of Batista's Cuba. But several things set Güero apart from Che, Lenin, Mao, and other revolutionary leaders in whose footsteps he hopes to follow. Communist revolutionaries have typically been men from educated classes who take up arms against injustices they understand in theory but have never suffered personally. Che was an allergist by profession; Lenin, an attorney; Mao, a schoolteacher and the son of a prosperous farmer. Ten years ago Güero was a landless peasant and traveling handicrafts hawker. Güero grew up illiterate; communist friends taught him to read as an adult. Lenin, Mao, and Che were self-taught revolutionaries. Güero went to China in 1969 to be trained. Other revolutionary leaders have been propagandists, but the PPUA does not even publish a newspaper. "The people will be in revolt before we have time to do much educational work," Güero says.

Güero was born in 1945 in the little town of Limón Grande, Guerrero. The Medrano clan was notorious long before Güero's time for agitating in favor of land reform; three generations ago, Güero's ancestors fought alongside Zapata. During Güero's childhood, the family more than once clashed with pistoleros and the army. He remembers one Christmas when 27 of his relatives were jailed for taking part in a land seizure.

"When I was about 15, I had to join in the struggle with the other men in my family, the struggle for land." Outwitting the pistoleros became Güero's occupation. But after several gunfights with pistoleros and one clash with the army, he quit to seek work in Mexico City. There he had to face up to not knowing how to read. "Several times I went out to buy tortillas and couldn't find my way back home. All the streets looked the same to me, and I couldn't read the signs. Nobody would give me a job because I hadn't finished primary school." For a few days he pushed a fruit cart in La Merced market, then he moved on, first to Cuernavaca, where he worked for a short time as a bricklayer's apprentice, next to join the army. Nine months later he quit. Within weeks, he had joined a group of traveling artisans. While on tour with them, Güero made friends with members of a now-defunct communist political faction. At their discussion sessions, he was awakened to the Medrano heritage.

"Before, I always thought that our enemy was only in Limón Grande. But the more I studied and thought, the more I understood that the landlord problem affects all of Mexico. There are hundreds of thousands of peasants in the same condition as my family," Güero says. His Maoist friends invited Güero to join them on a trip to China. He was there for six months, and when he returned, he began to organize the peasants.

In 1973, Güero and his younger brother, Primo, led a handful of homeless Cuernavacans in the takeover of a large tract of undeveloped land owned by a politically prominent landlord. Within weeks 20,000 other squatters, most of them dispossessed peasants who had come to the city seeking work, joined the seven families who led the invasion. The encampment, dubbed Rubén Jaramillo in honor of a martyred land-movement leader, was nonviolent by default: the only weapon available was an M-l rifle Mario Cantú had given Primo. When the army came into Rubén Jaramillo to arrest its leaders, Primo fired away while the others escaped. Primo was killed, but the survivors, along with Chicano supporters like Cantú, regrouped as the PPUA. The army has been hunting Güero ever since.

Güero is a man who disdains words. He tells me that Mexico is about to explode, but does not follow with the usual Marxist sermon about why the masses ought to rise up. Instead, he orders an Indian youth at the doorway to guide me through half a dozen named villages. Then he opens his billfold and gives my guide 500 pesos for expenses. I note that the wallet is bulging, both with pesos and American greenbacks—whether sent by supporters or taken in ransom I do not know. Güero dictates a note to the youth who will accompany me, signs it with flourishes, then writes his name legibly below. I now have my passport to the war zone.

TRUENO: ROCKING GUERRILLA

My broad-faced mahogany guide is Trueno, a twenty-year-old Zapotec from Oaxaca. Though he speaks Spanish without an Indian accent, Trueno's thick muscular limbs, his squatness, his complexion and his straight, shimmering black hair that stands nearly straight up mark him as an *indígena*, or Indian. Yet Trueno is more like my younger brother, Joe, than any of his tribal ancestors. Like millions of young people north of the border, Trueno worships a music box. His particular icon is a battery-powered GE tape player and radio that he carries everywhere and without whose companionship he cannot fall asleep. The questions Trueno asks me about the U.S. are not about politics, economics, or history; they are questions about Alice Cooper, Elton John, the Grateful Dead, and the Doors. Trueno's pockets and his backpack are crammed with cassettes of their songs, whose words he cannot understand.

Trueno became a guerrilla less for ideological reasons than because he is surging with physical vigor in need of an outlet. Though he ran away from home at fifteen because his village had no high school, he is not inclined to intellectual pursuits. One day during our journey Trueno picked up my copy of the Mexican gun law. He read for less than five minutes, then said, "Hell, you don't need to study that. All it says is that everything is illegal." Two months earlier, when a kidnap ransom was paid, Güero gave him 194,000 pesos (about $8,200) to make an arms purchase on the black market. Trueno completed his mission without difficulty, so why study the law? He showed no interest in my other pamphlet explaining the agrarian reform law.

When I ask Trueno why he joined the PPUA his answer is: *"¡Hijo, hombre, es la honda! Las chamacas de la universidad se vuelvan locas por los guerrilleros"* ("Damn, man, that's the groove! College girls go crazy over guerrillas"). He does not talk freely about his past, and we travel together for nearly a week before I can piece it together.

Trueno is the second-oldest son born to peasants in a region of rural Oaxaca, where life is especially cheap and survival unusually dear. By his own account, his family was more prosperous than others. "We had electricity in our house," he says. An older brother, Jaime, ran off to Mexico City, where he educated himself and became a primary school teacher. Five years ago, Trueno joined Jaime in a waterless, unheated one-bedroom apartment in the city and shined shoes in neighborhood bars for pocket change. Three years later he graduated from a technical school and found work as a drill-press operator in an electronics factory. Hundreds of thousands of unemployed peasants in Mexico City pray every day for such luck. But Trueno could not abide the discipline of industry. "That was the toughest time of my life, there in the factory. I couldn't stand to have the foreman looking over my shoulder all the time. I wanted to quit every minute I was there." Trueno was never assimilated into urban life, and when a cousin in Oaxaca who had joined the PPUA invited him back to the hills to organize, he left the city at once. The PPUA gave Trueno what the Oaxacan economy could not: a sense of belonging, a mission. At last he was no longer burdened by the lowly status and monotony that go with the word indígena. Now villagers regard Trueno as a man of the world, a leader whose heart is in the countryside, but whose head has urban savvy.

Trueno has been with the PPUA only six months, yet already he is "burned"—known to the police. His frightened parents forbid him to visit their home. Trueno has not yet killed anybody, but he says he undoubtedly will when the order is given. He regards violence as a natural fact that only cowards and the naive would question. "They have always killed us, haven't they? So why not kill a few of them?" He studies the crime pages of newspapers, keeping score of every new kidnapping as though revolution were a soccer game and the kidnappings goals for his side. "But the articles don't say who does these things or why," I point out. "What difference does that make? They have it coming," he retorts. "They" includes American businessmen, diplomats from every capitalist country, the rich of all nations, all policemen, and military officers and politicians.

Despite his icy bravado, Trueno is full of the sentimentality and openness of youth. He plays with children on the streets and chats expansively with ticket clerks in bus stations, farmers in their fields, Indian women in their huts. Engaged to marry when he joined the PPUA, he now refuses his fiancée's pleas for a wedding date. He confides to me that he has never slept with her because he does not want to make promises he may not be able to carry out. Like most young men his age, he is often homesick. Every night before going to bed, he places a special tape into his machine, a song by revolutionary balladeer José de Molina:

> Madre, me voy a la sierra,
> Madre, dispuesto a luchar.
> Me llevo un puño de tierra,
> Pa' recordar el hogar.
>
> (Mother, I am going to the mountains,
> Mother, ready to fight.
> I carry with me a fistful of dirt,
> To remind me of our home.)

THE MAYOR: NO MORE WAITING

At the *Ejido Miguel Allende,* a three-hour walk into the hills from the highway, Trueno introduces me to a dark, squat, graying man who speaks in near-falsetto. He is the mayor of this community as well as one of its founders. In 1971, along with 200 other landless peasants, he petitioned the agrarian reform agency for an ejido on the square mile of ranchland where their fields and homes now sit. For five years, representatives of the peasants' committee signed papers—the verb "to sign" has become local scatological slang—and kept appointments with the bureaucracy's regional offices. But nothing happened. In early 1976, a few militants, armed only with machetes and hatchets, decided to seize the land in time to clear it for spring planting. As soon as they erected huts on a knoll, pistoleros moved in and harassed them unmercifully, fencing over their plots and turning cattle loose to trample their crops. The community survived by splitting up the harvests from fields that withstood the Santa Gertrudis invasion and, I suspect, by income from a small and well-hidden harvest of marijuana as well. But the ejido's spirit was broken. Families began moving out, some to seek work in far-off cities, some to return to the employ of patrones whom they had proudly told good-bye just six months earlier. Only those who had little future apart from the ejido decided to stay and fight.

Most peasants in southern Mexico know the name Güero Medrano. They whisper of his exploits in bus stations—the nerve centers that connect mountain villages with the rest of the world—and tell of them openly in the ejidos. Güero's organizers circulate through the backcountry, carrying the message of class struggle. The leaders of Miguel Allende had been hearing about Güero for six months or more; finally, they contacted an organizer and sent for him, in the hope he could help their ejido survive.

Güero showed up alone and empty-handed, but brought promises of guns and a tractor for the embattled community. He asked in return that the settlers aid other peasants in the land war and that they pledge allegiance to revolution if problems of campesinos could not be solved by ordinary means—in effect, that the village join PPUA. All of Miguel Allende discussed the proposal for a week at midday meetings. A vote was taken, and the PPUA won. Six dissident families left the community, and the rest awaited the inevitable confrontation with the pistoleros. Before spring planting time, the PPUA sent a tractor and a cache of Mausers, .22 automatic pistols, and M-l carbines. Party organizers cleared a spot of land further up in the hills to train villagers in the use of firearms.

On the evening of May 1, the men gathered in the *ejido* assembly hut for the attack. There were 77 altogether, 22 with guns and the rest with machetes and hoes. They grouped in a crescent on a ridge above the hollow where the pistoleros had built their huts. A warning shot initiated the fighting.

The mayor tells me the rest: "They shot back, about twenty rounds. One person was hit in the ankle. We started giving them thunder from all sides, and they skipped out, running for the highway. We got one as he ran off. He just lay there and we waited, not shooting anymore because we were short on ammunition. After dark, a pickup pulled up down there, and two men laid the pistolero in the back and drove off. We don't know if he was dead or alive."

Nothing has been heard from the pistoleros since the shoot-out. New families have joined the ejido, taking over homes abandoned by those who left last year. "Some who moved out on us back when things looked bad now want to return. But we've voted to keep them out, because they ran out in our time of trouble," the mayor explains.

Shooting a pistolero, of course, is a far cry from waging revolution, but the people of Miguel Allende have no concept of this. Miguel Allende's revolutionaries dream not about taking over the government but about taking a piece of land and holding it. For them, revolution means taking up arms against foot soldiers. They believe that if they can get enough M-ls, they will have all the advantages on their side. It is a simple equation: rifles plus geography means victory. The army must come up from highways below their village. No one in the village is aware of fragmentation or napalm bombs; only a few have ever heard of Viet Nam.

One family in the ejido does have a broader perspective. A father and his adult son came from Guerrero, the southern state where Acapulco is located and the former base of Che-style guerrilla leader Lucio Cabañas, killed by the army in 1974. "When we lived in Guerrero," the father says, "some people in our ejido helped Cabañas, but we were afraid. But here we decided to join this organization [villagers almost never say PPUA because they have been told the party's name is a matter of security] because people said it was for the same things Cabañas was. The farmer is suffering everywhere in Mexico and we're tired of it."

The son, about twenty, takes off his cowboy hat before speaking to me. "I have two boys who will someday want land. Unless we get rid of this government of the rich bourgeoisie [some PPUA visitor must have taught him that phrase] my children won't have the dirt to bury themselves in." But for most of the villagers, including the mayor, the world they know is limited to the Oaxacan jungle, and the idea of a national revolution is beyond them.

I ask the mayor whether the government could head off peasant insurgency simply by delivering a tractor to every ejido. He agrees with my proposition, but has no faith in the government. His skepticism has nothing to do with the government's economic crisis, of which he is unaware. "If the government would help us. . . . If, if," he repeats. "I have lived sixty-three years, and the only government I ever saw that gave a damn for campesinos was the Cárdenas government, way back in the thirties."

The peasants' distaste for governments and landlords is rivaled only by their faith in Güero, the only leader most have ever trusted. They reward him with near worship. When I ask the mayor why he decided to support Güero, his answer is a hearty *"¡Porqué el Güero es tan cabrón!,"* which translates to something like, "Because Güero is such a son of a bitch!"

"You see, Güero doesn't care what will happen if they catch him. All he thinks about is what we have to do to get out of this hole we're in. He is macho enough to do whatever it takes. We all waited for years, suffering, doing as we were told, hoping a new leader would come along. Now he has come, and we are ready and this time we won't forgive. Now we are cabrones, too. You see, when the people get mad, they are cabrones, and it takes one big cabrón to lead them."

Two mornings later, I see just how serious the mayor is about being cabrón. I am awakened by the voices of several town elders, including the mayor, who are talking to Trueno. The topic is Alfonso, a founder of Miguel Allende, its first PPUA leader and the very man who invited Güero in. But the elders say he tried to sell ejido memberships to landless peasants in the region, a common but illegal practice of corrupt ejido leaders. Peasants who buy into an ejido in this manner often are merely front men for big landowners who want to expand onto the ejido. The peasant stands aside while cattle are run onto his plot (and others), and pistoleros stand by with automatic weapons to protect him from irate ejidatarios. Suspicions about Alfonso were confirmed some weeks ago when he came back from Ocotopec, the nearest market town, with new knee-high boots and a feathered cowboy hat. "Where else could he get that kind of money? The rest of us barely have enough to feed the cockroaches," one of the elders declares. "We've got to kill Alfonso, the mayor says, and all nod assent.

The visitors have noticed that I am listening, but no one pays any mind. A little boy and a dog wander in and sit down together in the dirt; they too are ignored. The leaders want Trueno to approve their decision about Alfonso, but he wants a question answered first. "What about his family?" Alfonso is divorced and has no children in Miguel Allende. He lives with two sisters, one of whom has a child. The child is already an orphan, and therefore killing Alfonso will not deprive him of anything, the mayor says. Trueno hesitates a moment, sitting at his table in thought. Then he looks straight at the villagers and grins. "Yeah, man, you're right. Alfonso deserves to be thundered. But don't you provoke him in any way. Wait until you can ambush him in the jungle."

Father Antonio: The Church Leans Left

There are no regular religious observances in Miguel Allende. The village is one of 24 visited by Father Antonio, a beleaguered itinerant priest. The padre is a curly-haired, white-skinned man of about forty, a native of Mexico City with an urbane, middle-class accent. Though he has a sturdy lumberjack's build, he seems gentle, intense and, in a way, sad. He tells me he knows Alfonso but won't talk about him in the village. We agree to meet the following night in Ocotopec.

The encounter is set for a snack bar on a side street, and the padre, dressed in street clothes and a clerical collar, is waiting when I arrive. As soon as I am seated he leans towards me and whispers rapidly, "Do you know that they're going to kill Alfonso?" I ask the padre what he has done to save him. The priest stares at me with his green eyes; my question has distressed him, not because it provokes a moral crisis, but because it tells him I do not understand.

"Alfonso brought a pistol to Mass last week, and I threw him out. Afterwards, I went by his house to persuade him to give up the ejido. His sisters agree, but he's determined to show that he cannot be scared off."

He says he has not tried to talk the villagers out of murdering Alfonso. "What good would it do? They know and I know that Alfonso tried to make side deals on the ejido. People here in Ocotopec have told me that he offered to make them members for a fee." The padre does not consider his inaction tantamount to condoning murder. He tells me a parable about a man who committed seven sins and was forgiven; but when the man committed seventy times seven sins, there was no pardon from man or God.

In fact, the point of the parable related in the Book of Matthew is that there is no limit to mercy: Jesus tells Peter that even seventy times seven sins should be forgiven. Father Antonio's inventive interpretation of Scripture reveals a great deal about the role of the Church in Mexico today. Since the Church no longer has extensive land holdings to protect, priests for some time have had greater political latitude than they did before the 1910 Revolution. Especially in rural parishes, many priests have begun to embrace radical social and political ideas. Even the hierarchy is gradually being transformed. In Cuernavaca, Bishop Méndez Arceo, whom newspapers have labeled the Red Bishop, instructs his clergy on the sacred duty of advocating the cause of the poor. His priests are social agitators as much as men of the cloth, and they are not alone; all over Latin America, the Church is leaning left.

The padre orders Cokes for us both. *"Aguas negras del imperialismo"* ("black waters of imperialism"), he calls them; he frequently drops the rhetoric of revolution into the conversation. He tells me about his conversion, not to the priesthood, but to socialist politics. "Two years ago, I came out here to care for the spiritual needs of the indígenas, not knowing anything about how important material needs are. You see, my father was a merchant, and my brother is a judge; I come from a very petit-bourgeois family. Or I should say I did. Today I see things in the light of poverty."

Three months ago, Father Antonio asked the Church to set up a technical training school for ejidatarios, primarily because inexperienced peasants ruined a PPUA-bought tractor. But he does not know if his request was favorably received, and he, like his flock, is impatient with duly delegated bureaucracy. "You know, the revolution for independence was led by a priest, Miguel Hidalgo, who had Indian parishioners like mine. Hidalgo didn't wait for the whole Church to develop a full-blown social conscience, and sometimes I wonder what I should do." But Father Antonio has not joined the PPUA, nor is he likely to, because he has found a disconcerting verse in the scriptures of Engels: "Every premature attempt at an insurrection can only end in a new, perhaps still more horrible defeat."

Pablo de la O: A Time To Die

Trueno and I return to the countryside, but to a different ejido, Cuesta del Sol, a four-hour walk uphill from the highway. After we cross a muddy river in a dugout, a peasant boy leads us through a patch of jungle, which, many turns later, opens onto a hut on the far edge of the settlement. He has brought us this roundabout way because in Cuesta del Sol's center there are 17 uniformed policemen with Mausers; this in a village of about 350 inhabitants clustered in a little over a square mile. The squad was sent from Ocotopec some two months before, after an ejidatario suspected by his townspeople of spying for the government was found shot dead in the jungle. The police have not bothered to investigate, presumably because they already know that two tractors on the village square were paid for by the PPUA—and because they know, too, that the townspeople are armed. Each Saturday, the police force is rotated. Otherwise, the cops keep to their quarters, venturing out only to raise and lower a flag each day. The PPUA has issued orders not to harm them. "If one of us were to kill a cop, a thousand soldiers would come in his place," the party's local chairman tells me.

On my second day in the village, I meet a lanky young man who speaks knowledgeably about both Mexican and American affairs and professes a passion for books. After he has twice grilled Trueno about my reliability and inspected the signature on my pass from Güero, he tells me he is not Hector Calzado, as the villagers believe, but Pablo de la O Castareña. I recognize the name from newspapers. His sister, Maricela, is imprisoned for her participation in the Davis kidnapping.

Pablo, who is now 26, was working in a brickyard near Cuernavaca when Maricela prevailed on him to drive the getaway car for the Davis kidnapping. It was his first taste of revolutionary involvement. The next morning he began reading Lenin. "I found my whole life there. Everything that I had seen or felt since my childhood was explained," he says. After the ransom was paid, Pablo was dispatched to the U.S., where he arranged to smuggle a gun shipment into Mexico. Eighteen months ago, he was arrested at a checkpoint, taken to Monterrey, and warned that he would be tortured until he confessed to all he knew about the arms trade. Pablo decided it would be less painful and more valorous to die. He passed his belt around his neck and over a shower pipe in his cell. "Just as I was losing consciousness, the damn pipe broke," he says. When the guards discovered his attempt, they promptly took him for the "heating" he had dreaded. They forced water, lemonade, and alcohol down his mouth and nostrils. "For part of that time, they held my nose shut and stuck a hose down my throat. I had to swallow. When my belly was full, the cops gave me karate punches in the gut." Pablo vomited. The "heating" was repeated several times over four hours, until Pablo promised to tell all.

The guards hauled him upstairs, where he was unbound. Pablo told them he was a street hoodlum who traded in guns for profit, but they knew he was lying and ordered him taken down for another treatment.

"I knew I'd rather die than suffer through that again, and I knew that if they kept up, I would talk," Pablo recalls, telling the story with obvious relish. "We were going downstairs and the handcuffs were still off. So I told them that if they didn't shoot me right there, I would make a run for it."

They didn't, and Pablo did. There were shots, but the only casualty was a young passerby. After Pablo eluded the police, he looked for a way to go south.

"I found the poorest house in the poorest part of town, and I asked for help. The people let me stay overnight, and when I left, they gave me nine pesos and a pair of old socks." Pablo's picture was in the newspapers, which listed him as a leader of the American Terrorist International, a name the police invented and have never used since. Radio reports said that helicopters over Monterrey were looking for him and that all hitchhikers were being asked for identification. So Pablo went downtown and begged handouts until he had collected bus fare to Mexico City.

He is now living in Cuesta del Sol by day, sleeping in the jungle at night in a hut the villagers built for him. Looking upward from its door at night, I can't see the stars through the dense foliage of the jungle. If, as Pablo likes to believe, the helicopters are still looking for him—which they aren't—he is well hidden.

Pablo lights a kerosene lantern and reads aloud passages from Mao. "A revolutionary," he tells me, "is someone who has given himself to death. A true revolutionary knows that the struggle must be bought with blood, and he has made the decision to give his own life. Once you have decided to die, then nothing the enemy does can stop you. You become invincible." Trueno disagrees. "The point isn't like that, man. A revolutionary has to be ready to kill, not die."

CONCHIS: THE WIDOW'S LAMENT

Cuesta del Sol, like every town controlled by the PPUA, has refugees from ejidos where insurgent peasants failed. Those here are from Valencia, an ejido deserted last spring after an invasion by some two dozen armed men in federate uniforms; the refugees swear they were pistoleros in disguise. Among the refugees is Conchis, a widow of 24 who has three children, one only a few months old. Her husband, Miguel, was a native of Valencia, a leader of its ejidatarios, and a clandestine member of the PPUA. After fleeing Valencia, Miguel regrouped the refugees for a legal battle to regain their land and homes. As is usual in peasant affairs, they had no money to pay lawyers and none came forward to help; the peasants themselves scratched out denunciations and appeals to the government. Miguel and a companion left their huts in Cuesta del Sol last June 9 bound for Mexico City and an appointment with agrarian reform investigators. But they never arrived. Two pistol-toting men intercepted their bus about 15 kilometers west of the Cuesta del Sol bus stop. The two pistoleros took Miguel off the bus and, with 50 passengers as witnesses, shot him dead on the roadside. His companion, also hauled off the bus, received a flesh wound as a warning to the refugees from Valencia. There are no widow's benefits for ejidatarias in Mexico, and Conchis survives now on the slim resources other refugees provide her.

As we talk, she tends a clay pot of rice with one hand, holding her newest-born to her breast with the other. The infant is clubfooted, as is her second-born child, a two-year-old girl. Conchis talks to me through a missing front tooth, but without an Indian accent. "My husband practically left me in the streets when he died. He never worried about anything but the ejido during the whole three years we were married." She grimaces at the rotting roof of the hut. "When we came here the people in town donated us this hut. Miguel kept promising to fix it up, because the roof leaks. But he never did. Now he is gone, and I have no one to do it. The men here have promised to put on a new roof for me, but I can't pay for it, so you can see—they've done nothing." Conchis sits down in a hand-hewn chair, rocking the baby in her arms. She smiles at me, and places one bare foot on top of the other. "Señor, do you know where I might find a doctor for my two kids? I have been told that their feet can be fixed, but I don't know who will help. The priest who sometimes gives Mass here told me he would ask for a doctor, but no one has come."

It is true, as Conchis says, that the villagers are not helping her. "That woman goes into town at night and comes home in the morning with new clothes. She doesn't need our help because she's getting money from men in town," an ejido gossip tells me. A local PPUA leader says, "She talks against us so much, you'd think she had joined the enemy. We will help her someday, but not until she quits blaming us for her husband's death." Conchis and her children can be fed for about ten dollars a week; they could survive for a year on no more money than it takes to buy a single M-l on the black market. But the PPUA has asked its members to refuse her aid until she silences her critical tongue.

Conchis, however, is unlikely to give verbal or any other kind of support to the PPUA's enemies or, for that matter, to the PPUA itself. Like most women in the Oaxacan hills, she simply wants to survive. Politics are not her affair, by her own choice. Like most Mexican peasants, male or female, she is not curious about her place in history and asks only that history leave her alone. But that is no longer possible in Oaxaca. The whole rural expanse of southern Mexico is bristling with pistoleros, soldiers, and revolutionaries. No one is likely to answer her appeals for food, shelter or medical care, and she is beginning to realize that her future is out of her hands. The last thing she said to me as I prepared to leave the village was, "Señor, is there any way I could get help from people in the United States?"

It has now been six months since I first saw Güero and his PPUA. Since then, I have made another trip into the mountains. Alfonso, the intended murder victim, took Father Antonio's advice and abandoned Miguel Allende. Pistoleros ambushed Pablo de la O in October and left him for dead. With five bullets in his torso, he nonetheless survived and today is organizing in a new locale. The widow Conchis, still despised by her townspeople, has been joined by another widow, whose husband was killed by police just days after I left the village. Trueno carried the PPUA's message into his home region, where he won such support that he now visits his parents in broad daylight. Güero's headquarters today is an ejido in the state of Veracruz; six months ago, Trueno and I were asked to leave there because its villagers were fearful of government reprisals. It was apparent on my second trip that the PPUA is growing even faster than its leaders expected.

Its success is directly attributable to the persistent crisis that plagues the Mexican countryside. The statistics testify that the crisis is real, but anyone who has ventured into the backcountry requires no mathematical proof. I see the campesino's plight most clearly in my own memory: the peasants of Oaxaca live no better today than they did in my childhood, a quarter-century ago, when I first set eyes on them. In the market towns, one now sees with frequency scenes that a generation ago could only be witnessed in far-off places like Calcutta or Hong Kong: multitudes thronging around vegetable stands and bus stations, a great crush of people spilling into the streets, the flesh of the population explosion, dressed in bright colors. Urban Mexico may be entering the modern age—it is true that ordinary workers now purchase televisions and used cars—but in the mountains, nothing has changed.

Official peasant organizations assembled January 7 in Veracruz to protest conditions in the countryside, and President José López Portillo responded with a promise to put agricultural reform on a par with petroleum development. But what can the government do? It can neither create jobs by the thousands nor fashion new lands from the ocean. It lacks even the elementary resources to supply each ejido a tractor.

The government can't even effectively mobilize against the PPUA and the half-dozen other insurgent groups operating in the countryside. It has taken some symbolic steps: the new governor of Oaxaca is the general whose troops tracked down and killed Lucio Cabañas, and the army recently went on maneuvers in the Oaxacan mountains. Several cities I saw on my return were under guard at night, and sentries were posted around the clock at bus stations that connect with the ejidos. But the police are as clumsy and corrupt as they are portrayed in legend. Revolutionaries fear only the army, and with every passing day the insurgents are better armed for battle. Of course, they would lose any serious confrontation, but they don't plan to engage in direct combat. For the foreseeable future, their fight is with the landowners and their pistoleros.

It is, of course, unthinkable that the PPUA or its kindred organizations might bring off a successful revolution in Mexico within this decade or the next. But the PPUA just might lead thousands into massive land seizures, leading to who knows what kind of retaliation and accompanying turmoil in the cities. In the meantime, the threat posed by the PPUA is neither so great that the party must be dealt with, nor so insignificant that it can be ignored.

Recently, the PPUA has defined itself as a "Marxist-Leninist party." But that change is a calculated one aimed at winning support from the radical movement in urban Mexico. The PPUA's real character was described long ago by a now-forgotten general in Pancho Villa's army. The general told an American correspondent, "I am not an educated man, but I know that to fight is the last thing for any people. Only when things get too bad to stand, eh? And, if we are going to kill our brothers, something fine must come out of it, eh?" It is that simple faith—"something fine must come out of it, eh?"—which keeps revolution alive in Mexico.

In this piece, which appeared in *Texas Monthly*, October, 1978, Reavis finds employment at Rusk State Hospital, which at the time was a maximum-security unit of the Texas prison system set aside for inmates with mental disabilities. Reavis explores the banal and brutal world of both the attendants and the inmates, neglected by society and underfunded by the state, drawing attention to how dehumanizing language always antedates physical violence.

A Season in Hell

Two tall chain-link fences topped by concertina wire set off the dormitories for the criminally insane from the rest of Rusk State Hospital. To get inside this fortress in a forsaken corner of the Piney Woods, you have to go through gates operated by remote control from guard towers and pass half a dozen bored, blue-uniformed security men who lounge in folding chairs at the main entrance, staring hard at all who enter. I have no difficulty getting past them because my nametag identifies me as an attendant, or, in the institutional parlance, a Psychiatric Security Technician—a PST.

Getting the job was easy. Turnover is high, 60 percent annually among the 137 PSTs. On the day I applied, there were 15 openings. I lied about my identity, presenting the Social Security card of another man, along with an educational and employment record I had simply dreamed up. I listed the street address of a motel as my home and claimed that my previous employer was a man who had recently moved out of the region. No one cared to investigate. Rusk State Hospital pays PSTs $610 a month, so it has to hire whoever it can get. Few men in their prime will go to work here, and, understandably, few women want to work in the Maximum Security Unit, because most of its three hundred or so inhabitants are males, either felons or accused men sent for pretrial examination.

Some are timid and confused. Their connections with reality are fragile, they do not understand what criminality is, and their most serious offenses may have been stealing hymnals from chapels or writing checks in Clark Kent's name. Any violent urges they may have are numbed by drug therapy. Others, those whom the psychologists call sociopaths, are habitually drawn to violence and deceit. These men, as often as not, see Rusk as a gambit for avoiding prison. At the hospital, they continue to defy control, committing crimes—usually assault on other prisoners—while there.

The Maximum Security Unit at Rusk is different from other mental-care facilities because it houses some men who ought to be in prison, and it is different from other penal institutions because it houses some men who are fairly harmless and only in need of psychiatric care. This dual function is the source of most of the problems in the unit. The dorm where I work, Skyview II, like the three other Maximum Security wards, locks with keys that only attendants carry. Heavy metal screens cover all the windows. Otherwise, the four Skyview units resemble one-story college dorms. They are the newest—less than five years old—and the most comfortable buildings at Rusk. Each contains four residence wings, with four rooms on each wing; patients sleep six to a room in conditions similar to those you'd find in the enlisted men's quarters on a military base. In Skyview II, one wing is vacant now, one is populated by male patients under 21, one is reserved for adult drug addicts, and the fourth is for newly admitted adult males. In addition to residence wings, each of the four Skyview units contains a cafeteria, a laundry room, a recreation center, administrative offices, a pharmacy, and a nursing station.

The other attendants on my shift—except Billy Handsome—are already congregated at the nursing station when I come in about fifteen minutes late, as usual. Being late is not a concern here; the atmosphere is lax. Billy Handsome, a thirty-year-old, long-haired bachelor, spent last night at a rock concert in Dallas, and he has already gone to the drug-abuse ward to sleep off his hangover. The others—Big Boy, John Henry, and our foreman, Slim—all got here before starting time because none slept well. They were called back to work in the middle of the night because of a bomb threat. Even though they had to work when I didn't, nobody begrudges my absence. Because the state does not pay for overtime, dodging it is an accepted practice. "You're lucky you don't have a phone, that's what," Slim says good-naturedly.

There is camaraderie among the attendants—not because the work is hectic and dangerous, but because it usually isn't. Were it not for companionship (and an occasional fistfight among the patients) our routine would be unbearably dull. On morning shifts, we PSTs wake up our charges, watch them take medication, serve breakfast, and wait for lunch. After lunch we wait for 2 p.m., quitting time. When we are on the evening shift we wait for supper and afterward lock the patients into residence wings for the night. Then we wait for 10 p.m., when we can check out and go home. Men on the night crew do little more than baby-sit. They pass their time gossiping, watching television, and playing Foosball. A PST who does not enjoy those pursuits will not be popular with his co-workers, nor will he want to stay on the job, for there is little else to do. The patients, for their part, are as bored as we are.

This morning it is John Henry who tells the patients to wake up, speaking over the intercom. I set the shaving mugs and razors with locking blades on a counter just outside the door of the nursing station. Big Boy goes to the intercom to give the cigarette call and, when the patients come to him, tosses each one a white package of harsh cigarettes, actually little cigars, with the letters RSH printed on the wrappers. Then sunburned, white-suited Nurse Johnny comes out of his office, where he has been sorting and counting pills, to call patients to the "pill line." Within a few minutes, about half the fifty men on our dorm are queued up in front of him, ready for their morning doses. Some are dressed in brightly colored Western shirts and gray or light-blue pants, clothes which the hospital dispenses. Most of them are unkempt, especially the younger patients, many of whom do not shave. If there is a characteristic common to the disturbed inmates, it is their posture. The men in line slump, lean to one side, hang their hands low, or turn their torsos nearly sideways.

Standing in the hallway beside the water fountain are two young men from the adolescent ward, Roy and Ruben, both twenty. Roy is wearing blue Levi's and yellow-embroidered boots sent by his sentimental parents, who believe he is innocent of the rape he boasts about. Ruben, who looks like Sal Mineo, has a towel curled around his neck, its ends drooping down onto his white T-shirt. His orange pointed-toe shoes have been shined to a high gloss. Both youths are classified in the records as sociopaths, and both are here for having committed crimes involving carnal desire. Roy is a rapist; Ruben was a homosexual prostitute who one night quarreled with and then stabbed two of his clients. Neither of them has been prescribed any medication: although hallucinations can be suppressed by drugs, a propensity to crime cannot. So they come to the pill line every morning to extort, barter, or beg drugs from patients who have a legitimate need for them.

The most visible patient in the dorm, and the one most despised by the others, is El General, who has not shown up for the pill line. El General, who speaks only Spanish, is a hulking twenty-one-year-old who is severely retarded and epileptic. He has spent most of his life in institutions without learning much. Sometimes El General defecates in bathtubs and sometimes he urinates in water fountains. He is usually the most amiable man on the ward, but, if angered, he is difficult to subdue. El General is here because he struck out at patients who harassed him at another hospital.

Like the other patients, he has been assigned a sleeping bunk and a locker for his belongings. But El General does not understand what property and place are—he can't even remember where he slept the night, or the hour, before. Like a street urchin, home for him is wherever he happens to be when drowsiness overtakes him. John Henry and I find him asleep on an unassigned bed in the adolescent wing. There are no sheets on the plastic mattress, but that is unremarkable; sheets are one of the comforts for which El General has no appreciation. He is wearing the maroon jeans and suede running shoes that his mother brought him two months ago.

I grab El General by the ankles and shake him, moving his legs like the blades of scissors. He doesn't budge. I try pushing hard on his ribs, rocking him back and forth, while John Henry, standing behind me with his arms folded, stares down at El General, grinning. I lean over, putting my hands behind El General's shoulder blades, and strain to raise him. With some difficulty I lift his torso about six inches above the bed and let him fall back. He doesn't blink. John Henry chuckles in a high-pitched, feminine tone, which seems wildly incongruous with his colossal physique, but he offers no help, so I raise El General's torso again, letting him fall back on the bed again, and again I get no result.

It is obvious that my methods won't awaken El General. So John

Henry leans across the bed and gently backhands El General across the cheek. El General stirs. John Henry slaps him again, and this time El General opens his eyes.

"Why are you hitting me? Why are you hitting me?" he says in Spanish, scrambling out of the bed.

"Let's go. It's pill time," he tells El General, who thinks he is about to be hit again. He dodges past the attendant and ducks behind a locker, hoping we will not notice him there. John Henry approaches the locker like a wrestler coming out of his corner. El General sees him and turns his face the other way, toward the wall.

"No, no me vas a pegar," El General wails, stiffening his body.

I tell El General that we are not going to hit him. John Henry, resigned for the moment to the idea of persuading El General, does his best with the Spanish he has picked up on the ward.

"Medicina, General, medicina."

El General is too frightened to believe it, and we know why. Last night, according to the night log the attendants keep, several other patients, including Ruben, Roy, and another sociopath, Killer Duke, attacked El General. That is how they have fun. While they were chasing him around the wing, El General went into a seizure. He fell, or was knocked, against a Sheetrock wall panel, in which there is now an indentation stained with his blood. Several strands of hair protrude from the crack made by his head. The night crew, as always, found out about the incident too late to stop it, and El General was already having his seizure when they arrived on the scene. El General can't understand that John Henry and I are attendants, not patients, or that there are rules against brutality. We are, in his mind, just two nameless men—I doubt he remembers seeing us yesterday or the day before—and our apparent intentions are violent.

John Henry throws a wrestling hold around El General's neck and pulls him away from the locker. Then he stretches out the patient's right arm, holding it stiff while encircling El General's face with his other arm. With El General thus under rein, John Henry marches him down the hallway, toward the pill line.

"Medicina, medicina," he tells El General.

"Me-di-ci-na. Me-di-ci-na. Me-di-cina," El General chants over and over. El General often repeats what we tell him, not because he is sarcastic but because he is afflicted with echolalia, a disorder characterized by a fascination with sounds. At the nursing station El General realizes what is going on and relaxes.

John Henry lets him go. Like the others, El General takes his place in line.

Most people in mental hospitals have come there by voluntary or civil commitment. Either they have asked to be let into a mental hospital—a common enough request, made especially by alcoholics in need of drying out—or their families have gone to court alleging that Uncle Ted or Brother Joe is behaving strangely and have gotten commitment orders from a judge. The presumption in both kinds of cases is that the person committed is helpless, because he or she does not firmly grasp reality, and harmless, because he or she has committed no crime. Patients who voluntarily commit themselves may walk out at will; those who are committed in civil proceedings may leave when review boards deem that they have been sufficiently treated or restored to sanity.

No one, however, may commit himself to the Maximum Security Unit, nor can anyone walk away from it when he wants to. No one may be brought in until accused of a crime. Patients are brought to the MSU, often in shackles and waistcuffs, from three sources: other mental hospitals, prisons, and courts.

The crimes that MSU inmates have committed range from breaking into automobiles to multiple murder. Hippie Fred, a patient in my dorm, was brought here from Austin State Hospital, where one sunny afternoon he jumped the fence and ran away. When hunger overtook him hours later, he entered someone's house, went to the kitchen, and began preparing a peanut butter and jelly sandwich. The owners of the house called the police, who booked Fred for burglary and returned him to the hospital. From there he was sent to Rusk, where he wanders about looking confused and sheepish.

Patients come directly to Rusk from courtrooms and jails when they have been judged not guilty of crimes by reason of insanity or when their competence to stand trial is in doubt. No one is sentenced to serve time here, though defendants who are either incompetent or insane or both must remain until they are judged able to stand trial.

The distinction between incompetence and insanity is an important one for many of our patients, especially ones like Solomon, a nineteen-year-old Black kid sent here for competency training.

Solomon killed his grandmother with a butcher knife one autumn night in Fort Worth nearly two years ago. His court-appointed attorney could not communicate with Solomon and therefore secured a competency examination, held in the office of a psychiatrist. In Solomon's court dossier, I found a record of that conversation.

Psychiatrist: "What is the function of a district attorney?"
Solomon: "He labors a portion of the kind of success that you do and what you include in. He tells you who the caseworker is. He is for to manage your main subject and verb."
Psychiatrist: "What is the function of a judge?"
Solomon: "If you was to be eliminated one night, tough to be sustained. Trial with your producers. Like if you was under pressure and any persuasion, it would affect you or be in your midsection."

Answers like these persuaded a Tarrant County judge that Solomon was incompetent. He was brought to Rusk, where he has been taught better civics. Today, thanks to his competency classes, he knows by rote what a judge and jury are. He now admits that he is a murderer, though he often writes letters home to the grandmother he killed. Because he can parrot the rules of courtroom procedure, a review board has found him competent to stand trial. In a few weeks Solomon could be back in the dock. If his attorney requests a sanity hearing for him and a jury finds him insane, he will be returned to Rusk. With time, therapy, and medication, he may improve.

When he is no longer deemed dangerous, he may be transferred to another mental hospital. If he is ever restored to sanity, he may be released without facing trial. Solomon is presently in danger of his competency being taken for sanity when he is returned to Fort Worth. If that happens, he could be convicted of murder and sentenced to Huntsville. A careless or callous defense attorney might even persuade Solomon to plead guilty.

Solomon belongs in the Maximum Security Unit because he is crazy and in all likelihood unwittingly dangerous too. But others here are willfully dangerous and not in the least insane. Often, they were charged with drug abuse—usually heroin addiction—and sent to Rusk for pretrial examination. Roy, the rapist, is one of these people. Six months ago he pulled a black stocking over his head and visited the home of a family friend expressly to rape her ("Because I hated the bitch," he explained to me). Afterward he fled and made coolheaded attempts to evade identification. Carelessness, not insanity, was his downfall. Caught with incriminating evidence, he pleaded insanity and was sent to Rusk for evaluation. "It's a lot better doing time here than in the county jail," he says. In my dorm there are others like him: Ruben, Killer Duke, who murdered his partner in a dope deal, Juanito the armed bandit, and several more.

But to the general public, Rusk State Hospital does not have a pleasant reputation. During the summer of 1977, journalists and investigators from the Texas Department of Mental Health and Mental Retardation, which is supposed to oversee the hospital, swarmed over Rusk, looking for and finding evidence that the attendants were brutal. That autumn, 124 employees were fired, and the Cherokee County attorney filed criminal charges against 14 of them, though none of them was brought to trial. Nevertheless, the revelations and the employee purge were effective. Inside the hospital today, sustained beating of patients is rare. Most attendants now prefer keeping their jobs to hitting unruly or annoying patients, and patients are now told when they come in that if they are struck they have the right to file an abuse complaint. So far this year, sixty of them have. Most of their complaints have been dismissed, but not before a board of MHMR employees and community volunteers has interrogated the parties named in each one.

If the beatings have largely ended, another problem that was discovered—patients beating patients—still exists, and there is statistical evidence that it may have grown worse. During the first seven months of 1978, 190 injuries to patients were recorded in the Maximum Security Unit, compared to 249 in the twelve months before the investigation. That works out to 27 patient injuries a month this year (most of them the result of fistfights), compared to 20 a month last year, and there are only three-fourths as many patients in the Maximum Security Unit today. Attendants blame the increase on the new regulations they operate under, which forbid them to take punitive or deterrent action against brutal patients. Before the 1977 investigations, attendants often locked the bullies in isolation cells. Today those cells may be used only under orders from a Rusk physician, who can prescribe isolation only to keep suicidal or epileptic patients from hurting themselves.

Behavior modification, another means of control, has also been proscribed on the criminal wards. Most psychologists favor it; as one told me, "Let me control cigarettes, coffee, and Cokes, and I'll control those three hundred patients in ways you wouldn't believe." The personnel at Rusk would like to have the power to give or deny amenities. But B-mod, as it is called, has been limited to a small program in Skyview III, the women's dorm, largely because administrators fear that its wide use might prompt another investigation. The lesson of the 1977 investigation is that patients, unlike prisoners, must be treated with respect; they are presumed to have the same rights as any other citizen. If they are allowed access to telephones and the mails, if they may not be confined, or even forced to bathe, the administration reasons, who is to say that denying them cigarettes is not also infringing on their civil rights?

The result is that police power at Rusk has in some ways shifted from the attendants to those sociopathic patients who are cunning enough to manipulate the others. These patients, who have filled the vacuum left by the attendants, need not fear the courts, which are unlikely to prosecute misdemeanor complaints against them, or the people in authority, especially the attendants. Some have even learned to manipulate the abuse-complaint system. If an attendant strikes him or curses him or even shouts at him, a calculating sociopath will threaten to file an abuse complaint. If the attendant ignores the threat, the patient may actually file the complaint, causing the attendant to come under suspicion. Today on the Maximum Security wards, there are sociopaths who spend most of their time looking for opportunities to maul other patients, and there are attendants who spend most of their time waiting to record the resultant injuries.

The attendants on the dorm this morning tacitly assume that Roy, Ruben, or others of their gang from the adolescent ward will renew last night's attack on El General. Everyone has seen the pattern before. Normally harmless, El General, after several turns as the victim of harassment, becomes cross, punchy, and unmanageable, a danger to anyone who comes within his reach. After a few days his equanimity returns, and the sociopaths begin another round of taunting him. I am in the nursing station with Slim, waiting for the inevitable, when El General strides up, in a good mood despite last night's incident.

He walks into the room confidently, as if he worked here; El General is the only patient allowed this privilege, because we know he is too innocent to take advantage of it. I hand him the nearly empty can of Coke I am drinking. El General is a walking disposal; he downs it all in one gulp, then looks around for more food or drink.

"Hey, General, throw that can away," Slim tells him. El General opens the drawer of the nursing desk and drops the can in.

"Not in the drawer, you dumb ass. In the wastebasket, General. Over there in the wastebasket," Slim says, this time pointing at the trash can.

Slowly, El General pulls the can out of the drawer and turns toward Slim, watching for new instructions, unsure what he has been told, and probably afraid someone will hit him.

"Over there, dumb ass," Slim repeats.

El General turns to the wastebasket, but does not fix his eyes on it.

"En el basurero," I tell him.

He obeys.

"Say, you must speak that Spanish pretty good. Ask that General how old he is, why don't you?" says Slim.

El General says he is five. I insist that he is not, but he will not reconsider.

"Yeah, that's what he always says," Slim tells me. "He had a real bad fever of something like 104 for three days when he was five, and that burned his brain up, the doctors say."

I ask El General why he has never mastered English.

"Because there are no chocolates," he tells me. Then he begins to mutter something about a dog, pointing at the glass wall that looks out on the hallway.

"El General, vámonos. Yeah, vamoose. That's right, get out of here," Slim says. El General meekly complies, and Slim begins to tell me at great length about the Opelousas catfish he caught yesterday. Fortunately, we are interrupted by another patient.

It is Roy, the rapist. He has come to get a light for his cigarette.

"Hey, Roy," says Slim, "was that lady you raped in Lubbock any good?"

"She sure was."

"Good enough for thirty years, huh?" Roy says that even if he's sentenced to sixty years, he'll spend the time thinking about the pleasures of the rape.

One of the Maximum Security Unit's three doctors walks in. Slim introduces me to him—he's called Doctor Benji and is a native of India somehow transplanted to the Piney Woods.

"Hey, Doc, you ever heard of a woman having a headache for five days?" As usual, Slim is in a teasing mood.

Doctor Benji says he hasn't.

"I thought not. I don't know what my old lady is pulling on me, you know? It's been five days, and she won't put out. I may have to get Roy here to show me how to get it," he says, nodding at Roy. The doctor, embarrassed by the conversation, edges off down the hallway toward the administrative office.

I slip out the door, hoping to discover what dark deeds are hatching in the adolescent wing.

Solomon, Killer Dave, Juanito the bandit, and Ruben are slouched in chairs around the television set. A commentator is interviewing Myron Farber, a *New York Times* reporter who is being sent to jail. The four patients understand nothing that is said. They are watching because they don't have anything else to do.

When I sit down, Ruben gets up to show me three burns on his right arm, two above and one below his tattoo, a skull and crossbones emblazoned with the legend "Born to Lose." Ruben burned himself last night with a match, but he says he doesn't know why. He also set fire to a photograph of his old girlfriend from Corpus Christi. I ask him whether he burned the picture because he is now enamored of Clara, a Maximum Security patient to whom he waves every night through the screened glass on the dorm's south side.

"No, man, it wasn't her. I don't want nothing to do with that bitch Clara. She's a *mayatera*," he explains in Spanish. *Mayatera* is a word I don't understand. Juanito tells me that it comes from *mayate*, a demeaning Chicano term for Blacks. A mayatera is a woman who prefers Black men to Mexican Americans.

Juanito tells me that Clara is indeed a mayatera and that Ruben burned himself because he was high on toothpaste cigarettes. I have never heard of them, so Juanito promises a demonstration. The technique is a relatively new one to him; it was brought here only last week by Killer Dave, who, I suspect, also smuggled in the matches Ruben used to burn himself.

Dave gets up to prepare me a toothpaste cigarette, as Juanito explains the process. New patients on the criminal wards are given a packet of toiletries, which includes a tube of fluoride toothpaste. Killer Dave spreads the paste across a cigarette paper, then blows on it to dry it out. He hands it to me, and I light up.

The cigarette pops like marijuana and leaves long, flaky, black ashes that don't fall off. I inhale deeply and soon feel a high, which I believe is from lack of oxygen. It's a crude feeling, like the feeling of smoking your first cigarette. The taste is foul and the smoke stings my already abused lungs. I refuse to light up a second of these jailhouse joints, but Juanito, Ruben, and Killer Dave assure me that if I smoked several, I would come to appreciate the high. It's the fluoride that produced the buzz in my head, Juanito tells me.

Solomon sits staring at the television all the while, rocking back and forth in his chair, transfixed. When I ask him what he did with the knife he used to kill his grandmother, consciousness returns to him. He looks over at me, starts to stutter, then says plainly, "She just swallowed it, I think." He also tells me that his brothers and sisters did not call the police. "They just came automatically. They always do when something happens." Without inquiring about who had the matches last night—no one will tell me, I know—I go back to the nursing station.

I mention the matches and the toothpaste cigarettes to Slim, who assures me that there is nothing we can do. "Hell, if it wasn't that, it would be something else," he says. "We can't search them whenever we want, you know. Last week they were smoking tea back there."

After lunch, I return to the nursing station to prepare the paperwork for Killer Dave's EEG brain-wave test later in the afternoon. Before I have finished, El General comes to the door, wailing. His head is bowed and he holds his hands over his eyes and nose. I put an arm around his shoulder and with a little prodding get him to show me his face. The bridge of his nose is red and swollen.

"They hit me, they hit me," he says.

"Who hit you? Which ones did it?"

El General looks at me wistfully, dropping his arms to his sides. *"El doctor? Mi papa?"*

He has never learned to call anyone by name. Whether he really thinks a doctor or his father hit him, I don't know; he may believe that all males are included in those two categories—except for his brothers, for he also knows the word *hermano.*

I do not have to wonder long who his attackers were. Ruben and Roy are soon standing in the doorway, savoring the scene.

"Why did you guys mess with him? Can't you pick on somebody who can defend himself, like Dave?"

Grinning mischievously, Ruben tells me that he did not intend to hurt El General.

Slim, who has been reading the sports section of a newspaper, casts an irritated glance at Ruben."Yeah, you're sorry, real sorry. Just like you're sorry you stabbed those two queers in Corpus, aren't you?"

Ruben takes this as his cue to leave and shamefacedly backs away from the door. He and Roy lean against the outer wall of the hallway, waiting for El General to step outside.

Ruben is upset. He does not like to hear homosexuality mentioned. Though he will argue in self-defense that any form of sexual release in confinement is honorable, he is not proud of his role as the "dorm whore." On the outside, before his arrest and transfer to Rusk, he was a gay prostitute. He insists that he was well paid. Here, he has several times been found in the showers, or even in his bunk, performing a variety of acts with other patients, none of whom is normally gay. Ruben feels ashamed about this because here on the ward his services usually cannot be paid for. One of the indignities he suffers at Rusk is being called queer.

Slim looks up from his newspaper again and glances at El General and me, then at the hallway.

"Don't worry about El General," he tells me. "It won't do you no good. There's nothing we can do."

"I'd like to take Ruben and Roy to the laundry room and give them a taste of their own medicine," I suggest.

"Shit! You know the rules. We can't even put them in isolation. Patients have all the rights today. Pretty soon, I tell you what, they're going to be running the ward."

Slim's advice doesn't calm me. "Ruben and Roy, why don't you get your chicken asses out of here," I tell them.

They slink off down the hall toward the adolescent wing. When El General quits sobbing, I let him go. He ambles off toward the adolescent wing, where I know Ruben and Roy will waylay him again. I want to follow him, but Slim advises me not to.

I turn back to my paperwork, but before I can finish a single form, Roy comes down the hallway, shuffling toward our door with El General in tow.

"Look at El General. His eyes are rolling back in his head."

It is true. El General's eyes are rolling up and down, as if operated by some unseen lever permitting him to take peeks at the top of his skull and the inside of his cheekbones.

"Aw, that ain't nothing," Slim says. "The doctors say his medication makes him do that."

I call Nurse Johnny, who is in his office on the other side of the nursing station. Johnny cranes his head out the door as Roy and I lead El General over.

"Aw, he's fixing to have his seizure. Just lay him down and let him get it over with," Johnny advises us.

Roy and I lead El General into one of the ward's two rarely used isolation rooms, a narrow wood-paneled cubicle with a bed and a door that locks from the outside.

El General, who vaguely understands that he is being put to bed, grabs hold of a blanket and lifts it up. Then he freezes, his hand holding the blanket, his head cast down, his eyes fixed straight ahead, seeing nothing.

Roy shakes him by the shoulder. "General, General, get in bed."

El General does not respond. "

¿General, nos escuchas? ¿Puedes escuchar?" I ask.

But he doesn't hear a thing.

Together, Roy and I force him down on the edge of the bed, then push his torso fiat. He is lying on his back, but with his forearms raised, the edge of the blanket still in one fist.

Roy bends El General's forearms down to his sides and puts a pillow under his head. He passes a hand over El General's eyes, but El General doesn't see it. He makes no sound.

We hear a rustling behind us. It is Ruben, come to see the fruit of his bullying. "Get the hell out of here, you *pinche maricón.*" I have now raised my voice at Ruben and cursed him as well. That, our regulations say, constitutes patient abuse. Ruben ducks out the door.

A deep growl, like that of a dog about to bite, comes from El General's half-open mouth. It wanes when he inhales, grows louder when he exhales. For ten minutes, the low roar reassures us that he's alive.

Roy steps out into the hallway, where Ruben is loitering. They exchange whispers as Roy combs his long, duck-tailed hair. When Roy steps back into the room, El General sees something, probably his profile. He sits up in bed, then freezes again. We force him back into a prone position and wait perhaps ten minutes more.

Nurse Johnny is now fidgety. El General's seizures do not usually last this long. Johnny comes into the isolation cell to take his blood pressure.

He measures twice before pronouncing El General's pulse and blood pressure normal. Then he picks up his equipment and goes back to the nursing station, where I hear him teasing John Henry.

I go out to ask Slim for permission to stay at El General's side. John Henry, I suggest, can take my place in accompanying Killer Dave to his EEG session. Slim frowns, even though John Henry readily volunteers. I can tell by his glare that he is wondering whether I will ever be good PST material. It is not part of the macho ethic of psychiatric attendants in East Texas to show pity for the helpless.

After a moment, Slim relents. "All right, you go stay with your girlfriend. John Henry can take Dave down to the infirmary. But I'll tell you something. This falling in love with the patients won't cut it."

"He'll get over that love business, that's for sure," John Henry chimes in. "Just wait till one of these patients lays into him."

I turn away to rejoin Roy in the vigil at El General's side. Roy, I know, was undoubtedly in on the beating. But at least he had the humanity to be shocked at its result.

El General does not move for ten more minutes. Then his fingers begin to tremble. Little tremors pass through his feet, causing his shoes to vibrate. This continues for four or five minutes, and then El General sits up.

He still apparently sees nothing. He drops the blanket he has been holding and stands up as if to walk. But he does not move forward. He is frozen again. We lay him down. The tremors resume. Then his body goes still, as if his spirit had departed. I notice that El General has wet his pants. Before long he rises again, this time almost fully conscious. When we move toward him he draws back, thinking, I suppose, that we are going to strike him.

"No tengas miedo, General," I tell him. "Don't be afraid."

He looks at me out of the corner of his eye and bellows—a long, savage, childish laugh. He is happy now, even if he doesn't know why, or where he is, or who is addressing him.

"El General," I ask in Spanish, "why did you have that seizure?"

"Because there are no chocolates," he booms, pleased by the sound of his own voice.

My tension slips away. Almost joyfully, I go into the nursing station to report that El General's siege of unconsciousness has ended.

"Oh, yeah? Well, that's fine," says Slim. "I told you it would happen like that."

Then he turns to Nurse Billy, who is visiting in the nursing station. "Hey, Billy Boy," he says, "I want to take my trotline out tomorrow. You think that creek where you fish is wide enough for a fifty-foot line?"

I slink off to the adolescent ward. Somebody has to make sure El General puts on some clean clothes.

In 1978 Reavis published his social history of Mexican immigration, *Without Documents* (New York: Condor Publishing Company, 1978), building the case that the problems involved in immigration cannot be addressed on a local level but require much larger political engagement. The book works methodically to undermine well-established narratives and stereotypes about the people who cross the Mexican–U.S. border by documenting the lived experience of those without documents, and the causes and consequences of their immigration.

Selections from *Without Documents*

CHAPTER 1: A TALE OF TWO COUNTRIES

On the afternoon of May 26, 1976, Border Patrolman Kent Nyguarrd apprehended a Mexican citizen, Silverio Hernandez, inside the city dump at Eagle Pass, Texas, just yards away from the Rio Grande. Nyguarrd handcuffed Hernandez to an abandoned refrigerator and then chased off after other suspected *sin papeles* [literally, "paperless," as in undocumented] in the area. When he returned minutes later, his prisoner was gone. Hernandez had moved about 10 yards back down the riverbank, where he pushed himself and the refrigerator over a five-foot mudbank, off into the depths of the Rio Grande. His apparent plan was to use the rusting appliance as a raft to carry himself back to the Mexican shore. Instead, it took in water and dragged him down. This is the story Border Patrolmen told newsmen.

Hernandez, 24, was a resident of Piedras Negras, the Mexican town across the Rio Grande from Eagle Pass, His friends say that he had no reason to flee from custody, and that he must have known from its very weightiness that he could not raft the refrigerator across the river. They think he was pushed in to drown. Yet no grand jury was called to investigate the death of Silverio Hernandez, nor were any charges filed. Nyguarrd was reportedly transferred to another Border Patrol station within weeks after the May 26 incident.

The bizarre death of Silverio Hernandez is perhaps an atypical listing in the daily reports of the Border Patrol, but his desperate bid to enter the U.S. is increasingly common. Each year, hundreds of thousands of undocumented Mexican immigrants come to the U.S. and succeed in their attempts to get a toehold on survival. Though many are apprehended and returned to Mexico, most of them return to the U.S.—illegally—in a matter of weeks.

Had Silverio Hernandez survived, he would have been returned home, one of nearly a million Mexicans now turned back annually in a rising wave of deportations that has swollen to 10 times the crest reached in 1964, following the cancellation of seasonal labor import programs with Mexico. The influx of undocumented immigrants has created a carryover population estimated as high as eight million, but probably much lower. The rising number of *sin papeles*—which former Immigration Service Commissioner Leonard F. Chapman called a "silent invasion"—is predominantly Spanish-speaking. Chapman estimated that five million of America's undocumented immigrants are Mexican nationals, with Central and South Americans accounting for another million or more. Of the Mexican majority, nearly 90 percent come to the United States without any immigration documents whatever, chiefly by crossing the dry California desert or the wet Rio Grande undetected.

The fate of Silverio Hernandez and that of thousands who cross the Mexican border successfully each month is no longer a question of regional significance alone. For four generations, undocumented Mexican immigrants have made Southwestern harvests profitable, and today, the destinations they stake out before leaving home run as far north as Seattle, Salt Lake City, and Chicago. The arrest of some 80 Mexican illegals at the Belmont race track in New York, and the deportation of others found working as janitors at INS headquarters in Washington, D.C., are indicators that the *scope* of undocumented immigration—if not its *base*—is widening eastward.

Whether he heads for San Diego or Detroit, the aim of the sin papeles is to get a job and hold it, either to work up a nest egg for survival on return to Mexico, or to establish himself in America. As simple and constructive as that goal may be, the sin papeles finds himself in a hostile environment. He is the hunted species of the Border Patrol, the police agency of the Immigration and Naturalization Service (INS)—which itself is a branch of the federal Justice Department. The sin papeles is an object of dislike inside the Spanish-speaking community where he settles, for he is seen as a job competitor. Outside, the sin papeles is viewed as a disposable source of cheap labor, as a welfare chiseler and tax evader, as a carrier of dreaded diseases and of poverty-in short, he is seen as a character to fit nearly every role of shame. The sin papeles as "illegal alien" is the subject of politicians' speeches and the object of racial discrimination, the stowaway in the Statue of Liberty. He is, in a word, an unwelcomed immigrant, but also an immigrant without any choice, for he cannot turn back to Mexico, whose myriad crises mount higher daily with no amelioration in sight. The sin papeles is forced by hunger in his homeland to seek out the status of a social outcast in America.

Since 1970, the presence of sin papeles in the United States has been developed into a public issue of major importance. Popular fears of a "Mexican invasion" have already lead several state legislatures—and one city government—to pass laws prohibiting the hiring of undocumented workers. Congress is again on the brink of passing anti-alien measures, including a proposal that would require all Americans to prove their citizenship when applying for work, or welfare, or even admission to hospital emergency rooms. The ultimate effect of these laws may be to lead us nearer to a police state, libertarians say—and Chicano leaders without exception predict that passage of the bills will intensify discrimination against the Spanish-speaking minority.

America today is in the breach of a historic decision, which in long-range terms is reducible to but two alternatives: latinization or xenophobia. For the near future, the choice is one between welcoming Mexican immigrants and erecting an electronic wall, buttressed by armed guards, along nearly 2,000 miles of borderland. The course Congress and the people will choose is presumably based on the truth of the information brought to light, on realism in assessing the present. The task of this work, then, is to dig out the basis for claims that America should hail or repel the millions of poor who are banging on the doors of our southern border.

CHAPTER 2: PROFILE OF *SIN PAPELES*

A Labor Department study released in 1975 provides a statistical profile of undocumented immigrants. The study, by Linton and Company, shows that Mexicans account for both the majority and the poorest segment of America's undocumented millions. The study divided seven hundred ninety-three undocumented immigrants it interviewed into three categories: Mexicans, other Western Hemisphere (WH) people, and Eastern Hemisphere (EH) natives. Of the 481 Mexicans interviewed, 90 percent said they came to the U.S. to find a job, compared to 60 percent of the WH immigrants and only 23 percent of the Europeans. The Mexicans averaged but 4.9 years of schooling, the WH respondents 8.7 years, and the Europeans 11.9 years, a figure close to the U.S. norm. In their homelands, the, Mexicans were most likely to have been farmworkers—49 percent were—and least likely to have held white-collar jobs; only 6.8 percent. Nearly 48 percent of the Europeans were office workers in their homelands, as were 34 percent of the Western Hemisphere immigrants interviewed.

Once in the U.S., the Mexicans continued to be the poorest among undocumented immigrants. The average wage of those interviewed for the study was $2.34 an hour, compared to $4.08 for Europeans and $3.05 for the Western Hemisphere sample. These wages compared to an average of $4.47 for American labor as a whole in 1976.

All of those interviewed by the Linton teams had worked two weeks or more in the U.S. Data from the study indicates that undocumented workers, on the whole, are younger than most workers in the domestic labor force. The average age of Mexicans interviewed for the study was 27.6 years; the average age of American workers is 39 years. This contention—that undocumented labor is youthful labor—is further buttressed by the finding that 46 percent of the Mexicans in the sample were between 16 and 24 years old. In the U.S. work force, only 23 percent fit into that age category. Not only were the Mexicans younger than most American workers, they were younger than the Europeans in the study group, who averaged 30.7 years of age, and younger than the Western Hemisphere aliens, whose average age was 30.

Mexicans were found to have the largest family obligation. On the average, Mexican sin papeles reported 5.4 dependents in their home country, compared to 3.6 for the WH group, and 1.8 for the European sample, again, a figure close to the U.S. norm.

The Linton study found that 48 percent of the Mexicans and WH immigrants were married, compared to 30 percent of the EH group.

Marriage characteristics differed sharply from those of the American population at large. Only 55 percent of the undocumented immigrants age 25 to 34 were married, compared to some 80 percent of the population as a whole. More than a third of those in this age group were never married, compared to only 15 percent of the U.S. population. Of those undocumented immigrants questioned, 39 percent had spouses in the U.S. Of 135 married aliens questioned, 82 indicated that their spouses were also undocumented. While there is some dispute about sex ratios among undocumented immigrants, 90 percent of those interviewed by the Linton study were males; the INS estimates that less than 10 percent of the nation's sin papeles are women.

The picture of the Mexican sin papeles that emerges from the Linton study is one of a young peasant, married and with children, uneducated and unemployed before coming to the U.S., poor by American standards even after his arrival, and separated from his family while be is here. The typical sin papeles hardly fits the description signaled by two words Congressmen and Border Patrolmen frequently use—the words "alien invader." Instead, undocumented Mexicans resemble the European "poor, hungry, wretched masses" once welcomed to Ellis Island.

Chapter 3: *Sin Papeles* Made Good

The problems of undocumented Mexican immigration were unstudied as late as five years ago. Since then, scholars and social planners have produced more than two dozen volumes in separate attempts to find ways of preventing unauthorized immigration, or adjusting to it. Though several recent studies have turned up details of statistical relevance, only a few have begun where public policy investigations must being to be successful— with the human subjects to whom any new policy would apply. For obvious reasons, sin papeles who have established themselves are difficult to reach and untalkative. Therefore, most sociologists have interviewed sin papeles in Border Patrol custody. This circumstance has led to the creation of a statistical profile of only the sin papeles who *fail* in their bids to advance themselves by coming here.

The story that follows is the true account of a successful sin papeles, whose last name is abbreviated with the letter "T" to protect his identity. Quotes are translated from the Spanish.

Martin T., 29, now lives in the Texas Panhandle town of Dalhart (pop. 7,000). Today this former sin papeles is a citizen, a union member, and an officer in the local Knights of Columbus chapter. He has proved to himself that the American dream can still come true: for today, in addition to being a homeowner, he is also a small-time landlord. Martin has succeeded where most men with his background of poverty—even native-born citizens—have failed.

Martin does not speak English with the ease of a native. He sometimes confuses "he" and "she," and also indulges a tendency to assign gender to all nouns as Spanish does: "See the hammer, he is over there," Martin might say. His style of dress is also reminiscent of Mexico, pointed-toe cowboy boots, plaid western shirts, with Presley-style hair, combed back and oiled. Some of Martin's friends wear metal tips over the toes of their cowboy boots, a sure sign that they are from south of the Rio Grande.

Martin comes from a farm community near Meoqui, in the Mexican state of Chihuahua. Meoqui lies about 150 miles south through the desert land from El Paso, Texas. It is but a village no larger than Dalhart, and intensely poor, because Mexico is a desperately poor country and the parched fields of Chihuahua produce little without irrigation. Like most sin papeles, Martin comes from a large family; he was the second son born to parents who had six children. He first came to the U.S. in 1968, at the age of 19. In his own words, Martin describes what he left behind.

"Before I came to the United States, my father owned a little piece of land, but the family couldn't make much of a living from it. In Mexico, you have to go to school for six years, and I went. It was hard for me sometimes, because I didn't always have shoes, and the other kids laughed at me. When I finished school—I guess I was about 14—I went to work in the fields other people owned."

When work was available, Martin earned about $1.15 per day: "I would work several days for one farmer, then be without work for a few days. Then I would find somebody else who needed help and work again as long as he needed me. I don't think I ever worked on the same farm for more than a month, because there never was enough work to do, and there were always other people looking for jobs, too."

The family home was a four-room adobe dwelling with dirt floors. In each room, a light bulb hung from a single strand of wire. There was no indoor plumbing; younger members of the family brought water from a hand-operated pump about 15 yards outside the house. Martin says the family's diet was far below standards for even the poorest Americans.

"Mainly we ate beans and tortillas, with a little salt and some peppers for seasoning. For a few months after each harvest, we would have meat maybe once a month. But we had chicken every week, because we owned chickens ourselves. A lot of people around Meoqui were not as lucky as we were, and never had chicken or eggs."

Like most peasant families, Martin's family believed that the way out of poverty lay in renting more land, or buying it. However, the family had no money for land acquisition. Emigration was not favored as a solution by anybody, because it would mean the separation of the family. Martin's father would not go the U.S., for if he were jailed or injured there, no one would be left to care for the family. When Alberto, Martin's older brother, reached the age of 20, however, he volunteered to go to *el norte*.

"It was about 1965 when Alberto came to the U.S. for the first time. He began sending money back to us, which we used for necessary things. But most of what he sent, we put in the bank to buy land. Finally, about 1970 or 1971, he and my dad leased some land and bought a tractor to farm it. Now the family is doing alright," Martin says.

Alberto did not come back to Meoqui for visits during the years he spent in the U.S. But early in 1968, he wrote home advising that Martin come north to join him. Inside his letter was a money order for $75 and instructions for dealing with Paco, a *pollero* or alien smuggler, who operates in Meoqui.

Paco is a native-born American citizen whose parents settled in the U.S. some 60 years ago during the last Mexican revolution. Weekdays, Paco works at an industrial job in the Texas Panhandle. Every other weekend he visits Meoqui to check into the accounts of a taxi service he owns there, and to make arrangements with the sin papeles whom he carries with him on return trips. Through employees of the taxi company, Martin secured an appointment with Paco, who drove by Pedro's house to pick him up the following day, a Sunday.

"When Paco came by the house, he had two other men with him, Ramon and Chelito. I already knew Ramon, because we had gone to school together. Paco drove us up to the border, and then took us down to a little shack on the Mexican side. He told us to wait until nightfall, then to cross the river and walk up to the first highway. He said he would flash his turn indicators as he drove along the highway and that we should come out of the bushes when we saw him. Then he took our money and left."

About two hours later, at sundown, a Border Patrol jeep passed by on the opposite bank of the Rio Grande, about 100 yards away. Sensing, or seeing—perhaps knowing—that the four men were waiting to cross, the jeep moved upriver about a quarter mile, then doubled back, crossing the point opposite them and going downriver several hundred yards. The jeep continued patrolling back and forth along the spot where Martin and his companions had hoped to touch American soil. Darkness came, and still the Border Patrol jeep made its rounds, at times flashing a spotlight on the river below. Martin and his companions knew well that there are hundreds of "safe houses" along the Rio Grande, too many for constant Border Patrol vigilance of them all. They concluded that someone had tipped off the American agents to their plan. After several hours of waiting, during which time the green jeep did not cease to rove the area, Martin, Ramon, and Chelito decided to give up. They began walking back toward home, a journey of nearly three days.

Two weeks later, Martin drove the three men, along with Hector, another Meoqui area farmworker, to the cover house again. No additional payment was made by the three men who had already been there two weeks ago; the rule in dealing with *polleros* is payment in advance, but for successful crossings only. Since Martin, Chelito, and Ramon had paid two weeks earlier, Paco now owed them a crossing. This time, the procedure was uncomplicated.

"The river was deep enough that I had to take my pants off, but nothing more. It was like wading across a flooded street," Martin says.

When the four men reached the highway on the U.S. side of the river, Paco was waiting with his car. The course he set out drove them over isolated ranch roads, away from Border Patrol checkpoints. "We weren't in danger of the Border Patrol there, but on some of those roads early in the morning I saw sheep and deer jumping out on the road in front of the car. I thought we might hit one of them," Martin recalls. By sunup, they were in Odessa, where Paco left the other three men with a *coyote*, or labor contractor. Paco drove Martin on to Alberto's house on a ranch about 20 miles outside of Dalhart. It was nearly noon when they arrived.

Several days later, a Chicano ranch hand took Martin into Dalhart to apply for a Social Security card. The Chicano translated questions on the application form to Martin, who answered all the questions truthfully: in the pre-Nixon era, there was no requirement that card applicants prove legal residency. The clerk in the Social Security station did not ask Martin about his immigration status, either, nor did she call policemen to investigate. Sin papeles are common in towns like Dalhart, so much so that they are almost an unquestioned institution. In West Texas, and across most of the Southwest, few people see any reason why Mexican immigration should be halted.

It was nearly six weeks before Martin's Social Security card came in the mail. In the interval, he helped the ranch crew replace fence posts, and was paid a gratuity by Alberto's employer. When the card arrived, through relatives of Chicano workers on the ranch, Martin found a job in Dalhart as a cement worker with a construction company. He was pleased with his new circumstances.

"A lot of places, they pay wetbacks less than other people, sometimes as little as $5 a day. But my checks came out the same as the other guys on the job. The company either thought I was legal here, or they decided to treat me fair anyway. Nobody ever asked if I was 'wet,' and I never said anything about it. All the foremen but one were Chicanos, so I didn't have any trouble communicating in Spanish."

Martin moved away from the ranch house into Dalhart, closer to his job. There he shared an apartment with a Chicano co-worker. After spending his first paychecks on clothing, he began saving.

"I wanted to send money home to my family, and someday, to buy a new car. I tried to save all I could, but you know, it gets kind of lonely when you don't know anyone, so I did go to the dances. It was the only luxury I had."

In a period of six months Martin saved some $1,800.

The dances Martin attended were sponsored by Chicano and Catholic church organizations in the area. They usually featured *ranchera* music, the same genre that Martin and nearly all Mexican peasants prefer in their homeland. At the dances Martin met young Chicanos his own age, and even several acquaintances from Meoque, as well. Like him, many of the Mexicans he met were sin papeles. But there was no reason to fear, because by long local tradition, lawmen did inquire into the immigration status of anyone who otherwise stayed within the law. From time to time, there were fights at the dances, usually between men who were legal residents. Sin papeles as a rule backed down from bullies, and were careful not to drink in excess; arrest for them could mean deportation.

Late one Saturday night as Martin and his roommate, who owned a car, returned from a dance, they were stopped by a city policeman on patrol. The left headlight on their car was burned out, and Martin's roommate smelled of beer. "The cop had both of us come down to the police station where they gave my roommate a ticket for driving the car with the headlight out. They also asked him about immigration papers. Since he could speak English, he didn't have any trouble. Then they asked me.

"I really didn't understand the question, so my friend translated for me. Everybody had told me that if I lied, *La Migra* might rough me up. So I told the cop in Spanish that I didn't have any papers, and my roommate translated what I said. Then the cops let him go, but they kept me there for Immigration."

Two days later, Border Patrolmen came to Dalhart to question Martin. He again confessed that he had no documents. The Border Patrolmen asked if he would pay his passage back to Mexico, and Martin agreed; "The way people had told me, you don't get in much trouble if you pay your own way back."

The Patrolmen locked him in a van with other sin papeles rounded up in the area, and drove him to a jail in Lubbock, some three hours to the south. The following morning all of them were put on a green-and-white Border Patrol bus, with bars on the windows. The bus headed south toward Mexico. A single Border Patrolman rode in it as guard.

The bus stopped at Marfa, Texas, on its way south. There, Martin and the other prisoners were processed through a deportation center. Border Patrolmen interrogated them, noting information on white index cards. The deportees were fingerprinted, and those who had money paid $26 for the trip from Lubbock. After the brief processing-stop they were reboarded and taken to the Mexican side of the border. With Border Patrolmen and Mexican police watching, all of the men were boarded onto a train bound for Chihuahua, capital of the state of that name. A Mexican guard accompanied them but he did nothing when several of the deportees jumped off the train as it pulled out of the station; these men were planning to make a quick return to the U.S. Martin rode with the others to Chihuahua, where all of them were released from custody. From the capital, Martin caught a bus to Meoque.

"I was afraid that when I got back people would laugh at me. But nothing like that happened. It was almost Christmas, and everybody was glad I could be home for the holidays."

His deportation did not alter Martin's plans to make a new life for himself in Texas. In Dalhart he had left behind a brother, a good job—and a fiancée.

His fiancée, Teresa, was a senior at Dalhart High School, a Chicana whom Martin had met at a dance some six months earlier. The young sin papeles knew that marriage to Teresa would open the door to permanent legal residency in the U.S., but he had not set a wedding date; Teresa wanted to graduate from school before marrying, and Martin, for his part, wanted to save up enough money to establish a household with her. He had been back in Meoque about 10 days when a letter came from Teresa, urging him to come back to Dalhart for an immediate marriage. In effect, Martin's deportation served as a catalyst to the couple's plans.

Martin again made arrangements to see Paco. But this time the pollero's fee was higher. "Paco wanted $100 instead of $70 like before. He told me that he charged me less the first time just to help me set myself up in Texas. I argued with him, but finally I had to pay what he asked. It's always that way in Mexico; if people know you have money, they're going to make sure they get their share of it."

Martin's return to Dalhart was uneventful, but once there, he encountered new problems. "I couldn't go back to my old apartment, except to get my things out, because once people know you've been deported, a lot of things are different. People are afraid to live with you, because they don't want *La Migra* coming around. And then there are always some people, especially among the Chicanos, who will turn you in if they see you. Every community has its informers for the Immigration."

After taking his belongings out of his old apartment, Martin took them to his brother Alberto's place on the ranch. Then he went to Teresa's house to plan for the wedding.

"We had wanted a big wedding, with a dance afterwards and everything else that is traditional. But both Teresa and I were afraid that Immigration would get me again, so we decided not to tell anyone else that I was back in town. Her parents didn't like the way we had to do it, but there was no choice. We didn't even send out wedding invitations for fear somebody would denounce me.

"We decided to have the little ceremony the following Saturday, six days away. I had to be careful, so I went back to my brother's house and stayed there all week. I only went out of the house twice, once to get the blood test, and once to sign the marriage license."

Teresa's relatives and Alberto were present at the bride's home that Saturday afternoon, when the couple was wed. After the brief Catholic ceremony, Martin moved his belongings to a bedroom in Teresa's family home.

"We would have rented a place of our own, but both of us wanted to save up some money for putting my papers in order. I figured that if I went back to work and saved, we could hire a lawyer within a couple months."

"I went back to my old job. Everybody there knew that I had been deported, but nobody cared anyway. I was a good worker, and in this country, that's what is important. Here, they don't care who you are or what family you come from. All they care about is how hard you work."

But six weeks after he returned to work, Martin was picked up again.

"Two Border Patrolmen came out to the job we were working on, looking for another 'wetback' who worked with us. This particular guy was in a restroom across the street from our job, and nobody told the *Migras* anything. They looked around for a while, and when they couldn't find him, they started questioning me because I was the only other Mexican around. I told them I was married to a citizen, but it didn't do any good. One of them argued with the other that I should be given a delayed deportation order. But the other one of them, who must have been the chief, didn't want to."

Martin pleaded with the Border Patrolmen for a chance to say good-bye to Teresa, and they relented. Both agents waited at the curbside while Martin went in to bid her farewell. He gave Teresa the money he carried, except for the fee he knew he would be asked to pay for transportation home. Teresa and her mother wept, for it was clear now that the wedding had been hurried for no good purpose, and once again, they feared Martin was in danger. He assured them that the Border Patrolmen were courteous, and that he had no fears about being deported. Teresa promised to meet him the following week in Meoqui, and Martin left. Once again he was taken to Lubbock, to Marfa, and back to Chihuahua. Three days later he was home in Meoqui again.

Marriage to an American citizen does not confer automatic immigration rights to Mexicans. The "beneficiary," or prospective immigrant, must provide documentation of several kinds. Martin's first task was to journey to Mexico City, 24 hours away, the only place in his homeland where Mexican citizens are issued passports. When Teresa came, she brought a document saying that Martin had not been convicted of any offenses in Texas, as well as a letter from his employer, saying that his job was waiting for him. Some three weeks after Martin's deportation, he and Teresa presented themselves at the U.S. Consulate in Chihuahua.

Martin saw an irony in the requirements: "You have to have money to get all the paperwork done, and you have to have a job in the U.S. to get in. The only way to get those things, at least for most of us in Mexico, is to go to the U.S. Or in other words, you have to break the immigration laws before you can ever make yourself legal."

The irony was deepened when Martin told the consul officer that he had been deported twice. "They said if I had been deported, it would take special permission for me to get it legally. So we waited nearly a month for them to check up on my deportations. When it was all done, they said they could find no record of them, so no special permission was needed." What actually happened, as Martin learned, was that his deportations were what the Immigration Services calls "voluntary departures." Normally, no criminal charges are filed against deportees who admit their illegal status and pay their fares home. Instead, these deportees, far and away the majority, are classified as voluntary returns. The voluntary return process saves the Immigration Service the costs of long-term jailings and court actions. It saves the deportee from prejudicing his future, because records of voluntary departures are not indexed as criminal records in Justice Department files. The consulate was unable to find any record for Martin as a deportee because technically he never was. Finding his voluntary departure records would not have barred him from legal immigration, and therefore, no check of these records was made.

By the time his forms were processed and ready, Martin and Teresa had spent two months waiting. It was then too late for Teresa to make up lost weeks in school. She never graduated, but neither she nor Martin were embittered, for at last they had legalized their future. Martin succeeded where most sin papeles fail.

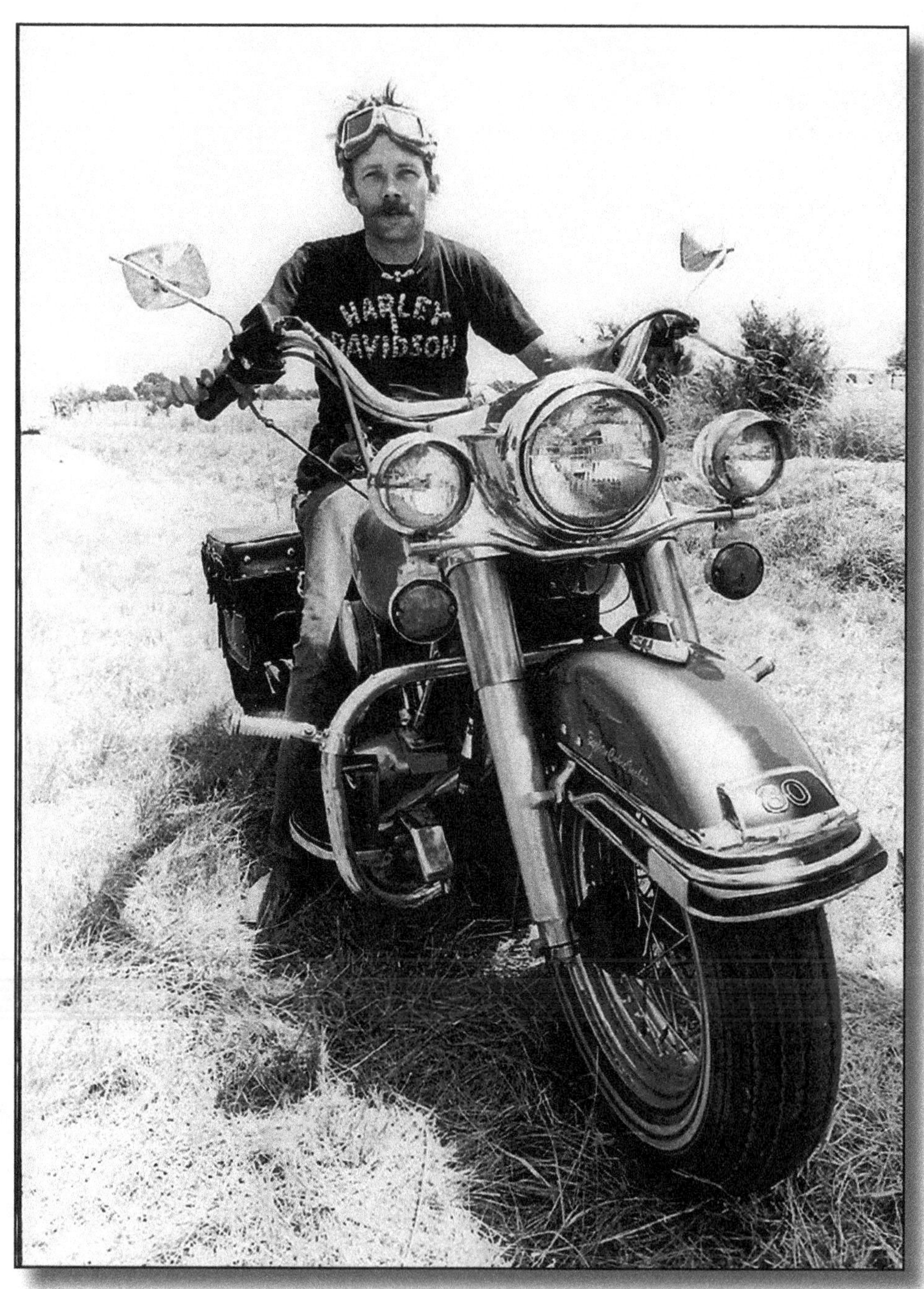

Reavis on his motorcycle, circa 1980. Photographer unknown. Image courtesy of the Wittliff Collections.

Despite his near-fatal accident in 1978, when he was hit on his motorcycle by a drunk driver, Reavis was an avid biker, writing numerous articles for a variety of magazines as well as collecting photos of bikers. Many of these photos are now held in the Dick J. Reavis Papers in the Wittliff Collections at Texas State University. This article first appeared in *Texas Monthly,* May 1979.

Never Love a Bandido

Big Jim sits astride his Harley, waiting for a red light to change. It's long after midnight and there's not a car in sight, but Jim doesn't think about running the light. A cop car could be sitting in the darkness around the corner, its cruising lights turned off. And now is no time for a Bandido to be getting into even minor trouble in Fort Worth. Ever since that fight at Trader's Village and the arrests that followed, the cops have been chasing down Bandidos on any charge at all, even for minor traffic infractions. Now not only the cops, but someone else—nobody knows who—has joined the game. At midnight three weeks ago, chapter president Johnny Ray Lightsey was blasted with a .38, and he fell dead in the street. Jim blinks a little, remembering that Johnny Ray was gunned down while waiting at a lonely intersection for a red light to change. He knows it could happen again.

Part of the trouble with police is a Bandido tradition. Ever since the club's first chapter was formed fifteen years ago in Houston, police and Bandidos have been instinctive enemies. The Texas Organized Crime Prevention Council has called the Bandidos a little Mafia, and with encouragement like that, Jim tells himself, it's no wonder that every two-bit police recruit in the state thinks that he has to earn his uniform by harassing Bandits. The club's founding president, Don Chambers, is locked up in Huntsville for a life term on a murder charge, and Jim believes Chambers is not the only Bandit wrongly in prison. "Free Don Chambers," say white letters on the front of Jim's black T-shirt. "Support Your Local Bandidos—Or Else," they say on the back.

Run-ins with the police have not limited the growth of the Bandidos; if anything, their legal troubles have made them more attractive to their potential members. Leaders won't divulge the group's size, but today there are Bandido chapters in seven states, and probably 1500 members or more—enough to warrant the claim that the Bandidos are the nation's second-largest outlaw biker clan, after California's Hell's Angels. Before joining up, most would-be Bandidos tell themselves, as Jim did, that being a Bandido means risking arrest and imprisonment every day. Rather than pale before that prospect, those Bandidos who stay in learn to welcome it, because if there are any qualities the macho motorcyclists respect, fearlessness tops the list, way ahead of honesty, intelligence, dexterity with a pistol, or even brotherliness.

Jim joined the Bandidos four months ago, just when a new wave of police harassment was unfolding in the wake of arrests at the Trader's Village chili cook-off in Grand Prairie. As both the police and the Bandidos reconstruct it, a young Dallas woman took leave of her boyfriend to beg a ride on a Bandido motorcycle. Half an hour later, when she and the Bandido rode back to the cook-off, the young lady leaped from the bike and screamed to her boyfriend that she had been raped. A free-for-all between bikers and onlookers ensued. The Bandidos joined forces and "all came together like a kind of magnet" one witness observed. At the end of the brawl, seven cook-off patrons were hospitalized, some for stab wounds. The Bandidos got off physically unscathed, but eight of them were jailed on charges ranging from rape to misdemeanor assault. As the Bandidos tell it, there had been no rape, and the member who gave the young lady a ride was Herbert Brown, not Ronald Kim Tobin, whom police charged with the crime. The incident was a classic case of confrontation between outlaw bikers and the citizenry, and the highly publicized charges that came out of it gave the police a reason to come down on the Bandidos, whenever and wherever they could. It became almost impossible for a Bandido to cross town without being stopped for a flickering taillight or having to show title to his Harley. Club members in Fort Worth pooled their resources—and even took jobs—to bail members out of jail or to pay off bondsmen who held Bandido bikes as collateral. Jim, who had been in and out of outlaw biker groups for most of his adult life, had never seen teamwork and defiance like the Bandidos showed after the Trader's Village bust. So he joined up with them, damn the police

"Damn the cops, anyway," Jim thinks to himself, chuckling a little. He'd had trouble with them virtually all his life. His mother, lacking anyone else to call for help, telephoned the police when her labor pains began. A patrol car came for her, but before it reached the hospital, Jim was born, right there in the back seat. The first event in his life had not been the caress of his mother, but a butt-beating by a cop, and life had followed that pattern pretty closely ever since. If there was anything Jim aspired to in his good-natured moments, it was getting a chance to give some cop a good butt-beating, just to even the score. As a Bandit, he might sooner or later get the chance.

The front wheel and the headlight of Jim's Harley flutter up and down, vibrating unnaturally. The vibration comes from underneath him, from the motorcycle's frame, which is broken in three places—two of the breaks are at the back, where the engine joins the transmission. When the light changes, Jim eases out, hoping to keep the vibration down. He can hear his motor squirming around as he gains speed. If he doesn't weld those breaks in the frame, it won't be long before the engine twists loose from its mounts. He promises himself to do something about it soon.

Every night at this hour for the past ten days, Jim has ridden this road over to the Nevada Club, a topless bar on the East Side, to pick up Doe at closing time. He never asked her to move in—that would have been too much trouble—but she had anyway, thinking herself privileged to be able to. The money she brought in from her dancing job wasn't half bad, he knew, but that wasn't all Doe had going for her. Unlike the other women he'd known, Doe wasn't a troublesome bitch, always giving orders or complaining. If she keeps behaving right, Jim tells himself, she might be worth making into a permanent old lady. He hadn't given her a Bandido jacket patch for old ladies, but he might, in about another month. Another month would give him time to see her react to trouble. Within a month, there would probably be a big bust, or somebody else would get shot. An incident like that would give Jim the opportunity to see if Doe was worth being made a Bandido old lady, because it would put her through the test of Bandido bad times.

The vibration in his engine quiets as Jim speeds on the final stretch going out to the Nevada, but it comes back as he slows down to enter the sandy parking lot. He parks his bike and goes through the small throng of hangers-on gathered around the front door. Everyone but employees has cleared out of the club. Inside, Doe is sitting with Julie, also a dancer at the club, and the girl who had introduced Jim to her. Julie liked to consider herself Jim's old lady, but he had never taken her in.

Doe follows Big Jim out to his bike, but she doesn't move to mount it as usual. Jim looks up. She raises a pale hand to her mouth and yells out over the din, "Jim, I've got to talk to you." He pushes the kill switch and his motor goes dead.

Doe, a frail young woman of about twenty, runs her hand through the black, almost kinky hair that clings close to her head. Jim looks down at her waist, where the ends of her blouse are tied, about three inches above the belt buckle on her jeans. He stares up at her cleavage, where the butterfly tattoo is. Around her neck is the same little bare silver chain she always wears, in all important aspects, she looks the same to him. Jim wonders what she could want.

"So, yeah, you want to talk to me?" he mumbles.

"Jim, I don't want to go home with you tonight. I don't want to be your old lady."

Jim strokes down on his shaggy beard and spreads his legs out stiffly, one on each side of the Harley. The skin on his broad face is drawn tight now, and he stares at Doe over the handlebars, nailing her with his pale blue eyes.

"Yeah, why not?" he growls after a minute.

As she explains, he shrugs his shoulders, and, with his left hand, takes off his Harley cap, running a palm over his thinning hair.

"Jim, I've been kidding myself. I can't be a biker's old lady anymore. I've tried before, and it just won't work. I need a man who works forty hours a week, just like me; not somebody who's going to spend all day puttin' around with his buddies."

Jim has heard these gripes before but never paid them any mind. He's hacked now that she would take them so seriously, "Lookit, I've already heard it, right? What are you going to do, tell me about your first old man again?"

"Well, Jim, it's for real. My old man was as much a one-percenter as you are, and you know it. Then that truck hit him and—poof—he was gone. I'm not ready for that again. I can't handle it. And here you are, a Bandido. You could get blown away anytime, and you know it. A woman can't live with that, thinking her man may die just any minute."

"If you talk like that, you ain't ready to be a Bandit's old lady," Jim drawls, smiling ironically.

"That's right. I don't want to be no Bandido's old lady."

"Well, that's it, I guess," Jim mutters. As she stands there a little distraught and unsure of herself, Jim fires up his motor. He could hang around and argue with her, maybe even change her mind, but he doesn't see much point in it. That would be conduct unbecoming to a Bandido. Without another word, he rolls his machine back away from the sidewalk and roars off.

He heads his bike to the north side of town, toward Nasty's house, where he knows his Bandido brothers will be tinkering with their motors in the garage. But the incident with Doe has disturbed him more than he would like to admit. He has known and lived with several females, but none like Doe. For one thing, she is headstrong, and, reluctantly, he admired that in her, even as she was telling him off. Not many women, he thought, had the nerve to come straight out and rebuff him like that, right on the street. The others would have run off, leaving notes behind or telling him good-bye over the phone. But not Doe. She was ferocious, despite her size.

Nasty's garage is a center for the Bandidos and has been for about six months, ever since the police raided their last clubhouse after the Trader's Village arrests. Nasty's two bikes are usually parked inside amid the refuse of another half-dozen bikes and parts from perhaps twenty more. Around its pine walls are several mechanic's tables, and on its greasy floor a scattering of tools. Centerfolds from *Easyriders*, a biker magazine, and photos of two or three of the looser women who hang around with members of the Fort Worth chapter are nailed to the walls.

The windows in Nasty's simple frame house are dark when Jim rides up, a sign that Nasty's wife and son are in bed. As he rounds the corner, headed for the garage in back, the garage lights go out, and the four Bandidos inside, on guard against the sound of any bike—for it might carry Lightsey's killer—come creeping out the doors, taking cover with their weapons. But they recognize Jim and, with a round of laughter, go back into the garage. When they switch the lights on, Nasty and E. J. are over by the red refrigerator drinking beer. Both have just come in with the night's receipts from the Magic Lounge, a bar on the Jacksboro Highway that Nasty operates. Jim gets off his bike and saunters up to the refrigerator to take out a beer.

Though Jim has grown accustomed to him, Nasty is a terror to behold. He is a satanic reincarnation of Abe Lincoln. Dark eyes peer out from his narrow face, which is surrounded by a thin, straight, glistening black beard. Like the Great Emancipator, he speaks in a high-pitched, gentle voice that contrasts with his lankiness and his dead-serious demeanor. On one wrist he wears a studded leather band. From his hip pocket sticks the narrow, heavy handle of a 9mm automatic pistol, and above his bed, Jim knows, hangs a Thompson semiautomatic. Seeing Nasty loitering in the garage or behind the bar at the Magic Lounge, there is little to show that the man is a father, a homeowner, a decorated veteran, and the husband of an entirely traditional wife whose occupation is nursing.

E. J., the short, squat figure next to Nasty, is Jim's oldest friend. He is wearing a black Bandido T-shirt, his tattooed arms are akimbo, and he has a beer in one pudgy fist. E. J. seems to balance, not stand, on tiny feet shod in blue and yellow jogging shoes rather than black motorcycle boots. Wiry black hair sprouts wildly from the top of his head, and his unshaven chin. His paunch overhangs his jeans all around the waistband.

E. J. and Jim had ridden together even before both became Bandidos. Once, when Jim's bike was down, he borrowed a car from E. J. and drunkenly drove it through the plate-glass window of an orthopedic supply house, which brought suit against them both. It was Jim who was riding with

E. J. the night that E. J. plowed his Harley into the front seat of a Toyota as it made a left turn. The Toyota simply collapsed, and its driver was killed by the impact. E. J. was thrown over the car's roof and suffered two broken legs. Someone remarked that the Toyota looked as if it had been hit by an unidentified flying object, and ever since then, E. J. had been nicknamed UFO. "That means Unidentified Fat Object," he sometimes jokes when introducing himself. E. J.'s strongest asset was his sense of humor, and Jim knew it well, because when Jim didn't have an apartment of his own—and that was most of the time—he lived with E. J. and his old lady, Trisha, a dancer at the Magic Lounge.

The two other Bandidos in the garage are Rockin' John and the club's pledge, Ken, usually called by his title, Prospect. Rockin' John spilled his bike on one of Fort Worth's remaining brick streets last weekend; only today did he get out of the hospital, and the beer he is drinking doesn't quell the pain that still plagues him. Rockin' John is kneeling at his Harley, trying to wrest off the seat. Prospect is helping. Nobody notes that Jim is perturbed. After a few seconds, Rockin' John, disgusted with a rusted bolt on his wrecked bike, bellows out an obscenity.

Jim chuckles. "You think you've got troubles. Well, brother, I just lost my old lady."

"So what's that?" Rockin' John spits back. For Bandidos, bikes are more important than women.

Jim doesn't know how to reply at first. Then he blurts out, "Well, if nothing else, that's going to be a helluva blow to my income."

Everybody laughs, especially E. J., whose roar can be heard halfway down the block. When the garage has quieted down again, Rockin' John continues needling Jim.

"Man, I can see you could sure use some of that income. Look there at your pants," he says, pointing at Jim's crotch.

Jim, who has sat down on a wire milk carton, casts his eyes down to his legs. His faded denims are ripped at the seam on the left side. He is not worried by that, because he has another pair in his room at E. J.'s place. But somehow this problem with Doe has not come to an end that he can live with,

"Don't worry, bro, if she don't come crawling back tomorrow, I'll give you my old lady," E. J. says, putting a pudgy arm around Jim's neck.

"Say, now, don't do me no favors," Jim drawls.

About noon, E. J. stumbles into Jim's room in the house they share, grabs Jim by the shoulders, and shakes him.

"Say, bro, wake up. It's Doe on the phone. Says she wants you back."

Jim blinks. "Huh? Doe? Shit!"

"Do what you want, bro. I'm just giving you the message," E. J. growls, trundling back off to his and Trisha's room.

Still in the ripped pants he wore last night, but shirtless and barefoot, Jim rises and makes his way to the wall telephone in the kitchen.

"This is Big Jim. Who is it?"

"Jim, I have to tell you that I screwed up last night."

"Huh! Yeah, you can say that again."

"I'm serious, Jim. I still want to be your old lady."

"Well, you're going to have to earn it now. Things won't be the same." He grins, awaiting her response.

"Jim, I mean it. I'm sorry. I want you to come get me so we can talk."

"Well, I ain't got much to say."

"Jim, I'm serious. Come get me now. I'm at the Nevada."

"You hold on there. It's going to take me a while, you know. I just got up," Jim explains. He holds the yellow receiver at arm's length and blinks at it. Little noises are still coming out; Doe is talking. He blinks again, and hangs the receiver in its cradle.

He tells himself that it was probably some guy. Some jerk came to the club and Doe wanted to hop in bed with him. That's why she dreamed up that whole rap about not wanting to be a Bandido's old lady. But there's no sense in bringing up anything about another guy, he decides. After all, he is back in command.

He brushes his teeth, finds his boots, shirt, and Harley cap. In the kitchen he makes a cup of coffee, and sits at the table, groggily mulling things over. There's really no sense in going over to see her. He could just pick her up tonight at closing time as usual. But he decides to go over to the Nevada anyway.

Fort Worth in autumn is a nearly ideal town for biking. The winds are not high and the cold has not bitten hard yet. The streets are wide and traffic is relatively thin. With practiced ease, Jim cuts in and out, passing cars that are already exceeding the speed limit. Only one stoplight halts him en route to the east-west freeway.

The freeway was resurfaced last spring, and the new finish is not good for motorcycles. Grooves half an inch deep snake along the pavement, to reduce hydroplaning on rainy days, the highway department claims. But the new surface steals traction from narrow motorcycle tires. The treads of Jim's front tire catch in the grooves, causing the wheel to bob and bounce. Jim feels the traction slip, but he has learned how to deal with it. The higher the speed, the less noticeable the loss of traction. He races down the freeway at 80 mph, not because he wants to see Doe, he tells himself, but because he doesn't want his bike to spill on the pavement. In minutes, he is at the exit nearest the Nevada.

Doe is waiting for him outside. He rides up next to her, and she mounts the bike without saying a word. Pressing her hands hard against his waist, she leans forward, and with her lips next to his ear, speaks over the hum of the Harley's engine.

"Honey, let's get some lunch."

Jim nods.

They ride back to the north end of town, to a favorite Bandido diner, where both of them order without saying anything to one another. Jim is waiting for her to speak first, but Doe says nothing. When they have finished eating, she pays the tab and they walk out. Jim starts his Harley up and she climbs on back.

"Coming to get me tonight?" she asks as they pull out.

Jim doesn't answer. When they pull up at the Nevada a few minutes later, she asks again, as if Jim hadn't heard the first time.

"Well, I think it would be better if you met me at Kim's house," he mumbles.

"If that's the way you want it," she drawls, as slowly as she can. Jim turns his Harley and rides off without nodding her way.

Nine figures kneel in a circle in the shadows of dusk on a parking lot behind a beer joint on Fort Worth's South Side. Each Friday evening the Bandidos come here for their weekly meeting. The owner of the stark tavern was an admirer of Johnny Ray Lightsey, and he still welcomes the Bandidos; if nothing else, they buy a few beers before and after their powwows. Now that Lightsey is gone, the chairman of the meetings is Kim Tobin, 28, a husky six-footer who works weekdays as a diesel mechanic. His long blond hair is pulled back into a ponytail. He listens more than he speaks, and when he does speak, it is in the manner of a still-shy adult. The chief business tonight is filling a vacancy for vice president. There is no show of hands to make it formal, but Tobin, voicing the consensus, tells E. J. he's it. Elated, E. J. challenges everyone to a game of pool back in the bar, where Prospect, several women, and a couple of Bandidos from out of town are waiting.

In the group of well-wishers is a gargantuan, swarthy young man with a beard stubble and bushy black hair. His filmy pink shirt is unbuttoned above the waist, and there are two chains around his neck, a bear claw hanging from one, a five-pointed silver star on the other. This kid, Lloyd Tobin, is Kim's nephew. The Bandidos protect him, perhaps because he is unable to fend and befriend for himself, even when sober. Tonight he is staggering drunk. He wanders from the sidewalk out front to the bar and pool tables inside, giving everyone strong-arm embraces they could do without. Apparently penniless, he guzzles the drinks others offer him.

Jim circles through the crowd. There's no sense saying so, but he's a little ticked by the incident with Doe last night. She's got no right to tell him to work, Jim thinks. Besides, she's not the only woman he can have; there are others. One of them is Nadine, a barmaid at the Acapulco Club. Jim hasn't seen her in several weeks, because he hasn't wanted to. If he shows up tonight, he reasons, she'll probably be so overwhelmed that he can wheedle free beers from her for the whole Bandido club. He proposes to Kim that they ride over to the Acapulco, and when Kim nods okay, everyone prepares to go.

There are a dozen black Harleys outside, all of them belonging to Bandidos. One by one, the riders crank them up. Kim leads out across the street, and the others fall in behind. Nasty brings up the rear, fishtailing for fun every time they stop at a light. The Bandidos are masters at riding in packs, handlebar to handlebar. When their line rides up on motorists, the cars slow down to let them pass. The Bandidos whip through traffic at more than 50 mph, while Lloyd weaves drunkenly in his Chevy, following about twenty yards behind. A cop comes in sight and, bypassing Lloyd's swerving vehicle, tails the Bandidos, five yards off Nasty's taillight. The Bandidos slow to 35 and creep onto the parking lot of the Acapulco, as the cop rolls slowly by, peering as if trying to pick out a particular member. The Bandidos pretend not to see him and file inside.

The Acapulco is a neighborhood club that on weekends attracts single females as well as men, most of them Mexican American. There is a small dance floor in one corner and pool tables against another wall. The sleek U-shaped bar is heavily populated tonight.

Most of the Latinos sport shiny print shirts open at the chest, wedge heels, and Sansabelt pants, and at least half of the young gallos wear gold medallions around their necks. When the Bandidos come in, the Acapulco's male patrons frown a bit, staring at them from corners of the room and the other side of the bar. Several look up from the pool tables, mystified as much as irritated. The women move a little closer to their dates, seeking shelter; those without men turn their heads away. The Bandidos are now in a situation biker patois describes as "being ugly in a no-ugly zone."

Suddenly, there is a commotion over by the pool tables. Everyone, Chicano and Bandido, rises to look. Lloyd is scuffling with one of the Latinos, a young man with a neatly trimmed black goatee. A knife pops up, its blade glinting beneath the Tiffany-style lamp that lights the billiard table. The Chicano now has the knife, having wrested it from Lloyd's fist. Flustered, Lloyd spins away and picks up a pool cue. Then he advances on the goateed Latin with his head lowered, like a swordsman stalking his opponent.

Kim strides in through the back door, the entrance nearest the pool table. He steps between Lloyd and the Latin, lays a hand on Lloyd's cue, and with an authoritative flick of the arm shoves his nephew backward. Bandidos spring out of other nooks of the bar, grab Lloyd, and drag him out the back door; Lloyd shouts as he goes. The Bandidos form a cordon around the pool table, sealing off the area of conflict. Some stand with legs spread wide, their hands twisting pool cues held waist high. Everyone is waiting for an order from Kim.

The Latins congregate on the other side of the room, spouting Spanish. Some of them glare over at the Bandidos, but others are merely watching curiously, *"¿Mano, qué pasará next?"*

A second Latin has somehow wedged himself in at the pool table, a man older than the goateed youth who took Lloyd's knife away. The older one holds the other by the shoulder. Tobin is talking to them, but the music is too loud; no one else can hear. He is not apologizing, it seems; his gray eyes are intent on the two men confronting him.

The goateed Latin stomps away from the pool table over to the bar, where two male friends and a woman gather around him, telling him to cool down. Instead, he breaks away for an instant and, pointing at the Bandido line, screams, "They're just a bunch of pussies. Pussies—that's all they are!" His friends pull him back to the bar, but the Bandidos, stung, tense up on their pool cues, itching for action. Tobin, however, gives no signal to move. The older man, apparently an uncle of the goateed youth, is now nodding his head in agreement with something Tobin says. Tobin sits down on the edge of the pool table and, calling Prospect over, orders him to bring a beer. Then he lays aside his cue, and looks at his hands as he chats with the older man. He pulls from time to time on the brim of his black Gimme Cap. When Prospect brings him the beer, he fondles it as he speaks. The dispute isn't resolved yet, but the Bandidos can see that

Kim won't be calling them to combat. The Latins drift apart, and most of the Bandidos slink outdoors, where their bikes are. Tobin and the older man are left alone, conversing at the pool table.

Ten minutes later, Tobin comes out of the bar. He wants no part of their banter. Instead, he picks Lloyd out of the circle and upbraids him. "Now, listen up, Lloyd, I know you got riled, but you had no right to. You've got to think about these things more. You know you've already been to the joint once, but you're about to get us all into trouble for you. Listen, you're not alone anymore. You've got us; you've got a family now. We'll take care of you, but you've got to understand that now you have more people to think about than just yourself." Lloyd, who is mute throughout the little lecture, is overwhelmed and blubbering by the time Kim finishes. He throws his arms around Kim, who returns the embrace. Pretty soon, the other Bandidos pass by, patting Lloyd on the back. When he raises his bushy head and asks who has a cigarette, everyone knows he has regained composure. The trouble with Lloyd, everyone agrees, is that he's not Bandido material. He should know that with Lightsey's killer running loose, Bandidos must guard their violent urges. "We've got to save ourselves for the shithead that shot Big Johnny," one of them tells Lloyd.

Bandido Weird Larry is sitting on his haunches over by the bikes when Big Jim steps out of the club with Nadine, the barmaid. Larry rises to his feet to join the crowd around her. Though married for more than fifteen years, Larry has been quarreling with his wife ever since he joined the Bandidos four years ago. This afternoon they were spatting again—over his paycheck from the fencing company he works for—and tonight Larry is looking for a diversion from his troubles at home.

A fair-skinned girl with shoulder-length auburn hair, Nadine can't be a day older than eighteen. She is also either stoned or drunk. Big Jim dwarfs her, his arm around her neck. She scissors her legs nervously back and forth, answering the Bandidos' jive questions, hugging closer to Jim when they laugh. Before long, Larry belts out the perennial biker demand: "Show Us Your Tits!" There is a general murmur of glee as she raises her cotton pullover and exposes an apple-colored nipple on a spotless white breast nearly as large as a football. "How about that!" Weird Larry exclaims as she puts an arm around him. Big Jim momentarily leaves her side, and she looks up at Larry from under his wing, asking, "Aren't you one of my brothers, too?" Larry points to his Harley hat festooned with a dozen trinkets, then shows her the Bandit patch on the back of his denim jacket. Then he raises her blouse again, and she looks at him, and says, giggling, "Go ahead, lick it." Larry bends over her, and another Bandit takes over the other breast.

"Say, Nadine, you're going to ball us all, aren't you?" Larry squeals out.

"Sure," she stutters. "You're all my brothers, aren't you?" Somebody assents, and she assures them, "I'll give y'all anything you want, 'cause you're my brothers and I'm your sister." There is drunken or drugged pride in her voice.

But Big Jim comes from the back of the circle to intervene.

"Listen, brother, this chick has got to go back inside right now. She's got work to do." Obediently, the girl turns to go, and as she walks off, Jim tells her to bring some beer. A few minutes later, she comes back with cans of Coors and Budweiser. There are cries for more beer, and she returns inside with Jim close at her heels. She goes behind the bar and gives him a beer. Then, a moment later, when the bartender and manager are not looking, she sets up another. The can is still unopened. Jim lowers it into a pocket of his black leather jacket. She passes him another and another. Five minutes later, Jim goes back to the street with half a dozen beers in his jacket. A few seconds behind him, the girl steals out, a beer under her blouse.

For the next hour, Nadine pivots back and forth, inside and out, as if the club gave curb service to Bandidos. When closing time comes, she steps out with Big Jim at one side, Larry at the other.

Everyone mounts and rides to Tobin's house, a sparsely furnished shack on the North Side. An out-of-town Bandido and two locals crowd around the rear door of a van, preparing its bed for the gang bang. Doe, still in the clothes she wore this morning and looking aged with fatigue, and Julie, outfitted in cowgirl garb, pull up in Julie's pickup. Both have just gotten off from their stage jobs at the Nevada. Instinctively, they know what is afoot. Doe makes straightway for the living room, where Nadine stands under the arms of Big Jim and Larry. She, or someone else, has removed her blouse. Doe stops just inside the doorway, listening.

Larry and Jim are arguing like farmers disputing ownership of a cow.

"Jim, there ain't no way this girl can be your old lady."

"Huh, where'd you come from with this shit?" Jim asks Larry, blinking puzzledly.

"If she's your old lady, have you got a patch on her?"

"I ain't got to," Jim slurs, a little drunkenly. He has not turned to see Doe standing behind him.

"What do you mean you ain't got to have a patch on her? Ain't you never heard of an old lady patch?"

"Man, I got three old ladies now, and they only give you one patch. On top of that, brother, I ain't given an old lady patch to none of my old ladies."

"That's just the point, see. You got to have a patch on your old lady. One patch, one old lady. You got to have a patch on all your property."

"What do you mean, I've got to have a patch on all my property. I ain't got no patch on my pocketknife, and it's mine."

"Yeah, but you got to have a patch for an old lady."

"Look, Larry, the girl is with me and you can't claim her. She's going to be my old lady, not yours, and that's it, brother."

Only a few minutes earlier, Jim planned to give Nadine to the club for a gang bang. But Larry's insistence, his off-the-wall lecturing, has gotten on Jim's nerves. Now he claims Nadine as an old lady and is convinced he always planned to. Nadine, however, has run off in the confusion—Doe and Julie have handed her a blouse and hustled her off to the back of the pickup where all three are talking low. Jim doesn't know where Nadine has gone, but he fears that if the argument with Larry continues, he and a brother Bandido will come to blows. He wheels and goes outside.

On a sheet of notebook paper, Big Jim's first two old ladies are writing out a set of rules for the new recruit, who has enthusiastically grasped the prospect of old ladyhood. As Doe writes, Julie explains to Nadine what each rule means. The rules, which have apparently never been written out before—the men in the yard laugh when they are told what the project is—are common sense to Bandidos. They say that old ladies must help keep their men and motorcycles in good order, contributing to the financial needs of both. They forbid a Bandido's old lady to gossip about club members when women gather together, and they command above all obedience, cleanliness, and truthfulness. There is a prohibition against unauthorized adultery, though it isn't called that.

By now, everyone knows that there isn't going to be any turn-out. Some club members, like E. J., have already gone off with their own old ladies, and others, like Nasty, who did not bring their wives, have gone home.

Even Larry has left for his house. Jim, nearly alone now, walks gingerly over to the pickup. He steps quietly up to the back and puts a forearm on Doe's neck. She cranes her neck to see him. "Yeah, what's up now?"

"Let's go home," Jim mumbles.

Doe looks at him, then turns her head back to Julie and Nadine, who have heard, and are staring at Jim, waiting for him to beckon. But Jim says nothing more.

"What about your other old ladies?" Doe demands sharply.

"I ain't got no other old ladies," Jim mutters, glancing downward. Then he looks up at her again. "All I got is just one."

Nadine only vaguely understands what is said, but Julie catches it.

"You goddamn scooter slime, you lousy damn scooter slime!" she wails.

Jim winces but turns away. Doe stands up in the pickup bed, then jumps over to follow behind him.

When Doe awakens the next morning, Jim is not in bed with her. The kitchen door is open, and Doe looks out. There sits Jim, on the back of his bike, legs outstretched, feet crossed on the gas tank, the chrome studs on the brim of his Harley hat gleaming in the September sun. Gingerly, and with the cheer that carried over from last night's victory over the other women, she opens the screen door and calls out to him.

"Honey, do you want some coffee?"

Jim looks up from his musing.

"Naw, never mind."

"Is there anything I can do for you?"

Jim chuckles, then looks down his legs to his feet again. "Now that I think of it, you might buy me a new bike."

She giggles and steps out onto the porch, but Jim, raising a hand in the air, halts her before she can come to his side.

"Listen, baby, don't bother me now. I've got some thinking to do."

"What about?"

"Aw, about them Hondas. I can't see why anybody wants to ride 'em," he quips. The Bandidos' antipathy toward Hondas is endemic. A real man can only ride a Harley.

Doe goes back inside without saying anything. Today is Sunday, a day off for her, and waiting in the house for Jim to think through some silliness—probably something about his bike—is not what she had planned for the day.

Jim looks up at the tree branches overhead, which have already lost their leaves. It's nearly October. Winter will be coming and that will make his pickup a necessity. But the old Datsun, parked a few feet away in the back yard, won't run anymore. It will take money to fix it. He's a month behind on the payments for it, too. The finance company will be wanting money before long. What Doe brings in will help, but that alone is not enough to make it through the winter.

Winter isn't the only problem, either. There's self-defense. Jim doesn't own a weapon; he borrows a pistol when he can from one Bandit or another, but most of the time he's unarmed. Lightsey's killer might come back, and Jim needs a gun—to greet him, he thinks, chuckling aloud.

Getting an income is a problem almost too big to think about. What Jim would like is to go into some kind of business. The trouble is, he doesn't know what kind of business to start up. He's never given business or money that much thought before, and now, because he has no money, he can't go into business no matter how much he may want to. There's no sense in thinking about that, he tells himself.

There are other options, of course. He could let Julie come in as his second old lady, like she wants to; that would give him the income of two dancing girls. But both of them would have to eat, too. And they'd probably be continually harping at him about something. It's not worth it, Jim thinks. Women are too much trouble to manage. There's running dope, or selling hot bikes, or burglary, but Jim decides against those pursuits, too. Jails are cold in winter, he recalls. Sooner or later, a man with dealings like that has to go to jail. Being a Bandido is jail risk enough.

But all that only leaves one thing: work. It's hard to work for a boss, he reminds himself. But what else is there to do? He considers his assets. He has no skills, except being a Harley mechanic—and there's no market for that. He has an equivalency diploma, an honorable discharge from the Navy, and a prison record for auto theft: not much to offer. He'd have to lie about most of his life to get a job. Nobody would trust him. He'd have to pretend he wasn't a Bandit, and that prospect chills him. About sunset, he crawls down from his bike and goes indoors. He still doesn't know what to do about an income. One thing is for sure, though. He's not going to tell Doe about any plan to look for work. That would make the bitch think she's running the show.

The next day, after taking Doe to the Nevada, Jim stops by the diesel shop where Kim works, hoping that Kim will have some advice. Kim has more than that. If Jim wants to come on as a mechanic's helper, he says, there will be a job open next week, right there in the same diesel garage. Jim agrees to try it out.

Back at home, however, he sees new problems with working. For one thing, his bike won't hold up long, and if he starts a job, he won't have time to fix it. He will need the Harley to ride to work on, and that means he'll need to be finished with the repairs by Monday. Jim starts in immediately. By nightfall, he has the Harley on a box and the wheels off and he's ready to pull the engine.

The next day, Doe takes on her assigned role as parts cleaner, without knowing why Jim is impatient to rebuild the bike now. E. J. joins in, too, but as an equal.

"There's two important skills you've gotta have for a job like this," E. J. counsels. "You got to have the know-how and the know-where. You've got to know how to do the work, and you'd better know where to get the parts."

They visit other bikers, even several who are not Bandidos. The parts come in, almost all of them from trades with other Harley riders. A few items, like piston rings, they buy from the dealership, though neither of them enjoys giving the dealer their trade. In their eyes, Harley dealers are little more than profiteering pirates. By Thursday afternoon they have reworked the motor inside and out and have also borrowed a welding rig for work on Friday. It is dark as they lay the engine aside—time for E. J. to take over the Magic Lounge from Nasty, who is getting off early that night. When E. J. gets in his car to leave, Jim jumps in with him.

Several Bandidos are already on hand at the lounge. Prospect, Herbie Brown, and Kim are there. About 11:30, Lloyd comes in and sits down with the Bandidos, who welcome him as they always do, with free beer.

About midnight, twenty blocks away, Nasty is awakened by the sounds of banging at both the front and rear doors of his house. Naked, he leaps from bed, picking up his automatic pistol and running toward the rear of the house. As he peeks out through a curtain, his kitchen door is thrown open by a cop.

"Get your family out of the house!" the patrolman bellows.

The garage, fifteen yards from the back door, is in flames. Nasty pulls on his jeans and ushers his wife and child out the front door. Still barefoot, he runs to the rear of the house and begins hosing it down; paint on the wooden structure is already blistering under the heat.

After the fire crew has come and gone, he gets a flashlight and tallies up the ashen, soggy remains inside. Two bikes and hundreds of parts are ruined. A padlock from the rear door of the garage is missing and so is a set of Harley gas tanks. Somebody has broken into the garage, taken what he wanted, and set it on fire.

The Bandidos at the Magic Lounge do not hear about the arson until much later that night. At almost the same instant that Nasty is awakened, Kim and Lloyd step outside the lounge. Kim wants to show Lloyd the changes he has made to convert his '36 Harley to electrical starting. As he bends over to point out a wiring detail, he feels a searing blow at his waist and tumbles down. Lloyd, too, falls, struck by a bullet that enters his chest and dances across his body, exiting at his shoulder. Gravel flies about them, kicked up by automatic-rifle fire. By the time the others reach the front door, pistols in hand, the assailants have driven on down Jacksboro Highway. Later, the Bandidos easily connect the two events: whoever torched Nasty's garage drove immediately to the lounge and opened fire on the Tobins. The attacker, they reason, was probably the same man who shot Johnny Ray Lightsey off his bike. Kim and Lloyd are hospitalized, and once again the Bandidos sleep with their pistols.

Two nights later, Big Jim squats in the kitchen of E. J.'s house, over his cycle work. That afternoon he welded up the cracks in the bike's frame; now he is picking at the transmission. Earlier that night, another club brother kept watch on the house, but now it is nearly 4 a.m., too late for prudence. Big Jim is out of cigarettes, and neither Doe, sitting tiredly at the kitchen table, nor the Bandidos drinking in the living room have any left. Jim and Doe decide to buy more.

It is a somewhat ambitious plan. The only means of transportation at their disposal is Prospect's battered old pickup, which he left in the back yard early that evening. It has a leaking radiator hose. But he can drive it, Big Jim thinks. He'll have to remove the hose, cut away its tattered end, and clamp it back on again. He picks up a screwdriver and steps out the back door, onto the porch. Doe is a few steps behind him. As he turns toward the pickup, he sees a flash and hears a boom. He collapses back into the doorway. Blood jets from his belly.

Before he can clutch the wound, another flash comes, from a shotgun about fifteen feet away. This time his forearm is hit. "Get out of the door!" a Bandido yells from inside. But Jim can't move. He falls backward through the still-open door, landing beside his engine. There is another boom; this time, his side is crushed. He leans his uninjured right arm over the Harley engine, lying down, playing dead. Now he hears return fire. Two Bandidos are at the kitchen window, discharging their pistols at a figure in the darkness.

A moment later, there is silence. The assailant has run away.

Doe has turned away from Jim; she is weeping.

Jim, still conscious, shouts for an ambulance. But already his vision is blurred.

"E. J., brother E. J.," he moans.

E. J. kneels at his side, a revolver in his fist.

"Take it easy, brother. We've called an ambulance for you."

"E. J., you take my bike. It's yours, brother."

"Nah, no need to say that, brother," E. J. mumbles. "You're going to make it all right," he says, not believing himself. He looks around the room; all the other Bandidos are worried, too. No one thinks Jim will live. Doe will not look his way. She moans as Trisha comes and leads her off to the bedroom.

Jim does not lose consciousness. When the ambulance comes, he asks the driver to let E. J. ride along to the hospital. But E. J. does not go to the hospital, not immediately. There is other business to take care of. The cops are searching the kitchen, demanding to see the weapons the Bandits used in self-defense. And there's the matter of the dog, too. E. J.'s black-and-brown mutt failed to bark when the phantom gunman came into the yard. As soon as the cops are gone—taking one Bandit pistol with them—E. J. paces up to the dog, which is playing at another Bandit's heels. When the animal looks up at him, E. J., with a swift, straight-armed motion, aims his revolver and fires. The dog falls dead without a whimper.

"I never gave that dog a name," E. J. explains to his startled club brother. "But now I don't have to. We can just call him Dead."

And a few seconds later, he adds, "Yeah, and the same goes for the dude who shot Big Jim and Kim and Lightsey. We'll just call him Dead, too."

Half an hour later, two patrolmen in Richland Hills on Fort Worth's northeast end stop their car behind a van parked in a lower-middle-class residential district. The garage doors of the nearest house are open, and so are the rear doors of the van, which carries two Harleys. Suspecting a burglary, the patrolmen question the tall, long-haired man attending the vehicle. By radio, they ask for a registration check on the motorcycles. Their suspect, Steven Daniel Vance, 22, turns out to be a resident of the nearby house. But both motorcycles were reported stolen earlier that week. Vance is arrested for theft.

The two patrolmen search the van for other contraband and weapons. They find six handguns and a twelve-gauge pump shotgun. All are loaded, the shotgun with green Federal Express shells like the spent cartridges found in the yard where Big Jim was shot. The weapons are turned over to Fort Worth investigators for ballistics testing.

Two days later, Vance is charged with the shooting death of Johnny Ray Lightsey. Fort Worth homicide officers say that bullets fired in ballistics tests of a .38 caliber pistol found in the van match up with slugs taken from Lightsey's body. They also report that marks on shells fired from the suspect's shotgun match those on the spent ammunition found where Big Jim's assailant stood. In addition, bullets fired from the semiautomatic rifle taken from Vance pair with a slug in Kim Tobin's bloodied leather jacket.

Though the evidence neatly implicates Vance, it is unlikely that he was the only actor in the Bandido shootings. Fort Worth homicide investigators and Bandits alike believe that at least two men are responsible—one who drove the vehicles from which Lightsey and the Tobins were shot and one who fired upon the victims. The Bandits also believe that Vance could not have been alone that night North Richland Hills policemen arrested him: unloading motorcycles from a van is ordinarily a two-man undertaking. Vance, however, refused to discuss his associates or accomplices with prosecutors. All winter he was mum as he sat in jail awaiting trial.

For several years both police and Bandidos have known Steven Daniel Vance as Trapper John, a member of the Ghost Riders club, a local organization which, though originally formed as a Bandit farm league, has drifted beyond the control of its founders. The Ghost Riders have in recent years been closely allied with the Dallas Banshee chapter, which is also hostile to Bandits. On the night of July 9, 1977, outside a bar on Harry Hines Boulevard in Dallas, Steven Vance was wounded by a shotgun blast fired from a passing car. A police report filed on the incident indicates that Vance told investigating officers the Bandits had shot him.

The morning after Johnny Ray Lightsey was killed, two Banshees were shot off their motorcycles at Madisonville, between Houston and Dallas. One of them, before he died, identified his attackers as three men in a tan Lincoln Continental, and gasped, "The Bandits hit me." Banshee national president Ronald Bush took up the accusation, telling reporters, "The Bandidos don't want any other motorcycle club in Texas and the only way they can get us out is to kill us off." He further said that if the Bandidos wanted war they would get it.

An Austin Bandido who drove a tan Lincoln, and who had business dealings in the Fort Worth-Dallas area, Jan Colvin, 31, turned up dead on a vacant lot in Irving last November. His death may be part of a Banshee "payback" for the Madisonville killings. But Bandidos believe Colvin was killed by disgruntled business associates, not Banshees.

The Texas Bandidos enforce a hegemony all their own over the 75 other outlaw biker clubs in Texas. Bandidos forbid members of other clubs to wear various regalia items on denim membership jackets, or "colors." On the list of prohibited adornments are rocker patches that say Texas—for the Bandidos consider that their native, exclusive turf. Last spring, the Fort Worth Bandidos demanded that a mid-cities club of black bikers, the African Bandits, change their name. To avoid war, the blacks chose compliance: today they call themselves the Mandinkas.

The clubs that Bandidos regard as imitators sometimes pull public stunts, like beer raids or showdowns with the police, which the Bandidos believe are best left to experts like themselves. As the Bandidos see it, the trouble always comes home to them anyway, no matter what club is involved. They say that practically every crime committed by bikers in Texas is attributed to them, because they are the most notorious club in business. Taking the heat for others, the Bandits believe, gives them the right to call the shots.

Dozens of smaller clubs have been absorbed into the Bandidos. But from time to time, other clubs have defied Bandido dictates. Almost every member of the Fort Worth Bandit chapter has "battle patches" sewn on his jeans, patches forcibly taken from the members of other clubs in sovereignty disputes. The chapter's battle flag, too, has its swastika surrounded with such trophies—patches taken from the Ghost Riders, the Diablos, the Damned Few. Some clubs, like the Freewheelers, though still organized elsewhere in Texas, no longer have chapters in Fort Worth because absorptions and forcible "patch pullings" have decimated their numbers. Like Jim, who was a Freewheeler, most Fort Worth Bandidos once rode with smaller clubs.

The Bandidos frequently fight with the members of other clubs, but usually win, and they are probably right to believe that none of the other clubs are nervy enough to declare an all-out war on them. That is why, from the first, they have suspected that Lightsey's killers were individuals seeking to settle some private score—a private score against Bandidos, perhaps, but not a club complaint. In their own search for the men behind the Fort Worth shootings, they are looking for Vance's friends, not for fellow club members or allies. All winter long they kept their ears open to rumors, but apparently learned little.

The winter was not a good season for the Bandidos. Kim, when he recovered, was brought to trial for the rape alleged to have occurred at Trader's Village. Despite protestations from Herbie Brown and the other Bandidos that Kim had nothing to do with the Dallas woman, Kim Tobin was convicted of raping her and was sentenced to an eighteen-year prison term. Weird Larry, or Larry Dale Sparks, was also placed in the dock for a chili cookoff stabbing. Though eligible for probation, he was handed down a seven-year sentence.

Steven Vance initially fared much better in court. Prosecutors did not ask for his indictment on the Tobin shootings, and a grand jury no-billed him for the Lightsey murder. On January 26 he pleaded guilty to the shotgun shooting of Big Jim Bagent and received a probated ten-year sentence. As soon as he left the jailhouse, he went into hiding from the Bandits and, perhaps, from everyone except his attorney and probation officer. But twelve days later he was behind bars again. Local officers working on a felony fugitive warrant picked him up for return to Louisiana where he had skipped out on a one-year probated sentence for drug possession. At his new mid-city apartment they found a van reported stolen from a Dallas floral shop a slim three days after his release from custody in Fort Worth. Probably because he suspected the Bandidos were trying to hunt him down Vance was well armed. The police took a .357 Magnum revolver from him a the door of his apartment; inside they found a sawed-off shotgun and a rifle. All three arms are forbidden to probationers, and mere possession of the short-barreled shotgun is an offense. Trapper John will be a prisoner for years to come, but at least guards will stand between him and the Fort Worth Bandidos, even if they all meet up in Huntsville.

If better days were ahead for the Fort Worth Bandidos over the winter, the first sign came from Houston. Bandido national president Ronald Hodge of Houston sent the Fort Worth chapter a new leader. Butch Goodwin, 34, a stocky, bearded ex-convict with the words "I love my Bandit brothers" tattooed on one arm. Goodwin put a stop to the chapter's laxity: its members began riding armed and in pairs. Not a shot was fired at them, perhaps because Vance's accomplices were cowed or because they simply lost heart when Trapper John was jailed. Then in mid-March, Judge Howard Fender overturned Kim Tobin's eighteen-year sentence and Kim was freed on bond. There is little likelihood that he will ever be brought to court again for the alleged Trader's Village rape, but the trial had cost Kim his most precious resource. On the Sunday after his release, he sold his Harley to pay off his attorney's fees.

Three months after his wounding, Big Jim, flanked by Butch and E. J., paid me a visit. His comrades helped him up the front steps, and Jim came through the door gingerly, balancing his hulk on a four-pronged cane. I received these Bandidos from my bed, where I lay recuperating in a body cast, the payoff from an October head-on crash between my own Harley and a pickup. E. J. and Butch quickly left to carouse in Austin's topless bars, while Jim and I talked until daybreak, empathetically trading hospital trauma tales. He showed me the gashes surgeons left on his abdomen, the cast covering the bone blasted out of his arm, the brace on his paralyzed left foot.

He had suffered in other ways as well. His old Datsun was repossessed and Doe left him. Jim had no insurance, but he believes that he has something better, the Bandidos. "You know, I haven't had a cent all this time. My brothers give me what I need," he told me.

Jim did not want to talk about anything he might have known about Vance or his phantom accomplices. When I asked him why he was shot, his answer was evasive, if witty: "I really don't know why they did it, but I'll tell you one thing, that's what. I don't think it was no accident, they convinced me of that."

E. J. also told me little: "If we ever find out who was involved, I can assure you that he will be duly reprimanded," he said.

Bandidos I spoke with later were equally sly and closemouthed, and that is as good an indicator as any that if they can, they will carry out a vengeance in their own style. Their judgment, we may assume, will come as a crack in the night.

Reavis (center) with Fort Worth Bandidos, 1978. Photographer: Chris Wahlberg. Image courtesy of Dick J. Reavis.

The 1980s

This article, which appeared in the *Texas Observer,* July 25, 1980, should be read in conjunction with his earlier articles, "At War in the Mexican Jungle" and "The Smoldering Fire." Here Reavis continues his reporting on the fate of Mario Cantú.

Unreliable Witness

INDEBTED

I did not want to be a witness in Mario Cantú's probation hearing last April. I had problems of my own. My wife was in Honduras visiting her family, and my solitude disoriented me. I couldn't do anything right. I forgot to feed her dog. I let him eat up household objects. I put clothes into the washer but forgot to take them out; I exhausted my supply of razor blades and let food in the refrigerator rot. I sat behind my typewriter, hour after hour, pecking out writings that will never be published, and in the middle of one of these nerve-work stories, I ran out of paper. When I reached for a cigarette, I found that there were only two left.

The telephone rang. Mario Cantú was calling from San Antonio. He told me that his probation hearing was scheduled for the following week. He said he wanted me to testify on his behalf. Images of our relationship dashed across my consciousness like lightning during an electrical storm.

I first met Mario some three years ago, because he was in touch with Mexican guerillas whom I wanted to write about. Three times I went into the mountains of the state of Oaxaca to witness their activities. On two of those trips, Mario accompanied me. After the last of them, in October

1978, Mario was summoned to appear before federal District Judge John Wood to determine whether Mario had violated the law by going to Mexico.

Instead, Mario split for Europe.

I missed him while he was gone. Mario was more than a source for my guerilla stories. In early 1977, I had written a book about illegal immigration. Mario had provided me with telephone numbers and introductions to Chicano spokesmen who were decrying *la migra*.

He also gave me his ideas on the subject. Then as now, his theories were odd, unique, and without any hope of achieving immediate popularity. Other Chicano leaders essentially favor immigration, by legal or other means. Mario does not. He says immigration to *el norte* is an escape valve for the Mexican economy: if immigration were halted, revolutionary pressures would build in the ranks of Mexico's displaced peasants and marginal workers. Mario wants to see revolutionary socialism take hold in Mexico.

If there is to be massive immigration—and, everyone concedes, we have it—Cantú says it should be policed in a humane manner. He and other Chicano leaders charge that the lower ranks of the Immigration and Naturalization Services are chocked full of racists. But the other Chicano spokesmen want no truck with revolutionary socialism. In Texas, Mario walks alone, and to their left.

I gave Mario but a brief mention in my book on immigration [*Without Documents,* Condor Publishing Company, 1978], which did not praise him at all; I had theories of my own to tout. Nevertheless, he continued to aid me. Because I wanted to do an article on the rarity of honest reporting in Mexico, Mario called me up, invited me over, and made introductions whenever a Mexican reporter came to interview him, which was often. If today I am on terms of confidence with some Mexican journalists, it is in part because Mario gave me openings.

Always, Mario was eager to help. When he called asking that I testify, I felt obliged.

I knew that other people who have been involved with Mario would have felt indebted, too, even if for somewhat different reasons. Cantú has been *padre o partero* to a dozen infant causes called Chicano, though he orphaned many of them in their adolescences. In the early 1970's, he put together a broadly-supported San Antonio movement against police brutality. He helped found La Raza Unida Party. When the Texas Farm

Workers Union was not much more than an idea in Antonio Orendain's head, Mario gave him money and introductions. He edited *Sin Fronteras,* the newspaper of the once far-flung Centro de Acción Social Annónima, an organization which defended immigrants facing deportations. When San Antonio's garbage workers went out on wildcat strike in 1978, Mario went to jail with them. His character was nowhere more evident, though, than in 1970, when he cancelled a contract his restaurant had to provide lunches to inductees. Mario didn't care about passing up Army money; he cared about protest.

Journalists, however, are more indebted to the truth than to any movements, or to any individuals, with the possible exception of their mothers: if nothing were true, journalists would soon run out of stories to write. Mindful that I knew some things about Cantú that his lawyers wouldn't want aired in court, I warned him that I would testify truthfully.

"Sure," he said, "don't worry about it."

Still reluctant, and mindful of my disorientation, I told him that if he wanted me to appear, he'd have to subpoena me. I hung up, and went out for smokes.

Mario must have gone straight to the courthouse. Two days later, the subpoena I demanded was delivered. I called Mario. "Now what do I do?," I asked. He told me to be at the downtown Holiday Inn in San Antonio April 2, the day before the court hearing. I was to meet with his attorney, William Kuntsler.

Whether we like him or not—and I don't like him—the profile of gangling William Kuntsler is familiar to anyone who keeps tabs on contemporary history. Kuntsler is the Darrow of our day. He is best known for representing the Chicago 8, who convened the 1968 Democratic convention protests in Chicago. Over the past 15 years, Kuntsler has defended the nation's most publicized black agitators, white agitators and Indian agitators, both armed and unarmed. It was time for him to defend a Chicano agitator.

Of course, I wanted to meet Kuntsler: but not about legal business. My experiences as a participant in the judicial process had all been of one kind, as one of the *accused.* I was a civil rights worker in Alabama during the mid-sixties, and got all the first-hand courtroom experience I'll ever need. Every time I stood trial, I had a civil liberties lawyer like Kuntsler, except for one time, when my lawyer was jailed, essentially for being a New York Jew. Kuntsler got him out, but I languished in jail three weeks. It was not a personal grudge that I held against Kuntsler, but a grudge against his kind, the let's-make-a-precedent lawyer. Every time I stood trial, I was convicted. I was sure that Mario would be, too, with representation like Kuntsler. "Why didn't you hire Gerald Goldstein or some other good Mafia lawyer?," I asked Cantú.

"We've already been through that," said Mario.

Believe me, we had. Last December I went to Paris, where Mario had been in exile more than a year, continuously speaking out about injustices to Chicanos and Mexicans. I needed to see him about several matters. Coming back was one of them. At his family's request, in personal conversations I urged him to return. I told him I thought it was best to come back and face the music in silence, head bowed. "If the reporters ask why you've returned, tell them that it is because you left your toothbrush behind." That was my advice to him.

Gathering

Part of it, he took. We flew from Paris into Mexico together. Then he stayed south, in Monterrey, for two months. The weekend before his return and surrender in February 1980, I went to Monterrey to see him, perhaps for the last time, I told myself. Again, I urged him to come back quietly.

Mario by then would hear none of it. He said that his original 1976 sentence was patently unjust. I could not disagree. Only two people have ever been convicted of shielding illegal aliens. In Mario's case, the charge came because he refused to let immigration agents raid his restaurant until they obtained a search warrant; they regarded his insistence as obstruction. He was convicted because he was guilty; but then, so are thousands who are never molested or jailed. Even alien *smugglers* rarely receive five-year sentences for first offenses, and many of *them* are never charged simply because the federal courts and the INS are backlogged with work. Injustice, however, comes from many sources, not only the courts. Most of us have to live with our heads bowed at some times in our lives. I thought Mario's time had come, and that he must endure the outrage if he wished to proceed with his politics.

When I arrived in San Antonio and met Mario in Kuntsler's hotel room, I immediately understood that Mario had cast off all ties to caution. Sitting across from Kuntsler was Herman Baca, a Chicano firebrand from

California. In 1977, the Ku Klux Klan staged show patrols along the border to put the fear of vigilanteism into the hearts of illegal immigrants. When the Kluxers came to maraud at San Diego, Baca and his associates met them with picket signs. A riot was narrowly averted. I could see a similar scenario on script at the federal courthouse the following morning.

My worst fears were eased a few minutes later when Monsieur Daniel Jacoby stepped into the room. Jacoby, whom I had met in Paris, is a human rights attorney of record and stature.

He is accredited by the International Federation for Human Rights, Amnesty International, the United Nations, and a half-dozen other goodnik agencies and organizations. I am quite sure he would shriek in case of riot. Like me, Jacoby had come as a witness.

I didn't take notes during this meeting. I didn't plan to write a story. This experience, I thought, was a chapter from the personal life—or demise—of a journalist, not something meant to be published.

I told Kuntsler I was hesitant to testify because, as I'd indicated to Mario, I might know things about Mario which could hurt his case. He asked me what sort of things I knew. I wasn't sure what to say, especially in the presence of other witnesses. Mario, I figured, would know what to worry about. He knew, better than me, what the terms of his probation were. I looked over at Mario, who was sitting on the bed opposite Kuntsler, and Mario looked over at Kuntsler. "Ah, don't worry about it," Mario told him.

Kuntsler then told me and the other witnesses something we hadn't expected to hear. Mario already had told the court that his October 1978 trip to Mexico was made without permission from his probation officer. Guilt was a matter of record; tomorrow's hearing was only to establish mitigation.

I was an important witness, Kuntsler said, because I had accompanied Mario (rather, he accompanied me) on that clandestine trip. The other witnesses would speak only about political issues or Mario's character.

The last man to enter Kuntsler's room that afternoon was big, brash, red-faced Ruben Sandoval, Cantú' s San Antonio attorney. In a few words, Sandoval told us that his own plan for the defense had been subordinated to politics. Sandoval had wanted to rely on what Mario called "onions." He had wanted to bring out the human side of Mario's life, to talk about the family's fears for Mario's safety, about the difficulties of separation from them, about business problems which arose in the wake of Mario's departure for Europe.

Kuntsler, on the other hand, wanted to get a political message across, and so did Mario. Commentary on the disagreement was brief, because it was time for Cantú and Kuntsler to show up at a cocktail party sponsored in honor of the New York lawyer at the downtown offices of MALDEF, the Mexican-America Legal Defense and Education Fund.

I went along, probably because I was hungry for something sardonic. MALDEF, you see, is an organization of liberal attorneys, liberal legal secretaries, and just plain old liberals. They wear business suits, sip Margaritas, and are usually to be found chattering light-heartedly, but with seemingly sincere titillation, about "programs," elections and racism. Marx had a phrase for this sort of people: he called them "beer-quaffing philistines." But Cantú and Kuntsler, who hold themselves out as Marxists (Cantú does not accept, completely, any political ideology), begrudgingly accept them as kin. I took refuge with Luis, Mario's cousin, the one person present who I was sure would not mention "programs," elections, or race to me. Luis was there to serve tacos. I ate several of the tacos, which were brought over from the restaurant. They were good.

RALLIES, OLD FRIENDS

When the Margaritas were gone, those of us in Mario's lengthening train piled into cars and went over to a protest rally being held on his behalf at the Mexican-American Unity Council's big office in that grand old pinkish building on Commerce. I don't know what the Unity Council does, but it is to be commended for preserving that building, a monument to a graceful time in San Antonio before the military bases were big, back in those pre-war days when the city's leading daily was the Spanish-language *La Prensa*. I urge the reader to take a close look at the Unity Council's building someday. Titans should live there.

On the west side of the Unity Council's building is a large cement courtyard. That's where Mario's forces had set up their rally. More than a half-dozen invited speakers sat on the outdoor stage, a big protest banner above them. To their left was a canopy, where *chalupas compuestas* were served, and in front of them, some 20 rows of 10 folding metal chairs each. I sat down in one of those chairs, next to Romulo "Chacho" Munguia, a thin, sixtyish man who has been Mario's confidant for 35 years. We listened as one by one, speakers came to the microphone and made their addresses.

The speeches bored me, and they made Chacho mad. Chacho is a Republican, and he is not at all ready to agree with what radicals say about America. Herman Baca, or else Corky Gonzales—Denver's Mario Cantú—summed up most of the speeches in a single phrase: "It's not Mario Cantú who is on trial, it is the *system* that is on trial." Chacho and I don't agree about politics, but we did agree that there wouldn't be any judges going to jail after the morrow's hearing.

Chacho has aided Mario by writing leaflets and giving advice for most of the ten years since Mario became a radical. He had done so, not through love for Mario's domestic ideology, but because of his strong feelings for Mexico. Chacho's own parents were radicals, refugees from the Mexican revolution in its latter days, when it became radical to be honest in office. As Chacho and many other second-generation San Antonians see it, Mario has inherited the mantle of his Mexican parents. The Mexican government has taken on the legacy of the thieves who drove the honest people out. I suspect that Chacho would stop short of advocating the overthrow of Mexico's government, but I cannot be sure: all sons and grandsons of that nation believe sins go uncounted there.

When the bombast from on stage passed the limits of his tolerance, Chacho began telling me of his relationship with Mario. It was a saddening account. Although Chacho had aided in the defense campaign, he had done so only out of personal loyalty. The idea of a show trial ran counter to his very conservative instincts. During the months Cantú had been back in San Antonio, Chacho said, neither man had made overtures to the other. Chacho felt that Mario owed him first courtesies; Mario, I'm sure, knew that Chacho wanted to discourage further protests, and didn't want to hear that advice. Their old friendship had grown distant, and that distance promised to become vertical when Mario climbed on stage. Chacho went home before Mario's speech.

Mario said what all of us expected. He talked about the suppression of political liberties in Mexico and of Mexico's economic subservience to American interests. If his words were not exceptional, his tone promised hope. Mario stood back from the podium, leaned towards it and spoke with timidity. He appeared to be thoughtful, or frightened: it was hard to tell which. Perhaps Mario is tired, I told myself. But I knew better: Mario is tireless in politics. It was his supporters, men like Chacho, who were tired.

THE HEARING

I was bleary and still tired when I walked into the federal courthouse on Durango the morning of April 3. The architecture of the place did nothing to cheer me up. The courthouse is made of pre-fab, textured concrete, and it is newy-newish and white. I am sure it was intended as a judicial tribute to airports. Just inside its plate glass entrance, security guards sit around a metal detector. There are no smoking sections in the public areas of the courthouse, not even in the foyers.

An absurd sort of decorum was in force in the courtroom. As I entered, I pulled off my leather jacket. Before I had it in my hands, however, an individual in a polyester suit grabbed me by the shoulder and told me, in command voice, that I'd have to put it back on. Many of the males who came to wish Mario well were without coats. Someone in the foyer outside passed coats around, while the supply lasted. As a result of federal lending, several men in the courtroom soon were attired in topcoats, all-weather coats and raincoats. I'm sure the men in the raincoats looked over at me and whispered, "who's that *petit bourgeois* in the motorcycle jacket?"

At ten o'clock sharp, Judge William B. Sessions strode in from a door off to the side of the room, buttoning his cloak as he came so as not to waste a second. Judge Sessions is a thin, white-headed, fiftyish man, whose pronunciation is precise, and whose eyes are clear blue attentive. He is one of those rare individuals who really does sit erect, all the time. He promptly began to page through the letters sent to him about the case, noting each one for the record. Several of the some 50 letters came from prominent San Antonians: Archbishop Patricio Flores, grocery king Eloy Centeno, and three legislators, including Rep. Matt Garcia, presumptive nominee to head the immigration service. Other letters came from Chicano movement leaders: LULAC chief Ruben Bonilla's name figured among them.

Most of these letters, which I'd heard read at the rally the night before, were of a similar tone. They said that their authors, while often in disagreement with Cantú, believed his conviction had been unjust and that his absence had caused a hardship on his family. They said Mario was of an honorable character, and that he merited mercy.

Letters of a different sort came from radicals like Angela Davis. Several of these letters said that the judicial system is racist or otherwise unjust. Without showing any offense at all, Sessions noted his exception to such statements. Ruben Sandoval asked the judge to pardon their authors, on grounds that they were laymen at law. Sessions said he hoped ignorance accounted for the tone of those letters, and then proceeded to count the petitions which Mario's supporters had signed. Sandoval presented the judge with some 500 additional signatures, accounting for 50 or more pages. Judge Sessions turned each page, noting that there were no photocopies.

When each item of paperwork had been noted, Sessions called witnesses to the front and swore us in. A marshal led us away to a room down a curved hallway that opened off one side of the courtroom. The room was dominated by a big, round, mahogany-colored table with a Formica top. Twenty-five people could have sat around it. There were about six of us, including Richard Avena, the Civil Rights Commissioner. He told us about the vacation he planned to take in Central America. Corky Gonzales was seated across from him. Another witness, a frail man about 40 years old, who was apparently a federal official, drew Gonzales into a conversation about boxing. Corky had been a professional fighter in the fifties; the frail little man was one of his fans. I had known nothing about Corky's pugilist past, but when I looked him over carefully, I saw that there was no reason for surprise. His nose was flattened and muscles bulged out of the silver filmy shirt he was wearing. Only boxers and wrestlers show off their muscles in shirts like that, and wrestlers do not have flat noses.

M. Jacoby also was in the room, reading over his notes. Bexar County Judge Albert Peña and I sat near one another, listening to the woman who, before the morning was out, was to enthrall all of us—Señora Rosario Ibarra de Piedra. She's not nearly as tall as her name. Sra. Ibarra is a petite, well-dressed woman, still pretty despite her 53 years and the trouble she's seen. The wife of a physician, she was until five years ago a Monterrey housewife. In 1975, her son, a college student, was arrested—or perhaps, kidnapped—in Mexico City. Sra. Ibarra found him in Campo Militar Numero Uno, an army installation where suspected subversives are interrogated. Several months after his confinement there he was taken away, reportedly to another prison. He never arrived. Sra. Piedra has learned nothing of his fate in the years since, despite persistent appeals to his captors, despite continual contact with other political prisoners. Her son is *un desaparecido*, one of the some 400 Mexican students and peasants who, human rights agencies say, simply disappeared while in government custody. During her search for him, Sra. Piedra encountered other mothers who were searching for their sons. They banded together to demand explanations from the Mexican government, and were soon joined by representatives of Mexico's leftist parties. Today, Sra. Piedra maintains a house in Mexico City. Traveling nation to nation, she protests the loss of her son.

Sra. Piedra told us of her family's suffering, but with optimism: it would help produce a more civilized world, she said. We did not, I suppose, discuss the Cantú case: what was there to discuss? All of us knew Mario in distinct ways, and a conspiracy between us was not conceivable. Nevertheless, the prosecution had asked that we be sequestered away from the court proceedings. I suspect that the others, like me, felt the sequestration was harassment. What was going on in the courtroom, we suspected, was a teach-in of sorts, and might have been worth watching.

One by one, we were called to testify. Only three or four of us had not been called by lunch, when we were given permission to leave the building. I ran into Chacho outside, and during the break, we agreed on a common attitude towards the outcome of the hearing. I think its formulation was my work: "If Mario goes free, we are happy, because he is our friend. If he goes to prison, that's fine too, because he hasn't asked for our advice lately." Anyway, it went something like that. I wondered how many others were thinking the same way.

I TESTIFY

About 2:30 p.m. 1 was called to the stand. Kuntsler, attempting to explain Mario's purpose in breaking the terms of his probation, asked me several questions about why Mario had gone to Mexico in October 1978. I said Mario had gone to make sure that an NBC crew could safely film a land seizure by armed peasants. I had been hired to do that job but could not have performed it alone. Had he and I both not gone along, NBC would have failed. Mario was the man who, in a tight spot, persuaded the guerillas to allow NBC to continue its mission.

Kuntsler failed to question me thoroughly: I could have told the court that Mario did not tell me of his plans to make the trip until two hours before I was scheduled to leave; his wife did not find out until after I did; and NBC knew nothing until its crew was in Mexico. Mario took these precautions because the guerillas had asked him to. They could not have been persuaded to cooperate with us had Mario insisted on telling his plans to a probation officer two weeks before the scheduled invasion.

As things turned out, the guerillas misinformed us about their plans. We had planned to arrive three weeks before the invasion, to film mere preparations. The rebels advanced their date for action without telling us. We arrived three hours before they set off in march.

When Kuntsler had finished with me, a short, balding prosecutor, Fred Rodriguez, edged up. He looked stern and I felt menaced. He asked me a startling question.

"Mr. Reavis, didn't Mario Cantú tell you that he wanted the revolution to be televised?"

I couldn't believe it. I didn't know what revolution was being talked about, and I didn't know how Mario would have told me that he wanted it televised. What was Mario supposed to have said? "Listen Reavis, we've got a big revolution planned for 10:15 Monday morning, corner of Fredericksburg and Zarzamora. Everybody will be there, grenade launchers in hand. Can you call up the networks and see if they'll send out a crew?"

I did not voice these thoughts in court, of course. Instead, I gave an answer in decorum.

"No."

Rodriguez started flapping through papers on his table. He snapped up a sheaf of them and came towards me. He was halted, mid-way, by the voice of Judge Sessions, I believe, telling him that the papers had not been entered into evidence. The prosecutor handed them to the clerk, the clerk handed them to the stenographer, the stenographer put a fluorescent sticker on them, and the prosecutor laid them down on the railing in front of me.

What he had was a photocopy of a *Texas Monthly* story I'd written about Cantú.

I hadn't reviewed the story before coming to San Antonio, and neither Kuntsler nor Cantú nor Sandoval had mentioned it. I didn't recall what I'd said in that story, but I was sure I hadn't said that Mario had told me he wanted the proverbial revolution on television. I try not to be ludicrous in print.

The prosecutor pointed to several lines he had underscored in red: "The incident received ample news coverage, helping to fulfill Cantú's desire that the revolution, whether in Mexico or the U.S., be publicized on television and in print."

I urge the reader to go over that statement twice, noting the word "desire."

I admit it: the notion of publicizing a revolution, by advance notice of some kind, is ludicrous. I didn't say so in court, but I beg the reader's forgiveness: I was in a body cast and under the influence of a stomach tranquilizer called Soma when I wrote that story.

But no defense need be made of my choice of the words "his desire." The word *desire* is not equivalent to the words *said* or told.

Prosecutor Rodriguez then repeated his question, with a little jaw-boning. He said something like, "Now you've identified this article, and that statement, as yours. Do you still intend to tell this court that Mario Cantú never told you he wanted the revolution on TV?"

Prosecutors, being literate men, are supposed to recognize the differences between words like desire and said or told. The prosecutor, I'm sure, has at some time desired to sleep with an actress. But he never *told* me that.

I repeated my denial, and may have explained the difference between desiring and saying, without mentioning actresses, of course.

Mr. Rodriguez was not pleased.

He asked me if Mario Cantú didn't advocate revolution.

I told him Mario did.

"In the United States as well as Mexico?"

I told him that, as far as I knew, Mario had gone out of his way to make his feelings known. He's never concealed his sympathy for revolutions, not to my knowledge.

Rodriguez was not satisfied.

"A peaceful or violent revolution," he peppered.

I told him that revolutions are not peaceful. I think that is a fact of history as well as of English.

The prosecutor would have gotten a lot more out of me had he merely asked me to explain what Mario believed. But his tactic was to picture me as an adversary of the government, so as to ready his audience, or the judge, for any evasion of mine when he asked his hardball question:

He asked me if Mario Cantú had ever been a gun-runner.

It was one of those questions I had feared without formulating. No objection to the question was voiced from the defense table, or if any was, I didn't hear it. I was too frightened to hear. My reply leaped out in an instant.

I told the court that as far as I knew, Mario had been involved in a gun-running incident discovered and halted some years before in Monterrey.

The prosecutor asked me exactly when the incident took place.

I said I wasn't sure.

He then showed me my article again. On a second or third page, these words were underlined in red: "He has admitted to smuggling guns into Mexico as late as 1976."

Rodriguez asked me why I didn't want to say that the year was 1976.

I told him that I'd written the article some 15 months ago, hadn't read it since it was written, and didn't possess a perfect memory. Even journalists have their faults.

Then he asked me how I knew about the gun-running incident. I told him that I'd read clippings from the Mexican press which made reference to it, and to Mario. I said that Mario had given me those clippings, and that I had asked him about the claims they made. Mario never denied involvement. In fact, he once called a press conference in San Antonio to claim responsibility.

Rodriguez then asked if I was aware of any State Department licenses for arms shipments to other countries.

I told him that I was quite sure that the State Department or the government sent arms overseas all the time.

He was startled. Someone at his table helped him rephrase the question.

He asked if I knew of any State Department authorizations to ship guns to Mexico.

I told him that if what he was probing for was a statement that Mario Cantú was not authorized to be a gun-runner, it was probably true. Mario, I said, had spoken to me on the subject in a way that caused me to presume the shipment he was involved in was illegal.

Sandoval and Kuntsler were by now plainly distressed. They took me on re-direct examination. One of them asked me why Mario had allowed himself to have anything to do with gun smuggling. I said that if I knew Mario, it was because he believed that the peasants needed guns to defend themselves.

Prosecutor Rodriguez then took me on re-cross. He asked me if I hadn't ever asked Mario if he didn't feel responsible for violence in Mexico, since "guns cause violence."

I told him that I had never felt that a question like that would provide me with useful information. Journalists are not the guardians of Mexican peace. Nobody is. Nobody can be.

The prosecutor may have asked me more questions, but if he did, they weren't worthy of memory.

I stepped down and went outside. Cantú's supporters, I noted, were staring anxiously at me as I left. I didn't care. I wanted a cigarette, not popular acclaim.

Chacho Munguia followed me out. He reached over and shook my hand. I had spoken the truth, he said. No one could complain against me. We stared at one another, as if for a last time, and then he went off. I think he went home.

A recess was called. During it, Cantú huddled with his attorneys. When the recess was over, they called him to the stand. That was a surprise to everyone.

Cantú Is Called

Kuntsler questioned Cantú about gun-running, and then Rodriguez took his turn. Cantú told both of them that he had given money to Mexican revolutionaries who had bought guns and taken them across the border. He said that he had not told them to buy any armaments. He also said he hadn't told them not to.

His tone was that of a man trying to win sympathy after a failure. It said, "Look, there is misery in Mexico, and I was trying to do something about it. I can't help what those guys did with my money." But it also carried a trace of defiance, as if what went unsaid was "They really *did* need those guns." I suspect that Mario told everything he knew, but only half of what he felt. (During the land seizure, hostages were taken by the guerillas. I saw them, and cringed with the feeling that keeps timid men away from lynch mobs; I was afraid to see violence inflicted. The hostages were not harmed, but Mario, I recall, showed only passing concern for them. His mood was one of boyish pleasure at the larger events of the seizure, which ultimately failed.)

I doubt that when questioning of Mario was done, Sandoval and Kuntsler felt that, as lawyers say, they had rehabilitated their client.

Prosecutor Rodriguez must have been sure he had Cantú nailed, even though no one, I believe, had established any conflict between the gun incident and Cantú's probationary status. Sitting in the audience, I asked a reporter how he thought Sessions would rule. We discussed possible sentences by note, and agreed on an estimate: Mario Cantú would be sentenced to three years in prison.

Bill Kuntsler began his summation. He told the court that Mario was a man like those who led the American Revolution, principled and unafraid. It was a facile, and I thought, vapid comparison.

Mario spoke last. He spoke quietly. There was pain and hesitation in his voice, as if he were taking a stand he feared to take. He talked about his political commitments, and said that in Europe he had accomplished an agitational mission. I know Mario well enough; he never is afraid to say these things. Something more had to be coming, I told myself.

"I have come back to face whatever it is that I must face," Mario said after a minute. He went on to say other things, but I did not listen. The strain in his voice eased off. Mario had said what was most difficult for him. He had admitted that the court could punish him, and that he was afraid it would. He had summed up everything I had advised him to say. I hope Chacho was in the courtroom to hear that one sentence. It was the only sentence I've ever heard Mario speak in a tone of resignation. I believe that Mario was ready to go to jail, perhaps even quietly. His voice was unusually quiet.

MEN, IDEALS, LOYALTIES

Radicals are, by and large, a feisty and overbearing lot. They survive on the forbearance of their followers and associates. Ultimately, if they do not slack up on their demands for sympathy, their associates denounce or desert them. Defections, purge trials and de-Stalinizations are all testimony to this. During the years I have known him, I have seen Mario Cantú drive off more supporters than he is likely to have today.

Over the past 10 years, the period of his activism, Mario Cantú has inconvenienced not only the authorities, but many of the rest of us: family, friends, business peers, even sectors of the press. Perhaps our discomfort is necessary. Mario is, after all, the first prominent Texan to espouse revolutionary socialism in public since the McCarthy era, when the legislature required all communists to register as foreign agents or face felony prosecution. In the two decades since witch hunts waned, red celebrities have arisen in other states—William Kuntsler is one. Texas has seen only Cantú, and it is not surprising that he draws his inspiration from Mexico, where revolutionary socialism is almost voguish. Because of our nearness to Mexico, Mario Cantú, or someone very much like him, is an inevitable figure in our political life, if only at its fringes. He has chosen to walk down a trail strewn with legal, moral, historical and religious issues as prickly as cactus.

I do not think Mario has learned to be politic, but, as later events of the day may have shown, he may at last be on his way.

After Mario spoke, Kuntsler told the Judge that the defense was concluded. Sessions proceeded immediately into observations on the case. He began with what radicals of the '60s would have called a *de-obfuscation*, had the pronouncement been made by one of them. Sessions denied that Kuntsler's comparison of John Adams and James Madison to Cantú went far enough. They organized revolution knowing that it meant victory or imprisonment. No Bill of Rights protected their advocacy. Cantú, however, was liable to imprisonment for violating the rules of the closed world of probation, a world in which, as in pre-Revolutionary days, many ordinary liberties are proscribed.

Sessions said that as he understood it, the defense had argued, without saying so, that Mario's violation was mitigated by First Amendment considerations: Mario had violated his probation agreement in order to aid the press and to espouse his own political opinions. Sessions said that another judge, whom he did not name (Wood), had rendered the verdict which placed Cantú on probation. While he made no criticism of the case, he referred again to the letters which showed that Mario's sentence was an unpopular and unusual one. He then cited my testimony and that of Jacoby as having buttressed the argument that Cantú was honorable, if defiant.

Sessions sentenced Mario Cantú to five months in a San Antonio halfway house, and a return to probationary supervision. He also said that in the future, he, not Cantú's probation officer, would make decisions about Mario's travel requests.

Cantú and his attorneys regarded the decision as favorable. After statements were made to reporters, they recessed to Mario's restaurant, where followers were already grouping for a victory celebration. Several long tables were joined together, and Mario ordered drinks on the house.

I went, but did not join in the festivities. Instead, I sat in a booth with Sra. Piedra and her daughter. We talked of other things.

After half an hour, one of Mario's collegiate supporters, in a fresh summer suit, came over to our booth. "Mr. Reavis," he told me, "we have just named you Unreliable Witness of the Day. Your prize is a one-way bus ticket back to Austin."

There is an old saying in Spanish: "Don't talk to the clowns, talk to the head of the circus." I rose and walked over towards Mario. Conversation at the long tables stopped. In a voice for all to hear, I asked Mario if he wanted to step outside to settle a grievance. I wasn't really looking for a fight. Rather, I wanted to make a demand on Mario's soul. I felt no remorse for my testimony, that's for sure—and I didn't think that he could blame anything on me.

Mario stood up halfway, then waved. "Ah, don't worry about these people," he said. "Don't pay attention to them. You did all right."

Mario's supporters, I am sure, thought that he was kowtowing to the press, but he and I knew better. Mario was speaking for himself, not for his movement, not for his lawyers. For the second time that day, he had spoken as I'd never seen him speak before: not as an advocate, but as an individual. Long ago, he convinced me that he is unquestionably a man of principle. That afternoon, he convinced me that he is something much more important: a man. Had Chacho Munguia been there, I am sure he would have offered a handshake to Mario. Perhaps he will yet.

About the Klu Klux Klan in Texas, this article, published in the *Texas Observer,* September 19, 1980, is also about Reavis's style of reporting. What is at stake, he asserts, when one listens to others—is the possibility and fear of *conversion.* Although nascent in his earlier writings, conversion—be it religious, political, or ideological—became a central theme of his subsequent work.

Klan on the Ropes

By the standards of the industry, I am a writer who still needs polishing. I can't engage in literary talk. My favorite novels are dime westerns, and as far as I know, "Ruby Don't Take Your Love to Town" is *the* poetic expression of my generation. My etiquette is lacking, too. A couple of months ago, two writers, a man and a woman, invited me to their house for supper. I did not use the salad bowl they set out, because I saw no soup, and had no idea that salad bowls are used in homes as well as in restaurants.

I'm not entirely comfortable with rednecks, either. They scare me. They are tough and sunburned and close-lipped, and I have trouble duplicating the act. But I am more comfortable with rednecks than with writers, because rednecks do not espouse standards of literacy or conduct more refined than my own.

Magazines have tolerated me largely because my lack of refinement is an aid of sorts, if only in doing stories no one else wants to do. Hard-luck characters accept me as a member of their class, I need acceptance of any kind, and magazines need stories about the underclass. Editors indulge their charitable instincts by paying me to write tales about that class. A few months ago, displeased by articles I'd read about the Ku Klux Klan,

I decided to get to know them myself.

I put on my best Wrangler shirt, my pointed-toe cowboy boots, and a laundry-creased set of jeans, the costume of a rodeo reporter. I rented a car and drove from my home in Austin to Houston, where I crossed the ship channel to Pasadena, a refinery town. I passed by a local landmark, an X-rated drive-in with a saggy wooden fence, and drove up to a cement block building which in better days housed a motorcycle shop. Today, it is a bookstore and headquarters for the Texas Knights of the Ku Klux Klan.

The Knights are the fastest-growing of some half-dozen Klans, and their Texas organization is probably the most strident of all Knights groupings. Even its sign says so: across the Pasadena office is hung the biggest Ku Klux Klan sign in the world, twenty times bigger than the plaque that hangs in New Orleans, outside the national office of the Knights. I parked my car and walked inside.

I introduced myself to Louis Beam, who is Grand Dragon, or top dog, for the Knights in Texas. Our first words were mere pleasantries, but the interval it took to speak them gave me an opportunity to size up the man. Louis is in his early thirties. His face is ruddy and acne-scarred, his eyes, deep-set, black and beady. He had a short, but broad, mustache, and curly dark hair, shaved to barracks' shortness on the sides. Muscularity came across in his handshake, and sincerity in his voice.

The Klan's office-bookstore suits Louis just fine. It fits his personality. There is nothing composite about it. It is a single-story, single-tenant, flat-roofed structure with walls of strong, steady—unadorning—concrete block. The bookshelves and tables inside are of brush-stroked lumberyard pine, cut, sanded and nailed at home. The windows that once went around the building have been boarded over because the occupants cannot afford to look out on the world, or have it throw firebombs in. Corporate towers, which have tinted or one-way mirror windows, allow occupants to look down unseen on an unaware world. At the Klan office, there is no need for such guile. Here, contempt for the world is up-front, without veneer or acoustic carpeting. Hatred is proclaimed on the big sign outside, and the office does not smell of malice. It smells of dust and the concrete floor.

Louis was not wearing jeans, or boots, or a western shirt (as I was, on the theory that Klansmen are rednecks). No, he was in the uniform of the underpaid clerical: cotton casual pants, dark loafers, and a dress shirt with shiny yellow thread in the pattern. His red nylon windbreaker reminded me of bowling team regalia, despite the Ku Klux Klan emblem stenciled in white on its front. As far as I could see, there was nothing scary about the man. In a setting more tranquil than Pasadena, in piney East Texas, for example, he might be taken for a deacon. I immediately took a liking to him, despite contrary urgings from my conscience.

Then I went a step further. I tried to win rapport from him, not only because I liked him, but because journalism demands it: rapport is essential to insight. To get on his good side, I told Louis Beam that I hate New York and everybody who lives there. After all, New Yorkers control the publishing industry without abandoning home or the East Coast way of intellectualizing things. Louis told me that it was true. He agreed that New York is an odious place, but he said it is because of the Jews. The Jews and the Blacks and the Puerto Ricans, but mainly the Jews, he said. I didn't challenge him. The important thing, I told myself, was to let him draw me into what was shortly, and by my design, to be an encounter, a prize fight of sorts—a game. One of the Klan's oldest games: conversion.

The process of conversion is not nearly so benign as missionary and political societies would have us think, and it is similar regardless of the ideology it serves. Religious and radical sects are the rings where conversions are best battled out, sometimes for the highest stakes. Jimmy Jones and Charles Manson are world-class fighters at the conversion art, whose reigning champion is the Ayatollah Khomeini. The object of hard-core conversions is the knockout punch. Once the crusader has connected one or more of these blows to the head of the convert, the convert's heart and soul are no longer his own.

News reports I had read told me little about the Klan except that it is racist. That's not news to anybody. That is like saying, "Ali punches hard." "How hard, and how?" I wanted to know. I wanted to see the Klan's conversion style and I was willing to take a bruising to do it.

Round One

After my remark about New York, Louis Beam seemed to sense in me the making of a convert—at least that was my hope—for finding out "How hard, and how." My hope seemed well-based when I perceived he was looking for another weakness, and, presumably, a quick conversion—a moral knockout. He began questioning me about my political leanings and background. When I told him that I felt uneasy about having lapsed as a

Southern Baptist, he thought he'd found his opening. The fight was on.

He said that the following morning the Ku Klux Klan would hold religious services, right there in the bookstore. He, too, had been an ardent Southern Baptist in his youth, he said. He invited me to Klan church.

I told him that I found my religious guide in a Johnny Paycheck song called "Outlaw's Prayer," and I quoted him these lyrics.

> So if this is what religion is,
> A big car, a suit and a tie,
> Then I may as well forget it, Lord,
> 'Cause I can't qualify
>
> — *written by B. Sherril and G. Sutton* [*Armed and Dangerous, Epic KE 35444*]

Lewis said *those* lyrics were good, and that the churches deserve them. Then, like anyone who has become an intellectual and thinks he has risen above his people, he began an argument based on literary comparisons. He compared other lyrics of "Outlaw's Prayer" to scriptures in the Bible.

In "Outlaw's Prayer," Johnny Paycheck says that Jesus had long hair. But the Bible says (I Corinthians 11:14) "Doth not even nature itself teach you, that if a man have long hair, it is a shame unto him?" Jesus did not do shameful things. Therefore, Louis told me, Jesus did not have long hair, and we cannot rely on Johnny Paycheck for spiritual advice.

It was fortunate for me that Louis and I were not alone. A few feet away, behind the open doorway to the storeroom, stood another Klansman, Charles Lee, an affable, pot-bellied biker with strawberry blond hair—pulled back in a ponytail.

I pointed towards Charles: "What about that guy? He's got long hair, and I'll bet he's in the Klan."

The scriptural integrity of the Klan was against the ropes. I'd parried his hook and landed a good blow of my own.

"And what about tattoos?" I pressed. "The Bible is against them, too."

(I didn't know it at the time, but Louis Beam has two tattoos, inky souvenirs from his wilder youth. One of them says "Born to Lose," an inscription appropriate to small-time hoodlums, perhaps, but not to a Grand Dragon of the white race.)

Louis nodded but said nothing. I decided that he was phased. The possibility astounded me. 1 decided to test his defensive abilities further.

I took my lead from my father-in-law, who is always trying to convert me to the Pentecostal faith. Several weeks after I was seriously injured in a motorcycle accident, he wrote to inform me that I must repent, because according to scripture he cited, broken bones are a specific punishment for sins. Several of my bones were broken in the accident, and I was left with a cold-weather limp.

I moved in close on Louis. "See my bad leg?" I told him. "Well, it got that way when it was broken, see, and if you really go for all this Bible stuff, you've got to tell me that I deserve it, 'cause it's a punishment for sins."

Louis played for time.

"Naw, God doesn't punish us like that," he said. "If he did, why, we'd all be dead."

I thought I had him quivering at the knees. I stepped back, relieved.

"God doesn't punish us that way because our ignorance is not our own fault," he continued.

He moved his hands limply, as if in a weak attempt to defend himself, and then he began his diversion.

"Our enemy, the Jews, have gone to great lengths to keep us ignorant, even of our own book, the Bible."

There was no possible interpretation to the words "our" and "us" except one: they referred to the white race, "our" race.

It was an attempt, racist and blatant but straightforward, comradely, to draw me in.

"Now I'm not saying that ignorance is anything to be ashamed of because I am ignorant, too," he continued. "I'm not an authority on physics, so I'm ignorant of physics. And I'm not a mathematician, so I'm ignorant of mathematics."

Having drawn me near, he probed to see what, if any, counter punches I might offer. I am sure he felt I was still a potential convert, but I was going to be a tough card.

"Now I graduated from college," he said, "as I'm sure you did. I got my degree in history, so I'm not ignorant of that. But both of us are still ignorant of a lot of things, I'm sure."

At the mention of college, Charles Lee, who had been listening in, turned his attention back to a manual task. He had been repainting the surface of a wooden literature table which was damaged in a November firebombing at the Klan bookshop. Charles, who dropped out of school, in junior high, probably figured that the discussion to follow would be over his head.

I did not pick up the challenge to battle Louis on the grounds of history. Had I done it, my political persuasions, considerably to the left of the Klan, would have leaped out and betrayed the match. I said nothing. He must have taken my silence for weakness. He came out of his Rope-a-Dope act and advanced.

"Most of the churches," he said, "have fallen under Zionist influence. God is the original segregationist, but the churches have become derelict in both duty and doctrine by preaching integration. If you ask me, that's one of the big reasons why a lot of good, white, patriotic Americans, who love Jesus in their hearts, have fallen away from their churches."

If Louis had sought to co-opt me, racially, with the words "us" and "our," now he was pushing me back. He was saying, not "we" or "us" white Christian blah blahs, but simply "white Christian . . ."—without the us. It was bullshit, subtle, and effective. I could not counter by saying that I wasn't white, and I was no longer in a position to say that I wasn't a Christian, or wasn't patriotic: I had thrown those punches away.

I felt as if a bell had rung, end of round. I went into my mental corner to hear advice. Journalism told me to come out fighting, to brave the challenge of Klan church, and to bring back the truth of its nature. But another voice told me not to do that.

Going to Klan church would have made for interesting *reportage*, but it would have required me to join in the prayers of fascists. I may be a skeptic, but standing there in the bookstore of the Ku Klux Klan, I realized that I have not bleached the faith of my heritage from the marrow of my bones. I decided I could not go to Klan church because that would be like lying to God. His knockout punch is more to be feared than anything in the Klan's repertoire.

I did not answer the bell that would have rung in the next round. Instead, I meekly told Louis that I couldn't show disrespect for his, or any religion, by entering a worship temple in an insincere frame of mind. I said that I would think about attending Klan church, but could not promise to be there.

Louis had won the fight, but he was plainly disappointed. He hadn't gotten a chance to throw his knockout punch, i.e., I had left unconverted. It was as if a decision had been handed down which said that in not accepting the invitation to Klan church I was a weak-willed fighter, neither worthy of great respect nor capable of doing great harm. Louis told me he had other business to tend, and he ignored me, even though we were both at near quarters in the bookstore.

SIGNING UP

I spent the rest of the day sitting behind a literature table with Charley, talking about motorcycles and watching as he waited on customers. Two of these who came in will never ease out of my memory.

One was a chunky, burr-headed, sixtyish man in a brown corduroy jumpsuit, a persona from some drama about the Klan's past. He had come from a little Central Texas town all the way to Pasadena to ask the Klan for help. His son, he said, had been run over and killed by a Black motorist whom the highway patrol wouldn't arrest. The man brought a copy of the police report filed in the accident. It gave information on the driver—his name and license number, birthdate and other items—but the address given, the man said, wasn't right.

Louis came over to take the matter in hand. He asked the man a few questions—none that I heard were about the circumstances of the accident—then took down some notes, shook hands with the fellow and told him to return next Saturday, when the bookstore would be open for business again. Louis promised that unnamed friends of the police force would get the Black man's address if it could be gotten.

Later in the day, a short, muscled, bearded man in his mid-thirties parked his pickup outside and stepped in. A black cowboy hat with a feather band was on his head, and there were shiny boots on his feet. His blue T-shirt was illustrated with the figure of a cowboy on skis, and the legend, "If God had meant for Texans to ski, He would have made bullshit white." Both Charles Lee and I chuckled and grinned when we read the legend. This man, the representative of the Klan's present, was outgoing and optimistic, not embittered and cranky.

He sifted through the pamphlets and books which were laid out on shelves and tables around the room, eyeing each one with a slow, grave stare. His eyes didn't move an inch from the print before them. His good humor had turned to a steely seriousness.

In a moment he drew in his breath, as if he'd made up his mind about something, then spoke in a voice as rough as sandpaper: "Gimme a membership form."

Charles Lee reached into a drawer and pulled one out. It is a standard sort of form, one page long, but on its back there is a photo of a 1910 lynching, a nostalgic bit of "white humor," the Klan calls it. After looking it over, the bearded young man picked up a ballpoint pen and began completing the blanks. When he was finished, he gave the form to Charles Lee. I looked over Charles' shoulder to see what responses the man had supplied.

My eyes fell upon the question which asks, "What are your reasons for joining the Knights of the Ku Klux Klan?" The man penned in only two words: "My children." It was an answer so basic and all-encompassing that it frightened me. There is nothing some men will not do in the name of their children.

Louis came over about this time, took the form from Charles Lee, looked it over and talked to the bearded applicant.

The form said the man was from the little town of Clute.

"We're organizing a den out in Clute, and if you're accepted, we'll send our Kleagle, or organizer, over to see you. You'll be surprised at who he is."

Somewhere in Clute, there's a police chief, sheriff, minister, popular bartender or prominent businessman with Klan regalia hidden in his closet.

The bearded customer smiled. It was as if he'd been presented proof that this Invisible Empire, with its Dragons and Wizards and Kleagles and klaverns and dens were really a serious and stable—and far flung—organization after all. It had secret members in Clute!

The bearded man nodded to Louis, shook hands and strode out of the bookstore, carrying a poster and some pamphlets with him.

THE PROTOCOLS

About sundown I excused myself to go to supper. I took with me a book Louis had urged upon me, an anti-Semitic classic called *The Protocols of the Learned Elders of Zion*. The *Protocols*, Louis told me, were taken from the minutes of a meeting held in Vienna in 1897, and led by the Zionist intellectual Theodore Herzl. Since the meeting—if it ever took place—was held in secret, there is no proof of authenticity; most scholars, I believe, think the *Protocols* are a fake. Louis, however, cited me Henry Ford's opinion of the document: the *Protocols* are true because they fit the world situation. One finds in them, for example, statements like the following: "We shall raise the rate of wages which, however, will not bring any advantage to the workers, for at the same time, we shall produce a rise in prices of the first necessities. . . ." Predictions like that are perhaps powerful potions in an industrial town like Pasadena today.

Over supper, however, I found something far more predictive in the hoary *Protocols*. I found passages, all saying the same thing, which, I believed, revealed to me the future of the Klan. I pondered over the prospect, and decided not to ask Louis about these passages until after the Klan meeting that night.

The Klan meeting opened about 7:30 in the bookstore, whose tables and magazine racks were cleared away to make room for rented folding chairs. I showed up a half hour early to study the setting and the Klansmen who came to hear the message. Klansmen's wives, like Klansmen, are ordinary, down-home, poor and working-class whites. Kara, Louis Beam's strawberry-cheeked, 18-year-old spouse, was pregnant. As we waited for the speeches to begin, she told me about the Lamaze classes she and Louis were attending in preparation for delivery, some three or four weeks away. Charles Lee was at the meeting, in clean jeans and a dress shirt now, his hair washed and combed down at the sides. Next to him sat his big-boned, black-headed wife, a woman who, if I remember well, had on a polyester blouse and slacks. The atmosphere of the hall was like that of a country church half an hour before services begin on a Sunday morning. Only it was Saturday night: something deep within me told me that the 20 kids who showed up, most of whom were under 30, should have been out at Gilley's high-steppin' and drinking beer.

The guest speaker that night was an aging little man from San Antonio, Dr. R. J. C. Brown. He is short, grey-headed, bulldog-faced and given to leisure suits and red-white-and-blue ties. He has a certain stern look about him; had I not been told of his laurels, I might have dismissed him as a crank ne'er-do-well, as one of those men who is smart, but not yet rich. He is not anything so bland, common, or benign. Brown was a brigadier general with the allied resistance forces in Europe during World War II. He says that he holds two PhD's, one in psychology and one in Christian theology. He is a former Grand Dragon of the original Ku Klux Klan, a group which in Texas, I was told, had been absorbed by the Knights. Dr. Brown today is Grand Kludd, or chaplain, for the Texas Knights. He is also an expert in karate, judo and lesser-known martial arts, and, from what I heard, has a reputation for musical talent as well.

Dr. Brown rose to the podium and looked around the room, studying the faces of individuals in the audience as if to determine their racial characters. Then he opened his address by saying that—hallelujah!—he had no doubt that the Klan would restore sovereignty to white people, just as it had done in 1876, at the end of that bloody resistance which brought down the *N*******r*, carpetbag, Reconstruction government. He told the crowd that white, Christian, patriotic Americans would win the struggle because they were the true Israelites. To prove the point, he reviewed genealogies of the Bible. Mary, he said, was the descendant of a union between Judah, an Israelite, and his daughter-in-law, Tamar, also an Israelite. The Jews, on the other hand, were descended of an *illicit* union between Judah and a Canaanite woman—and of other race-mixtures as well. In the veins of Jews, Brown said, there flows the blood of Hittites, Maobites, Babylonians, and other heathens. Jesus could not have been a Jew, Brown stressed, because he was the son of Mary, an Israelite, and God. Who—assured Brown—was certainly no Jew. If there was an Israel in the world today, Brown said that it would have to be the American, British, Scandinavian, and Germanic nations, not some strip of land that Jews had wrested from Arabs.

Had I not spent the day with Klansmen and their pamphlets, I would have understood almost nothing of Dr. Brown's discourse. He laced his statements with sectarian, obscure terms whose meaning is unintelligible to the uninitiated. For example, he calls Jews, not Jews, but Khazars, Khazar Yids, and International Zionist Khazar Yids. Whenever he spoke of people, I had to make a hurried mental adjustment: in Dr. Brown's reading of the Bible, there are no races, only people and two-legged beasts. People, of course, are white. Sometimes when he mentioned "the enemy," it was plain from the context that he meant the Communists. At other times, the word would have been capitalized, the Enemy, in reference to the Jews; there were times when I could not distinguish which form of the word he intended, and I would not be surprised if, in accurate translation, the word at those points referred to Jewish Reds. (Earlier, I had asked biker Charles Lee how he waded through the morass of anti-Semitic terminology. He told me he no longer had a problem doing it. "I guess the Klan gave me an education," he said.)

The crest of Dr. Brown's speech came when he began to talk about the upcoming struggle to rid America of un-Christian, nonwhite influences.

At about that point, Louis, who had been shooting pictures of Brown, laid his camera aside. He couldn't focus well; his eyes were reddened, their lids swollen with tears.

Dr. Brown's voice boomed as he drew a picture of carnage. "Now I'm no prophet," he cried, "but I think that you and I will live to see the day for war upon the beasts, the day when the Enemy will hang from telephone posts and trees, right here in Pasadena, the day when blood will *literally* flow in the streets." His speech was interrupted with cheers and applause. "I believe that we may be given a commandment from God to deal with our Enemy, in the same way He ordered our ancestors, the children of Israel, to deal with the Canaanites—by killing every man, woman, and child among them!"

The fifteen metal chairs rocked back and forth a bit, and the Klansmen and their wives rose and roared "White Power! White Power!" and Lewis started snapping pictures again, and Charles Lee stomped his feet, so moved was he by the sledgehammer climax Dr. Brown had put on his speech. I sat frozen to my chair, wishing I had a pistol to shoot my way out of the place. I would have been outgunned, though: a Klansman stood outside the front door, a semi-automatic rifle in hand. There were pistols behind the podium, I knew. Klansmen are a minority in comparison to their guns.

Dr. Brown continued to speak for some minutes, but in a calmer tone. One of his observations was that American youth have been made wayward today by "N****rization." People should not mourn the death of Elvis Presley, he commented, because Presley was partly responsible for the low state of the nation's youth: he had led "the N****rization of American music." Brown did not explain further, but other Klansmen had already advised me that in their eyes, only classical music is of respectable parentage.

Brown's commentary on youth and music reminded me of the passages I'd read in the *Protocols*, the ones which I felt held the secret of the Klan's future. Brown's attack on Presley was so strikingly parallel and I was by now so disgusted with the Klan that I decided to raise the issue as soon as he quit speaking.

There is a passage, or several similar passages, in the *Protocols*, which say that Christians "bemuse" themselves with alcohol, and from the contexts, the conclusion to be drawn is that booze is a Zionist scheme to undermine civilization. This implication, I thought, was no less odd than another one I'd run onto in Klan literature; namely, that the Soviet Union is a Jewish-controlled state.

I stepped up to Louis, who was chatting with Brown beside the podium at the front of the room. I told him about the passages in the *Protocols*, and what I made of them. Then I asked if the Knights were as prohibitionist as the Klans of the Twenties had been.

"Well," he drawled with caution, "I wouldn't say that Klansmen were prohibitionists, but I don't think the Bible approves of alcoholic beverages except maybe for wine used in religious services."

Of course, any Baptist would have told me that. We were sparring again, but the punches were harder now. I had to toughen my attack.

"Is that how the Klan thinks the Jews control Russia—with vodka?" I tried to keep a straight face.

"You could say that was one factor," Lewis snapped, perhaps aware of my feint.

Then, without warning, he threw me a cross. Vodka wasn't the only beverage the Jews used on Christians, he said. Before I had time to react, he threw his desperation punch.

"In Texas, they use Lone Star beer."

Those were his exact words. I swear it. He was dead serious.

I fell back, really dazed. It was more than a minute before I could get my bearings again, and when I did, I was still too stunned to speak. I decided to get the hell out of there, without good-byes. Louis Beam had not knocked me out, but he had frightened and maddened me so much that I knew I had to jump out of the ring.

Charles Lee met me as I headed for the door, and as I stepped aside, with a few quick words, I asked him how anybody, anybody at all, could possibly endorse Dr. Brown's evaluation of Elvis Presley. Charles didn't answer me, however, for two quite distinct reasons. One, he is quietly a fan of Presley and Paycheck and the others, despite his Klan robes. Two, I think he had me figured out, in his own way.

Charles Lee had told me that the Klan gets most of its harassment not from Blacks and Chicanos, but from whites. Ignorant whites, unenlightened rednecks, he told me. He recalled to me how, a few days after the Klan's Pasadena bookstore was firebombed last fall, somebody had painted "Earl Campbell #1" on one of its outer walls. The Klan, which is opposed to integrated sports, regarded the act as defacement: its members suspect that it was the work of an ignorant white football fan. If Charles Lee heard the questions I put to Louis—and I think he must have—he no doubt put me in the same category. For the first time in my life, I got certified as a redneck, albeit an "unenlightened" one.

THE KLAN LOSES

The Klan had perhaps not correctly understood me, but I had understood them. The Knights, and America's half-dozen other Klans, are experiencing a new vigor and growth, probably because Americans are seeing that the nation's problems are obdurate—and some of us are becoming desperate. Young men like the fellow in the cowboy hat with the feather band *are* being enticed into the Klan, but they cannot stay in: very few Texans will forsake longnecks or the Oilers in the name of any cause, and besides, Lone Star and the Oilers are causes in themselves. In the throes of a crisis, people will turn more seriously to these diversions.

Louis Beam and his associates have done nothing more than draw the conclusions which must be drawn, by force of logic, from the archaic texts and tenets to which all Klansmen subscribe. Country and western music has been deeply influenced by Blacks. It was Jimmy Rodgers who thought he was singing the blues, Hank Williams who learned a guitar style from Black railroadmen, Bob Wills who named Bessie Smith as his favorite vocalist; need Charley Pride be mentioned when the roots of Black involvement run so deep? By the same token, one cannot put faith in the authenticity of the *Protocols* and still defend the amusements of alcohol. Other Klan leaders and other Klans may finesse around these points, but in the end, they will only buy time with the tactic.

Fundamentally, it is too late for the Ku Klux Klan. Some advances, like integration in sports and music, cannot be turned back, because white people will defend them, too. The Klan cannot become a broadly popular organization while it is moored to theories and texts so archaic that they condemn our daily pleasures. Country and western music, football, and Lone Star beer, may not be popular with leftists, but they are popular with rednecks and they are progressive if only because they protect us all from the return of hoary white-sheeted legions from the past.

There is a real, if unlikely, parallel or analog to the Klan in our national past. During the Fifties, the once-sizeable Communist Party was withered to a stump by the blizzard winds of McCarthyism. Yet those who had professional or moral gains to make by proving that America needed jingoists—men like J. Edgar Hoover and Billy James Hargis—kept the Red Spectre alive. A phantom Party provided them with influence and respect.

The Ku Klux Klan, with an estimated 10,000 members nationwide in 1980, compared to 16,800 in 1967 and 4,000 in 1971, is a minuscule organization composed of the young and impressionable. It is not destined to be anything much more significant. Its members will indeed carry out isolated acts of vandalism and terror but they *will not* lead the nation. When all is said and done, the Ku Klux Klan has no future except in our imaginations. It is nothing if not the bogeyman of American liberalism.

In this article, which originally appeared in the May 1980 issue of *Texas Monthly,* Reavis explored, through numerous quickly shifting perspectives, the experiences of those who visit, and those who live in, one of the many Mexican brothel districts existing along the Texas border since at least the early 1900s. Such communities, microcosms with their own rules, continue to reveal systemic and economic exploitation that perpetuates sexist, economic, racist, and nationalist interactions and aggressions.

Town Without Pity

Elizabeth couldn't find her hairbrush when she awoke Saturday afternoon. She poked through the clutter of cosmetic bottles on her dresser—mostly Leta's cosmetics, not her own—and still didn't find it. Maybe Leta had taken it again, she told herself.

The missing hairbrush didn't worry Elizabeth, but buxom little Leta did. The girl was eighteen, new to cabaret life, and still impressed with the appeal her figure held for men. She had a thirst for work—*¡Hijo!,* eight men, just last night!—and her head was full of dreams about solving all her family's problems with cash. Elizabeth and the other girls at Nuevo Laredo's Tamyko Club didn't have the heart to disillusion Leta by saying so, but they knew that plans like hers just didn't work out, ever. The truth of the matter was quite simple, Elizabeth believed: nothing good ever comes from men, except children—and brandy.

As Elizabeth sat in front of the dresser, her fingers parted her straight, pitch-black hair and her eyes stared at the face in the mirror before her. She noted that her coloration, once mahogany, had paled and that the skin across her cheekbones seemed more tightly drawn than ever. *¡Ay!* I'm drying up!" Elizabeth lowered her hands and felt the surface of her face. Her fingers told her that the pimples were still there; they couldn't be seen, perhaps, but they could be felt. All the evils of age were creeping up on her—she was 31—without any of the benefits, which were few enough anyway. Those pimples, they should have been gone years ago.

She rose and quickly dressed herself in the canary-yellow summer suit that she had promised her son Julito she would wear today. She dropped her key ring into a matching but empty purse, slipped on her brightest yellow high heels, and went out the door, leaving it unlocked for Leta who had no key. She scurried down the walkway, past other rooms like hers, then knelt at the altar in an alcove by the dining room where the girls at the Tamyko were served meals. After crossing herself, she hurried over the arched cement bridge that spanned the "Oriental Courtyard" and patio, and seeing Leta inside the club snuggled up to a balding gringo, she went in to exchange greetings.

"I belt you're going to see your boyfriend," the old gringo bellowed, noticing Elizabeth's attire. Leta, who did not understand much English except sexual terms and numbers, smiled and leaned back against the man's arm.

"No, I go see my son," Elizabeth replied, as politely as she could.

"Your son, my ass," he snorted.

Elizabeth backed away, went out the door, waved at the cop who stood guard, and got into her battered red Toyota. As she came to the checkpoint at the entrance to the district she noticed a blue Chevrolet pickup wallowing down the road toward her. A husky, red-haired, fortyish gringo was driving, and a pudgy, pale, white-shirted man sat at his side.

"Hey, angel, let's go off to heaven together," the man in the white shirt hollered.

"You devil, go to Hell," she snarled in a voice loud enough for him to hear. As she turned the Toyota to the right, the pickup passed the checkpoint booth and drove inside the walls of Boys' Town.

Boys' Town wasn't the name Elizabeth or any other Mexican used when speaking of this district—the gringos called it that. In Nuevo Laredo, it was known as *La Zona de Tolerancia*. Tolerance was a part of its name for reasons well known to any seasoned prostitute. Prostitution is outlawed by federal statute in Mexico, so where it existed, it existed in forbearance. And forbearance, like the sexual favors available in La Zona, must be paid for. Payoffs and licenses and dispensations of one sort or another came to nearly 10 percent of a club's gross. Elizabeth and the other girls didn't pay a great many bribes; they couldn't afford to. But they did pay their share, like everybody who worked in La Zona except *las autoridades*. There were so many laws being broken and so many bribes being paid on all sides that the police and other officials who worked in La Zona—those who put rowdy customers in the district's little jail, those who collected exit fees from the girls when they left in the company of clients, and those who worked in La Zona's state-run venereal disease clinic—were parasites as much as they were protectors. Sometimes, in fact, Elizabeth wondered who was tolerating whom.

Every Saturday or Sunday Elizabeth drove out to the house of Señora Jiménez, a woman ten years her senior who had only one child of her own and who kept eleven-year-old Julito in exchange for 600 pesos a week. As usual, Julito was dressed up and waiting in the living room when Elizabeth arrived.

"Mónica wants to go with you and Julito today," Señora Jiménez told Elizabeth.

"No, Mama, I don't want Mónica," Julito whined. "Her shoes are dirty," he said, pointing at the black vinyl flats the little girl wore with her fluffy dress.

"Oh, this Julito!" Elizabeth exclaimed as Señora Jiménez went to the kitchen for a rag. "If you weren't so cute, I'd say you were too demanding. "Where do you want to go today?" She asked her son.

"To the Ola," he said, naming a local restaurant.

"*No, hay que cola en la Ola.* We'll have to wait in line at the Ola," Elizabeth rhymed.

"Mama, don't say things like '*cola en la Ola*.' It sounds silly," Julito protested.

The Ola, on Avenida Obregón, was the sort of place where small children are welcome and the waiters don't wear coats, but where the fare, being seafood, is not inexpensive by local standards. Elizabeth, not sure what she wanted and hesitant to spend anything on food for herself—her meals at the Tamyko were free—allowed Julito to order for all of them. His choice for everyone was 'snapper *filete*,' priced at 70 pesos.

Julito also told the waiter to bring his mother a glass of *vino tinto*, red dinner wine. The Ola was out of tinto, the waiter said, but other wines and beverages were available.

"No, no, it won't do," Julito chided. "Mother likes vino tinto before her meals."

Elizabeth nodded and smiled, proud that Julito knew her tastes. But if only he knew, she thought to herself, just how much his mother liked brandy. "Could I have something else to drink?" she asked her son.

"No, no," Julito said, waving the waiter off. "They are supposed to have red wine for you, Mother."

"But Julito, I have a headache," she implored.

"Why didn't you say so? We'll have the waiter bring you Alka-Seltzer," Julito promised.

Sometimes Elizabeth wished Julito were not quite so much a gentleman.

By the time she and the children were served, the two men from the blue Chevrolet pickup were walking Boys' Town's rutted caliche streets. The roads in the district were broad enough for a dozen cars to line up abreast but were a peril to drive on because they were cratered with a thousand potholes big enough to sink washtubs in.

What both men had in mind was a big meal followed by a few shots of whiskey. They had spent all morning and half the afternoon on the hot griddle that was the road from Houston to Laredo. They hadn't eaten all day. And they'd passed the two weeks before in the steam kettle of the Louisiana Gulf, where they worked on an offshore oil platform.

As they walked around the district, Wayne-O, the red-headed one, kept count of the little stucco-fronted rooms that opened onto the street, rooms from which shopworn prostitutes hawked their services. There were 120 of these rooms, though only some 80 showed signs of occupancy. They were ugly little niches, the interior walls painted a dull yellow or a dirty turquoise, and they contained only the essentials: a bed (usually sagging), a wardrobe for clothes, a stand with a washbasin, and sometimes a dresser. No plumbing was evident; the rooms opened onto common courtyards that usually had cold-water hydrants and sometimes commodes and showers concealed by wooden blinds.

As they rounded one corner on the south side of La Zona, Mike, the white-shirted one, stumbled up to one of the women who stood in the doorway of a room.

She is fat and ugly, Wayne-O thought, what could Mike want with her? Mike embraced the woman, and Wayne-O moved closer to watch.

"Say, baby, I want to take you home and marry you. Yeah," he teased, turning toward Wayne-O, "I want you to meet Mom and Dad."

The woman, who couldn't have been many years short of fifty, smiled and reached for his crotch, without showing that she had understood a word.

"Yeah, how 'bout it, baby? Let's go," Mike continued.

"Go my room? Ten dollars," the woman said.

"Ten dollars? No, *two* dollars," Mike replied.

"Two dollars? Room two dollars," the woman said, dropping her hands.

"The room costs you two dollars?" Mike said, hesitating. "Well, baby, won't you do it for love? For love?"

The woman gave a throaty laugh, leaned her head out the doorway, and called something in Spanish to another woman in a room down the street.

"I tell you what, baby, I'll give you four dollars," Mike said, leaning a little closer now, as if he were serious.

"No, ten dollars," she said, adamant.

He took some bills from his pocket and counted out four of them. The woman raised a palm between herself and Mike, shaking her head no, no. He turned back to his companion, and they shuffled away.

"Hey, you," the woman hollered after them, "give me cigarette."

The men paid no attention, but she came out of her room, taking hurried steps toward them. She grabbed Mike by the shirt.

"Give me cigarette," she demanded. With reluctance he reached into the pocket of his shirt. She grabbed his arm. "Come to my room," she said.

"No, no," Mike said.

"I give you good time," she pestered.

"No," he repeated, trying to turn away. But the woman wouldn't let go of his arm.

"Gimme light," she said.

With his free hand Mike reached into his shirt pocket again.

He brought out a disposable lighter and stuck it under the cigarette between the woman's lips. As he did, the woman put both hands on his crotch, beginning a clumsy massage. The lighter went out. He flicked it again. A flame caught and again went out.

"Your lighter's bad, buddy," said Wayne-O.

He struck a match and reached over to light the woman's cigarette. But the match went out too.

"Did you see that?" Wayne-O laughed. "Hell, she's blowing out our lights." Mike didn't think it was funny. He tried to pull himself away, but the woman was holding his arm again.

"Gimme light, gimme light," she kept repeating.

"Hell, no, you old whore," Mike shouted.

The woman backed off and began cursing him in Spanish.

The two visitors turned away and headed down the street again.

By the time Mike and Wayne-O had made a second circuit of the district, Elizabeth was saying good-bye to Julito across town at Señora Jiménez's house.

"Julito, is there anything you need?" she asked him.

"No, Mama," he said.

"Do you need money? Do you want me to buy you something?"

"Mama, there is one thing," he said, watching her eyes carefully to see if he was charming her. Elizabeth said nothing. "Mama, you have a yellow dress and a yellow purse and shoes, but look at me. My shirt and pants are yellow, but I want some yellow shoes, too."

"Well, Julito, I don't know where I would get them," she murmured.

"I saw some in the store over by school. Running shoes!" he exclaimed.

"Well, all right, we'll get them tomorrow," she said.

"And a green set, too? I want a green shirt, like those baseball shirts, and some green-colored jeans, and maybe some green running shoes, too."

Elizabeth sighed, then smiled. Julito's demands weren't really impertinent. But she didn't have the money to satisfy them, either. She owed Señora Jiménez for the week's child care, and she had no savings to draw on. Last week had been one of those weeks when she just hadn't felt like working, and she was sure her reluctance wouldn't wane with the evening sun.

Prostitution had not lifted Elizabeth far above the poverty of her childhood, but it provided adornments like the Toyota and Julito's outing to the Ola. Elizabeth didn't expect much more. Going to bed with drunks who needed a bath—most Boys' Town patrons fit that description—was an undertaking that daunted dreams of great wealth. Prostitution did promise a new life in the future, she knew, but its night-by-night realities were so beastly that Elizabeth recoiled from most of its options. She could stretch her body and spirit year after year until eventually she became a rich but infamous madam, owner of a club worth a half-million dollars, like the Tamyko; a woman whose children reached for her money but cringed at her touch. She could hoard her earnings, dollar by dollar and peso by peso, until she had amassed enough to purchase a small beauty shop or restaurant in which to risk earning less over a lifetime than a halfhearted whore took in during a decade. She could marry an American client, as little Letita dreamed of doing, and spend her life fearing a husband who at every spat would call Julito a bastard and fling her *puta* past in her face. Or, and this was the choice she found convenient, she could accept prostitution on its simplest terms: by day, it gave her food, lodging, and pocket money for Julito; by night, it gave her brandy. If from time to time her trade turned her stomach, the brandy made it tolerable. In fact, sometimes when she was *full* of brandy Elizabeth believed that were she stone sober she might find a physical pleasure in making love to a few of her clients. Prostitution, it was true, had not made her rich or perpetually happy, but it had shown her the way to consolation.

Elizabeth drew Julito to her, looking closely into his face and kissing his forehead. Her son had large, pale brown eyes and a fair complexion, just like his father, and he had the same lush, crisscrossed eyelashes. He was a handsome child, the very picture of a man who'd abandoned her years before.

"Yes, tomorrow we'll buy you anything you want," she told Julito.

The two men from the oil fields couldn't find a restaurant. They had rounded corner after corner, looking into the face of nearly three dozen faded stucco-fronted bars, nightclubs, and pool halls, most of them dark and empty though it was late afternoon. Even the canopied *barbacoa* stands were unattended and latched.

Some of the clubs, like the old 1-2-3, had from the looks of things been closed for years.

"I guess that's what massage parlors and the so-called sexual revolution have done for this place," Wayne-O observed.

"It's them amateur whores making competition in the singles bars," Mike added.

Ultimately the two men strayed into the oval-shaped Marabú, a club surrounded, in this walled-in district, by high, white walls of its own, walls topped with bits of broken glass, walls that enclosed a shady courtyard and garden on one side of the club and a broad, smooth parking lot on the other. Inside, they sat sipping drinks at a table on the perimeter of the Marabú's elevated, waxed, wooden dance floor. At other tables and booths around the big room sat an array of women, none of them glamorous, perhaps, but most of them attractive. Each had attired herself in her own style, some in lacy nighties, others in vested business suits.

"Some of these broads look like librarians or teachers," Mike grumbled.

"Yeah, but look at that one!" Wayne-O whooped, pointing across the dance floor. She was impossible to overlook: tall, lithe, and as white as talc. Platinum hair hung down past her waist, and she was almost nude; a scant filmy garment concealed very little of her body. "I'd like to take on that one," Wayne-O said.

"You and me ain't handsome enough for her," Mike complained, reaching in his pocket for a cigarette.

"Hell, not long ago you were telling me that the girls in this place only wanted money," Wayne-O reminded him.

"Yeah, but you know that ain't all, Wayne-O. They want, well, someone a little more handsome or richer than us."

"Speak for yourself." The trouble with Mike, Wayne-O had long ago decided, was that for some reason he felt he was inferior to everybody. He was always talking about how stupid he was. Yet Wayne-O knew him as a co-worker; he did good work.c"Aw, we'd better be going," Wayne-O muttered, a little disappointed because the blonde had seated herself with a group of clients across the room.

It suited Mike fine that they were leaving—deep down, he was just plain uneasy around women. "I'll get some amateur whore when we get back to Houston," Mike said as they stepped into the street again.

Wayne-O didn't say anything.

"Say, what's eating you?" Mike asked. By his sights, Wayne-O was acting nervous and moody. "Ain't you been here before?"

Wayne-O didn't answer. He didn't see why he should explain his whole life to Mike, though he had sometimes confided in others. No, it would probably sound like some kind of *lecture* to Mike, or worse, like some kind of joke. There were some things that Mike wasn't ready to face up to, things married men a few years older would readily understand.

For Wayne-O, this trip was a step back some twenty-odd years, to his adolescence, to a time when there were plenty of whorehouses in Nuevo Laredo (though no walled-in Boys' Town) and more Americans on the streets around them. Wayne-O had driven long nights to Laredo then, when he was legally a minor in Texas but could drink in Mexico. Like many other Texas youths since the advent of the automobile, he and several high school buddies had driven down eager to get loaded and afraid to get laid; eventually they'd all done that, too. Two of them, Wayne-O and his buddy George, had kept going back for more—until Wayne-O had gotten a dose.

Wayne-O, who had just turned forty, now felt old enough, and weathered enough, to admit to some men—but not Mike—that he'd actually fallen in love with one of the girls in Laredo. He'd seen her every two weeks during that dusky summer and fall, even thought of marrying her, until he'd gotten that bite of gonorrhea.

Wayne-O wasn't entirely certain what returning to Laredo meant for him, though he had thought up the idea of taking the trip and had invited Mike along to help drive back home. Whatever it was that was pushing him, however, Wayne-O was sure it had something to do with pain—and lost youth.

"I don't know, Mike," he lied. "I guess I'm worried because I was thinking that this would be a good place for someone to roll us."

"Aw, come on, man," Mike said, a little disturbed. "What the hell is bugging you, man? You think your old lady will find out or something?"

"I don't know. I might just tell her."

"Huh! I wouldn't do that," Mike said.

Wayne-O glanced sideways, resting his pale blue eyes on Mike. "Well, Mike, a man might do a lot of things when he's married, but me, I think one of the worst of them is lying."

"Why did you come anyway?" Mike asked.

Wayne-O didn't answer for a minute. He just kept walking. "Well,

Hell, Mike, he said slowly, "I've been married a long time, you know—nearly twenty years. I see the girls in the stores and all, you know—and I just kind of got to thinking, 'What would it be like?'"

"What you need is one of them amateur whores," Mike assured him with feigned authority.

"Naw, them girls around Houston, they might try to make trouble, get me divorced or something."

Mike was silent. He hadn't thought of that.

A street opened off to their left. About halfway down the block was what looked like a pagoda with Chinese characters painted in white on its orange tower. Wayne-O ambled toward it, Mike trailing behind. It was a club, all right—cars parked all around, men going in and out in the early darkness, people selling cigarettes in front. Wayne-O decided they should try out this place—the Tamyko.

As the two men crossed the threshold, Leta, topless except for the suspenders on her black hot pants, came up to Mike and put her arm around his waist.

"Yeah, let's sit down," he blurted. The trio took a table and Leta began her pitch.

"Whiskey?"

"Aw, all you want is for us to buy you a drink," Mike said, a little irritated now.

Leta nodded.

"How much?" Wayne-O asked.

"Dollar half," she said.

"A dollar and a half, hell," Mike groaned. A waiter stepped over from the bar at the back of the room.

"Well, are you going to buy the girl a drink?" Wayne-O asked.

"Aw, I don't know," Mike said. "A dollar and a half ain't much, but why?"

Wayne-O turned his head toward the waiter. "Yeah, bring us two rum and Cokes, and whatever the girl wants."

"Shit. It's you who's paying, Wayne-O," Mike said. Leta pulled her suspenders aside, showing Mike her deep brown nipples and turning away when he tried to touch them.

"No," she said. "Thirty dollars."

"Thirty dollars!" Mike exclaimed. "Hell, babe, I can't afford it," he lied. He pulled out the bills he had in one pants pocket—a twenty, a ten, a five, and a one. "Look, babe, I've just got thirty-six dollars."

"Okay," said Leta, and she rose from his knee, reaching for his money.

"No, you dumb broad, I ain't going to give you that. I'll give you sixteen dollars, that's all."

"How much?" Leta asked, raising her eyebrows, trying to understand.

"Sixteen," Mike said.

Leta shook her head no, no, and sat back down on Mike's knee. Looking up, she waved to someone standing outside the door leading to the courtyard. Wayne-O peered through the glass and saw a sharp-featured woman about his own age, wearing a yellow suit. She waved back at Leta and started toward them.

"Your friend?" Wayne-O asked.

"Yes, Elizabeth. Too skinny, no?" Leta giggled. Wayne-O didn't respond.

"Buy friend drink?" Leta asked, poking Mike in the ribs as Elizabeth sat down. He looked over at Wayne-O.

"Okay, I'll buy her a drink," Wayne-O said. Elizabeth turned her head away.

"What's matter?" Leta asked her. Elizabeth didn't answer. The waiter came, took her order, and returned, slipping a quarter to Elizabeth with her drink. Elizabeth covered the quarter with her hand, then looked at Wayne-O to see if he had noticed. He hadn't. He watched as she and Leta conversed in Spanish. Elizabeth's tiny black eyes brightened as the minutes went by, whether from the drink or the gossip Wayne-O couldn't tell.

"Do you want another drink?" he asked Elizabeth.

"Did I ask for one?" she shot back.

"Well, no. I was just trying to be polite," Wayne-O said.

"You buy Leta a drink, too?" Elizabeth asked.

"Yeah, go ahead," he said.

The waiter brought the drinks and again handed quarters to the two girls. With no hesitation, Leta tucked hers into a pocket of her hot pants. Elizabeth looked over at Wayne-O.

"Here, your quarter," she said, extending her hand toward him.

"Did I ask you for that?" he said. Elizabeth laughed.

Mike was haggling with Leta again. "Sixteen dollars," he said. Leta again shook her head no. "Why not, am I too ugly?" he asked.

"*¿Qué dijo este maje?*" Leta asked Elizabeth.

"He said, is he too ugly?" Elizabeth answered in English.

"Ugly," Leta parroted.

"You whore," Mike swore, rising from his chair and dumping Leta off his lap. Frightened, she skipped off to another prospective customer.

Elizabeth laughed and then, drink in hand, started to leave too.

"Why don't you stay? You ain't even told me your name," Wayne-O said. Elizabeth turned back and looked at him. "Yeah, sit down. Don't mind my friend here," he coaxed.

Elizabeth sat, still across the table from Wayne-O. She told him her name and said she was from Matamoros.

"Well, how old are you?" Wayne-O queried.

"Forty-five," she said, her broad lips opening wide in a smile.

Wayne-O chuckled. The girl was obviously not 17, but she wasn't 45, not by a long shot.

"Yeah, sure, and I'm sixty," he said, smiling. "Do you like old men?"

"What's wrong with old men?" she said, giggling.

When the waiter came, Elizabeth boldly took the three quarters he gave her.

"Why didn't you give me the quarters back?" Wayne-O asked her.

"I like money," she said.

Wayne-O by now had decided that this girl was worth his time. Her figure was acceptable, by his standards, and there was something about her spunkiness that held him on. She was a little more honest than some of the whores, and she might not pretend to enjoy him in bed when she really didn't. It was important to Wayne-O to measure his prowess against the incompetence he'd felt twenty years ago.

"Well, you ready to take my thirty dollars?" he asked.

Elizabeth thought about the green pants and shirt and the yellow shoes and the green shoes Julito wanted. She also remembered that she had a headache and a hangover. "I don't know," she told Wayne-O.

"Yeah, well, how about for all night?"

"I don't know."

"Aw, come on," Wayne-O coaxed. "I ain't going to be on top of you all night."

Elizabeth stiffened her neck a little. It had been a long time—months—since anyone had asked her for that. All night, an expensive proposition. "We can watch TV? Elizabeth asked. "There is a boxing fight."

"Okay, it's a deal," said Wayne-O, reaching for his back pocket. Then he hesitated. "How much?"

"Hundred dollars," she said. It was less than the price usually asked on weekends.

"A hundred dollars!" Mike interjected. The price seemed out of the question to him.

"Well, okay, but you have to give me all the quarters from our drinks," Wayne-O teased.

Elizabeth laughed. She took the money to the bar, paid the manager $25 for use of a room, and came back to the table.

"You ready to go to room?" she asked Wayne-O.

"Naw, let's take a walk around outside, go look at this neighborhood," he said.

It was an unusual request. Still, it was harmless, and there was time, now that he had paid her for the night.

"Buy me drink before we go?" she asked him.

Wayne-O nodded, and Elizabeth ordered another El Presidente with soda. When the waiter gave her the quarter she pushed it across to Wayne-O, but as he reached for it she snapped it back.

"Man, you better make that broad give you the money," Mike spoke out. "She's taking you for a fool."

Wayne-O faced him.

"Is that what you think, brother?" His tone warned Mike not to reply.

The three went outdoors, toward the street. The guard came slinking up behind them. Elizabeth turned and said something to him in Spanish.

"What was that?" Wayne-O asked.

"I told him you had pay my room for the night," she explained. The guard casually saluted her and left. They walked up the street, Wayne-O and Elizabeth hand in hand and Mike tagging along behind.

There were clubs along one side of the street, and walls—the exterior walls of another club—on the other side. Gringos in jeans and cowboy hats and Mexicans wearing *guayabera* shirts with business slacks sauntered in and out of the clubs, whose billboard-size neon signs were beginning to give light to the darkened street. They came to a *conjunto ranchero* playing on a sidewalk outside another club.

The lyrics were sung entirely in Spanish, but Mike liked the music. In the middle of a song, he stepped up to a guitarist. "Can you play 'El Paso'?" he asked.

The guitarist kept strumming and singing. Only when his ballad was finished did he acknowledge Mike.

"Can you play 'El Paso'?" Mike repeated.

The guitarist, though he did not understand English, nodded as if to say yes, he knew the song.

"How much?" Mike asked excitedly.

"Three dollars" one of the band members said.

"Three dollars!" Mike said. "No, one dollar, one song." The *conjunto* members refused and prepared to move on.

"One dollar," Mike hollered out again.

A Mexican standing nearby handed a dollar to the guitarist in front of Mike. "Here," the Mexican said loudly in English, "I'll give you one dollar, just for free. This gringo is a cheapskate." Everyone in the throng around the *conjunto* laughed, except Mike. The band members walked on.

Mike watched them for a moment. "I'm going to find that four-dollar whore," he told Wayne-O and Elizabeth.

She was still standing in her doorway, two streets away.

"Hey, baby, four dollar," he said, mimicking her English and suggesting fellatio.

"No, ten dollars," the woman shot back, folding her arms. Mike pulled the bills from his pocket. He shoved the five out toward her. The whore took it and stepped back into her room, motioning him in. He turned and waved at Wayne-O and Elizabeth from inside.

Elizabeth stood on tiptoe, speaking into Wayne-O's ear. "She not do it. She fool him," Elizabeth said.

Wayne-O was hungry again. He asked Elizabeth to pick out a restaurant. Instead, she led him back to the Tamyko and into the dining room. Seated at a long wooden table inside were half a dozen of the girls from the club and one of the cops who worked outside. Elizabeth and Wayne-O took chairs and the cook brought a dish of *mole* with rice for each of them.

Then he poured them coffee. One of the women, a robust, brown-skinned woman whose slim breasts hung out of an open-front maroon evening dress, turned to Wayne-O and asked in broken English if he thought the girls at the Tamyko were fat. Then she translated her question into Spanish for the listeners at the table.

"Well, no," Wayne-O said, as soon as he was sure what she'd asked. Everyone chuckled but Wayne-O and the cop.

"You see," the woman explained, "we have three girls who are pregnant. The waiter say they too fat."

"Pregnant?" Wayne-O said, a little startled. "How can they be pregnant?" Laughs went around the table this time a little ahead of the woman's translation. Wayne-O and Elizabeth scowled at the others.

"Those girls, they have no children," Elizabeth told him, speaking quietly. "They want be mothers."

"But who are the fathers?" Wayne-O asked in a whisper.

"Oh," she said, "who knows?"

"But why don't they get abortions?" he insisted, obviously disturbed.

"I told you, they *want* be mothers."

It was plain to Elizabeth that Wayne-O did not understand women. Sooner or later, a child was what every cabaret girl lived for. Most of the girls, like Leta, had children before they married—premarital motherhood was the burden that drove them here. Others came to the club after divorce and economic troubles had pared away their alternatives; a job as a beauty operator after her own divorce hadn't offered Elizabeth the income she wanted for raising Julito. But even if children didn't come to a woman before she came to the Tamyko, Elizabeth knew, they would come afterward. Being a mother was a station of dignity inside La Zona.

"Do these women still, uh, work when they're pregnant?" Wayne-O asked, speaking into Elizabeth's ear.

Yes, she said, they found clients as always. Some men preferred them over the other girls.

Wayne-O was shocked. It would be different, he felt, if the men involved were the women's husbands."Would you work if you were pregnant?" he asked Elizabeth.

"Yes," she said. Then, in a louder voice that all could hear, she said something in Spanish to the woman in the maroon dress. Everyone at the table but Wayne-O laughed.

The woman in the maroon dress leaned over his way, inadvertently exposing her paunch as well as her breasts."Elizabeth say maybe she get pregnant and not be so skinny," the woman told Wayne-O.

He leaned back in his chair and did his best to put on an amused look.

Elizabeth saw that he was uncomfortable, grasped his hand in hers, and kissed him on the cheek. "I just lying," she whispered to him.

Wayne-O tipped the club's cook for their meal and followed Elizabeth to her room. Leta was there, combing her hair into place; her last client had mussed it up. Wayne-O looked around the room. There were fluffy gray throw rugs on its red tile floor and a maroon-and-white Texas A&M pennant on one wall. It was a gift, Elizabeth told him, from one of her clients, whose friendship ring she wore next to the cheap wedding band that she had never removed even after her divorce. At Elizabeth's direction Wayne-O picked up her portable television and followed her down the hallway that fronted on the courtyard. Elizabeth stopped by the altar, placed a new candle in her holder, and moved on. A few paces later she called out to the matron who provided maid service for the rooms.

"Want another drink?" she asked Wayne-O. He shook his head no. She turned back to the cleaning woman, telling her to bring a brandy.

Wayne-O followed Elizabeth into a vacant room very much like hers, but unadorned. The cleaning woman came with Elizabeth's drink, and Elizabeth bolted the door shut. Then she disappeared into the bathroom, drink in hand. Wayne-O lay down on the bed without removing his boots Elizabeth came out of the bathroom a few minutes later, clad only in black bra and panties. She crawled in next to Wayne-O, pulling the bedclothes over her torso.

Outside, Mike stood on the sidewalk, trying to pick out the face of his friend in the stream of passersby that came and went in the shadows beneath the lights of the Tamyko. Wayne-O was not in sight. On the other side of the street he saw a curio shop. It was just what he needed, he told himself. He was a little dismayed by the night's events. He'd spent what he considered a small fortune on drinks for himself, and he had given the whore five bucks. She had rooked him in, in a sneaky sort of way, and left him ashamed. Maybe in the curio shop he could buy something good, and for a good price.

He stepped into the little pine lean-to store. Straw sombreros, bull horns, and nude paintings hung on the walls. He turned his back to the shop's attendant and spotted a painting on black velvet in one corner of the shanty. It was a portrait of Jesus. Grasping the painting by its wooden frame, he pulled it toward him to look at a similar work behind it. He reviewed several of the same genre and settled on the one he'd seen first. It showed Christ's head turned upward as if He were begging for mercy. A streak of crimson ran down one side of His tormented face, and there were drops of blood beneath the large thorns of His crown. Mike thought that maybe he would give the painting to his sister in Houston, or maybe he'd keep it for himself, take it back with him to the offshore platform where he worked.

"How much?" he asked the shops attendant.

"Twelve dollars," the man said.

Mike turned his back on the attendant again and, with caution, pulled his money from his pocket. He still had a ten and a one. He stuffed the one back in and faced the attendant. "Look I'm really sorry, but all I've got left is ten dollars," he said, showing the bill to the man.

The attendant hesitated, but only for a moment. "Okay," he said, smiling.

Mike handed him the money and picked up the portrait, holding it out at arm's length. He was pleased—it was the first real bargain he'd found all day—until he noticed that the lower edge of the velvet painting was covered with dust. "No, man, this is dirty," he complained.

The attendant went to a corner and brought out a nylon brush with short, soft bristles. He dusted off the portrait and handed it back to Mike, who was smiling now.

Mike stepped out of the shop, carrying the huge painting at his side. On the sidewalk in front of the Tamyko he sat down, crossing his legs under him, and settled in for the night.

About sunrise Wayne-O turned in his sleep, woke, opened his eyes, and looked around the bare room. Taking care not to disturb Elizabeth, he dressed and slipped out of the room, then went over the bridge and into the club. Leta was there, writing out her address for a bearded young man who looked like a college student.

Wayne-O opened the aluminum-framed glass door at the front of the club and looked to his right. There, a few yards away, Mike was sprawled out, his legs extending across the sidewalk, his right arm flung over the top of the Jesus portrait, his head leaning back against the club's outer wall. Wayne-O knelt down beside him. "Wake up, wake up, brother."

Inside the Tamyko, Elizabeth reached over to the nightstand for the half-empty glass of brandy. While she sipped it she found herself thinking that perhaps it was true—maybe she was just too skinny, like the other girls said. But as she drained the glass, the thought that always consoled her at these times resurfaced. No, she wasn't too skinny, and it wasn't her age that made men get up in the night. It was just—as she'd thought on so many other mornings—that nothing good ever comes from men, nothing except children and brandy.

While hospice care is no longer controversial, this article, which appeared in *Texas Monthly* in June 1981, shows that it was not always so. It faced opposition from the medical establishment and mainstream Americans, and those who sought it faced a myriad of problems.

Passing On

On November 18, 1980, Linda Mihlan, a 29-year-old mother and housewife in Mesquite, died of cancer of the cervix. She died in her living room, sitting next to her husband, Chuck.

At the moment of Linda's death, Chuck was talking on the phone to Cathy Little, who is a hospice nurse. Her job is a fairly new one in the world of health care. She looks after people who are dying, who are beyond medical help. Cathy has chosen to spend her life making other people's deaths slightly more bearable, an ever-larger calling in America, one that sometimes attracts mystics and kooks and one that utterly fails to satisfy the constant demand made of modern medicine—that it offer hope of recovery. And yet, for Linda and Chuck Mihlan, it undeniably eased the pain.

Linda's mother was already dying of lung cancer when Chuck and Linda began dating. In Chuck, Linda's mother saw a chance of security for her daughter; he had a kind voice, temperate habits, and the prospect of a good job. He was the sort of man, she believed, who would make a good father to the three children from Linda's first marriage.

Linda's life had always been a cause for worry. Reared in lower-middle-class poverty in the Garland-Mesquite-Balch Springs area, she had quit school after the ninth grade and married young. She worked as a waitress and bore three boys to her first husband, a hard-drinking, fast-driving man. Now the children were a burden to support. When Chuck came into Linda's life, Linda's mother asked them from her deathbed to marry before she passed away.

Chuck did not want to marry until he had known Linda for a full year, but he didn't want to frustrate a dying woman's wish, either. In November 1975, five months after he met Linda and only weeks before her mother died, Chuck and Linda were wed at her mother's home in Mesquite. They moved into a Dallas apartment. Linda stayed home with the kids, and Chuck took himself off every day to his new job as a hydraulics mechanic at an oil field supply plant.

Linda's health had never been good, and it did not improve after their marriage. Within three years she had her appendix removed, was diagnosed as diabetic, and had a benign tumor removed from her breast. In order to understand these and many other minor ailments, Linda sometimes paged through a set of medical encyclopedias inherited from her mother, the sort of books sold in grocery stores. But not until the fall of 1979, four years after her mother's death, could Linda read the chapters on cancer.

For more than a year Linda had been bothered by a vaginal discharge, especially on nights when she and Chuck made love. On two brief pages of *The New Illustrated Medical Encyclopedia for Home Use* she found such a discharge described as symptomatic of cervical cancer. Once she had diagnosed herself, Linda lost no time. She asked Chuck to accompany her to the doctor's office, and while she was being examined, he sat in the waiting room, ill-humored at having given up a day's work to placate his wife's insatiable obsession with illnesses. Half an hour later, when Chuck was called in, Linda was crying. "Your wife has cancer of the cervix, but she has a good chance of surviving," the physician told Chuck. But Chuck was distressed. After all, cancer is cancer, isn't it?

Tumors of the female organs, which 30 years ago accounted for 1 in 5 cancer deaths, account for only 1 in 10 today. In Texas deaths due to uterine cancer have declined from about 750 a year in 1950 to about 580 today, and across the nation, some 78 percent of women stricken with cancer of the cervix live for five years or more if diagnosis is early. In other words, a diagnosis of cervical cancer no longer means probable death, even in cases like Linda's where diagnosis comes late. Her doctor was within the statistical bounds of reason when he counseled hope and speed.

The doctor had scheduled further tests for Linda at Pleasant Grove Hospital the following Monday. After the tests Linda asked Chuck to see a lawyer about adopting the children, so that they would be his if she should die. She then called the children together so Chuck could tell them what was wrong. "Linda has cancer," Chuck said. "Do any of you guys know what that means?"

"Yes," blurted six-year-old Jimmy, "it means that Mommy is going to die!" Despite assurances that death was neither imminent nor certain, the boys wept. That Christmas Chuck and Linda gave the children everything they asked for. Under the tree the boys found a stereo set, racing cars, and a dozen lesser goodies.

But Linda's condition did not improve. At Easter she was in the Baylor University Medical Center hospital for a hysterectomy, which was followed by a brief and futile regimen of chemotherapy. By June her weight loss was noticeable, her strength was fading, and she was in pain. Unable to manage her responsibilities, she agreed to place the boys in the Buckner Baptist Children's Home in Dallas. They did not want to leave her, but Linda was in the hospital as much as she was home now, Chuck had an obligation to work, and there was no one to care for them.

Money was scarcer than it had ever been. Chuck had medical insurance for his family through his employer, but it paid an annual maximum of $10,000 per beneficiary. That amount was exhausted by the time summer began, as were the couple's savings. Because Linda could no longer drive, Chuck had to miss work in order to accompany her to hospitals and clinics; because there was no money, he had to go into debt to keep her out of pain. Even with the kids at Buckner, Chuck had more work at home than one man could handle.

Sympathetic hospital personnel advised Chuck to call upon the Home Hospice Program. The Dallas Visiting Nurse Association (VNA) hospice, established in 1978, is one of the nation's largest home care programs for terminally ill patients. At any given time VNA Home Hospice nurses, aides, and social workers are providing advice, treatment, and household help for one hundred terminal patients, most of them cancer victims.

The term "hospice," which denotes a place of shelter, has for three decades been used in Britain as a name for hospital wards devoted to the care of the terminally ill. The first modern hospice, St. Christopher's in London, opened in 1948 and set a standard for similar institutions. Hospices, wherever they are, provide staple medical services like oxygen administration and intravenous feeding, but because treatment in terminal cases is largely palliative, they specialize in pain control. Programs built on the British model also offer patients and their families a variety of counseling services, including advice on wills, funerals, and pensions. They deliver services to the patient through teams composed of doctors, nurses, social workers, and volunteers, many of whom are the survivors of former hospice patients. Hospices bring experienced personnel to the assistance of dying patients, but as Chuck Mihlan would learn, they cannot resolve all, or even the most painful, problems associated with death. In hospice theory, and in ordinary practice, the team members function as aides to the patient's family—upon whom final responsibility rests.

Last July—about the time Linda came into the Home Hospice Program—it and 25 similar projects across the nation were released from the Medicare system's restrictions on the type and number of visits that would be reimbursed. That federal endowment, though it did not directly affect Linda, did lessen the hospice's dependence on funds donated by survivors of former patients.

The hospice did not charge Linda and Chuck for hospice visits to their home. The VNA also used privately donated funds to hire household help for them for four hours a day. It dispatched David Overton, a bearded 27-year-old social worker, to assist the couple in facing the traumas of impending death and to help in maintaining contact with the three children in Buckner. The VNA hospice also assigned 26-year-old Cathy Little to visit Linda's bedside. Cathy had been a hospice nurse for less than a week when she drew the assignment. It proved to be a good test of her preparedness for the new job.

In many ways Cathy fit the profile of nurses whom hospice work attracts. She had not been a traditional nursing school student. Throughout her formal education she had enjoyed literature more than math or science, and in her personal and political views she was trendy and liberal, not staid or traditional. She was convinced that the hospital setting discouraged warmth and closeness. But Cathy pursued nursing anyway, because the work itself appealed to her. Times were changing, women's liberation was making inroads everywhere, nursing was winning a new dignity—and a new clout—and in that ambience Cathy hoped she could find a place for herself.

For three years after graduation Cathy shifted from job to job, looking for professional contentment. She worked for an oncology, or tumor, hospital; on a cardiac intensive care unit; and on a neurosurgical intensive care unit, all in the Dallas area. She was not favorably impressed. Hospitals were hurried, businesslike institutions, she thought—and working in them was like working in a factory or store. Her patients on the intensive care unit reminded her of greenhouse plants: silent, unmoving, and artificially maintained. Cathy wanted to get away from the chilly atmosphere of organized medicine.

Her superiors in the hospice program hired her because she had technical expertise, because she was experienced with terminal patients, and because she was reasonably well insulated against a common hazard of hospice work, career burnout: her boyfriend of three years, she said in a job interview, would know how to comfort her when the strain of working with dying people gave her doubts about her job. Though it meant a pay cut of $150 a month, Cathy was delighted to be hired by the hospice. No longer would she have to work under a regime of medical spit and polish. Now she would be a member of an irregular, or guerrilla, corps.

For all practical purposes, the American hospice movement dates to 1969 and the publication of *On Death and Dying*, a manual by Swiss-born psychiatrist Elisabeth Kübler-Ross. For several years Kübler-Ross was an associate professor at the University of Chicago and a staff psychiatrist at its Billings Hospital, where she talked with hundreds of terminal patients. Ultimately she turned her findings into a theory of death psychology. Patients facing death proceed through five stages, she said: denial, during which patients refuse to acknowledge a diagnosis; anger, a phase characterized by blaming survivors for impending death; depression; bargaining, or the attempt to prolong life by promises, often to deities; and finally, acceptance, the tranquil resignation to fate. In seminars and books, Kübler-Ross advocated training programs to enable lay and medical personnel to act as guides through these stages of the mind. By the time the first American hospice opened in 1974, Kübler-Ross had become a pop saint. She was given keys to the city in half a dozen locales, and she received eighteen honorary degrees in five years.

In actual practice, the five stages Kübler-Ross outlined turned out not to be stages at all, and even their formulator now waffles over the term. Most dying patients do experience denial, anger, depression, bargaining, and acceptance, but not in any sequence. The stages might more accurately be termed moods, because most patients experience them in an unpatterned way. Kübler-Ross's credibility was further damaged by accounts published in the late seventies of her participation in séances in which widows purportedly achieved sexual union with the spirits of their husbands by coupling with a middle-aged guru named Jay Barham. The Barham scandal would perhaps have finished off Kübler-Ross as an influential figure had the hospices she advocated not been so useful to terminal patients and their families.

Kübler-Ross followed *On Death and Dying* with more books, and death became a much-published topic: more than 400 popular works about death were in print in 1980, compared to less than 100 ten years before. Along with discussion of death came hospices.

Two types of institutions had been developed by the British: freestanding hospices, where all patients are terminally ill, and hospital-based hospices, usually wards of an ordinary hospital reserved for terminal care. But Kübler-Ross noted that most terminal patients she spoke to expressed a desire to die at home, and she called for the creation of home care hospice services. The idea has caught on like wildfire, but probably not as a response to the wishes of the dying. In the U.S. the expense of hospital care—more than $400 a day for cancer patients at Houston's M.D. Anderson Hospital, for example—is not borne by a program of national health insurance as it is in Great Britain. Some government and private insurance plans deny reimbursement for hospital care not aimed at healing the patient, and physicians are reluctant to authorize hospital admission for patients nearing death. In many cases terminal care may be most cheaply administered outside a hospital setting. The American medical tradition includes visiting nurse associations—the Dallas VNA was established in 1934—that have provided terminal care, if not the whole range of hospice services, for decades. The development of hospice care through VNAs was a logical step for both historical and fiscal reasons.

Logical or not, that development was viewed with suspicion in many quarters of the medical community. Two recent studies by the University of Texas Medical Branch in Galveston show that the hospice concept has won no great favor with Texas physicians. In both studies—one of UT Medical Branch staff, the other of practicing physicians across the state—only two of every five doctors interviewed expressed a desire for additional resources in matters related to death and dying.

One reason physicians have not taken up the hospice cause is that the very notion of terminal illness runs counter to their training and practice. For the best of reasons, physicians are sworn and accustomed to direct their efforts toward saving life. They are reluctant to prognosticate death, because even cases of advanced cancer are sometimes subject to spontaneous remission and there is almost always a method or medication or procedure that has not yet been fully explored. For the physician, the dying patient is not a financial burden—or a beloved relative.

Some of the medical establishment's distrust arose from more mundane concerns, however. In the absence of both clear standards defining hospice care and any licensing or legislative requirements, the field was ripe for experimentation and abuse. Nursing homes have in some cases merely restyled themselves as hospices without expanding their services. Nobody knows how many projects calling themselves hospices exist in the U.S., and even the fledgling National Hospice Organization (NHO) is unable to give an account of its membership. Many of the organizations affiliated with the NHO have not established hospice operations yet, and some existing programs may not measure up to the NHO's standards.

For their part, most hospice advocates are quick to point out that hospital and physician care is characterized by the commitment of expertise only. Medicine, in pursuit of technological miracles, has lost its human face, they say. Hospice programs aim to restore warmth, as well as familial and financial considerations, to the bedside manner of medical workers, and that's why hospice programs, generally speaking, are hotbeds of scorn for the medical establishment. Nurses like Cathy Little see themselves as leading a movement for the reform of not only terminal treatment but the whole medical profession. The typical hospice worker is part scientific provider—nurse or doctor or social worker—part chaplain, psychologist, or consoler, and part agitator or visionary.

Cathy Little took two six-packs of Ensure from the room where donated supplies were stored and carried them downstairs to her maroon Pontiac Phoenix. She put the squatty orange-and-white cans onto the back seat, between her briefcase and the catheters in plastic packages, above the bags of Chux pads on the floor. Then she drove northeast, toward the suburban territory she works for the Home Hospice Program. Cathy was taking the Ensure, a milkshake dietary supplement, to Linda Mihlan.

Ensure would improve Linda's life in two ways. She didn't like the taste of her methadone, a bitter narcotic, even though it came with a grape syrup additive, and Ensure would give the drug a more palatable chocolate flavor. It would also give her concentrated nutrients. Nothing could keep Linda, who was already using a walker, from growing even thinner and weaker, but Ensure might slow down the process.

As Cathy drove, she mapped out the day ahead of her. She would give the Ensure to Linda that afternoon. Other patients in Garland would come first, and then patients in Mesquite and Balch Springs. Six weeks earlier, when all twenty of Cathy's patients had been alive, Cathy sometimes had not returned home until nightfall. But even then she had planned her visits to Linda for late in the afternoon, in order to spend as much time there as Linda wanted. Linda was a special patient because she put Cathy to the test, not only as a nurse in a blue-and-white uniform but as a creature of empathy. Dying of cancer is not always painful, but Cathy knew that Linda Mihlan, with or without Ensure, was likely to suffer great misery. Cancer sometimes does not yield to even the best or most innovative interventions of the medical profession.

Cathy's task as Linda's nurse was essentially to supervise a regimen of pain control. After a month-long summer hospitalization, Linda had been prescribed Dilaudid capsules and injections of Demerol, a painkiller, with Thorazine, a calmative. Pain control is controversial among doctors and patients alike, and the results in Linda's case show why. Most physicians prescribe barbiturates with a sparing hand, lest patients develop dependencies, and many patients, believing that agony is preferable to addiction, hold themselves back from the medicine bottle. Linda had reached a point where relief came only when she was stuporous from high doses of her painkillers. When her injections were delayed she suffered both the psychic and the physical pain of withdrawal. In October, at Cathy's request, Linda's doctor began prescribing methadone for her.

Methadone is synthetic morphine, as potent as any painkiller available. Its euphoric effects have made it an alternative to heroin in medical therapy as well as on the black market. In the beginning it stupefies its users, and it is a powerful addictive agent even though, like any pain remedy, it is not effective for all patients or at all times. Linda's body usually responded well to the drug, and it enabled her to resume some of those activities that pain had taken away. She entertained her children on weekends and, supported by a walker, helped in the kitchen on weeknights. Sometimes, in the wheelchair that substituted for muscle strength, she went with Chuck to modest restaurants or to flea market sales.

But even methadone is not infallible. It did not end Linda Mihlan's—or Cathy's—suffering. The crisis for Cathy came one afternoon in October when she made a scheduled visit to Linda's home. Cathy's ring at the door was answered by the household aide, who, before Cathy crossed the threshold, warned that Linda's pain was out of control.

When Cathy walked in, Linda, at 29, just three years older than Cathy, was lying in a pink nylon gown atop an artificial sheepskin on the old green couch in her living room. On a coffee table at her side lay her usual appurtenances: a photo album, a Bible, and a bottle of diet Dr Pepper. The patient, now weighing less than one hundred pounds, barely noticed when Cathy approached and inquired about her condition in a quiet, tentative voice.

Linda didn't hear because she was moaning. "What is happening to me? Why do I hurt? Somebody please help me, tell me why I hurt."

"Linda, Linda," Cathy said, kneeling beside the couch, "why do you think you are in pain?"

But Linda continued her pleading. "Can't you give me a shot? Call the doctor! Do anything!"

There was no question, by that time, of giving Linda any injections. That route had already been tried and had lost its effectiveness. All that remained was to administer methadone. Cathy rose, measured the dose, mixed it with Ensure, as she had for weeks, and spooned it into Linda's mouth. Then, kneeling, she checked her patient's blood pressure and pulse, busying herself and comforting Linda while she waited for the drug to take effect.

But the drug did not take effect. Half an hour later, Linda's emaciated frame was still curled with pain, her mouth still strained. She begged for a mercy that, she knew, would not be forthcoming.

"Linda, there's nothing more I can do except just hold you," Cathy told her patient, trembling herself. She encircled Linda with her arms and in a quiet voice told her to breathe slowly, ever so slowly. Linda complied, and as her respiration rate slowed she nodded faintly and hummed or snored. In a few minutes she fell into an uneasy sleep. Cathy carefully slipped out of the house, late for her team conference meeting at the hospice.

As the other nurses, social workers, volunteers, and household aides compared notes and discussed treatments for patients, Cathy kept silent, offering no advice and asking none. When her turn came to report, conference leader Charles Kemp asked about Linda's condition. Cathy blurted out something about intractable pain, then broke into sobs.

Kemp, who sat on Cathy's left, put his arms around her, as did the nurse on her right. Rather than admonishing her to stop crying, both encouraged her to express herself. Phrase by phrase, Cathy explained her difficulties with Linda's pain control program. She also talked about how Linda's impending death frightened her. After all, Linda Mihlan was in many ways her double: they were the same age, they had both been born and raised in the Dallas area and spoke with the same accent, and, as her hospice co-workers had noted, they were both women of a somewhat serious disposition, friendly but sometimes somber. Before the discussion of Linda's status was over, half a dozen people were crying with Cathy. It was the sort of mutual support meeting that hospice workers claim they must have in order to face their jobs. They must give strength to families facing death, and in the course of their work they themselves often need emotional bolstering.

The Texas hospice movement's leading visionary was nurse Charles Kemp, 36, a tall, thin, bass-voiced, black-bearded man. Kemp was a Marine machine gunner during the Viet Nam War, and he returned home disillusioned and frightened. He became a counter-culturist, and even today he neither blinks nor grins when he cites Dr. Timothy Leary as an authority on matters of metaphysics. Like Kübler-Ross and other hospice pioneers, Kemp has unorthodox ideas about the afterlife, and though these views do not enter into his hospice or nursing work, they were in part responsible for his interest in the crises of dying patients. Kemp graduated from nursing school in 1975, with some help from the GI Bill, and three years later completed a master's degree at the University of Texas at Austin. He went home to Dallas, where he and a handful of associates began providing ad hoc hospice care to terminal patients, sometimes on a voluntary basis.

His efforts won approval in the nursing community, and in the fall of 1978, at the request of the VNA, he put together a hospice program. Though the project grew—it now has a paid staff of fifty and a $1.5 million annual budget—late last year Charles Kemp resigned as director and was replaced by a licensed nursing home administrator whose background was entirely orthodox and bureaucratic. Kemp had become a victim of career burnout. His new occupation, however temporary, is as a yardman and gardener. "I just got sick and tired of death," he says. But Charles Kemp was there when Cathy wept at the hospice meeting, and he, more than anyone, gave her the resolve to go on. Though he ultimately gave up himself, Kemp brought dozens of new hospice workers into the program and steeled them.

Linda's condition improved in early November, and once again she was able to venture out in her wheelchair. One of the few wishes she expressed was to visit a simple seafood restaurant on Buckner Boulevard; methadone allowed her its fulfillment. Though she was weak and by then weighed not more than ninety pounds, she and Chuck also went one Friday night to dinner at a Bonanza steakhouse in Mesquite, at the invitation of a co-worker of her husband's. That dinner was her last meal.

Over the weekend Linda weakened rapidly. She refused food and on Monday laid her cigarettes aside. She could no longer rise from bed and slip into her wheelchair; Chuck now carried her from room to room. Her complexion grew pale, her body turned cold, and her breathing became labored. On Monday, when Cathy Little visited the home, Linda's blood pressure was abnormally low. On Tuesday both Cathy and Chuck knew that she would not live long.

Chuck called Cathy outside the front door of his house. "I don't know, Cathy," he said, "but Linda is getting weak pretty fast. I don't see how she can make it another week."

"I think you're right," Cathy told him, reaching for his hand.

Chuck braced himself, as he had for months, in the belief that harsh news hurts less on a stiff backbone.

Some premonition told Cathy to give Chuck her home telephone number. She wrote it out on a slip of paper and, as she left, told Chuck to call her if he had any problems that night.

Linda lay on the old couch in the living room that evening, sometimes whimpering, sometimes wailing with pain that not even methadone could hold down. She hurt, as she had for days, in her right thigh, and she hurt in her bowels as well, for that evening diarrhea had come upon her.

About ten o'clock her multiple pains were severe enough that she began imploring Chuck to call an ambulance. She wanted to go to a hospital.

"Linda, we've discussed it before, and you know there's nothing they can do for you in a hospital," Chuck told his wife.

But Linda would not be content. She told Chuck that she loved him and repeated her plea for an ambulance.

By ten-thirty Chuck was perplexed and afraid. He sat down in the overstuffed chair next to the couch where Linda lay and picked up the telephone. He dialed Cathy's number. "I don't know what to do. Linda's in awful pain and she wants an ambulance," Chuck told Cathy.

Cathy made several inquiries about Linda's condition, then counseled Chuck to fend off the requests until the pain subsided, as it always had before.

"Just a minute," Chuck interrupted, turning his head toward his wife. Linda had moved one foot onto the floor and attempted to pull her torso erect, as if to rise up from the couch. Now she sat in that position, stiff, with eyes and mouth wide open.

Chuck laid the receiver on the floor, then checked his wife's respiration and pulse and looked into her eyes for dilation, as Cathy had taught him to do. In seconds, he knew that Linda was dead.

He picked up the receiver again. "Cathy, she's gone. It's all over now."

Cathy counseled him to accept what he had known was inevitable.

"I'll tell you what," Chuck said. "You go to your icebox and get a beer, and I'm going to get some margarita mix we've got here, so I can get drunk."

After Chuck had mixed his drink, he continued his conversation with Cathy. They planned out the steps that were required that night: telephone calls to a funeral home, to Chuck's best friend, to Linda's family. They hung up, and after he had made the phone calls, Chuck turned to look at the woman who only minutes before had been his wife.

"It's hard to say how I felt, but I felt so, so alone," he recalls. "I didn't know what to do, so I tried to close her eyelids. I couldn't get them closed, though, and I just sat there, not knowing what to do. Finally, about the time her family came in, I went into the bedroom and sat down and played the stereo with my headphones. It was a hard thing to handle." With Dave, the hospice social worker, Chuck visited the funeral home the following day. He selected a modest casket and looked at Linda.

"I wanted to make sure that she didn't look worse than when she died, or else I wouldn't have let her have an open-casket funeral," Chuck says. "It was a good job they did. They stuffed her cheeks with something so that she didn't look so thin. She looked better than she had in months."

After approving the morticians' work Chuck went to the Buckner Baptist Childrens' Home. The three boys were called into the chaplain's office where Chuck told them their mother was dead. All three wept, and one of them, who at times had beaten his mother about the waist, later blurted out, "It's my fault, it's my fault."

Two days later the children were out in their Sunday best to attend Linda's funeral, held on the fifth anniversary of her marriage to Chuck. The funeral was Baptist, simple, and well attended, like most services for the young. But it fell short, in some ways, of what Linda had wanted. She had requested that a popular country-and-western song, "I'll Go to My Grave Loving You," be sung at her service. Chuck could not arrange for it. Nor could he afford to give Linda's grave a headstone.

Wearing a sport coat of his own and a pair of pants borrowed from his father-in-law, Chuck showed up at the funeral to perform the tasks the widower's role required of him. But he was not comforted there. As soon as Linda was in the ground, he slunk off with Cathy, Dave, and a hospice volunteer—the people who he believed understood him best—for drinks in a Dallas restaurant where he and Linda had often dined. The four sat together for about two hours, reviewing the events that had brought them, a group of strangers, into family-like intimacy in the past weeks. By the time they left, all four were as clouded, and as comforted, as well-wishers at any whiskey wake.

Cathy Little, who had spent weeks preparing for Linda's death, found that the memory of her patient was, in many ways, a personal one. "Linda had always wanted to go to Colorado, and Chuck always said that if there had been any way he could have afforded it, even after Linda got sick, he would have taken her," Cathy says. "Well, after she died, I began to have the strangest new desire. I wanted to go to Colorado myself, as if for her, in her place. I haven't gone yet, but I will."

Chuck Mihlan has found solace hard to come by. For a few weeks after Linda's death he turned to drinking—hard. At Christmas he carried a small tree with an ornament on top to her grave. There he broke down and cried for the first time since hearing Linda's diagnosis. Social worker Dave Overton's objective advice to Chuck was to seek out the company of new women, but Chuck spurned that counsel. Instead, he turned for consolation to the Pentecostal faith of his adolescence. In a world where youth, family, medical science—and even the specialized services of a hospice—are not as extensive or protective as we would like, Chuck Mihlan is finding a way to cope with Linda's death: "You put your faith in God, you stay close to the one you love, and when she is gone, you pray that she is not alone."

Reavis, Neiman Fellow at Harvard, Cambridge, Massachusetts, 1990.
Photographer: Will Van Overbeek. Image courtesy of Will Van Overbeek.

Decades after publishing his early thoughts on labor issues in *The Rag* as a student at the University of Texas at Austin (*see* "The IWW: One Big Union and the Relevance of Anarchism"), Reavis returns in this article to labor conflicts, now as a reporter rather than an activist, with critical acumen that opens up more perspectives on such conflicts. This article first appeared in *Texas Monthly*, June 1986.

Unionbusters

It was still dark on the morning of January 2 when the meeting broke up at the union hiring hall in Houston's navigation district. Nearly 200 men, dressed in jeans, sweatshirts, and jackets, left the hall and piled into their cars and pickups as if to go to work. They crossed the Ship Channel at the Wayside overpass, then headed down Clinton Drive along the north side of the turning basin until they came to the road that leads to the public docks. Passing the guard station at the entrance, they continued for about a hundred yards to the foot of the S-shaped turnoff road, where they parked. Then in groups of 20 and 30 they wound their way on foot past the Strachan Shipping storage yard and behind the tin warehouses that face the water, emerging at the flat, open expanse of concrete at Public Dock 8. The men gathered in dark little knots there, in front of the *Samu*, a black ship that had moored during the night.

The *Samu* was carrying 6200 tons of Brazilian steel scheduled for unloading that morning. The men were members of the International Longshoremen's Association (ILA), and AFL-CIO union. ILA men had loaded and discharged all ships at Houston's public wharves for 50 years.

They had not been hired to unload the *Samu*, however. They had come to Dock 8 not to work, but, their leaders would say, to protest the awarding of the unloading contracts to Hank Milam and his company, Houston Stevedores, a firm that did not hire ILA men. But the massing of men on Dock 8, perhaps only because those men were longshoremen, gave another impression. It looked as if they had come to prevent the *Samu's* unloading.

Their protest was the sort of action that at best stood on the borders of, and at worst mocked, the law. A restraining order in force for months warned the ILA against "molesting, interfering with, threatening violence or bodily harm" to Milam and the men of Houston Stevedores. That morning ILA officers had called a special meeting at the union hall, taken a vote, and passed out picket signs. They had urged their men to go to Dock 8 to protest—clearly a legal activity—and had admonished them not to obstruct the performance of work, because obstruction was illegal. The vital question was, Would they obey? When Milam and his men set foot on Dock 8, would the unionists move aside?

Waiting for Milam's arrival beside the guard station were half a dozen of his foremen and about forty laborers he had contracted at $8 an hour from the International Brotherhood of Teamsters, which is not part of the AFL-CIO fold. One of Milam's foremen had driven down the turnoff road toward Dock 8 shortly after the protesting longshoremen arrived. Pickets blocked his path. The foreman was convinced that if he tried to take his crew to the dock the ILA men would attack. The situation promised to spark the biggest waterfront brawl in memory, and gave the foreman reason to hesitate. He held his crew at the guard station, a quarter mile from the docks.

What was brewing was a classic labor confrontation. It was also a drama that epitomized the plight of unions in both Texas and the United States. Unions had negotiated and mitigated the class struggle of the '30s and '40s. Even in Texas, a right-to-work state, they had organized refineries, auto and aircraft plants, meatpacking houses, and telephone companies. They had helped create a large, prosperous middle class in America, one that gave the nation political stability and insulation against radicalism. But now in the '80s, with hard times, a hostile White House, and employers poised for the kill, unions seemed to be in danger of extinction. One of the scripts being played out on Dock 8 called for longshoremen to reenact the bitter battles of their union's rise. Another called for them to surrender to the men like Hank Milam and economic forces that said that unions were of no use anymore.

Despite the unpopularity of unions in Texas, the ILA had gained a near monopoly as a supplier of labor to companies in the business of stevedoring, or the loading and unloading of ships. The union's dominance extended to 36 other ports on the Atlantic, the Gulf, and the Great Lakes. Time and again it had defended its role with a willingness to strike against management and to scrap with members of rival labor clans.

Hank Milam was a small-time Houston stevedore who had less than $20,000 worth of equipment and an office in a building whose chief attraction was a deferred-payment leasing plan. In the previous nine months, by underbidding stevedores who hired Houston's 2500 ILA members, Milam had won two dozen contracts for ships berthed in the navigation canal, but until the day the *Samu's* moored, he had never tried to set foot in the sanctum sanctorum of the ILA, the public docks. Alone, Milam was hardly a threat to the ILA's strength. But ever since 1981, when the nation's president had taken on the Professional Air Traffic Controllers Organization and flattened it, union members everywhere had been on the alert. Following PATCO's demise, unions like the United Auto Workers, whose employers faced Japanese competition, had been forced to forgo or postpone planned wage increases. Finally, even unions with no foreign competitors—the Amalgamated Transit Union, for example, which represented Greyhound bus drivers—had been pressed to give back the gains they had won. As the dollar grew stronger during 1984 and 1985, exports continued to decline, and because the oil market had gone to pot, Houston's maritime traffic was in a slump. Every time Milam underbid a unionized stevedore, managers of competing companies demanded that the ILA take cuts in work gang size, benefits, and pay. Milam's activities had inspired non-ILA stevedoring operations in other ports. The *Samu* had already called in Tampa Bay and New Orleans, and it had been unloaded in both places by non-ILA laborers. If Hank Milam wasn't stopped, Houston's ILA men believed, the union would be imperiled from Texas to Maine.

MILAM DECLARES WAR

Henry E. "Hank" Milam, 39, is a squat, pink-faced, blustering, brown-bearded businessman. He was born in Kentucky, where his mother is a union worker in a baked good factory. After earning a journalism degree in his home state during the late sixties, he served a tour of duty as an Army intelligence sergeant in Korea, then returned home to manage an uncle's trucking company. Through connections he made on a golf course, he arranged to become an executive for Dixie Stevedores in 1978, and he moved to Houston to begin the job. He was appalled by the double-digit wages that Dixie and other union stevedores grudgingly paid union men. "It didn't take a lot of intelligence to see that people were being hired all over town for six to eight dollars an hour," he says. "But nobody had the guts to bring them to the waterfront." In March 1984, with $2000 that he says he borrowed from a friend, Hank Milam founded Houston Stevedores. He hoped to get rich quick by outmaneuvering the ILA and its client companies.

The President's Commission on Organized Crime has cited the ILA as a union under mob influence, if only because leaders of some New York-New Jersey locals had personal business ties to suspected Mafiosi. But the specter of becoming the target of a Mafia hit team didn't deter Milam. He declared war by circulating brochures that offered stevedoring services at rates 25 to 50 percent below those of established ILA-employer firms. "I didn't have to base my prices on cost," boasts Milam. "I based them on competition." But shipping lines and cargo owners were reluctant to tempt the legendary and seemingly invincible ire of the ILA. During his first year of business, Milam won contracts to handle cargoes, but only on the ships that were safely berthed at out-of-the-way private docks. In April 1985 he bid to load 17,000 tons of grain onto a ship called the *Lone Star*. His bid, 55 cents a ton, was about a dime per ton below the bids of his competitors. The owners of the cargo gave Milam the stevedoring contract, even though the ship was to be loaded at the Cargill grain elevator, an important private facility just inside the Ship Channel waters traditionally worked by the ILA. On the morning when Milam and his crew, all nonunion men, arrived to load the *Lone Star*, about fifty ILA pickets stood at the entrance to the elevator. Milam's tactical and business sense told him that his men didn't need to charge the picket line. He hired a helicopter to fly them onto the ship and off, and he still made a handsome profit. Hank Milam had won his first skirmish with the ILA, and by the measure of Gulf maritime affairs, it was historic;

fifty years had passed since non-ILA men had loaded any grain ship in the region's deep-water ports.

Two months later eight employees of Houston Stevedores returned for another job at Cargill. They came to load the *General M. Macleef*, an Israeli vessel. No pickets awaited them, and they began work straightaway. But as they were eating lunch aboard the ship, at least fifty ILA men came up its gangplank. They cut the cables on Cargill's loading chutes and with punches, threats, and shoves ousted Milam's crew. The following day Milam went to court, asking for a restraining order against the ILA. When the damage at Cargill had been repaired, Milam's men returned under court protection to finish loading the *Macleef*. Completing the job was a second win over the ILA. The restraining order, Milam believed, was his biggest victory yet. It made clear to everyone that the law was on his side.

Milam then was ready to take his crusade to the public docks to unload the *Samu*. One of the lieutenants he chose for the operation was Grant Akers, 31, a burly, hard-drinking, black-haired foreman for Houston Stevedores and a veteran of the Cargill skirmish. Akers was committed to Milam's cause with the zeal of a convert—or a turncoat. For several years, though he never signed a union card, Grant worked out of the ILA hall on Harrisburg Boulevard, sharing in the jobs the union dispensed. He had come from a union family, which he says is now beset with "something kind of like a civil war." After Grant joined Milam's raiding party, his father, an ILA retiree, quit conversing with him. Grant's grandfather was Floyd Akers, an ILA member and veteran of the Gulf waterfront war of 1934–35. That conflict had first given everyone on the waterfront—union and management alike—a deserved reputation for brutality and lawlessness.

In two on-again, off-again strikes in 1934 and 1935, company guards, ILA men, non-ILA dockworkers, and assorted strikebreakers battled to exhaustion, time after time. In packs of a hundred, union men charged the Cotton Exchange building, where strikebreakers gathered every day to ride through Houston's navigation district—practically a shooting gallery—in armored trucks. When the vehicles were fired upon, guards fired back. Both sides ignored warnings from their foes and scoffed at court orders. When their partisans were arrested, both sides hired lawyers who helped even the guilty enter self-defense pleas. The strike spread east to Mobile, Alabama, and west to Corpus Christi and was violent everywhere. "We learned pretty quick that if you broke a scab's arm or leg, he wouldn't show up for work the next day, but if you only bloodied his nose, he'd go anyhow," recalls Gilbert Mers, 78, an ILA survivor of the strike. To ride herd on the feuding dockers, the City of Houston hired a special force of 41 policemen, and the port authority called in Frank Hamer, the former Texas Ranger credited with the ambush of Clyde Barrow and Bonnie Parker, as chief of security operations. Despite those measures, five of the strike's thirteen killings occurred in Houston.

THE FRUSTRATION OF YOUNG MEN

Calvin Akers, 33, stood with his fellow unionists at Dock 8 on the morning of January 2, waiting for his cousin Grant to come down the turnoff road with the other men from Houston Stevedores. Calvin is a tall, thin man with strawberry-blond hair. He kept an eye out for Grant because he had a bone to pick with him. Dock 8, Calvin thought, was the appropriate place. Like Grant, Calvin is a grandson of ILA progenitor Floyd Akers, but Calvin has remained steadfast to the family's union tradition. Calvin is grateful to the ILA; because of the union, he says, his and other longshoremen's families have been able to partake of the nation's prosperity. Calvin has not been able to vacation in Cozumel, as bachelor Grant has, nor have he and his wife, Michele, been able to travel outside of Texas more than once. They don't own a powerboat or a lake house or a Bronco or any of the other coveted totems of working-class life in East Texas. But they have been able to rear their three small children in a brick house in a wooded suburb, and thus far Michele hasn't had to seek work outside the home. Calvin believes that not only the union wage but also his willingness to work has made his relative security possible. "I'll take any job I can get, even sling bags of rice, and no matter how cold it is, I'll go to work because I know I've got to work to live," he says. Grant, Calvin maintains, was afraid of hard work long before he left the union fold. "Grant's problem is that he's just sorry. He didn't want to do the kind of hard work we have to do. He left the union because those other guys offered him a soft foreman's job."

The real difference between Calvin and Grant Akers has less to do with class, family loyalty, marital status, and an inclination to avoid work than with the fact of dates. Calvin quit high school at seventeen, went to work on the docks, and got married. The year was 1970. Grant, who is two years younger, finished high school, went to college for two years, then spent several years at an inland job. He didn't decide to become a longshoreman until 1978, eight years after Calvin had.

ILA jobs are meted out by seniority. The concrete floor of the union hall is divided by strips of yellow vinyl tape into large squares, each marked with a number corresponding to years of seniority. Each morning ILA crew foremen step out from behind a glassed-in enclosure onto the floor, clipboards in hand. The papers on the clipboards carry notations about the names, locations, and cargoes of ships and the number of longshoremen, winchmen, crane operators, and truck and lift drivers needed for each job. Men get to choose their jobs, but the picking starts at the high-seniority end of the floor, and the distance is great: Texas ILA workers average 49 years of age, and many have 25 years on the docks. In good times the seniority system is benign. Senior longshoremen claim the easiest jobs for themselves, but there are jobs for everyone. In bad times it becomes painfully evident to younger men that the union, which is supposed to wrest an equitable deal out of the waterfront's economic system, has imposed a hierarchy of its own. Plutocracy may rule the waterfront, but gerontocracy rules the union hall. Grant Akers began standing on a numbered square at the union hall during the oil-and-inflation-fueled boom of the late seventies. When the bust came and he hadn't advanced to a number high enough to be safe from the scarcity of jobs, his association with the ILA no longer made sense to him.

In 1979, 117 million tons of cargo moved through the Port of Houston. By 1983 that figure had dropped below 90 million tons, and by 1985 it was under 75 million. But tonnage figures don't include the weight of cargoes such as bulk petroleum—cargoes that longshoremen don't touch—and thus fail to show the depths of the depression that has descended on Houston's docks. General cargo movement and steel imports—big job sources for longshoremen—have fallen to half the levels of the late seventies. Grain exports have declined by nearly three quarters. The total number of man-hours worked by ILA members in the area from Lake Charles, Louisiana, to Brownsville dropped from a high of 9.9 million in 1980 to 5.2 million in 1985.

By 1985, when Grant Akers abandoned the ILA, he had accumulated enough working hours to qualify for only four years of seniority. His wages had fallen from about $25,000 a year during the boom to below

$18,000. Calvin, on the other hand, had fourteen years of seniority. In 1985, a year of job drought on the docks, he logged about 1800 hours at work, an average of 36 hours a week. His paychecks totaled $39,000. "I blame the union for not spreading out the work to low-seniority men," Grant says. "The trouble with Grant," Calvin says, "is that he didn't go to work even when he could have."

The frustration of young men like Grant Akers is traceable to the seniority system, but the loyalty and affluence of young men like Calvin Akers can be explained only by taking into account the paradoxical success of the ILA as a union. Senior ILA men owe their security and comfort to the threat of automation. The 1934–35 strikes established the union as a permanent fixture on the waterfront but did little to improve the longshoreman's daily life. The factor that made the ILA the dominant force in waterfront labor-management relations was the introduction in 1956 of the shipping container, an innovation that threatened to decimated the ranks of dockworkers. The specter presented the ILA with an unfeeling, visible foe, with a device for uniting its members in militant opposition to mutual extinction.

The shipping container is a metal box, originally eight by eight by twenty feet in size and now sometimes twice as long, in which fifteen to twenty tons of almost any cargo can be stored. Though the container came late to commodities, cotton—until recent years a big Texas export—offers telling evidence of the container's power. In 1935 and for more than thirty years afterward, cotton was stowed on ships by the sling method. Whereas Houston stevedores could load 200 bales of cotton per hour with slings, they can now load 1100 bales of containerized cotton in the same amount of time. Shorter loading times mean reduced hours for longshoremen, and reduced hours, when filtered through the ILA's seniority system, spell friction between younger and older union men.

Containerization gives rise to friction between unions too. Traditionally, dockside warehouse work is performed by members of the ILA. Inland warehousemen usually belong to the Teamsters. Since containers can be swiftly and cheaply transported inland, the work of packing and unpacking them, called stripping and stuffing, need not take place on the waterfront. The container makes the site of warehousing and unions a matter of choice. It pits ILA men against Teamsters, Teamsters against ILA men, wage scale against wage scale.

Because containers can be lifted by cranes from a ship directly onto a railroad car or a truck, containerization has created competition among ports. Today it is cheaper to import many cargoes through Atlantic ports for rail transfer to Houston than it is to bring them by ship across the Gulf. Containerization has made choosing a point of import or export less a question of geography than one of pure cost. It has pitted port against port.

Containers also exacerbated an accident of world economic history. The globe's developed nations lie along an east-west rather than a north-south axis. Containers and their cranes were expensive technological innovations; they came into use, first and foremost, in trade between industrial nations. The biggest U.S. container-handling ports are on the Atlantic and Pacific coasts, not on the Gulf, whose characteristic business has become the exchange of non-containerized mineral and agricultural goods with Third World nations. Containerization threatened Atlantic and Pacific dockers with the loss of their jobs to automation. It threatened Gulf dockers with a loss of their jobs as a result of the decline of their ports.

The ILA's fight against the effects of containerization began in 1964, when the union struck for the privilege of dictating the size of work gangs, a power formerly reserved for stevedores. The struggle continued throughout the sixties with efforts to impose a royalty on every container to be paid into pension funds and plans that guaranteed every ILA member a full, 52-week salary, regardless of the availability of work. The fight broke out again and again over demands that shippers hire ILA men and not the cheaper Teamsters for all stripping and stuffing performed within a fifty-mile radius of ports. Though Houston's ILA men had to back their demands with a 101-day strike in 1968 and 1969, the union was victorious from Maine to Texas. The ILA won because the Vietnam War, inflation, and a vigorous domestic economy boosted international trade and induced a labor shortage. It also won because management knew that the union's victory was Pyrrhic; containerization proceeded, and that meant that the future belonged to fewer longshoremen than had been needed in the past. The ILA's strategy was aimed at protecting the status of its veteran members, men like Calvin Akers, not at ensuring future jobs for men like his cousin Grant.

The triumphant ILA soon became arrogant. It won sixteen holidays for its members, including the birthday of Thomas W. "Teddy" Gleason, Sr., its longtime international president. It required stevedores to hire ILA winchmen and flagmen who weren't needed on every ship. Waterfront-wise seniors often signed up for two featherbed jobs at a time, collected two paychecks for a single eight-hour shift, and sometimes didn't even present themselves for work at either one. "Double-dipping," as the two-check scheme was called, disappeared during the late seventies, when waterfront payrolls were computerized, but another featherbedding tactic, double-barreling, continued. "I've seen times," Grant Akers says, "when there would be eight men sent to work on a vessel whose holds didn't have room for more than four. The extra four would just sit around, double-barreling, doing nothing. But they were still on the payroll." About a fifth of the 11,000 longshoremen from the Port of New York-New Jersey, largely a container port, are now living without working at all, on the basis of checks from the union's guaranteed annual income program. To finance the plan and an increasing pension burden, the ILA hiked the rates for employer-paid benefits. Today Calvin Akers earns $17 an hour in wages, but to hire him, employers must pay an additional $6.50 an hour into ILA benefit programs. When all labor expenses are tallied, including workmen's compensation and insurance, it costs about $35 an hour to employ an ILA longshoreman. Hank Milam brought his Teamsters to the public docks on January 2 for a total of $13.50 an hour.

A Prophet of Capitalism

It was nearly sunup when Hank Milam arrived at the guard station at the entrance to the docks. From where he stood, Milam could see the vehicles of protesters parked at the turnoff road, and from the reports of his foremen he knew that the ILA force was unruly and large. Hank Milam was caught off guard. He had expected a picket of perhaps fifty men, like the line he had crossed by helicopter at Cargill. But he had thought that his restraining order would prevent the unionists from massing or menacing; after all, hadn't it kept them from returning to the *General M. Macleef*? What Milam believed was that the union's leaders wouldn't allow their men to violate the terms of the restrainer order. By his lights he had won every encounter so far, and he intended to win again. If the gathering on Dock 8 wasn't legal, Milam reasoned, the wisest move was to have it dispersed by the police. With a foreman at his side, Hank

Milam went running to the Port Authority's security office, about half a mile from Dock 8.

The port's chief of security hadn't come to work yet. Milam telephoned him at home. When the security chief arrived at the turning basin, he decided that it was a problem bigger than his men could handle. He called the Houston Police Department, whose plainclothesmen did not arrive until about nine-thirty. The HPD officers, after sizing up the looming confrontation, decided that the men on Dock 8 could be dispersed, but only by riot cops. They promised to have a sufficient number of crowd-control officers gathered at the guard station by two o'clock.

The call for riot cops drew television, radio, and newspaper reporters to Dock 8. Men and women of the press, in sport coats and khaki pants and shirts, milled among the men in jeans, interviewing those who would talk. Hank Milam smothered his rage. He spoke in the politest terms. The confrontation over the *Samu*, he said, arouse because the ILA "would prefer to maintain a monopoly, and I would prefer to make the waterfront independent and competitive." He spoke expansively and in a spirit of nearly amused optimism, explaining his views on business and unions, frequently invoking the word "competition." In a way, the arrival of the press was Hank Milam's hour. It gave him a chance to take his crusade to the public, and it let him speak as a prophet of capitalism.

The morning passed slowly. In the early afternoon Milam and the reporters watched as longshoremen brazenly began laying a barricade. The ILA protesters took trucks, forklifts, and shipping containers from the Strachan Shipping storage yard and placed them across the turnoff road. Shortly after two, as they hastily finished their fortifications, nearly twenty blue-and-white patrol cars and several unmarked cars carrying plainclothesmen came int0 the turning basin and halted around the guard shack. Other patrol units took positions at both ends of Clinton Drive, sealing off the area. About four, black-suited, riot cops began adjusting their helmets with face shields, securing their canisters of tear gas, cinching the straps of their plastic shields. All of the elements for Milam's victory seemed to have come into place. He had a restraining order, which prohibited the ILA's interference. He had contracts authorizing him to unload the *Samu*. And with the arrival of the riot cops, he had enough troops to clear the protesters from Dock 8. There seemed to be no reason, in law or in tactics, why he should not proceed. Milam was ready to move in.

A Battle of Nerves

Hank Milam wasn't the only man with a stake in the *Samu* dispute. Shortly before the riot police pulled up at the guard station, Le Roy Bruner, president of ILA Local 24, still in his offices on Harrisburg Boulevard, decided that the protest on Dock 8 had gone on long enough. Burner, 49, is a short, brown-haired resident of Pasadena with the guarded demeanor and cautious mind of a deacon: he is a deacon, at Houston's Allendale Baptist Church. He is also the son of an ILA man and the nephew of no fewer than seven ILA men. As president of the union's local, Bruner had early that morning asked his members to protest the *Samu*'s arrival. But he hadn't asked them to prepare to fight. Bruner, as Milam had suspected, wasn't ready to go to jail. As he drove from the union hall down Wayside on his way to the docks, Bruner tried to find the words to ask his men to concede the *Samu* to the men in Hank Milam's crew.

This wasn't the first time he had gone to ask his men for concessions. It seemed to him as if he had been doing nothing else for months, ever since Milam's rise in Houston and the emergence of non-ILA stevedores in other ports. To help ILA employers compete with Milam and to help the Port of Houston compete with New Orleans, where union concessions had also been made, Bruner and the Houston ILA had agreed to substantial cuts in the size of work gangs. They had also made miscellaneous concessions on a day-by-day, ship-by-ship basis. But even their concessions had not stopped Milam's forward march.

Bruner's acceptance of the tactic of retreat was the mark of his brand of unionism. Fifty years ago, when most union men were brawling with guards and strikebreakers to establish their organizations, the labor movement was an evangelistic, nearly millenarian cause. Union spokesmen, by and large, were syndicalists, radicals, and socialists; some were thoroughly red. In the eyes of left-leaning leaders, union halls were not places of business but church houses, places to preach a doctrine and gather a congregation in pursuit of aims that lay not in the present but in a future, more egalitarian world. The union movement in those days, if it wasn't realistic, was at least inspired. Advocating concessions was akin to advocating sin.

The debate over radicalism had started early in the ILA. In the mid-thirties its West Coast locals, led by the leftist Harry Bridges, in defiance of instructions from the union's New York headquarters, had precipitated general strikes and participated in sympathy strikes, especially with seamen. By 1937 East-West relations in the ILA had grown so tense that Bridges bolted the ILA, establishing a new Pacific dockers organization, the International Longshoremen's and Warehousemen's Association. Stung by the loss of the union's western membership, ILA leaders helped spur the drive to purge radicals from labor's ranks, a process that began at the onset of World War II and was completed in the mid-fifties. The deradicalized union revived an older, more moderate school of union philosophy, sometimes called business unionism. Le Roy Bruner was a product of that outlook.

Advocates of business unionism regard themselves as salesmen of a commodity—labor—in an economy whose ground rules are essentially beyond question. The business unionist sees his role as one characterized by research, persuasion, mediation, and compromise; sincerity, brawn, and lawlessness are the weapons of the radical school. Le Roy Bruner, because he was a business unionist, did not feel that he had betrayed or failed his men by going to them with proposals for compromise. He was quite sure that the rise of Hank Milam was not because of evils inherent in the economic system but because of the decline in maritime commerce.

But advocating concessions was dangerous. Bruner had learned that union members are apt to distrust leaders who, like most ILA officers, live in relative ease. It had been more than ten years since Bruner had quit working "off the floor" to assume the white-collar duties of a local vice president. As the local's president for a year, he'd earned an annual salary of $93,000—enough to make him suspect. In November Le Roy Bruner will face reelection. He already knew that there were men in his local who believed that he hadn't taken a hard enough line with management. And Bruner had a special problem: his union critics included Teddy Gleason, the ILA's 85-year-old international president. In September, with Bruner's support, Gulf locals had voted to forgo a $1-an-hour raise for work on grain ships. But wages are one of the items in a seven-point master contract, uniform in all ILA ports, that is negotiated in New York by a committee of national union and management leaders. In late September, Gleason and the International, as the union's New York headquarters are called, had rebuked Gulf leaders for undermining the master contract and had ordered ILA locals to accept the wage hike, whether they wanted it or not. Thanks to hard times and Hank Milam, Le Roy Bruner had become a union leader who couldn't count on support from above or below.

Bruner arrived at Dock 8 about the time the riot squad was suiting up. He shook hands and chatted briefly with two or three union members, then stepped onto a pickup bed to address his men. In his measured, cautious deacon's style, he told them that the ILA had a long history and a big investment on the docks, and he talked about the virtues of lawfulness and the need to preserve a businesslike image. "You can say what you want," he told the protesters, "but we need to move out of here in a right way."

The men were skeptical. Not all of them believed, as Bruner insisted, that the union could hold its ground by resorting only to means within the law, such as protests and boycotts and strikes. Not all of them were inclined to take their leader's admonitions at face value either, because the docks are a special place. They are a place like the borderlands, where law and actuality are customarily different. On the border the most common attitude toward the law is expressed in a series of questions" "What is law? Who enforces it? How likely is enforcement?" They are places where men make deals and depart, usually before the long arm of the law can roll up its sleeve.

The longshoremen hesitated for another reason. Most of us work at jobs in which we have little reason to fear the future. We are sure that economic terms like "strong dollar" and "balance of trade" have some relation to us, but since we live in a workaday world largely made in the USA, we are not exactly sure what those terms might mean. Longshoremen are no better economists that the rest of us, yet every day when they go to the hiring hall, those vague economic terms determine whether longshoremen work today or hope for tomorrow. The strengthened dollar, more than any other factor, has minimized Houston's grain exports because Third World countries can't afford to buy our grain anymore. But longshoremen can't find consolation or a scapegoat in the economists' lexicon. Incorporeal demons can't be fought; cops and men like Hank Milam can. Most of the protesters on Dock 8 had decided not to square off with the riot squad—they figured that they would lose if they did—but they had also resolved not to back down until faced with an actual physical threat. They weren't ready to surrender in what thus far had been only a battle of nerves. "I figured that the police would settle the whole thing," Calvin Akers says, "but they hadn't come down there yet." When Bruner finished his speech, a few seconds passed in silence, and then someone in the crowd yelled, "We're staying right here, where are jobs are!" The cry was met with clinched-fist salutes and shouts of approval. A dismayed Le Roy Bruner looked into the cheering crowd, then stepped down from the pickup. He left Dock 8. The longshoremen stayed.

UNKNOWN FORCES

As Le Roy Bruner drove off from the turning basin on his way back to his office, he passed the guard station. Plainclothesmen were in a huddle there, talking to Hank Milam. They had taken a count of the protesters, about 260 of them in sight and perhaps as many as two dozen more lurking in the tin warehouse at Dock 9. Numerical superiority wasn't on the lawmen's side. "We were outnumbered and so was Milam, and the mood of those longshoremen was not conducive to peaceful resolution," recalls police captain M. C. Simmons. Furthermore, the lay of the land—the barricades and storage area, the scattered containers, and the open warehouse—was not favorable to a sweep. There were too many places for the dockers to duck out of the way. Any incident on the dock would take place in the full view of the press and might embarrass the whole waterfront business community, not to mention the police. The cops decided not to clear the dock. Milam was infuriated. "Had they wanted to go down there and bust up that situation, they could have," he grumbles. "But they were afraid of getting caught in the middle. They were afraid of public opinion." But Milam didn't argue with the policemen. He kept his composure. After all, he was on TV.

Outmanned, outsmarted, and feeling betrayed, Milam could think of only one recourse, to reach deeper into the recesses of law. All day he had been consulting his lawyer by telephone. Their plan was to rush into court, asking a judge to turn the restraining order into a permanent injunction—and to cite the ILA for contempt. Milam hoped to make his legal points before the end of the day and to unload the *Samu* by artificial lighting, if necessary, at night. About three, he left the turning basin for his attorney's office downtown.

Unknown to Milam and the men on Dock 8, forces outside of

Houston were already being brought to bear on the situation. In New Orleans shortly after midnight on January 2, Dale Revelle, 31, had gotten into his blue Ford mini-pickup and begun the drive to Texas. Revelle, a black-haired man who looks like a marine, is representative of the Commodity Ocean Transport Corporation of New York (COTCO), the firm that managed the *Samu*. Revelle's purpose in coming to Houston was to see that the ship's loading was accomplished quickly, because an idle ship meant idle capital. Minutes after his arrival in Houston at about sunup, he and another ship's agent had crossed the ILA's picket line, boarded the *Samu* to confer with its captain, and as they drove away, passed through a hail of bottles and junk. The ILA men at Dock 8 apparently were blaming the ship's agents too for their troubles with Milam and the Teamsters.

Revelle felt as if he and the owners of the *Samu* were bystanders to the Dock 8 conflict and its victims. In the liner trade, ship owners usually select stevedores. But the *Samu* was a tramper, and most of its cargo was being carried under "free in and out" contracts that left stevedore selection to cargo owners, agents, and brokers. He wanted to see that the *Samu* got a quick turnaround, and the face-off at Dock 8 was causing delay. The rowdiness Revelle had seen that morning convinced him that if the ILA didn't win the battle for the *Samu*, bloodshed—and more delay—were inevitable. He had gone to the waterfront offices of a Houston stevedore to use a phone, and from there he had reported his observations to COTCO's New York chieftains. Revelle expected them to persuade the owners and agents of the *Samu*'s cargo to back away from their contracts with Milam.

Control from the offices in New York has long been a fact of Gulf waterfront life. Most of the nation's container companies, shipping lines, and export-import handlers are based there. The classic case of intervention from New York dates back, as does so much else on the Houston waterfront, to the 1934-35 strikes. When New York's ILA locals, who were not on strike, voted to boycott the ships of any lines that had not come to terms with the union in the Gulf, the threat brought immediate results. Not being able to do business in Houston was a minor inconvenience to most lines, but not being able to do business in New York was cause for crisis. The New York home offices of the nation's shipping firms sent telegrams to their Houston affiliates, ordering capitulation to the ILA and ending the dispute.

While waiting in the offices of Houston Stevedore's Doyle Varner, for orders from New York, Dale Revelle also called Houston ILA leaders to invite them for a talk. By late afternoon more than half a dozen, including Le Roy Bruner, were gathered in Varner's offices for the meeting with Revelle. The union leaders fidgeted on the couch or paced about uneasily because they were accustomed to regarding their host not as a friend or partner who deserved to be privy to their business talks, but as an opponent and employer. Varner, 57, is a big, silver-haired man, an executive since 1958, and now head of Houston-based Empire-United stevedoring firm, one of the biggest ILA employers on the Gulf. Varner had allowed Revelle to use his office out of courtesy, and his attitude toward the COTCO agent's talks with the union was one of aloof neutrality.

Varner recognized the desperation of Bruner and other ILA leaders to score a victory on Dock 8, but his sympathies weren't easily swayed. He felt in many ways as if the ILA had invited trouble by abusing its contracts and clout. On the other hand, Varner recognized an opportunity to squeeze one-time concessions and maybe long-term goodwill out of the ILA—something a stevedore needs whenever a ship comes in.

When the union men asked him to be ready to discharge the *Samu*, Varner demurred. The proposition wasn't promising, he said, because at least two of the cargo owners and brokers had contracted with Milam at rates that a stevedore employing ILA men couldn't match. If he was going to arrange for the unloading of the *Samu*, Varner said, the ILA would have to make concessions for the job. His wish was granted on the spot.

About sundown Dale Revelle, now safely accompanied by Le Roy Bruner, again boarded the *Samu*, this time to look over its cargo with an eye to unloading arrangements. While the two men were in the hold of the ship, word reached them from New York that the cargo owners and brokers had agreed to bolt their contracts with Milam. Le Roy Bruner leaped to the deck of the *Samu*, then scurried down its gangplank. Standing on a level with the men on the dock and under the lights of television camera crew, he announced the ILA's victory. "Why did the cargo owners change their minds?" a reporter asked him. Bruner hesitated in the prudent manner of a deacon who's been asked to confess his sins and then with the slyness of a politician quipped, "I guess you could say that they decided that in the long run we would do the best job." The ILA men on Dock 8 roared with laughter. Their president, they decided, was a hero after all. He had won the day and had made a fool of the press. Anybody on the waterfront knew that the cargo owners and brokers had changed their minds not because the ILA was more efficient than Milam's men but because its numbers were greater and its men were bolder. Unlike the crew from Houston Stevedores, the ILA men knew how to prepare for a fight.

THE RULE OF LAW

Hank Milam's defeat at Dock 8 on January 2 was not nearly so bitter as it seemed. In a way, Milam had won: the terms of his surrender were so sweet as to be attractive. The broker for the bulk of the *Samu*'s cargo had paid Milam in advance. Milam had contracted to unload most of the ship's steel at the rate of $10 a ton. When Doyle Varner telephoned Milam's house to tell him that the cargo was reassigned, Milam stood his ground. "I told him," he says, "that I was willing to subcontract the job to him, but at six dollars a ton," a figure below Varner's profitability floor, even with ILA concessions. Varner, who says he never does anything out of the goodness of his heart, agreed to take the cargo to win goodwill from the ILA.

The public notice generated by Milam's scrapes with the ILA, on the docks and in court, was good advertising. In some quarters, he became a folk hero, the entrepreneur of the hour. Milam's office was deluged with inquiries and congratulations from cargo receivers, some from as far away as New England. Although several ships he had contracted backed away from using his services after the brouhaha on Dock 8, Hank Milam's chief business problem became not winning contracts but a shortage of capital for expansion. In early February Milam opened a Houston warehouse, putting non-ILA men to work stripping and stuffing the containers that passed through.

He also began operations in New Orleans and Mobile, and in March he opened offices in both ports. With supervisors from Houston and locally recruited Teamsters, his company unloaded a ship on the public docks in New Orleans—unthinkably, on Mardi Gras, and ILA holiday. In late March, Milam announced plans—which so startled the maritime shipping community that the story was carried on the front page of the

Journal of Commerce, the shipping industry's daily—to begin doing business in the port of New York-New Jersey, the hallowed ground of the International. Two months after he lost the *Samu*, Hank Milam could boast that he had become the biggest non-ILA stevedore in the nation. The honor was a small one, but it took on new significance with every passing week. The organization of the non-ILA stevedores that Milam and his cohorts had inaugurated in late 1985 had by the spring of this year claimed a total of 22 public affiliates and an undisclosed number of covert members. Waterfront businessmen speculated that the closet membership was an indication that companies bound by ILA contracts were about to father secretly owned subsidiaries that would hire non-ILA longshoremen. "Double-breasting," a tactic used in the construction industry to foil government minority hiring and prevailing wage rules, was on the agenda for companies that work the docks.

Milam had also sparked an aboveboard counterrevolution. On January 24 the West Gulf Maritime Association announced its refusal to join other employer groups in new ILA master contract talks. Within two weeks, employers' associations in New Orleans, Mobile, and eastern Florida joined the boycott. By the end of February only four management groups remained in the dozen-member committee that had negotiated previous master contracts, and even they postponed the opening of contract talks.

In early April, as the whole maritime industry watched, Houston's ILA longshoremen and negotiators for the WGMA began their own round of talks. On April 9, while the ILA and the WGMA were cooking up their new deal, Milam's men again challenged the ILA on the public docks. A grain barge, the *Producer*, was pushed into port by a tugboat out of New Orleans. The barge was to be loaded at Dock 14, site of a public grain elevator, with wheat bound for Haiti. On the morning of April 9, policemen escorted Hank Milam's men to work, barricaded the dock, and encircled the ship with as many as fifty patrol cars. Nobody but cops and Milam's men reached the barge—except for two representatives of Doyle Varner's company, Empire-United. Varner's men offered the tug's captain a competitive loading rate; he spurned them. Half a dozen ILA picket stood by, at a safe and legal distance, for three days while the *Producer* took on its cargo. Milam's men completed their work, and the barge was towed out of port without incident.

Milam had won, and he had won on ILA turf—the public docks. Ten days later, on April 21, Houston's ILA men voted to accept what amounted to a new contract, much of it effective immediately, which granted such large concessions that it was hailed as a "landmark" contract; the base wage was reduced to $14 an hour. The locals were ready to compete with Milam, but there was the question of whether the International would approve the contract or whether it would ask the ILA rank and file to vote for a strike in the fall. And there was the still larger question of whether the union would survive.

Like most other American unions, the ILA is now on the defensive. Yet it is important to recall that strong organizations like the ILA were built not on the general conditions for labor but as a defense against specific threats, such as the container. The evangelistic fervor of the union movement, without which many participants thought unions could not survive, has been gone for thirty years. Yet unions endure despite declines, as churches have endured. Billy Sunday died, but he has been superseded by evangelists of the electronic church, and nothing stands in the way of a future revival of unionism.

For the ILA, that revival may come this fall, when a national ILA referendum could force Houston's union longshoremen out on strike whether they want it or not. If a strike comes, Hank Milam will replace the shipping container as the inspiration for change. Union and management leaders are predicting that a strike won't happen, but then they always do. Prudent, self-interested men don't predict strikes or hurricanes. Like mayors of coastal tourist towns who don't want to speculate about the possibility of hurricanes, union and management men don't speculate about strikes. But strikes and hurricanes do happen, and on the waterfront both are potentially deadly and damaging.

The most likely beneficiaries of a fall ILA strike—in the short run anyhow—are non-ILA stevedores like Hank Milam. Most of them are already making preparations to get rich quick. They have made money by underbidding competitors who hire workers from the ILA, and now they are ready to make their fortunes when those employers are struck by the ILA. When union and management disagree, entrepreneurs like Hank Milam make bucks.

The 1990s

The two chapters included here from *The Ashes of Waco: An Investigation,* first published in 1995 by Simon & Schuster, provide the core of Reavis's argument. Contradicting government accounts and mainstream media, Reavis makes the case that the raid, siege, and ultimate destruction of the Branch Davidians' Mount Carmel Center near Waco, Texas—by the Bureau of Alcohol, Tobacco and Firearms (ATF) and the FBI—were unjustified and belligerent. In doing so he contextualizes David Koresh as a church leader of an established religious community, in contradiction to government accounts and mainstream media coverage.

Selections from *The Ashes of Waco: An Investigation*

CHAPTER 8: POOR GEORGE

> My father told me one month before he died, that I was the Man Whose Name is the Branch and that it was my responsibility to rebuild the temple in Jerusalem just like Solomon was to do so at the death of his father.
>
> —*George Roden*

When Vernon Howell [aka David Koresh] first came to Mt. Carmel, he was not a ready pick for leadership. He had memorized the Bible, perhaps, and had developed some theology of his own, but he did not show the aggressiveness that distinguishes those people who rise in group hierarchies. He would have to change the group before it could follow him. His ascension would require the Living Waters Branch to reorganize, and to adopt a new and developing theology to which only Howell had the keys. As things turned out, it also required the faithful, and at least one doubter, David Jones, to pass through a virtual birth of fire, a paramilitary campaign in which—foreshadowing 1993—Howell and his followers would raid the property, displacing the one who claimed to rule as messiah there. In the wake of the gunfight, Howell and his closest associates, like the survivors of the 1993 inferno, would face a jury on attempted murder charges. The young preacher and his comrades-in-arms won that fight, their first battle for Mt. Carmel, which was among the reasons why they didn't flinch when Koresh pegged Robert Rodriguez as a cop.

If Vernon Howell had been living in a fog during his first months at Mt. Carmel in 1981, his potential had not escaped the eye of one if its denizens, George Roden, Lois's barrel-chested, bearded, forty-three-year-old son. George had a future in mind for himself, and he instinctively feared that Howell would spoil it. Roden believed, on scriptural grounds, that when his mother died (she was not yet dead, or even ailing), he should take over leadership of the Branch.

Almost nobody bought George's message for a basketful of reasons. He was not a decorous leader, and most people referred to him, almost derisively, as "Poor George." The hulking, would-be heir was sorely afflicted. "You'd be standing there talking to him, and he'd all of a suddenly twitch and spit in your face," David Koresh [Howell] recalled. "Not that he meant it. He just couldn't control it. He would be sitting there and all of a sudden slam his hand down on the table and he'd—the soup would go everywhere. And your, your plate would fly off, you know. He couldn't control it."

Not even Lois supported her son's bid. Looking for a relief preacher, two years after Howell came into the Living Waters Branch she began letting him spell her at the pulpit. Howell came in and out of Mt. Carmel, leaving, he claimed, to take construction jobs in the cities, and coming back when he was flush. But during weeks when he stayed at Mt. Carmel followers saw him visit Lois's quarters at night. He told people that his visits were for private discussions of the theological issues that he would bring to his sermons.

Vernon would later confess that for several months in 1983 he'd also bedded Lois, in an attempt, inspired by a vision, to fulfill the scriptures (Isa 8:3), "And I went unto the prophetess; and she conceived, and bare a son." That Lois was years past menopause was no obstacle, Howell insisted: the Bible says (Gen 17:21) that thanks to God's intervention, at the age of ninety, Sarah, the mother of Israel, had borne Abraham a son.

Some detractors who did not distinguish between the imperatives of custom and those of Holy Writ—which celebrates several spring/autumn marriages—had been appalled by the forty-year difference in Lois and Vernon's ages. Others were aghast at their unwed status. George Roden, never to be outdone, claimed that his mother had been raped. Frustrated and politically jealous, he began issuing tracts in which he predicted Howell's demise.

"There are three men who represent Lucifer today," he'd written in a bulletin to the Branch. "That is because Lucifer has three sets of vocal cords. First voice—public relations, Second voice—printed word, Third voice—music. Perry Jones, Clive Doyle, and Vernon Howell in that order. . . . But they cannot win for they are defeated foes, Jesus and the Antitypical Immanuel George Roden have conquered and their doom is certain," he prophesied. Roden also assailed Howell for practicing cunnilingus, which, according to Roden, was a diabolical act.

In the spring of 1984, as tension rose, Howell and his followers left Mt. Carmel for the Palestine, Texas, encampment. David Jones was at the time living in his house trailer in Waco, steadfast in his refusal to return to the fold. But he was not indifferent to the event. His parents and in-laws, all in their fifties, were now living among the school buses, tents, and plywood shacks of the raw camp. He thought that they deserved better. "Mt. Carmel was his parents' home. That's all they ever had," Jones's ex-wife Kathy explains. Jones blamed George Roden—not Vernon Howell—for his parents' loss, because as far as he could see, it was obvious that Roden was nuts. Besides, Howell was now a part of David Jones's family.

Shortly before the exodus to Palestine, Howell had become Jones's brother-in-law by marrying Jones's sister, Rachel, who was only fourteen at the time. The marriage was made with the approval of her parents, it was legal, and in the biblically intensive circles of the Branch, nobody had to point out that Rachel was older than the Blessed Virgin Mary when she wed old man Joseph.

Howell's marriage and exodus vexed Lois Roden, who was still formally the leader of the Branch. For months she traveled back and forth from Palestine to Mt. Carmel, hoping to salvage the organization. But the dispute was still unresolved when she died in November 1986. By this time, George Roden was practically alone at Mt. Carmel; most people had left in fear of him.

Desperate to justify his claims to leadership George looked for a way to demonstrate that God was on his side. He dug up the casket of

Anna Hughes, a one-armed believer who had been buried at New Mt. Carmel nearly two decades earlier. The "Antitypical Immanuel" then issued a challenge: Whoever could raise Anna from the dead, Roden proposed, would be revealed as the rightful leader of the Branch. "Not today, George," Howell told him when Roden threw down the gauntlet.

Seeing an opportunity to dislodge Roden, Howell consulted with Douglas Wayne Martin, a lawyer who had joined the Palestine camp. Martin pointed out that it's illegal to disinter people in Texas without a permit; "corpse abuse," he called it. Howell then went to Waco to pay a visit to David Jones. He explained to the doubter that if George could be ousted, Jones's parents could return. The two went together to the McClennan County sheriff's office to demand that Roden be arrested. Jones told the sheriff's department that he was concerned on behalf of the memory of a brother who was buried there: If Roden could dig up one corpse, he might dig up others, he argued. But as Howell and Jones told the story, the department's deputies weren't impressed. On the advice of then-prosecutor Denise Wilkerson, they demanded a photo of the crime.

Sam Jones, a younger brother of David Jones, was one of the stragglers living at Mt. Carmel. He had even helped George Roden—in whom he didn't believe—dig up the casket of Anna Hughes, or so his brother thought. Howell wanted to persuade Sam to take the pictures he needed, but Howell could not set foot on the property—Roden had already fired on a busload of visitors from Palestine—and Sam couldn't be reached by telephone. David Jones was the solution. He persuaded his brother Sam to take photos of the casket. Howell provided an Instamatic for doing the job.

The photographer took a half-dozen shots, and when his pictures were ready David Jones and Vernon Howell went back to the sheriff's office to present the evidence. But the photographs didn't satisfy the lawmen. Sure enough, they showed a casket draped in an Israeli flag. But the deputies wanted a picture of a body, or bones. And getting a new photo didn't promise to be easy.

A few days after he'd taken the pictures, Sam Jones had gotten into a wrangle with Poor George, and had moved away. His departure meant that if Howell wanted new photos, he'd have to sneak onto the property, a perilous prospect because Roden had taken to toting an Uzi semi-automatic. "Be careful, boys, there's some rough customers out there," a deputy named Elijah had warned Jones and Howell on their last visit to the sheriff's office.

For a month, Howell planned a paramilitary action, either to obtain the photo, or to oust Roden, or both. He enlisted David Jones and seven disciples from Palestine, and went to Kmart and a hardware store to equip them for a raid. Because it was cold, Howell bought insulated deer hunter's coveralls for his army. He also bought an assortment of shotguns and small-caliber rifles, flashlights, and face paint. Just after midnight on November 2, 1987, the nine of them jumped out of a van on EE Ranch Road and crawled into the brushland around Mt. Carmel, sending one of the group, Mark Wendell, forward with a camera. When he came to the chapel building where Roden had kept the casket, Wendell found that it was gone. As he was returning to his comrades-in-hiding, Roden's dogs began howling and George emerged with his Uzi. The raiders decided to hunker down for the night.

The following day, they eased onto the property and began peeking into buildings, looking for Anna's casket. After they'd entered one of two of the structures, a "gentile," or non-religious woman who was living on the property—Koresh claimed that she was wearing short shorts and was bare-breasted at the time—spotted the group and immediately denounced them to Roden. The invaders promptly faced his Uzi again. Vernon's little army was trading shots with the Antitypical Immanuel when the sheriff's department came over the hill. Wendell, who must have seen them first, ran into the brush behind Mt. Carmel and wasn't discovered. But David Jones, Vernon Howell, and the others were nabbed. One of the arresting officers was a deputy named Bill Thorn, whom Jones greeted. "David, what are *you* doing here?" Thorn had asked, like Peeler, unable to place a postman in a shoot-out scene.

Howell best told the story of what happened after they got to jail. The group spent the first night in a holding cell. The following afternoon, deputies escorted them to a hallway, then slammed the bars behind them. "So, there's guys in there, boy, and I'm talking about they, they are like tough-looking guys," Howell said. "They're like, all like, you know, side by side down this hallway, this run. And they're going, 'Yeah, yeah, come on'—some black guys, 'Come on down here, we all, we all done cleared out a room just for you guys.' . . . And they treated us with such respect! And they treated us with such decency! And they were kind of standing back from us, you know?

"Well, we didn't know—we thought . . . we was going to get in there and get a lot of trouble, right? But these guys were just so nice. What had happened was . . . they had played on the news that eight PLO terrorists had assaulted Mt. Carmel Center."

The confusion, Howell liked to explain, came about because one of his Christian commandos was the young Hawaiian who would later become his gun show partner, Paul Fatta. Somebody (newsman or jailbird) had mistaken his name for Al-Fattah. Either that, or—heaven forbid!—their jailbirds had believed a *Waco Tribune* report in which Roden described the assault as a "jihad" and Howell's army as a branch of the then much-feared Palestine Liberation Organization.

Roden had been slightly injured, a bullet to the thumb. Howell and his captured commandos were charged with attempted murder, a felony. Howell and Fatta each paid $5,000 to a bondsman, and David Jones, fearful of losing his postal job, paid up, too. But when he reported for work, he learned that until the felony charge was cleared, he was suspended, and a petition people along his route circulated on his behalf couldn't change that. For the next six months, while five of his comrades remained in jail, David Jones became a roofer, a framer, and a handyman. "He did anything he could do to pay our bills," ex-wife Kathy says.

Then came the trial, which dragged on for ten days in April 1988. Again, it was Howell who told the best stories about the affair. "The district attorney would . . . hire these professional analysts to analyze certain things. . . . One guy was a professional in regards to paramilitary weapons and tactics. . . . So . . . they presented the jury some baling wire," he began. "And what happened was that Shabazz"—El Hadi Shabazz, the lead prosecutor—"stands in front of the jury and says. . . . 'Now what was this used for do you think? What was this intended for?'. . . And the guy goes on to explain that in certain paramilitary groups such a wire is used for strangling. . . . So the guy gets up . . . walks down in front of the jury, grabs the wire and puts it around Shabazz's neck, and—you know, this is, this is extreme, right? And so the jury . . . their eyes are getting real big, right?

"And so anyway," the story continued, "they also had some, a red piece of shirt, several pieces of red checkered shirt there. And Shabazz is saying, 'Now what might this possibly be used for?' And he says, 'Well . . . such things or items can be used as, as signaling devices, things to signal a, a movement or a, a preconceived intention, you know.' And so the jury is like well, wow, you know, all these neat paraphernalias here.

"And so what happened at that time is that Paul Fatta is there on the, on the stand, and Shabazz is asking him. He says, 'Well, Mr. Fatta, is it not true that, that you were using these things for signaling devices? Isn't that the way you communicated to everybody in regards to the way you'd move on the property, and, you know, you would flank Mr. Roden and, and, and kill him?' And he goes, 'No, sir, that is not true.' He goes, 'Well, just what is the truth about this then?' And Paul goes, 'Well, do you really want to know?'. . . And Shabazz goes, 'Oh, yes, I would like to know.' And he goes—Paul goes—'Toilet paper.' And Shabazz looks at him kind of funny. He goes, 'Would you explain that?' And Paul says, 'We were down at the barn, we'd been out all night. Some of the guys needed to relieve themselves and all we found down there was an old shirt. So we tore the shirt up and we gave it to different guys in case they had to relieve themselves for toilet paper.'"

The defense countered the charge that the raiders had carried garrotes with the testimony of Stan Sylvia, fifty, a New Englander who was the shortest and most muscular of the group of accused murderers. Sylvia demonstrated for the jury that the coveralls Howell had bought for him were four to five inches too long for his legs. Dressing in the garment for the jury, Sylvia "pulled up the bottoms of the pants . . . tucked them over and wrapped the wire around and around them to make them short so they wouldn't fall down below his shoes."

The government did not call George Roden as a witness. Defense attorney Gary Coker called him instead. On the stand, the cunnilingus foe admitted that he *had* tried to resurrect one-armed Anna, and that he sometimes closed prayers at Mt. Carmel with the words, "In the name of George B. Roden, amen."

That was enough for the jury. It acquitted the seven commandos and balked at any verdict regarding Howell. The case went down as a victory for the defendants, attorney Coker told the *Waco Tribune*, because "our witnesses are nice people with no criminal record who don't believe they're Jesus Christ."

Not only did the criminal trial turn against Roden and the state, but other events did, too. Nobody had paid taxes on the Mt. Carmel property for nineteen years, the assessments had accumulated a value of $62,000, and in mid-1987, the county had taken steps to exercise its lien. Poor George had over the past five years filed some fifty pro se civil suits, demanding a tax exemption on the Mr. Carmel acreage, and in one of them, filed shortly before the raid, he'd asked, "Who does the Texas Supreme Court think they are, 'God'?" Roden's brief answered the question by saying that "If you think your [*sic*] God then God would have taken the poor into account but you sons of bitches have your goddamn click [*sic*] to take care of. . . . You can't afford to allow the poor to get any benefit or you might loose [*sic*] your ass in the process. . . . Maybe God will make it up to you in the end and send you herpes and AIDS then seven last plagues and shove them up you goddamn bastards asses."

While George was assailing the judiciary, he was living at Mt. Carmel in violation of a 1979 restraining order that had never been rescinded—or forgotten. On March 23, 1988, about two weeks before the trial began, a federal judge sentenced him to six months in jail for contempt of court. That same day, a Waco State solon imposed the 1979 injunction ordering Roden not to return to Mt. Carmel. Poor George said that his persecution was obviously part of a Communist conspiracy, directed by the comrade Pope.

Taking advantage of Roden's myriad troubles, Howell's supporters rushed to pay the taxes owed upon the property, and to secure an order authorizing their return. When they moved back to Mt. Carmel in April 1988, they found Anna Hughes resting in her coffin in a mechanic's shed, and the roofs of their former quarters caving in from neglect. "Hogs wouldn't even go in my home," Bob Kendrick told the *Waco Tribune*. "But I'm glad to be back. I lived there 21 years. It's home."

Soon after his release, George Roden ceased to trouble Howell's followers entirely. He moved to Odessa, Texas, where in 1989 the Antitypical Immanuel hacked an ostensible follower to death because, Roden reportedly said, "I am a Jew and he said that he was a Nazi, and I felt threatened." George Roden remains in a hospital for the insane, reportedly giving interviews to reporters in exchange for black Stetson hats.

That first persecution, David Koresh had often told David Jones, showed that behind everything, God had a plan. True Christianity had been purified by the thinning of its ranks—Poor George was out of the picture, anyway—and the government's plot to imprison the raiders had been undone.

FROM CHAPTER 14: THE GOVERNMENT'S FLYING MACHINES

> Before a standing army can rule the people must be disarmed.
>
> —*Noah Webster, 1777*

> We use the military all the time, as does the FBI, Secret Service and other federal agencies.
>
> —*Daniel Hartnett, ATF executive*

If David Koresh's Bible interpretations were the stuff of fantasy, they met their match in the bold, flying leap that the ATF took at justice on February 28. Both Koresh's procreative activities and the ATF raid required their actors to spring high and long from the texts that justified their pronouncements and deeds. For the ATF, the foundational document analogous to Holy Writ was the United States Constitution and its reams of derivative law, counterparts to the writings of White, Houteff, and the Rodens [The former leaders of the Branch Davidians].

In a 1994 groundbreaking study of the historical background to the Constitution, published by Harvard University Press, Professor Joyce Lee Malcolm of Boston-area Bentley College—certainly not a hotbed of redneck mischief—provides evidence that the American legal tradition for untrammeled gun ownership dates back to the Plymouth Colony. In 1623, Plymouth's elders promulgated a measure ordering that:

> every freeman or other inhabitant of this colony provide for himselfe & each under him able to beare arms a sufficient musket & other serviceable peece for war . . . with what speede may be."

Most colonial enactments regarding firearms, Malcolm discovered, dealt with the need for arms, not their ill effects, in part because gun ownership was established as a right in England long before the American Revolution began.

American colonial and Revolutionary leaders, chaffed by the impositions of the British Army, generally took a reluctant view of standing armies. "Armies in time of peace are allowed on all hands to be an evil," James Madison noted. "I am for relying, for internal defence, on our militia solely, till actual invasion," wrote Thomas Jefferson. The preference of most of the American Founding Fathers was for a general, or universal militia, staffed by all able-bodied, free, adult male citizens, not selected by authorities, and called to service only in times of emergency. The Fathers were of course aware that in real life most citizens used their guns for private, not militia purposes. But like the English commentator William Blackstone, they argued that gun ownership was a part of a "natural right of resistance and self preservation."

Revolutionary-era preoccupation with the tyrannical potential of a standing army, and the liberating potential of universal gun ownership, made itself manifest in the Second Amendment, which reads: "A well regulated Militia being necessary to the security of a free State, the right of the people to keep and bear Arms, shall not be infringed."

The leading Constitutional argument for gun control renders the Bill of Rights as authorizing gun ownership by members of police forces, the army, and a "select militia," the National Guard—but not by the citizenry at large. But the framers of the Bill of Rights, Malcolm points out, rejected a proposal that the words "for the common defense" follow "to keep and bear Arms," precisely because they wanted to protect the private use of firearms. If control advocates are right, she says, then the Second Amendment granted gun ownership only to government entities, and not, as its language says, to "the people" as a whole. The Bill also grants freedom of speech and assembly to "the people," and Articles IV, IX, and X grant other rights to "the people"—not merely to those associated with military or police agencies.

"The Second Amendment was meant to accomplish two distinct goals, each perceived as crucial to the maintenance of liberty," Malcolm states. "First, it was meant to guarantee the individual's right to have arms for self-defense and self-preservation. Such an individual right was the legacy of the English Bill of Rights. . . . These privately owned arms were meant to serve a larger purpose as well . . . when, as Blackstone phrased it, 'the sanctions of society and laws are found insufficient to restrain the violence of oppression,' these private weapons would afford the people the means to vindicate their liberties.

"If the government and people in their wisdom come to the conclusion that . . . such a right does more harm than good," Professor Malcolm cautions, "then amendment is the course that should be followed. . . . To ignore all evidence regarding the meaning and intent of one of those rights included in the Bill of Rights is to create the most dangerous precedent, one whose consequences could . . . endanger the fabric of liberty."

If the findings of Professor Malcolm and other Constitutional scholars are trustworthy, the laws that the ATF sought to enforce at Mt. Carmel on February 28 were unconstitutional. But in an atmosphere in which an American president would, only months afterwards, call for a new wave of gun controls, the ATF was determined to enforce the laws that are now on the books.

The ATF did not act alone. Instead, the agency called upon military forces for support, bringing into play the historically delicate issue of the use of standing armies. As with the gun-control question, legal and historical scholars find that today's superfice of law is a slippery slide of citizen rights.

The statue governing the deployment of American soldiers against the civilian population is the Posse Comitatus Act, adopted by Congress in 1878. In its present form, the law imposes fines and prison terms upon "Whoever . . . willfully uses any part of the Army or the Air Force . . . to execute the laws . . ." In everyday terms, the act denies the American military the authority to conduct searches and seizures, or to arrest a citizen on criminal charges. DEA agents can riffle our desks, policemen can issue traffic tickets; soldiers can't.

The reasoning behind the law, a federal appeals court found in 1975, is that "It is the nature of their primary mission that military personnel must be trained to operate under circumstances where the protection of constitutional freedoms cannot receive the consideration needed . . ." It is the duty of soldiers to intimidate, maim, and kill declared enemies of the nation. Since the police are given authority not over national enemies, but over their statutory peers, more restrained behavior is expected of them.

The Posse Comitatus Act was originally drafted to prevent federal troops from supervising elections in the Reconstruction South. Its first apparent violation in modern times came during the fifties and sixties, when National Guard troops were dispatched to guard integrated schools, to guard demonstrators, and to restore order in riotous streets. Military actions like those were justified, the courts said, because "Congress intended to make unlawful the direct active participation of federal military troops in law enforcement activities; Congress did not intend to make unlawful the involvement of federal troops in a passive role in fulfilling law enforcement activities."

Along the way, the Coast Guard was exempted from the provisions of Posse Comitatus, and in 1981, Congress, in a sterling contribution to the nation's longest-running and most popular conflict, the Drug War, authorized the military to participate in interdiction efforts. When victory still didn't come, and in response to the designation of drug trafficking as a national security threat by Defense Secretary Richard Cheney, in 1989 Congress passed new legislation, authorizing military forces to train civilian drug warriors.

In the legal goulash created by such enactments and findings, all that remains clear is that the military may not take an "active" role in civilian law enforcement, except where drug interdiction is involved. Its "passive" role can be quite comprehensive. Military personnel can provide a civilian lawman with a rifle, teach him how to use it, supply him with ammunition, even load his weapon for him. But because of the wishes of the Founding Fathers and the authors of the Posse Comitatus Act, soldiers can't pull the trigger.

Just what the military can and can't do, and when, is of course, subject to interpretation. Governor Ann Richards, titular commander of the Texas National Guard, which, like the Army, was called up to assist the raid, took the position that only drug interdiction could justify the use of military resources. So did congressmen who quizzed the ATF's brass in a post-raid hearing.

The congressmen were, of course, themselves befuddled about the status of the law. "Is my understanding correct," Representative Peter Visclosky (D-Ind) asked the ATF executive whom he was supposed to be interrogating, "that the only nexus or connection to the operation which would allow United States military to participate with a civilian law enforcement agency on such an operation is the assertion that a drug crime has been committed and that there is a drug connection in terms of your operation?"

Dan Hartnett, the ATF's Associate Director for Law Enforcement, or ADLE—his subordinate, the Deputy Associate Director, is known as the DADLE—gave the agency's answer.

"No, that is not correct," the law enforcer said to the lawmaker. "We use the military all the time for law enforcement support. Many of the bureaus do . . . but it has to be with reimbursement."

"The issue is if they are going to provide us support in training . . . we reimburse them at their cost. . . . The military has a law-enforcement support plan, which means that you have to reimburse them, unless there is a drug nexus, then they are not reimbursed."

According to ADLE Hartnett, the intent of the Fathers and the Posse Comitatus Congress was not to ban military involvement in civilian police affairs, but to set forth rules governing reimbursement.

In connection with the February 28 raid and the fifty-one-day siege that followed, both the ATF and the FBI called upon military units for various kinds of assistance and equipment, including training sessions conducted by Green Berets, tanks, CS gas, and fixed-wing aircraft. The most striking item, however, involved the loan, with pilots, of the three National Guard helicopters that flew over Mt. Carmel seconds before the onset of hostilities below.

In making the initial request for use of the helicopters, on December 14, 1992, the ATF's Houston office did not mention any "drug nexus." "For the past six months, this investigation targeted persons believed to be involved in the unlawful manufacturing of machine guns and explosive devices. These targets are of a cult/survivalist group," its letter requesting the flying machines said. Four days later, however—just to be safe—the agency's Austin office followed with a similar request, which added that "the individual is suspected of unlawfully being in possession of firearms and possibly narcotics."

After the February 28 raid on Mt. Carmel, when the use of the helicopters became a matter of controversy, deputy director Hartnett hastened to assure Governor Richards that the "drug nexus" was firmly established. In a March 27 letter, he told her, "There are eleven members of the compound that have prior drug involvement, some with arrests for possession and trafficking. Additionally, open court testimony in Michigan in February 1992 documented Koresh's possession of a methamphetamine lab within the compound." When the hubbub reached Congress, in June 1993 hearings before a House subcommittee, Hartnett was equally sanguine about the "drug nexus." "First of all, there was any number of people inside the compound who had trafficking convictions, possession convictions," he told the hearing. "We have information from people inside the compound, of course, who have actually seen the meth lab."

The basis of the ATF's claims went back to 1987–88, to George Roden and his dispute with Vernon Howell over control of the Mt. Carmel property. During his period of waning influence, Roden had rented the family homes on the grounds to non-believers, including two men, Donny Joe Harvey and Roy "Boy" Wells, one of them an ex-convict. Howell's followers alleged that the two were making drugs on the grounds. Upon retaking the property in 1988, they found there either a manual for manufacturing methamphetamines, or a complete lab; memories of the survivors are sketchy, and do not correspond. In an unpublished memoir, Catherine Matteson recalls that "When we went in to clean up we found proof that George had allowed people to have an amphetamine lab. . . . When we found this, David called the sheriff's department. When they arrived he spread what we had found on the hoods of the cars. He showed them the powder and the other things that had turned up as we cleaned the building. The sheriff wet his finger and touched the power, touching it to his tongue, and then picked up everything off the hood of the car. They left very hurriedly, never saying a word." Howell then temporarily posted sentries at Mt. Carmel's entrances, to guard against any return by Harvey and Wells.

No one familiar with Howell, before or after his rise as Messiah, associates him with drug use, though he admitted that he'd once smoked marijuana, even confessed that he'd inhaled. He distrusted medicines that came in injectable and even pill form: after he was wounded in the February 28 raid, he wouldn't take so much as an aspirin.

Hartnett's "information from people inside the compound . . . who have actually seen the meth lab" was information from those who had seen the lab—if that's what it was—that Howell turned over to the sheriff's office. The "open court testimony in Michigan in February 1992" that, according to Hartnett, "documented Koresh's possession of a methamphetamine lab" was testimony by Marc Breault about the 1988 incident. Breault today insists that he never tried to link Howell with the drug trade. "There were no drugs of any kind used during my time in the group. I have no reason to believe that drugs were used afterwards," he says. "Never at any time did I accuse Vernon of . . . drug dealing or usage." The ATF's allegation about the methamphetamine lab was fabricated from the shreds of a misconstrued and bygone incident.

The agency's other claim, that Mt. Carmel was populated with "any number" of drug runners, is equally a product of bad faith. In a supplemental report to the House Appropriations Subcommittee, intended to document the testimony its personnel gave during the June 3 hearings, the ATF listed the specifics behind the charges that it had lobbed. "In November 1988," the document said, "Margaret Lawson was arrested by the U.S. Customs Service in Los Angeles, California, for possession of 4,970 grams of cocaine and failure to declare monetary instruments in excess of $5,000."

Margaret Kiyoko Hayashi Lawson is a diminutive woman of Japanese ancestry, one of the Adventists of the Hawaiian group who came to live at Mt. Carmel during the late 1980s. She was born in 1917, and would have been seventy-one years old at the time of the alleged offense. Lawson says that she came to Mr. Carmel in April 1988 and never left the place, until it—and any records of her prior whereabouts—were razed in its apocalyptic conflagration. The Customs Service says that it would have turned any seizure of some ten pounds of cocaine over to the Los Angeles Police Department for handling, and the LAPD says that if it did process a Margaret Lawson for cocaine possession in November of 1988, she wasn't the same Margaret Lawson.

Additionally, the ATF alleged that resident Kathryn Schroeder had been arrested in 1990 in El Paso for possession of cocaine and marijuana, and that her husband, Michael Schroeder, had been arrested in 1982—six years before he joined the Mt. Carmel group—on similar charges in Miami. Follower Brad Branch, the ATF said, had been arrested for pot possession in 1983 in San Antonio—five years before he came to Mt. Carmel. And Raymond Friesen, it reported, in 1989 "was a passenger in a motor home that was seized at the Port of Entry (POE) at Pembina, North Dakota, by the U.S. Customs Service. Allegations of marijuana smuggling and pornography were made."

In sum, the ATF alleged that five residents at Mt. Carmel—Lawson, Branch, the two Schroeders, and Friesen—had been involved in police incidents in which drugs were suspected, and that four of the five suspects had been arrested for drug possession. But as with Margaret Lawson, the allegations against the others were mainly bunk. The U.S. Customs Service says that it has no record of any detention or arrest of Kathryn or Michael Schroeder, anytime, anyplace. Only Brad Branch had been clearly implicated.

The "eleven members of the compound who have prior drug involvement," cited in Hartnett's letter to Governor Richards were identified by equally specious means. The eleven included the four innocents defamed in the ATF's report to Congress, and four others, cited as former drug users. "In correspondence between former cult member Breault and the ATF, Breault alleges that Oliver Gyarfas, Kevin Whitecliff, Greg Sommers, and Peter Gent all had a history of drug use," the report said, though it admitted that "Breault did not elaborate on a timeframe of drug use." In addition to the four innocent people mentioned earlier, and the four cited by Breault, plus Branch, two other associates of the flock were named: "Convicted narcotics trafficker Donny Joe Harvey and his associate, Roy Lee Wells, Jr.," the men whom Howell had evicted from Mt. Carmel for hoodiness.

Among the factors that the ATF did not take into account in compiling its misleading report to Congress is that higher arrest-and-usage levels characterize most National Guard and Army barracks, and that Governor Richards—who was on the campaign trail, and styled herself as a recovering addict—was, by the ATF's reckoning just as guilty of "drug involvement" as the former users named by Breault. But perhaps there was no need to be overly worried. As the Treasury Department pointed out in its investigation of the affair, "there is no formal standard by which the military defines a drug nexus."

Controversy over military involvement in the raid at Mt. Carmel might never have developed had the three helicopters dispatched by the National Guard been used as the ATF says that they were. The helicopters carried more than a dozen ATF troopers and brass, dressed in bulletproof vests, helmets, and other combat gear. These executives planned to supervise the raid from the air—the helicopters were to be what they termed a "command platform"—then take charge on the ground after the dangerous work was done. As a diversion, the arrival of the choppers at Mt. Carmel was timed to occur just seconds before the raiders piled out of cattle trailer rigs below, starting the land assault. "The helicopters arrived at an altitude of approximately 500 feet and a distance of approximately 300 to 500 meters off the backside of the compound. . . they were going to hover there until the raid teams secured the compound," ATF intelligence chief David Troy told the Congress.

But what actually happened, as the agency explained to the public in its 400-page report on the affair, was much different.

> The helicopters approached the rear of the Compound at approximately the same time the trucks pulled along the front, which failed to create the intended diversion. When they were approximately 350 meters from the rear of the Compound, the helicopters were fired upon, forcing them to pull back. . . . Two of the helicopters were forced to land in a field to inspect for damage. . . . The third helicopter, although also struck by gunfire, was able to remain airborne. It circled overhead to watch for additional attackers.

During the trial of eleven survivors of the Mt. Carmel events, held in San Antonio in early 1994, two warrant officers assigned to the National Guard helicopters provided details of what had happened to their plan. About 9:30 a.m. the helicopters left the airport near the command center at Texas State Technical College (TSTC), Warrant Officer Doyle Stone, Jr., testified. Believing that they were in danger of arriving too early at Mt. Carmel, the helicopters twice circled over the intersection of U.S. Highway 84 and Texas Highway 31, several miles from Mt. Carmel, he told the court. They then made one pass at their target, only to see that "the agents were already getting out of trucks" below. As the helicopters swooped over Mt. Carmel, somebody fired upon them from its rusting water tower. "Only his head popped out and you couldn't see it below," Stone recalled.

Warrant Officer Jerry Seagraves, whose helicopter carried eight agents and a "video man," testified that when the aircraft came within about 350 meters of Mt. Carmel, their occupants heard sounds like "popcorn" from the ground. Inside their craft, they heard banging noises "like a baseball hitting the side of a car." "We broke right, heard another bump, which was another round, and got out of there," he said. "At no time did I fly over that compound." A video from Seagrave's craft showed a single pass, at high altitude, turning rightward, as he described.

Almost none of the government's report squared with what two disinterested witnesses, John McLemore and Dan Mulloney, said during the same trial—nor with their videotape, introduced into evidence to document their claims. McLemore, a newsman, and Mulloney, a cameraman, both working for a local television station, had been driving along Farm-to-Market Road 2491 that morning, not far from its juncture with EE Ranch Road, about a half mile from Mt. Carmel. The two telenewsmen say that they saw the helicopters make first one, then another pass, not at the faraway intersection of Highways 84 and 31, but directly behind Mt. Carmel, at low altitude. The pair halted their Bronco a few yards from the juncture of 2491 and EE, removed their equipment, and captured the third pass of the aircraft on film: the footage shows a 'copter passing along Mt. Carmel's "north" side, within inches of the building's roof. As the pair finished recording the swoop on film, two cattle trailers loaded with agents passed by, speeding down 2491, then turning onto EE Ranch Road. McLemore and Mulloney tailed the raiders into Mt. Carmel.

McLemore and Mulloney's reports are consistent with the recollections of surviving inhabitants of Mt. Carmel, including those of government witnesses and apostates. Eyewitnesses who had been on the building's "north" and "west" sides tell most, because they had the best view. They claim that the helicopters strafed the complex.

Marjorie Thomas was an attractive, slender Afro-Brit, a practical nurse by trade, whose testimony was introduced by the prosecution during the trial of her co-religionists. On the morning of the 28th, she said, after his confrontation with undercover agent Rodriguez, David Koresh told Thomas and other women who had gathered in the chapel to return to their quarters. Thomas went to her room in the third-floor loft, and shortly afterward, noticed that two of the other women who lived there were staring out of one of the windows, on the building's "north" side. She joined them at the window.

Government prosecutors had called Thomas to testify, but because of her physical condition—during the April 19 fire, she received third-degree burns over some 50 percent of her body—they introduced a videotaped deposition instead. In her statement, given over a period of two days, Thomas reported that "I saw three helicopters approaching. . . . There was one at front and two behind, and the one at the front had very bright lights. I could see a person hanging from the side of the helicopter, because it was that close. . . . As the helicopter drew nearer, I heard a sound. It was a bullet coming—which came through the window and shattered the blinds. We all dived to the floor." While looking out of the window, Thomas told the court, she had not seen any raiders on the ground below.

Victorine Hollingsworth, who is a stout British Afro Caribbean in her late fifties, went from the chapel to her second-story room. When she heard the noise of the helicopters hovering overhead, she joined other women in the second-floor hallway. The women crouched or lay themselves over Mt. Carmel's children, hoping to protect them from harm. "There was firing above," she said in a deposition given to Texas Rangers. Kathy Schroeder, the government's key witness, from her room on the front or "west" side of the first floor, didn't see the helicopters and was not quizzed at trial about collateral observations. But today she declares that after the raid she inspected "holes in our water containers which I believed could only come from above. I also saw some holes from above because of the angle of the sheetrock around the holes."

The recollections of Catherine Matteson, a survivor who was not brought to trial, place the helicopters in an approximate time frame. Matteson says that she had not attended the meeting with the other women, but had instead gone downstairs in search of a copy of the *Waco Tribune*'s "Sinful Messiah" installment. "I picked up the story and started for my room," she writes in her memoir.

> As I crossed the floor, I noticed as I looked out the two windows and saw two cattle car-trailers coming down the road toward the house. . . . In my room I threw the paper on my bed and started to lay down when I heard the sound of helicopters roar in my ears. They sounded as if they were in the room with me. My room was at the back of the building on the second floor. As I went to the window to my amazement there were three helicopters in formation and facing David's room and firing as they came. As the helicopters came near the building they were between the second and third floor level. . . . As they made a turn toward the front of the building I realized there existed a great possibility of my getting shot, so I hit the floor. When they reached the front of the building, all hell broke loose and everyone at the front of the building started shooting.

Others who were inside confirm that the helicopters opened fire in the area just beyond the cylindrical water tower, some 25 yards "east" of the cafeteria, spraying bullets from its "southern" end, from which the residential tower rose—where Koresh had his bedroom—to its northern end, where three white vinyl tanks sat. The blasts of fire punctured Mt. Carmel's water tanks, and, most of the survivors say, killed three residents, Peter Gent, Peter Hipsman, and Winston Blake.

Matteson's account of the tanks dovetails with the observations of government witness Schroeder. "When the shooting stopped, I went down the hall between the rooms," the septuagenarian Matteson recalls. "Every window was shot out. The glass was all over the rooms and the venetian blinds all hung on one side of the window. I went downstairs and Kathy was filling containers with water. She said, 'Grab anything to hold water. They have shot holes in our water tanks!' So we both worked filling anything that was a clean container until there was nothing we could use.

Another of the arguments made by Mt. Carmel's survivors points to drawings made by children who were sent out of Mt. Carmel after the firefight. Their drawings, sketched with crayons while the children were in the custody of Texas welfare authorities, show bullet holes in Mt. Carmel's room and helicopters hovering overhead.

The autopsy findings regarding Peter Gent also provide the basis for a claim of aerial firing. Gent and the four others killed on Mt. Carmel's grounds on February 28 were buried by their peers during the siege, and their cadavers, unlike those recovered after the April 19 fire, were found with all limbs intact, and with what coroners called minimal decomposition. Dead men do not tell definitive stories, but they sometimes point toward truths that the living can confirm.

Gent was a twenty-four-year-old Australian whose twin sister, Nicole Little, also lived at Mt. Carmel, and whose father, Bruce, was an apostate member of the group, once again living Down Under. Peter, before he came to Mt. Carmel, had been the family's troubled child, dabbling in drugs, tobacco, drinking, and gang fights. He had cast off his worldly ways under the tutelage of Koresh and the Mt. Carmel work-study regime. For about two weeks before the assault, says survivor Clive Doyle, Gent had been working inside the property's old steel water tower, which had been in disuse for years. Gent had welded supports to its interior walls, erected scaffolding between them at several levels, and connected them with a ladder, under a plan to restore the tower to use, either as a water reservoir or storage bin. From perches on the scaffolding, we was chipping away the encrusted rust inside.

On the morning of February 28, Gent returned to the tower, perhaps armed, and alone: none of his comrades was on hand to witness his fate. At the tower's top was a hatch, which could be raised to peer outside. Gent did look out—or perhaps, shoot out—and was felled. During the San Antonio conspiracy trial of Doyle and eight others, an ATF ground trooper, Lowell Sprague, testified that Gent fired upon the pedestrian raiders, and that, in self-defense, he had dropped the Australian from his roost with a rifle shot. Other agents said that they'd seen Gent's AR-15 fall from the tower, apparently as he dropped inside. Like Sprague, two others claimed credit for dropping Gent.

The story as told by those who lived at Mt. Carmel was different, and more uniform. "And one young man," David Koresh told the FBI, "had climbed up on top of the water tower. . . . He heard helicopters and he climbed up and stuck his head through the tower. . . . See, he was working in that tower . . . getting it ready, to paint the inside of it to hold water. . . . He was in there when he heard everything going on outside, he climbed out and looked out the top and they shot him in the head, the helicopter."

The autopsy performed on Gent's body at the Tarrant County examiner's office in Fort Worth (site of all the autopsies done in the case) showed a single bullet wound, "located over the upper chest 53 inches about the heel," and "coming to rest near the right pulmonary hilus 53 inches above the heel." The heel-to-wound measurement indicates a level trajectory for the bullet that took his life. The finding is ostensibly consistent with Gent's death by helicopter fire, but inconsistent with the claim that he was shot from the ground, some four stories below. On the other hand, human bodies are not like buildings. They move. Had Gent been leaning downwards, an ascending bullet might have traveled a level path through his chest.

Peter Hipsman was a twenty-seven-year-old native of upstate New York, known at Mt. Carmel as an entertainer of its children. When he wasn't working or around the building or worshipping, he strummed an acoustic guitar, sang badly, and put his limited talent to best use by imitating Donald Duck and making up ditties for the kids. When the helicopters made their fatal swoop, survivors say that he was either in the area of the two rooms above the chapel, or the fourth-story bedroom where David Koresh slept and Hipsman died. In either case, they say, it was the helicopters that felled him.

Hipsman's autopsy showed four wounds, two of them to the body. One of the bullets that struck him passed on a level keel, between the seventh ribs on this left and right sides—a finding inconsistent with a shot delivered from ground level, but in accord with fire from an airborne source. A second round entered his left arm, on the back side, and exited

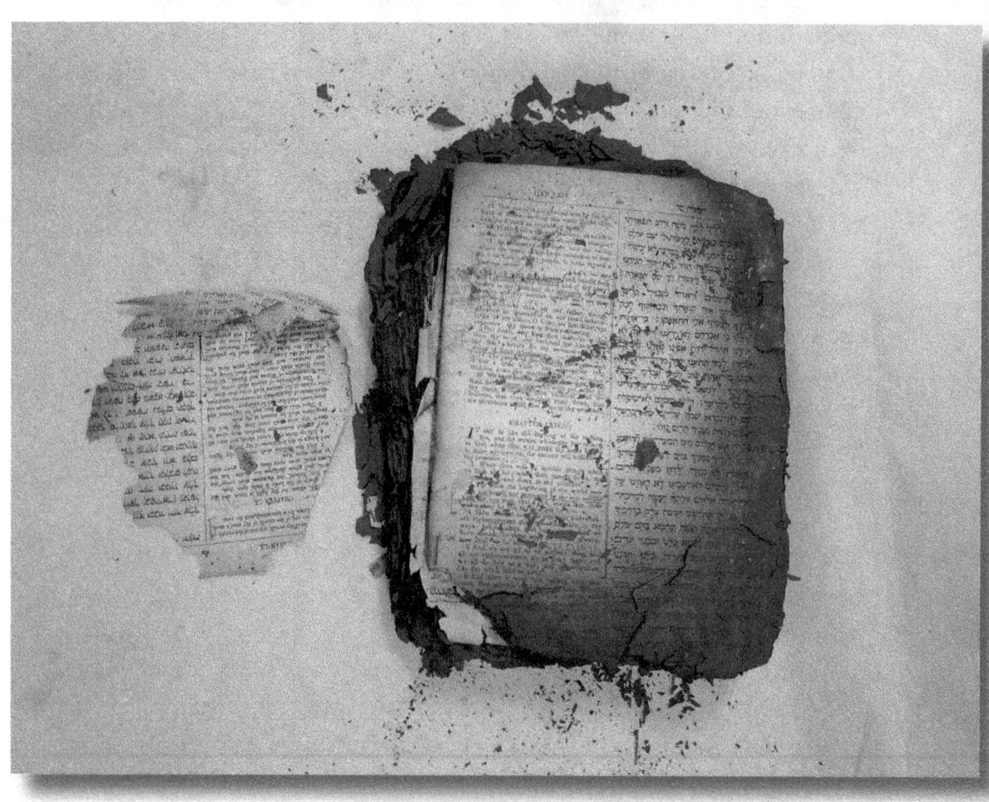

A Branch Davidian Study Bible, rescued after the 1993 fire by an FBI agent. Now held in the Waco Siege Collection, Newton Gresham Library at Sam Houston State University. Photographer: Trent Shotwell, 2020. Image courtesy of the Thomason Special Collections, Newton Gresham Library.

at a slightly lower position on his front side, again, in consistency with reports of aerial gunfire—provided, of course, that Hipsman was reclining or standing erect at the time that he received his wounds. The autopsy, oddly, also shows that Hipsman was wearing Steve Schneider's underwear.

The "holes from above" which Kathy Schroeder says that she witnessed were in the fourth-floor bedroom where Hipsman died. Those holes were also inspected by defense attorneys Dick DeGuerin and Jack Zimmermann, the latter a Marine Corps Reserve colonel and former combat artillery officer. DeGuerin and Zimmermann entered Mt. Carmel during the federal siege as representatives of two clients who are now dead, Koresh and his confidant Schneider; when their clients died, the attorneys' financial stake in the case died as well. Both men claim to have seen holes indicating an up-to-down trajectory in the bedroom's ceiling. Zimmermann told investigators from the Texas Rangers that "there were clearly exit holes in the ceiling. . . . . Exit holes," he explained, "meaning that the rounds had to be initiated outside coming in, and there was no question about that. . . . There are only two ways that could happen. You can have a guy standing on the roof shooting in, and it would look just like that, or you can have someone shooting from a helicopter that would look just like that." In similar testimony at the 1994 San Antonio trial, he told the court that the nearly one dozen holes that he had scrutinized in the bedroom had "paper and building material hanging down, punched in," in the pattern of descending fire.

Steve Schneider told the FBI that during the siege he had visited the wounded Hipsman after the gunfire stopped on February 28. Hipsman stated that his shoulder wound had come first, followed by the bullet that crossed his midsection. Hipsman was in "excruciating pain," Schneider said. Perhaps that explains his manner of death: Hipsman also suffered two head wounds, both, according to the coroner's office, fired at close range, one of them in an upward direction. Somebody inside of Mt. Carmel put Peter Hipsman out of his misery.

The Tarrant County autopsy report, which probes Winston Blake's remains, describes him as "a normally developed, obese, black male," and surviving comrades have little to add to that. He was twenty-eight years old, six-feet-two-inches tall, weighing some 190 pounds. His peers called him "Big Boy." Blake had come to Mt. Carmel from Great Britain several years earlier, along with his girlfriend, Beverly Elliot, who perished in the April 19 blaze. In England he'd been a baker. His room, where fellow residents say his cadaver was found, was on the back, or "east" side of the complex, just down the hallway from the cafeteria. The view from its window was eclipsed by the plastic water tanks just outside, the "water containers" in which Kathy Schroeder says she discerned bullet holes with descending trajectory. At the moment of his death, two eyewitnesses say, Blake was sitting on the edge of his bunk eating a piece of French toast. He was not alone; two comrades, one of them a roommate, were in the enclosure with him.

Blake was clad in a black "Beefy-T" knit shirt, bearing the legend: "david koresh/god rocks." Because it was cold and Mt. Carmel unheated, he had also wrapped himself in a long-sleeve turtleneck sweater. On top of the turtleneck, he had added a black V-necked sweater, and outside of it, he'd strapped on a black ammunition vest which bore the label, "David Koresh Survival Wear," a part of the gun show inventory. He was also wearing three pairs of trousers, the topmost, apparently, a pair of black jogging pants.

A single bullet entered Blake's head, just below the right ear, stopping at a shallow depth inside the skull. Projectile fragments from a .223-caliber or AR-15 bullet were recovered from the wound, but told nothing; both the raiders and the defenders utilized AR-15s. But coroners found traces of gunpowder on the surface of the skull and inside Blake's head, an indication that he was shot at close range. The coroner's report, if it is trustworthy, points to Winston Blake's death by friendly fire.

His black clothing and ammunition vest gave him an appearance similar to that of the agents outside, and a passing and panicked resident, spying him from behind, could easily have mistaken him for a raider. The weapons of his comrades inside the room, in the congestion and jostling that prevailed, could have gone off, especially since most of Mt. Carmel's defenders had only perfunctory training. The conspiracy buffs who've studied the case like to point out that wound caused by a short from afar can be faked as a near-range wound by firing a blank round into the opening. But if agents of the ATF or FBI tampered with the cadaver, they had to do so by stealth. Winston Blake's body was disinterred, not by federal agents, but by technicians from the Smithsonian Institution and the Fort Worth medical examiner's office. They turned it over, says examiner Rodney Crow, to a Waco funeral home. If there was foul play with Blake's corpse, the conspiracy that enveloped the February 28 raid extends far beyond the bureaucratic limits of federal police forces.

But no thesis can be discarded yet. Winston Blake's body was subject to a second autopsy, less than five months after his death, when it was returned to his family in the North of England. The physician who examined it for the Manchester Police Department came to a conclusion radically different from that reached in Texas. He found no powder burns on Blake's head, and paid special attention to the somewhat jagged shape traced into the victim's skull by the bullet that ultimately stopped within. "I formed the opinion," the British expert wrote in his findings, "that this injury had probably been caused by a destabilized high velocity rifle bullet of relatively low weight. This missile had probably been destabilized so as to cause it to yaw in flight prior to striking the victim. Such a destabilization could have been achieved if the bullet had previously passed through a light screening cover, such as the light-weight material reported to have been used in the construction of the building walls."

When examined on the other side of the Atlantic, Winston Blake's body told a tale, not of a bullet fired by someone close at hand, but of a shot that entered his room from outside.

Originally published in *The Met,* December 6, 1995, Reavis explores again anti-government political philosophy, interrogating its coherence and appeal after the Waco Siege.

Crazy Like a Fox: Robert Fox Is Not Nuts.

He Just Wants the Government to Pay Him $1 Million. In Gold. Every Day.

All the seats are taken and more than a dozen people are standing in a room with a low acoustic-tile ceiling in Rockwall, about 25 miles northeast of Dallas. The place looks like a motel meeting hall, but it's actually a courtroom in Rockwall County's new office building. The people in the room are mostly young men in jackets and jeans, defendants in two-bit criminal cases that will come before the bar today.

In their midst sits an odd figure, a portly middle-ager in rainbow suspenders and wire-frame eyeglasses. He has a long, flowing, reddish-brown beard and mischievous blue eyes. His name is Robert James Fox, and—sometimes with a chuckle—he calls himself an ambassador. Dime-store copies of the Texas and Christian flags poke out of his shirt pockets.

Contrary to appearances, the man is not nuts. In fact, Ambassador Fox is certifiably sane. The federal government has looked inside his head and found it in fine working order.

The Ambassador is here because, like most of the people in the crowd, he has been accused of a crime and ordered to enter a plea today. But his tricks are apparently working their magic again. When Fox's name is called, the court clerk tells him not to come back until January 9th, six weeks away.

The postponement of the case against Fox is an ostensible sign of victory. Either Rockwall is learning from the Ambassador what justice really is, or if not, it's learning, as other jurisdictions have, that it's best to leave him alone.

It's a lesson well-learned. If you are a policeman, a prosecutor, a judge, or even a humble bureaucrat, Robert James Fox can be trouble: big trouble, little trouble, and trouble in between, every day of the week. The Internal Revenue Service, the Immigration and Naturalization Service, and the federal courts have already caved in to this looming fact of life, and local authorities are toppling one by one, like dominoes in a line. The Ambassador's potency may not be evident in his demeanor or dress, but like a case of syphilis, it makes itself felt within a couple of weeks and can drive its victims mad as the years rage on.

Busted by Road Nazis

Robert Fox's alleged offense in Rockwall County is simple, on its face. He has been accused of "interfering with the duties of a public servant." But the accusation is quickly reduced to absurdity when viewed through the religious, political, and legal eyeglasses on Fox's blushing cheeks. What you see through Fox's eyes takes some interpretation, but it does make sense, if sometimes in a comical way.

There are three grounds on which, usually without much success, people in Texas commonly challenge received laws. First, there are religious grounds, the ground on which an old-line Mormon, for example, might claim a right to practice polygamy. Second, there are constitutional grounds, on the strength of which, for example, tax protesters claim immunity from prosecution by the IRS. Most common of all, though, there are the grounds that have been historically argued by jail-house lawyers and other schemers of the *lumpen* proletariat, people who claim that the whole legal system is just a racket for enriching judges, lawyers, and cops.

Ambassador Fox uses all three lines of argument against those whom his briefs refer to as "lawless road Nazis" (i.e., traffic cops), "pettifogger shysters for filthy lucre" (i.e., lawyers), and "imposters" (i.e., judges). Fox used his entire arsenal in the pending Rockwall case.

His arrest—or "kidnapping," as he calls it—grew out of a minor incident in Royse City, about 20 miles east of Dallas, on October 14. Fox says he exited a store to find policemen questioning a friend whose name Fox won't divulge and Royse City can't ascertain. The policemen were asking Fox's friend to identify himself; the friend was refusing to do so. Fox's friend, a small-framed man of middle age, was, after some wrangling, arrested for "failure to produce identification."

Failure to produce identification is, in turn, a fairly simple charge. If a policeman has reason to suspect a person of unlawful behavior, he can demand that the person identify himself. Or so the law says.

Because Fox's buddy didn't comply, he was booked into jail as John Doe. He spent about a week there, never revealing his name. Then the authorities sent him to the state mental hospital at Terrell, where he spent another week, undergoing evaluation, steadfastly silent about his name. After all of that, the Rockwall County district attorney's office let the matter pass, says Assistant District Attorney Rick Calvert, "because at some point you figure that a guy has been punished enough."

While the policemen were interrogating Doe on the day of his arrest, Ambassador Fox stood nearby. He didn't agree with the way that Doe was being handled. "They were threatening to arrest him because he couldn't do the impossible," he says. "And you can't be compelled to do the impossible!" Interpretation: If a man doesn't have any identification, you can't arrest him for failure to produce it, any more than you could arrest him for failure to tether a unicorn.

After John Doe was handcuffed and put into the squad car, Fox was arrested for interfering with the arrest. He has since threatened to sue, saying that he wasn't interfering with anything.

"If I am the public, and if alleged sergeant G. A. Hutchinson [the arresting officer] is my servant, then I would apparently have a duty to inform him of the error of his ways," Fox explains in a brief he penned for the case.

Furthermore, since the officer was violating John Doe's rights by requiring him to accomplish the impossible, Ambassador Fox claims that his own status was enhanced. According to his account, he became a witness to an official crime, the arrest of John Doe, and when Sgt. Hutchinson arrested him, too, the officer was actually attempting to intimidate a witness. Instead of suing Royse City for false arrest and intimidation, Ambassador Fox has offered the city a contract under which, for $1 million a day, paid in gold, it can violate his constitutional rights. However, there will be "no bulk discounts for wholesale violation of my rights," the tender's fine print warns.

Like John Doe, Ambassador Fox would have refused to identify himself on October 14, had that been asked of him. But it wasn't, because he'd just come out of jail following a Royce City arrest for . . . well, no charges were ever formally brought. Fox had been driving along Interstate 30 on October 9 when a Royse City policeman—Sgt. Hutchinson of the October 14 arrest—pulled him over. Fox refused to identify himself, for what he says are the soundest of reasons.

"If I'm standing in a bank and a guy comes in and shoots four tellers to death and takes a manager hostage, after the police come, yes, the state can force me to identify the suspect," Fox says. "That's my legal duty. But the officer didn't tell me that I had witnessed a crime that somebody else had committed, and so I had to assume that he wanted me to identify myself for a prosecution against me. The Fifth Amendment says that you can't be compelled to be a witness against yourself."

Robert Fox was taken to the Rockwall Country jail following the highway incident. A couple of days later, when the authorities offered to release him if he'd sign papers confessing his guilt, he demurred. "I told them, 'Oh, you would allow me to become a criminal and acquire a criminal record? No thanks!'" So they kicked him out of jail.

But before releasing him, they had hauled him before a judge who ordered Fox to submit to fingerprinting. He complied, while threatening to sue the judge. Filing suits isn't really an inconvenience for the Ambassador, who does all his own legal work, and in relative terms, it may be the easier way out. In the past, he did identify himself, and that caused even grander hassles. Fox's identity, you see, is a delicate matter that few lawmen properly understand.

IDENTITY CRISIS

In 1977, Robert Fox, a University of Manitoba dropout, was prospering as the owner of a Winnipeg, Canada business that set up audio and lighting systems for musical concerts and similar events, when, stone sober, he was involved in a fatal traffic accident. His van plowed into a motorcycle whose pilot and passenger were both killed. He was arrested, he made bond, and he started on a long and tortured trip through the Canadian court system, where, in 1980, he was sentenced to a term of nine months. But by then he'd fled to Dallas where he was living in the underground economy, recycling gold, silver, and scrap metals, he says. Fox has never returned to Canada, which has no extradition treaty with the United States.

"The accident was the beginning of a long spiritual quest," he says. After examining Islam and various Asian sects and beliefs, he came to faith in the Bible, not only as a divine scripture, but as a book of law. In his vocabulary, the Law—God's law—is superior to the Constitution, legislative enactments, regulations, and other man-made rules. As he sees it, he's bound to obey only laws that don't conflict with God's rules, which, according to his take, are extensive indeed.

When he was jailed in Royse City on October 9, for example, he refused to put on an orange, polyester-and-cotton prison suit. "It's made of mixed fabric, and that's against the Law," he declared. Strict Jewish sects interpret a biblical injunction, Deuteronomy 22:11 ('Thou shalt not wear a garment of diverse sorts, as of woolen and linen together'), the same way. Fox isn't crazy; he's literal. But, of course, his jailers didn't understand. They thought that he said, "That's against the law," with a lower-case "l." They locked him up in his underwear.

But back to the subject of identity. At least once in recent Dallas area history, Robert Fox did voluntarily identify himself. On October 9, 1990, he was stopped in Richardson while at the wheel of a 1990 Acura, a car that he'd paid for, he says, in gold. The Richardson officer stopped him because the Acura didn't have any license plates. Ambassador Fox offered to show him the car manufacturer's statement of origin instead.

An MSO, as the documents are sometimes called, is the original paperwork that describes a car. It comes from the maker, goes to the auto dealer, and, in the usual course of a new car purchase, is sent to the state, which, in exchange, issues a certificate of title. Ambassador Fox says that this procedure conceals a theft, and theft, of course, is against the Law.

Understanding his concept requires several interpretative moves. Fox defines God as "the Lawmaker." God commands, "Thou shalt have no other gods before me," and Fox takes that scripture to mean, "Thou shalt have no other lawmakers before me." If a government merely duplicate's God's Laws, passing statues against murder and theft, for example, it has not challenged God, but if it adds to God's Law or perverts it, it is competing as a rival god would.

"The god of Texas," Fox says (i.e., the state of Texas), "sends you a certificate of title. What that means is that a title exists, but you don't have one. The state, or the god of Texas, has it. A certificate of title is your permission to have the car that the state owns."

Ambassador Robert Fox wanted to own his car, so he hadn't traded his MSO for a blue title certificate. Doing so would have been irreligious, in his view, because it would have required him to agree to the switch. "Thou shalt make no covenant with . . . their gods," says Exodus 23:32.

Sensing an anomaly, the Richardson officer demanded that Fox identify himself. Fox complied, after a fashion. He handed over a document since forever lost in an exhibits box in some obscure courtroom or prosecuter's office. Fox calls the lost document a "passport from the Kingdom of Israel." Judicial records indicate that the "passport" identified him as an "ambassador" of the kingdom.

And that's why Fox, in jail in Richardson, soon found himself under interrogation by the Immigration and Naturalization Service, which charged him with using forged entry documents and with impersonating a diplomat. Both are federal offenses and felonies. The entry charge, at least, attained plausibility after the authorities discovered, quite without his cooperation, that Robert James Fox was (and presumably still is) a citizen of Canada.

But that's not what he thinks he is. According to his understanding of the Law, he is a "sovereign, *sui juris* . . . a follower of . . . Yahshua the Messiah" (i.e., Jesus), and that makes him a citizen of the Kingdom of Israel. When he wants to identify himself, he presents himself as the person whom he believes himself to be.

Since God doesn't operate a passport office, Fox makes up his Kingdom passports himself. His current identity card, for example, which has the look and feel of a driver's license, shows his photo, states his date of birth, height, names him as an ambassador, and carries what the unwary might mistake for a legal cite: "International Law FJ 2nd Kis 17. Para 35.36." It's a cite to the Lawbook: 2 Kings 17: 35–36.

Documents like this cannot be forged, nor are they false in any way, Fox maintains. True enough, he'll admit, the Kingdom of Israel isn't recognized by the Department of Public Safety or by the State Department or even by the United Nations. But Taiwan isn't recognized by the United Nations, yet Taiwanese passports are valid, and Cuba isn't recognized by the United States, yet Cuban passports are valid. "The fact that the Kingdom of Israel isn't recognized doesn't mean that it doesn't exist," Fox says, and reason is entirely on his side.

Essentially, what he is claiming is that, as he puts it, "citizenship is a political decision," and is therefore voluntary. Since he had not accepted the sovereignty of either the United States or Canada, he maintains that he can be judged only by the Law of the Kingdom to which he owes allegiance. In one of his pleadings, Fox gives an example of what he means: "If a police officer stops a stretch limo and comes to discover a man accompanied by his four wives, the officer would appear to be duty bound to bring the applicable bigamy or polygamy charges," the statement says. "However, once the man evidences that he is a Saudi Arabian citizen and declares his foreign law wherein pursuant to Islamic law he is entitled to have four wives . . . the officer and the courts must honor his legal position. I am a Citizen of the Kingdom of Israel and have declared the foreign law for all to know. . . ."

But what of his "ambassador" status? Well, Fox says, wasn't Jane Curtain of *Saturday Night Live* an ambassador for UNICEF? Wasn't Anita Bryant an ambassador for orange juice? There's nothing woefully official about the term. It is a generic word, as well as a specific. And if Robert James Fox claims to be an ambassador for God, who on earth can authoritatively dispute him? After all, doesn't the Bible talk about ambassadors of faith?

Arguments like these convinced the feds that Fox should have his head examined. He was shuttled off to a federal prison and mental facility in Missouri, where for two months shrinks examined him. Fox remembers the experience as something out of *Brave New World*. "There were these psychologists and stuff," he recalls, "and they called themselves 'my team.' But I got the feeling real quick that they weren't really on my team."

The Ambassador cooperated with the head shrinks however, only to learn, after he'd told the story of his Canadian "persecution," that they suspected him of having delusions. But his examiners called the Canadian authorities and, after investigating, ruled that Fox was sane. "I've always wondered if I wasn't having delusions, who was?" he says. "I mean, if I tell you the truth and you think it's a delusion, who is insane?"

Some eight months after his arrest, Ambassador Robert James Fox found himself facing Barefoot Sanders, the legendary federal judge. Fox represented himself in the proceeding. When the issue of his passport was discussed, he told the court that he had made it himself and that, "It is a genuine Kingdom of Israel passport, and I have made no attempt to impersonate myself. I am myself." Sanders listened, looked up the relevant precedents, and issued a written opinion that is now a page of the nation's case law. The judge noted that Canadians don't need entry documents to enter the United States in the first place, and thus one of the prosecution's arguments was "inconceivable." Sanders dismissed the charges. Fox went free.

But he hadn't entirely won. During the months of his incarceration, the IRS noticed that Fox had never filed a tax return. Its agents raided his North Dallas house—or embassy, as he called it—and took possession of his Acura, gold, and silver. "The Kingdom of Israel's treasury was stolen by force of arms in an attempt to diminish the sovereignty of said lawful kingdom," he alleges in legal pleadings. Ever since then he's been peppering the agency for the return of his "stolen" goods and property. But he hasn't paid any income taxes because that, he says would be against the Law.

If the IRS in now apparently ignoring the existence of Robert Fox, it is not alone. Before his 1990 arrest, Fox had applied to the Immigration and Naturalization Service for amnesty as an illegal alien. But that negotiation apparently fell through when he refused to obtain a Social Security card, and he hasn't heard from the INS in years, either. Ambassador Robert James Fox has become what millions wish they could be: a nonperson in federal files. Thousands of immigrants and plutocrats would pay dearly, if they could, to obtain the invisibility, or invincibility, that Fox has achieved.

His de facto immunity has come at no small cost, however. Over the past five years, the Ambassador has been deprived of three cars: in 1990, the '90 Acura in Richardson; in 1994, an '88 Honda in Garland; in 1995, a '78 Oldsmobile in Royse City. There's a pattern here: Each seizure is for an older and less valuable car.

FIGHTING FOR JESUS

Fox is no longer a prosperous entrepreneur, and the Kingdom's treasury is depleted. Though he says the IRS estimated his annual income at about $287,000 before 1990, and though he still tries to settle his accounts in gold and silver, the Ambassador is essentially homeless today, reduced to sleeping on couches in the apartments of friends. His embassy is a nest of legal papers, and with each move, some of them get lost. The Kingdom's archives are literally scattered all over the metroplex. Fox now makes his living, such as it is, by organizing seminars where other self-made barristers teach their tricks. He may have beaten the system, but it has beaten up on him, he says, even literally. He has filed claims with three area municipalities alleging police brutality, and sometimes he wears a brace as a result of an injury that he says came about when Lew Sterrett's goons stomped him in the back.

Law enforcement officers, judges, and prosecutors who've handled Ambassador Fox don't have much to say about the man; one thinks, because Fox has suits pending against most of them. Judge John Dietz of the 53rd Judicial District Court in Austin, however, doesn't yet know that he's being sued. In November, Fox brought the city of Garland before Dietz on a change-of-venue motion that arose from his suit to recover his '88 Honda.

"He was very coherent, very well-spoken, and extremely courteous in court," Dietz recalls. Then, chuckling, he says, "I'd never had a citizen of the Kingdom of Israel in my court." In ruling against the venue change, Dietz said, among other things, "I will respectfully decline to take notice of the Bible as law." Fox says that the ruling isn't kosher. After all, in 1982 (in what may be the most cynical act of elected officials to date), Congress unanimously adopted a resolution, Public Law 97-280, whose text declares that the Bible is "the Word of God." Now, is it or ain't it?

Rockwell Assistant District Attorney Calvert, who is the current legal point man against Ambassador Fox, notes that in the past five years his office has won several convictions against similar rebels, one of whom is now serving a year-long term in the county jail. "The amount of frivolous paperwork that these guys file is the main problem, and it's more annoying than anything else," Calvert says.

Ilse Bailey, an assistant district attorney of Kerr County (in the Texas Hill Country), last spring reported in *The Texas Prosecutor* that during one point in her '90s career, she spent nearly half of her time dealing with cases brought by litigants like Fox. "Remember when you are fighting with one of the litigants in court," she advised her peers, "that it is likely that he has the support and aid of hundreds of like-minded extremists backing him up. . . . They are numerous and they know how to play the system."

As they are doing in Rockwall County. When Fox leaves the courtroom, its congestion is greatly eased. Fifteen men and two women follow him out the door. All of them, including the lanky, black-bearded Rick Donaldson—Rockwell County's perennial Libertarian candidate—have come to show support for Fox. Not all of them call themselves citizens of the Kingdom of Israel, as Fox does. Not all of them believe that the federal government has become a front for the International Monetary Fund. Not all of them have declared an enmity to the IRS, and most of them don't drive around in cars without license plates. But they've all decided that the legal system is out of hand, that public servants have become our masters, and that something has to be done about it.

When the Ambassador and his retinue emerge from the county office building, Libertarian Donaldson calls them together. Something can be done to advance the struggle before Fox's next court date, he says. There is a sporty red Jeep on the other side of the building whose safety inspection sticker, he says, is two months expired. The assembled group considers itself a people's grand jury, and after looking over the suspect vehicle, the members decide to swear out affidavits demanding that the authorities prosecute the Jeep's owner. Of course, it helps motivate the group when Donaldson explains the vehicle's owner is an employee of the district attorney's office, a player on the opposing team. Once again the sovereign people—or maybe Lord Yahshua—is about to score a victory over official arrogance.

Expressing sentiments that stretch back to his early days when he was writing for Austin's underground newspaper, *The Rag*, this article, published in *The Met,* May 1, 1996, a year after *The Ashes of Waco: An Investigation* (1995), showcases Reavis's experience with and critique of mainstream media. Through this story of his attempt to get an interview with the Freemen of Montana, he foretells and laments the high price American's will pay if they turn their backs on old-school unbiased journalism, whose practices have the power to check governments. Interview or not, we see the way "Standoff in Montana" manages to "get the story" better than other mainstream media papers, airing opposing points of view as it unpacks their slanted language. It's instructive just to read the kind of questions an unbiased reporter would ask.

Standoff in Montana

Around me were the hills, the sky, and the snow of desolate eastern Montana. To my left stood a small, white, one-story farmhouse, sheathed in siding. A little farther down the road and off to the left stood a second farmhouse, a sibling of sorts, nearly alike. I was standing on the graded surface of a reddish dirt road, along which a dozen vans and station wagons were parked. The vehicles belonged to the television crews.

It was Thursday, April 4, and for about ten days I'd been reading the government's side of the Montana Freemen standoff. But I hadn't seen anything—in the mainstream press, the alternative press or on the Internet—that explained the conflict from the anti-government side of the barricades.

I was an expert witness to the FBI's last well-publicized standoff, which had ended with the fiery deaths of David Koresh and his followers at Mt. Carmel in Waco, and I knew that, in general, the media does a poor job reporting on the actions of government law-enforcement agents. As detailed in my book, *The Ashes of Waco: An Investigation*, the Mt. Carmel fire was almost certainly avoidable. But to put pressure on the government to act with restraint, first reporters had to do their jobs.

That's what I was doing in Montana—my job. I am a journalist. It's the job of journalists to "get the story" and to air different points of view or, at least, to try. Somebody, I figured, had to get the contrarian view, and I figured that since nobody else seemed to have tried, I should.

A White Flag and a Book

It was almost time for me to go into the Freemen's lair, counting down the minutes. I looked around to see if FBI men or Montana state troopers were near. They didn't seem to be. I could hear the hum of a small airplane overhead. The Federal Aviation Administration had declared the standoff area a no-fly zone, so the plane, I reckoned, could belong only to the FBI. Its pilots were the government's obvious eye, and if other lawmen happened to be watching, they were hunkered out of sight. Snipers were probably stationed around the area, and, perhaps, an undercover man was milling about among the crowd of reporters.

I walked over to one of the television guys and asked him which of the two farmhouses was the Freemen lair. "Here, step over to my camera and see for yourself," he said. A rig with a telephoto lens stood atop his tripod. I peeked into its viewfinder and saw a white house, but which one of the two it was, I couldn't tell. From the way the lens was pointing, I assumed it had to be the second of the pair.

"Why haven't any of you guys tried to go in?" I asked the TV man.

"Well, last week," he said, "a couple of guys from NBC drove down the road, past the imaginary line that the Freeman say marks their territory. Some of them came out with guns and took NBC's camera away."

"That's a problem for you photo guys," I muttered. I was planning to go in with only a notepad and a copy of *The Ashes of Waco.* The book, I believed, would persuade the Freemen to take me in, given its rather unflattering portrayal of the FBI and its actions at Mr. Carmel.

I walked a few paces down the road and accosted another television man.

"Why haven't you gone in?" I asked.

He eyed me suspiciously. "Among other things," he said, "they've got a sign at their gate warning us that they'll arrest us and try us before a common-law court and impose a fine."

I walked back to my Ford Explorer and counted my cash. Any fine the Freemen might extract from me, I figured, wouldn't exceed the amount of cash that I was carrying at the time. What were they going to do? Send me to the nearest cash machine, 100 miles away? I counted my resources: $600 in 20-dollar bills. I left $400 in the car's glove compartment, put the rest into my pocket, and returned to the television man.

"Hey, that fine business can be arranged. You just don't carry much money in," I advised.

"Yeah, but they might hold you awhile before trial, and if that happened, we'd become hostages, part of the equation, you know. Besides, these guys train their guns on us any time we move beyond where we are right now."

Oh, boy. "But have they fired upon you?"

"No, not that I know of. But you know," he added, "if we were to go in, the FBI could make our lives pretty miserable, couldn't they?"

I didn't reply. I couldn't believe these people. Sitting around waiting for the story to be handed to them on a press release or to be staged as a photo op.

I'm not the sharpest tool in the shed, but I knew enough to realize that no one was going to find out what was really going on by standing there talking to other reporters and cameramen.

I went back to my car. Casting off my gloves, I puffed on a cigarette and sipped from a cooler of tea, trying to figure out just what I should do. It seemed to me that going onto Freemen turf would require a white flag of some kind. I had just the thing, a red-and-white bandanna bearing the image of the Virgin of Guadalupe. I'd bought the bandanna in Mexico, during a February trip to the jungles of Campeche. The Virgin, Mexico's patron saint, was my patroness, too, as far as I was concerned. She'd protect me, if nothing else did.

I pulled a strand of dry brush from the ground and tied one end of the bandanna to it. Then I stashed the stick inside my coveralls, so that the TV men wouldn't notice it when I walked by. I slid a copy of my book inside the coveralls, too. Then I headed out, walking.

A couple of the television folks watched me leave. I was sure when I passed the point where their vehicles were parked they'd begin filming me. It was a mandatory trade-off; there was nothing I could do to stop them.

Besides, the arrangement worked to my benefit: with the cameras trained on me, I figured that the snipers wouldn't take me down. I had only the Freemen to worry about.

The road to the second farmhouse lay about a quarter-mile from the last of the press vans. By the time I'd gone half that distance, I'd pulled the Virgin flag out of my coveralls. I waved it with my right hand. I'd also removed my book. I pressed it to my chest with my left hand, like a priest approaching a pulpit, Bible at the ready.

I turned onto the dirt driveway leading up to the house. It was muddy, but the mud wasn't deep. Almost another quarter-mile lay ahead. I fixed my eyes on the farmhouse, which had a large picture window in what seemed to be its living room. As I approached it—my eyes glued on the window, looking for the glint of rifle steel—I turned over in my mind just what it was that had brought me here.

CONSPIRACY AND SLANDER

It was the newspaper stories, especially those in the *New York Times*, the nation's renowned "newspaper of record."

In its March 31 report on the standoff, for example, the *Times* quoted a source who called the Freemen a "cult," talked about a "bunker," and said, "The mental stability of some of those wielding weapons appears shaky." It mentioned the group's "powerful arsenal" and listed its contents, about a dozen rifles and shotguns and some 11,000 rounds of ammunition.

It also relayed, without comment, that, "officials say the Freemen run a forgery and financial fraud operation" as if the Freemen were merely con men. The flavor of the story was evident in a single sentence, alleging a certain Freeman "swaggers around the compound with a Glock pistol."

The "compound"? It was a couple of farmhouses. "Swaggers"? Lawmen carry Glock pistols. Do they swagger? The story once again raised my doubts about the ability of the mainstream press to report such matters with any fairness of understanding.

After all, one man's cult leader is another man's pope. The Freemen who have been in mental hospitals were sent there during criminal prosecutions, by the *Times*' own report. Anti-government protesters are commonly sent for sanity screenings these days, and they usually turn out to be no crazier than the Soviet dissidents of ten years past. Pretty Boy Floyd, now a folk hero of Depression days, robbed banks with a six-gun. The Freemen, indebted farmers like Floyd, have allegedly robbed them with a fountain pen. As for the "arsenal" signaled by the *Times*, keeping 1,000 rounds for every rifle one owns is common practice, and if 20 Freemen own 12 weapons, they're less well-armed than a lot of my neighbors in Dallas.

The "cult" and "swindling" charges were dubious. As *The Dallas Morning News* and other "objective" media have since explained, the Freemen are adherents to Identity Christianity. The media have lately even told us that Identity followers believe that white folks are the children of God—and the children of Israel, et cetera—and that Jews and non-whites are the sons of Satan. Or, in other words, the Freemen, according to our media, believe that God is a racist and anti-Semite.

But that description of the Freemen is not universally true. The big-time media haven't told you, but Identity believers are divided into at least a dozen competing camps, including "one seed" advocates and their rivals, "two seed" devotees. The "one seed" camp—the growing faction, I understand—believes that all of us are children of God and can become his chosen people, and great-great-multi-great-grandchildren of Israel, by obeying the many rules on conduct and worship set forth in the Good Book. If that's racist, I don't know why.

Among other things I wanted to learn from the Freeman was whether the "one-seed, two-seed" debate was going on in their circles, as I'd heard. It's a little matter of trying to get the facts straight.

The "financial fraud" run by the Freemen is complicated and certainly original but not completely without merit if you take U.S. law literally. A quick example: look at a dollar bill. Once upon a time, these bills said that the bearer could exchange them for gold, something of universal value. Today, the bills say only that they are Federal Reserve notes. A note is an IOU. A dollar bill says that a federal bank owes you one dollar, which is what you're holding in your hand. The federal banker has no means to pay you one dollar except to exchange one piece of paper for another or to give you a Susan B. Anthony dollar or a hundred pennies, none of which has the value of gold.

So far, the system has worked well enough for me, but the Freemen are skeptical. The Constitution says that Congress shall have the power "to coin money, regulate the value thereof," and not to make paper IOUs, they say. So what the Freemen and other groups have done is gotten assets of their own by filing what the media call "bogus liens" against public officials. The FBI says this has been done simply to cover up bad debt.

Such Rube Goldberg money schemes would border on entertainment if they were carried out as such. Instead, groups like the Freemen have cooked them up in what they call self-defense. At the core of the Freemen group is a handful of farmers and ranchers who, in law if not yet in fact, have lost their holdings to their lenders. Some blame them for bad farming. The Freemen say international cabals have used questionable laws to gut farmers and ranchers.

News coverage like I read in the *Times* is searched for hidden messages at places like the Freemen farm. Increasing numbers of ordinary Americans now believe that our country is firmly in the grasp of the International Monetary Fund and the Council on Foreign Relations, that our Constitution and our sovereignty have been usurped, and that shadowy schemers, bankers, and pols are in charge of things.

People like the Freemen believe that these cabals announce their intentions—or condition the public to accept their plans—with code words like "compound," "stockpile," and "suicide plan," delivered by journalists who are in the pay of the Council and the Monetary Fund.

When the fears of one's readers aren't addressed, when demonizing terms are printed as fact, the record shows that tragedy ensues. What I saw in the coverage of the Freemen standoff was the script of Waco being replayed. A conspiratorial group breaks the law, the government descends in force, the press brings in slander, and people die.

I wanted to get the story from the Freemen's point of view, before they were no more. I was prepared to stay to the end of the siege. I wanted to describe its finale, whatever that would be, from the target area. My instinct was that an eyewitness account would avoid all of the controversy that surrounded Mr. Carmel's fatal fire.

FLANNEL AND DENIM

Before long, I was within shouting distance of the farmhouse. I shouted, "Hello? Anybody here?"

No one answered. I shouted again. Again, no answer.

I kept walking, going a few yards to the right, until I was about 15 yards from the house, off a little to one side. I shouted again. No answer, no movement, nobody in sight. The house looked empty.

Maybe they're just hunkered down, I told myself.

Farther to my right and a little ahead of me lay a weathered building of some kind, maybe a small barn. A pickup was parked beside the barn, and if my memory serves me right, a travel trailer was parked beyond it, on the far side of the barn. A couple of chickens were on the property, pecking on the ground, clucking.

I didn't dare approach the front door, because as long as it was closed, I wouldn't be visible to anyone standing on the other side. I wanted the Freemen to get a view of me in a clearly harmless posture before I got any nearer to them.

I glanced back toward the press area. The photographers were bunched up at the end of their cars. They were looking my way.

Minutes passed. I shouted again. No answer, nothing moved. Then I heard a motor roar. It seemed to be coming from the other farmhouse. I looked to my left and I saw an old, brown pickup speeding down the main road, headed toward the gate where I'd come in. There were two occupants in the pickup's cab, a man and a woman in their 60s, both dressed in flannels and demin. They looked harmless. I raised my book to my chest and waved the Virgin flag as they pulled up beside me.

The woman rolled down her window.

"Are you folks Freemen or FBI?" I blurted.

"Well, who are you?" the woman said in a grumpy way. Her build seemed to be on the chunky side. Dumpy. These folks were dumpy, I told myself, not sleek and strong, like elite agents of the law.

I began explaining my presence.

"Well, you're in the wrong place," the woman said. The man nodded.

"What do you mean?"

"The Freemen don't live here; they live over there," the man said, pointing through his windshield. I looked. Farther down the main road, but far, far back from it, was a third white farmhouse, surrounded by pickups. It could have been the same place that I'd seen through the television lens.

"You mean I've come to the wrong house?"

"Yes, you have," the woman said. "This is where we live. The Freemen don't live here."

I felt like an idiot.

"What can I do?" I asked the couple.

They told me to go back to the road. I told them that I couldn't. The FBI would get me there.

"Are you running from the FBI?" the woman asked.

It was no use explaining.

"Let me cross over your property. I can get to the Freemen farm from here," I pleaded.

"No, we don't want anything to do with this," the woman said. "If all of you media people would go away, we wouldn't have any problems around here."

I couldn't argue with that. Humbled, I thanked the pair and started walking toward the road. I didn't even glance to where the cameras were. I knew those guys were laughing at me.

FBI or Freemen?

On my left, along the driveway that led back to the road, I came to a big barn. I hadn't even noticed it when I walked by, scared, a few minutes earlier. A tractor was parked at its side. About 30 yards beyond the tractor and the barn was barbed-wire fence.

That must be the property line, I told myself. If I could cross onto the Freemen property from the barn area, without going to the road, I'd be safe from FBI seizure. The farm couple wouldn't like it, but they seemed like nice folks and probably wouldn't shoot me for trying.

I headed toward the fence. When I got there, I slipped between its strands. One of them snagged my coveralls. I let the fabric rip. I was in a hurry now.

The snow was nearly two feet deep in the area beyond the fence. But I could see the Freemen house, beyond a ravine and over a ridge. To keep myself visible, I headed for the ridge. When I got atop of it, the Freemen would see me for sure. If they were going to shoot at me, that would be when.

I bogged down in the snow. The going was tough. My lungs, suffering from years of tobacco abuse, did not take to the trek. Before long, I was panting. But I kept moving forward.

At the top of the ridge, I looked down for a long while. A figure in dark clothing came out of the house. He seemed to be moving toward me. We were more than 100 yards apart. A gully lay between us. I headed down the ridge, going for the gully. Another fence came into view.

I ducked through it, just like the others. When I came up, the figure was in plain sight, maybe 30 yards away—shouting distance. I decided to keep my silence. The point was to move on, not to talk midway. The figure moving toward me was a middle-aged man, his torso clad in black, blue jeans on his legs. He had a small, brown mustache. A brown gimme cap was on his head. He looked like a farmer, not an agent.

"What do you want?" he shouted at me.

"Are you FBI or Freemen?" I called back.

"I'm neither."

"You're what?"

"I'm neutral; who are you?" he demanded.

We were closer now. I could see a lapel pin of some kind on his jacket or vest. Agents wear lapel pins; farmers don't. I looked to see if his was a bullet-proof vest, but I couldn't be sure.

We kept moving toward each other. He didn't seem to be armed, but in his right hand he was carrying a small walkie-talkie. It beeped and buzzed.

"Are you a Freeman?" he barked, frowning now. I figured that maybe the Freemen were expecting reinforcements to come in.

"Are you FBI?" I retorted without breaking my pace.

"No," he answered. We were 10 feet apart now.

The FBI had been allowing Freemen relatives to visit the farm, in the hopes that they could talk the group into surrender. I figured that maybe the Freemen had sent one of their kinsmen out to eyeball me.

I explained my situation. He toyed with the walkie-talkie but couldn't make contact.

"Look, my orders are for you to leave. These people don't want to talk to anybody," he said. The man seemed more afraid of me than I was of him. Maybe he thought I was a madman.

"Well, okay, I'll leave," I told him. "But first, let me give you this book." Inside was a note to the Freemen asking them to contact me. He took the book. I pressed my luck.

"Look, it's pretty hard going through that snow. If I'm going to leave, let me go that way," I said, pointing toward the Freemen house.

"No."

"Okay, let me go on the drive that leads up to the house. That way, I don't have to trudge through all of that snow again."

"No," he said.

"Well, how do you want me to leave?" I asked.

"You'd better go back just the way you came," he said, as if he wasn't sure how I'd come—and as though he was peeved that I'd ever shown my face.

I turned and headed back to the first farm, then back down the road. As I came into the press area, the cameramen formed a cordon across the road, their lenses aimed at me. I veered to the left, off of the road, hoping that they'd let me be. They swarmed around me instead. "Who are you? Who do you work for?" they screamed.

"I work for the International Monetary Fund and the Council of Foreign Relations," I shouted back.

They fell back, making way. Some of them later told me that they took me for a Freeman.

Forest and Trees

The Freemen made a fool of me, but they also made fools of themselves. Reporters are only pawns in the chess games of politics and revolution—but you should hang onto pawns when you can. The Freemen should have kept me, and if they are smart, before they die, they will hang a sheet out of a window, as the besieged at Mt. Carmel did, saying, "God Help Us. We Want the Press."

Four days after I made my fruitless run to the Freemen farm, Jim Pate of *Soldier of Fortune* magazine tried to get in. The Freemen knew where Pate stood. He'd spent several days with them last April. Nevertheless, when they spied him walking up the drive to their house, they escorted him swiftly back to the road.

The following morning, Pate returned. The Freemen took him into their farmhouse but only to lecture him about the Common Law for about an hour. Then they sent him packing again.

Their temporizing and reluctance gave the FBI time to design a policy for dealing with impertinent journalists. When Pate passed the federal checkpoint the next day, the FBI warned him that if he again returned to the Freemen farm, it would arrest him on three felony charges: encouraging fugitives, trespassing on a crime scene, and interfering with an investigation. The precise charged may not be appropriate but policemen do have a legal right to quarantine an area. Pate had to back away from his plans to visit the Freemen again, and so did I.

Nobody from the media has tried to reach the Freemen since Pate and I did. In the days since, several parties have tried, with FBI consent, to persuade the Freemen to give in. Retired colonel Bo Gritz and former fugitive

Randy Weaver, an Identity Christian, tried to go in some two weeks ago, but the FBI wouldn't let them pass. Finally, over the weekend of April 27, they were able to negotiate with the Freemen for several hours. If anybody known to the public can bring more Freemen out, it's Gritz and Weaver.

Pate, who knows most of those inside, believes that some take to heart the old battle cry "Give me liberty or give me death." I'm cautiously hopeful, though, that, as Gritz believes, they will surrender peacefully now that they are low on provisions.

Nevertheless, the media and the federal authorities are repeating the mistake of forest and trees. Ruby Ridge, Mt. Carmel, Justus Township, and the Oklahoma City bombing are not mere trees; they are something bigger. If we focus, as our media and political leaders do, on the singular or retail aspect of each incident, on the tree, more people are going to die. American headlines are already becoming like those from Israel, Bosnia, and Northern Ireland—a series of nearly identical reports about arrests of suspected "terrorists," carnage, and negotiation, leading to more arrests, carnage, and negotiation.

Everybody knows that millions of conformist, God-fearing, patriotic, hard-working Americans have, in the past few years, become radically discontent. As a group, they believe their personal fortunes are imperiled, that the nation is in decline, and that their good intentions have been betrayed. Thousands of them are reading our national history (they may be the only Americans who are still doing that), trying to figure out what led to the disaster they see. They have tried to bring their arguments to the public, as even Timothy McVeigh did, in letters to the editor, on talk radio, anywhere they can. The debate can be conducted by the usual means but not by the usual media, whose experts are off in Yuppieland, far from discontent, and whose reporters are standing by the road, waiting on their editors or the FBI.

But in this case, the Freemen must shoulder some blame as well. They are poor strategists at the game of politics, even politics styled as revolution. Journalism is a peon's move in that chess game, but even pawns are important. In revolutions, wars, and chess games alike, players who let the opponent neutralize their pieces, as the Freemen did in letting the press fall to the countermoves of the FBI, are probably headed for a less-than-memorable checkmate or death. Be it heroic or foolhardy, nobody is going to tell the eyewitness story of the Freemen's last struggle.

The 2000s

Reavis toured Texas, wrote guidebooks and documented his travels. In this *Texas Parks & Wildlife* article, published in the August 2004 issue, Reavis returns again to the Texas-Mexico border, presenting conflicts between immigrants, criminals, residents, and authorities.

Los Padillas

About 5 o'clock on a Monday afternoon in April, a half-dozen vintage, tri-hull Monarchs with 200 horsepower motors—sturdy work boats—begin their descents into the waters of Falcon Lake, which straddles the Mexican border between Laredo and McAllen. Their operators, Texas Parks and Wildlife Department game wardens, intend to reach their *sets,* or surveillance stations, without being spotted by lookouts on the Mexican bank, some 2 miles away. As the boats move out of their launch coves, they keep to the American shoreline, seeking concealment between the tops of trees and shrubs—huisache, retama, and mesquite—whose trunks are submerged beneath the surface. The lake's level has been rising with each passing storm. Some of the trees are freshly in bloom.

The game wardens keep their motors at low speeds, careful not to create white water, which is visible from afar. Within 30 minutes, all of them have reached their destinations. Rather than dropping anchor, the crews tie up on still-leafy branches.

From posts atop bluffs on the north bank, two wardens, spotters, scan the water and shorelines. One of them has the assistance of a Border Patrol agent and his *Snoopy truck*, as the men call it, a vehicle loaded with high-tech surveillance devices. When the sun goes down, the lawmen's radios begin to crackle with tantalizing coded messages.

"Hotel 9 on the Mike side, running white water," one of the transmissions says, citing the location of a suspect boat.

The dozen men upon the water are mostly game wardens, some accompanied by men from the Border Patrol's Special Response—or SWAT—Team, because the effort that's underway, called Operation Pescador, or Fisherman, is not simply a game-law affair.

CARP AND COCAINE

During the past 6 years, wardens at Falcon Lake—officially known as International Falcon Reservoir—have confiscated more than 150 boats and their motors, arrested more than 250 suspects and destroyed a quarter-million feet of gill net.

But in doing so, they've had to confront a duty that most of them didn't anticipate back when they were studying biology or wildlife management: They've become drug enforcers, soldier-sailors in a war that has no rules of engagement and knows no end.

Eliseo Padilla of Zapata, 56, is the mentor of the group. Retired in 2002 after nearly 30 years on Falcon Lake, over time he became so legendary that Mexican commercial fishermen in the area refer to all game wardens by his name: "Los Padillas," they call them.

Padilla still comes around to aid his successors, and to size up their challenge, which he describes with unblinking candor: "The commercial fishermen and the drug-runners are one and the same," he declares. "The purpose of the fishermen today is just to provide a legality, a legal covering."

Drug seizures on fishing boats back up his assessment. During the past 6 years, game wardens at Falcon Lake have confiscated more than 25 tons of marijuana and 200 kilos of cocaine.

The behavior of the fishermen that the game wardens have taken into custody on purely game-law charges seems to support the charge as well. Fishermen, even commercial fishermen, lead economically precarious lives in Mexico, yet the men don't complain about the punishments they face.

Netting is a Class C misdemeanor, penalized with fines of $250 to $500. Mexicans accused of netting usually plead guilty, then sit out their fines in the Zapata county jail, discharging their penalties at a rate of $50 a day; most are free within a week.

Jail time is less a hazard than the loss of their rigs, worth $2,000 to

$5,000, when the costs of boats, motors and nets are summed. But even a loss of that magnitude rarely inspires a cross word.

Photos of netters in custody show them joking and gesturing, carrying on as if at a backyard fiesta.

"You'll arrest two of them, and they'll tell you, 'Hey, you better go catch so-and-so and so-and-so.' And they'll tell you where they are, too. When you catch the others, those in the first group cheer. It's like they don't want to go to jail alone," says Marshall Davidson, 24, a Zapata-based warden.

The conclusion that game wardens draw is that most of the fishermen are front men, straw men, maybe even decoys: Somebody else, probably a smuggler, is covering their losses.

The apparent alliance between the fishermen and drug-runners has, during the past 10 years, redefined the job that Falcon-area game wardens do. It has turned every attempt to halt and inspect a boat into a possible shooting scene, every chase into an armed pursuit. The wardens, already trained as lawmen, have had to master military techniques as well.

Despite the blazing skies of the border country, the Falcon Lake wardens now wear bulletproof vests: "Better hot than shot," they say. After sundown, they peer through night-vision goggles that they've borrowed from their better-equipped federal colleagues. While on duty at Falcon, every warden carries a .40-calibre Glock, and on every boat there's a game-warden-issue Mini-14, a rifle that's not necessarily a match for the modern weapons that drug lords love. And in this wireless age, it's anybody's guess which side, outlaw or law enforcement, calls on the greater arsenal of cell phones.

When the game wardens at Falcon surprise a Mexican netting crew, they don't know whether they'll find carp or cocaine, pocket knives or pistols.

Sometimes they find all of those things.

And sometimes, they find only boats and nets, or maybe those things and a blanket or two.

Barbecue and Binoculars

Operation Pescador, staged in late April, began with a Monday meeting at a ranch near the lake. Just after noon, 13 game wardens in khaki uniforms, two plainclothes custom agents and three border patrol agents in camouflage fatigues, got together in a garage on the privately-owned spread. They were a burr-headed and electric lot, with wires and microphones hanging from their epaulets. With saddles, tires, chain saws, and welding tanks as witnesses, they mapped, for one last time, a plan of action.

They deliberated in metal folding chairs around a long table laden with barbecue. Some of them had come in the night before and taken bunks in an adjoining room whose sole virtue was air-conditioning. During the morning hours of a workday that would last past midnight, the early arrivals had prepared grub for them all. Bacon-wrapped jalapenos stuffed with cheese were the trademark delicacy of the operation, whose pre- and post-action meetings, during the course of four days, resembled campfires at a late-season deer camp more than meetings of any board.

As the men reviewed their written orders, nervous or distracted, they toyed with knives, flashlights, binoculars, the tools of their trade, and opened, closed, and stirred the ice chests that would supply them with sandwiches and soft drinks during the long nights ahead.

Several men grumbled that on cloudy, moonless nights, like the one awaiting them, their borrowed night-vision goggles would be needed more than ever, but would be of very little use, because where there's no light, the goggles don't help much. On the water, when one can't see much, they said, one hears things that only long experience can make sense of: the rhythm of oil pumps, the rumble of unlighted vehicles, and the wafting snatches of laughter and conversation.

Most of the men at the barbecue table had met before the operation began, but only a few were neighbors. Three wardens are assigned to Zapata County, where most of Falcon Lake lies. Supervisory and line personnel alike had been drawn from further reaches. Captain Chris Huff, 58, a short, graying Laredo native who learned his military skills in Vietnam, commanded the mission. He came from Hebbronville, 130 miles away in Jim Hogg County, which has no lakes for wardens to supervise. Others came from McMullen, Webb, and Atascosa counties, pulled away from their usual warm-weather chores.

Most of the men had taken part in a four-day hunt for Falcon netters two weeks before, an operation whose success—six suspects, five boats, and some 10,000 feet of net—gave them hope on that Monday. Some of them had also helped seized a couple of tons of marijuana in an operation the year before.

Their mood was optimistic, though it would turn doubtful before Operation Pescador was done.

The men said no departure prayers as they left the meeting, perhaps because they've grown accustomed to uncertainty and peril. But Huff's parting words to the group were chilling: "Don't be shooting at anybody unless they be shooting at us."

An International Border

Policing Falcon Lake, for either gill nets or dope, is, for diplomatic and logistical reasons, not a simple affair. Not only is the Lake expansive—120 square miles in size—and rising, but it also straddles an international boundary. Mexican laws and Mexican authorities govern the south side of the lake, Texas laws and American authorities, the opposite half.

The problem is that the two sides meet under water, and there can't be a white line running down the middle of a lakebed. Instead, the boundary is suggested by a series of small towers, planted about a mile apart along the center point of the Rio Grande's channel. Lawmen reckon the boundary by eyeball, lining up the boats they see with an imaginary line between the markers. When they can see the markers, that is.

"They used to be lighted by batteries, but commercial fishermen need batteries, too," quips Huff.

At night, the towers are sometimes dark profiles against a lighter sky, and sometimes it takes minutes to spot them.

Game wardens at Falcon are not authorized to pursue suspects across the line. If a chase starts on the north side of the boundary, they can't tail their subjects into Mexico, nor make an arrest on the Mexican bank. This forces them to lie in wait until boats cross into American waters, and usually, until they halt in a Texas-side cove. When—and if—that happens, the flotilla gathers at the mouth of the cove, its boats ready to foil any exit by shining spotlights into the suspects' eyes.

But even when they have their suspects bottled up, the chances of apprehending them are 50/50 at best. Treetops, brush, and miles of mesquite-studded ranchland aid getaways.

The wardens praise their sturdy Monarchs, but the boats that commercial fishermen use, made by Argos, a Mexican manufacturer, are nearly as narrow as a canoe.

"They can slither into those treetops, and in the darkness it gets hard to find them," complains Martin Oviedo, 32, one of the Zapata-based wardens.

Texas law allows TPWD agents to confiscate boats used in illegal fishing operations, and seizures are common. But once suspects realize that they're surrounded, they usually beach, abandon their craft, and take off in a run.

"Once they hit that brush, they're gone," says Huff, who has worked the lake for 29 years.

An Aquatic Stakeout

On that April Monday, shortly before sundown, a call comes over the wardens' radio network. The spotters see a watercraft, and a warden from his post on the lake notes that, "It sounds like a dude boat to me." A *dude boat,* in the argot of the wardens, is a sport-fishing craft, and at Falcon, pleasure craft appear mainly on weekends. The lake is notorious for a dearth of game fish, which some anglers blame on the netters. Other messages say that four people are aboard, too many for an ordinary netting expedition.

The suspicion of the wardens is aroused by the dude boat. During the past few years, smugglers have begun using speedy bass boats for what lawmen call *heat runs*—reconnaissance missions. When they spot what they take to be a heat run the wardens usually keep to their stations hoping that their presence won't be detected.

The dude boat that the flotilla puts under watch goes upriver and then beaches at a spot more than a half-mile from the nearest warden. Three of its occupants disappear into the brush onshore. Then its pilot turns and speeds back to Mexico. No one drops a net, nobody is seen unloading bundles, no vehicle is standing in wait. The flotilla's boats keep near the banks.

"Maybe he was just dropping off some guys that work on a ranch," somebody comments by radio.

Entering the United States across Falcon Lake is not legal, even for citizens, but on the border, informal crossings are an old and enduring custom. The men of Operation Pescador don't want to tip their hands for the sake of an offense that, in the region's courts, might not appear offensive in the least.

The sky turns black and the wind gains speed, creating waves almost like those of the Gulf. The wardens say that Mexican commercial fishermen do go netting in choppy water, even on moonless nights, but none are seen or heard.

The chief tools of *the commercials*, as wardens call them, are indiscriminate gill and hoop nets—both illegal in Texas. Their catch consists mostly of rough fish, carp, and tilapia, whose retail market is limited on the northern bank. But those species are stewed and fried in Mexico, and even if they weren't, fishermen might still venture onto the lake because some are either lookouts or decoys for drug smugglers, or smugglers themselves.

Hours pass. Nobody is seen, nothing is heard. Midnight comes, and still the radio remains silent. About 1 a.m., Huff calls the effort to a close. The wardens, still keeping their motors at low speeds, slip back into their coves and their pickups. Using only dim running lights, they lumber back to the bunkhouse in which most will pass the rest of the night.

Tuesday the team returns to the lake, for a similarly uneventful experience, concluded at 3 a.m. On Wednesday it's the same, and Huff, sensing disappointment in his ranks, ends the operation at 11 p.m. Before turning in, the men compare speculations. Most believe that Operation Pescador has been detected. The ranch that is their staging ground has civilian guards at its gates, and oil company trucks work the area every day until sundown. Somebody has a cell phone and a brother-in-law among the fishermen; somehow there has been a tip-off, they believe.

Even Captain Huff has lost his confidence.

"It's like a cat and mouse game," he muses. "Our surveillance gets better and then their intelligence gets better. Right now I think that their intelligence must be better than it was."

But he doesn't lose his determination. Skeptical, sleepy, a little unkempt, and by now, tired of bunkhouse life and longing for home, on Thursday the men of Operation Pescador return to their coves to repeat their daylight-sneak routine. Then they wait, as they have waited for three nights.

On Monday and Tuesday, as they passed the hours, the wardens chatted quietly about mutual friends, family members, and food. By Wednesday, some were talking shop, trading agency gossip, even discussing the apparent looming futility of their mission. On Thursday, there wasn't much talk. Everybody was simply pooped.

And bored.

Bored, that is, between 10 p.m. and midnight.

Early in the evening, the wardens on the south end of the night's operation, whose area spanned 6 miles of water, spied a boat with four occupants. It passed a marker and then suddenly turned in the opposite direction and came to a stop, apparently in response to another boat, near another marker, whose two crewmen were waving oars—a signal of some kind. The occupants of the two boats chatted for a few minutes, then drifted southward as night fell. A few minutes later, both of them, Huff believed, "boogied to the Mexican side," though he admits that in the darkness one of the boats may have slipped unseen to the American shore.

Not long afterwards, game wardens Bubba Shelton, 47, and David Murray, 40, both of Tilden, found a net strung beneath the waters. They tied up nearby, keeping their eyes peeled. Nobody came to tend it. The wardens didn't know whether its owners were hidden in the cove or on the Mexican side of the lake. They waited.

Nothing happened. For hours.

Then Zapata's Oviedo, on duty as a spotter atop the dam, which lies at the south or downriver end of the lake, saw a boat slide past.

"It was idling as quiet as could be about midnight," he recalls.

He informed the others by radio, but the boat slipped between treetops near the shore and was lost from sight.

The flotilla began closing in. Shelton and Murray cruised along the shore of their cove looking for the netters for nearly an hour. They didn't see any boat or anybody.

About 1 a.m., Captain Huff, who had been spotting, came to the cove on foot. He probed the shoreline for what seemed to be an eternity and finally stumbled onto a boat—freshly abandoned.

Nothing had been heard or seen in the other cove some two hours later when Huff set off to find the boat that Oviedo had glimpsed before it vanished into the night. But before he reached it, warden Davidson came upon the craft in his Monarch. Its occupants had taken to the brush, too.

The interlopers had made their getaways, but they'd left behind a 16-foot and an 18-foot craft, along with nets, motors and gasoline rigs.

The crew of one of the boats had also run off without their sleeping gear—a couple of cotton blankets. Apparently, they too, had planned on waiting until near-sunup. What's not known is whether they were waiting on fish to fill their net, or for smugglers to make contact.

When the second boat was recovered, Huff called it a day, ending the search that had brought his flotilla to Falcon.

Operation Pescador had not been a striking success, but it hadn't failed; stakeout jobs often end with such mixed results, any lawman knows. The wardens and their federal colleagues had prevented the netters from profiting for a night—and most likely, had nicked their dope-dealing backers for thousands of dollars in replacement costs.

They had done something else as well, and the blankets showed it. Though it wasn't important in the greater scheme of things, because of their own exhaustion, it loomed large in the game wardens' minds: By staying on the water until the wee hours, they had deprived their elusive prey of some badly needed sleep.

From the Johnson administration to the Bush administration, Reavis consistently reflects upon radical agitation, as he does here in an article that originally appeared in the *Independent Weekly*, March 23, 2005.

What's It Take to Get an Anti-War Movement Going?

It's hard to believe, but turnout for the March 19 anti-war festival in Fayetteville—headquarters of the Green Berets and 82nd Airborne Division—may have been unmatched in any other American locale.

But Fayetteville's achievement—rallying more than 4,000 people in a city of 120,000—only underscores a setback for American peace forces on March 19.

London and Istanbul staged six-figure rallies, but according to the mainstream media, San Francisco, New York, and Washington, D.C. may have failed to top not only their past performances, but the turnout in an isolated North Carolina town a mere fraction of their size.

The numbers may be forever in dispute, but the news reports that about 4,000 demonstrators marched on Saturday in Los Angeles, and "several [uncounted] thousand" in New York and San Francisco, both of which would have had to field more than 100,000 protestors to match Fayetteville's relative success. Across the board, *The New York Times* pointed out, anti-war actions were "nowhere as big as those in February 2003."

Even by the standards of its sponsors the Fayetteville rally was not an unqualified triumph. Only 13 buses arrived from out of town, four times as many as in 2004, but a fifth of what this year's organizers hoped to bring.

The Fayetteville action, more like an Americana July 4th picnic than any Days of Rage, was as placid and serene as the weather that day—temperatures in the lower 60s, dry, cloudy skies. No one keened or got red in the face, nobody clashed with the fascists, and policemen's boots didn't lose their spit-shines. The protestors were clad in loose-fitting, informal garb—jeans, cotton windbreakers and sweatshirts, athletics shoes and baseball caps. More than 90 percent of them were white—"middle-class hippies" of all ages, one participant quipped.

The North Carolina Peace and Justice Coalition had called the Fayetteville action to place Iraq-war veterans, bereaved families, active-duty soldiers, and their kin in the center of the anti-war crusade. The rally probably accomplished that aim.

But the vexing question is whether even an anti-war surge from within the military—if that's what Fayetteville inspired—will be able to bring sanity to our times.

"President Bush did not comment on the protests, which seemed unlikely to have any significant effect on national policy or on the glacial movement of public opinion," *The New York Times* opined at the end of the day.

The march formed on a downtown parking lot before noon, buses disgorging pilgrims from afar, contingents gathering beneath banners and signs. Led by a woman blowing a bagpipe—as if in a military parade—about 1,200 marchers, led by some 200 soldiers, ex-servicemen, and kin, strolled some 20 minutes over gently sloping residential streets to the north side of Rowan Park, a 50-foot depression surrounded by natural mounds.

From the park's pavilion at the bottom of the Rowan bowl, a 10-foot banner bearing the slogan of the event—*Support the Troops for Real! Bring Them Home Now!*—beckoned in a gentle wind.

Sheriff's deputies at two entry points conducted airport-style security checks, metal-detecting wands in hand. The procedure was congestive—some participants stood in line for nearly an hour waiting to pass—inspiring a chant that has become a litany from shore to American shore: "This is what democracy looks like!" the protestors intoned, pointing at their own ranks. "This is what a police state looks like!" turning toward the police.

"This is what democracy looks like in a police state," one of them observed; Rowan Park is one of those "free speech areas" that are out of sight, out of mind. From street level, you can't see what's transpiring down in the bowl.

But after a few minutes, almost nobody complained about the security screening because on the north side of the scene, along the rim of the park, stood about 100 counter-demonstrators with lynching on their minds: "Fry Mumia," their T-shirts harrumphed.

A cadre of seasoned regional activists—one of whom, gray-bearded Quaker Chuck Fager, 62, has been agitating since the days of the Selma voting rights march—had spent six months making national appeals and local arrangements to build the protests. As the marchers passed through the security screens it seemed as if the effort had failed; the first Fayetteville Iraq-war rally, in 2004, had drawn as many participants as had come from downtown.

But a couple of hundred peace advocates were already lounging on the greens, and as late afternoon warmed into spring, latecomers arrived by the score. By the time music groups and speakers began addressing the assembly, about 1 p.m., the crowd had doubled its size—and it didn't quit building for an hour after that.

The Associated Press put Fayetteville's turnout at 3,000, and march organizers claimed 1,800 more. By my own estimate, 4,200 people were gathered at the protest at its peak, about 2 p.m. Saturday.

Americans, complain as they may, are never, ever, alone. Commerce accompanies us from conception to—perhaps the far side of the Golden Gates. By the time the marchers arrived, politically correct vendors had laid merchandise atop 40 tables on the east side of the speaker's kiosk. Merchants at this Green-Beret-city bazaar brought with them pins and buttons of 900 designs, and possibly more books than escaped the looting and fires at libraries in Iraq.

Most of the merchants represented pastel peace groups and mild-mannered petition societies, but Trotsky's disciples—of a half-dozen stripes—brought tables, too, laden with literature that scientifically proves that pacifists, peace Democrats, and former comrades from the adjoining Trotsky tables have all taken part in the Revolution Betrayed.

At a table in the middle of the money-and-mailing-list exchanges stood two Seventh-Day Adventists, collecting signatures for a petition against Sunday closing laws.

On the west side of the grass-lined bowl, just across a tiny creek that courses in front of the speaker's pavilion, vinyl doors were opened and shut on 19 portable outhouses, a number sufficient to prevent the formation of lines. But the rally's half-dozen "poppers," or food-and-drink stands, weren't up to speed; demonstrators stood 20 minutes in line for plates of curry and hastily steamed hotdogs.

As they stood in line the participants gazed southwards up the hillside at 100 mock caskets draped in flags. Dozens of black umbrellas, resting on the ground, were strewn across the eastern incline, their surfaces inscribed at previous protests with the names and ranks of the war dead. Children daubed flower motifs and adults lettered slogans on new umbrellas, just to pass the time. The supervisors of this project, called Parasols for Peace, supplied brushes and colors. "We are doing this to provide a free and cheap way of breaking the silence in this time of fear," one of them told me.

About 1 p.m. the procession of speakers got under way. Among those who addressed the crowd were the stars of Fager's burgeoning submovement: pacifist Camilio Mejia, only two days earlier let out of an Army brig; retired Green Beret Sgt. Stan Goff; and Cindy Sheehan, the sparkplug in a group called Gold Star Families for Peace. Sheehan wore a white T-shirt stenciled with a photo of a soldier in uniform: her son, Casey, killed last year in Iraq.

But it was the content of the speeches—some of them lively and a couple powered with pathos—that exemplified the weakness of the March 19 protests, not only in Fayetteville, but from coast to coast.

In Rowan Park, and in locales elsewhere, organizational democracy precluded inspiration. The rally's organizers drew a list of nearly 30 speakers, practically one for every group in the coalition's fold. Apparently guided by a principle that might be called One Organization, One Speech, the rally's steering committee limited addresses to three minutes each. Admirably, most of those who stepped up to the microphone stayed within their allotted time.

But not even a Jefferson, a Frederick Douglass, or Karl Marx can convey a nation-transforming message, nor present any significant analysis, in a 90-second span. Perhaps for brevity's sake, almost all of the speakers drew from a well-worn repertoire of 10:

1. Iraq had no weapons of mass destruction.
2. Terrorists didn't take harbor there.
3. Most of the world disapproves of the invasion.
4. 1,500 American soldiers have died in combat.
5. American troops were sent to war in ignorance, with insufficient tools.
6. Many can't know when, or if, they're coming home.
7. American weapons have killed as many as 100,000 civilians.
8. The war is a luxury that our nation can ill afford.
9. The "War on Terror" has put American civil liberties in peril.
10. George W. Bush is unfit for the presidency.

It's all like a game of Texas Sweat: players draw distinct hands, arrange their cards into suits, and with individual styles and rhetorical flourishes, stake their hopes and livelihoods. But the house of Bush is dealing us a losing hand, as turnout for the March 19 demonstrations makes plain.

It may be that you can't fight city hall, that rulers have been hoisting and crucifying their subjects since the days of Spartacus, and always will. But our pose, or posture, and even our performance could be improved—or at least that's the message from North Carolina's leading leftist sage.

Michael Hardt, 45, a literature professor at Duke University, is co-author with Italian Antonio Negri of two recent tomes on globalization and the perspectives of resistance. Hardt, an admirer of the multifaceted Seattle protests of 1999 who is frequently pummeled as a producer of inscrutable postmodernist prose, lost little time in getting his bearings after the downturn of March 19.

Though he did not attend the Fayetteville action—he was on a plane returning from France—he says he knows why the demonstrations were not bigger and better, everywhere.

"When movements grow is when they propose the agenda for change," he declares. "One of the effects of the war on terror is that all we are doing is reacting. The anti-war movement has become a failure because it has conceded the terrain of issues to the pro-war people."

Hardt's general argument is that oppositionists should struggle to implement their unredacted dreams for a full vision of the lives they want to live, not for a list of reforms or bargain items underlined in red.

To return to a stage of growth, Hardt argues, the movement will have to recall what it hoped to gain by closing ranks to challenge Bush's adventurism in the first place.

Was it only a preemption of war, or peace once the invasion came? Or was it that, as the slogan went, *Another World Is Possible*—and that we wanted to live there today?

Although most of Reavis's articles were written for Texas print magazines, he also wrote for national publications, pushing beyond traditional print media to internet magazines. Reavis wrote this piece (July 10, 2006) for *Salon*. Salon.com, is a politically progressive news and editorial website, founded in 1995.

The Real Winners in Mexico

When Andrès Manuel López Obrador, leftist candidate and ostensible loser of Mexico's still contested presidential election, called a rally Saturday afternoon in the Zocalo, Mexico City's main square, 300,000 people answered. It was three times the turnout for the biggest rally held by his rival and the declared winner of the election, Felipe Calderón. The crowd greeted López Obrador's claims that Calderón's rightist allies stole the election with a chant of, "Andrès, hang on, the people are rising!" As the rally dispersed, the crush was so intense that a more common cry was, "Don't push, there are children here!"

Official results, however, put Calderón and his party, *Partido Acción Nacional* (PAN) ahead of López Obrador by about the number of people gathered in the Zocalo. López Obrador presented his formal protest of the final tally to the Federal Electoral Tribunal on Sunday, July 9, the day after the Zocalo rally, but soothsayers in all three of Mexico's major parties still expect the Tribunal to declare Calderón the winner.

Yet no matter how the Tribunal ultimately rules, neither López Obrador nor Calderón will win the power he seeks. The real winners of the July 2 presidential election are the Televisa and Azteca television networks, the Institutional Revolutionary Party, or PRI, which ran Mexico from 1929 to 2000, and Subcomandante Marcos, the leftist guerrilla turned pop culture icon.

Television was an obvious winner, and in Mexico TV means the twin behemoths Televisa and Azteca. The PAN spent $68 million for 70,000 commercial spots, about $4.50 for each of the 15 million votes Calderón received. The poorly capitalized Democratic Revolutionary Party (PRD), López Obrador's party, spent half Calderón and PAN's total for a nearly identical number of votes, while the PRI burned through $40 million for fewer than 10 million votes. Half the Mexican population lives on less than $10 a day. If the Mexican population remains evenly split between three competitive parties, the networks will continue to reap the benefits in coming elections.

The party that came in third, the PRI, also came out a winner. It will now hold few important national offices, but its stamp on Mexican politics endures. The PRI, which once ran Mexico as a single-party state, still makes the rules by which the other parties play the game.

Part of that dominance is purely cultural, as was evident on Sunday, June 25, when Calderón held his traditional cierre, or closing rally, in Mexico City.

The PAN would've preferred to stage the finale elsewhere, both because it advocates the decentralization of Mexican life and because its strength lies in the nation's north and west. But during its 71 years in power the PRI always staged everything in Mexico City, making it unthinkable for any party to close a political campaign anywhere else.

The PRI also always did everything over-the-top, citing Aztec tradition, and the austere, conservative PAN was forced to follow suit. Since Mexico City is PRD territory, the PAN had to import supporters to fill the 100,000-seat Azteca soccer stadium, bussing in bodies from the provinces, even flying in volunteers from the Yucatan. A soap opera star, a dozen bands, and a pro wrestler named the Blue Demon provided the entertainment, before Calderón delivered a 40-minute speech with the aid of a radio receiver strapped to his body. Blue, white, and orange balloons flooded the stadium, and cannons shot confetti into the sky.

More important than symbols, however, the PRI also won a share of power. No matter what the outcome of any ballot recount, the Mexican Congress will be almost evenly divided between the PAN and PRD. In the 500-seat lower house the PAN will have 210 seats, the PRD 163, and the PRI 113. Because any coalition between the PAN and the PRD is inconceivable, the PRI will have the swing vote.

To get any program passed, Calderón or López Obrador will have to buy votes, and Congress became a seller's market with the July 2 stalemate. The PRI ran third in the balloting, but it won the race by the rules under which it has played for the past 25 years. In the bad old days I once interviewed a mayoral candidate who told me he declined a PRI nomination after he was told he'd have to pay the governor of his state $15,000 to get it. I also witnessed journalists being bribed to write favorable stories. After this election, I believe nothing will move in Mexico unless the PRI's men get paid.

The third unannounced winner of the July 2 vote was the ex-guerrilla leader Subcomandante Marcos. A dozen years ago, this charismatic, ski-masked figure acquired a heady popularity when the forces of his Zapatista Liberation Army briefly took over five southern Mexican towns. Until last year, most Mexicans were saying, *"Marcos, ya pasó"*— "Marcos, he's over."

But last August, the anarchist became a TV talking head, albeit a ski-masked one, a sort of left-wing version of such American cable pundits as Bill Bennett and Pat Buchanan. The authorities did not arrest Marcos when he came in from the heat of Chiapas, perhaps out of fear of rousing the left. Soon his followers were out in the open too, lending their support to the López Obrador candidacy. The Marcos movement, which called itself "the Other Campaign," claimed only 15,000 formal affiliates, but when it held a rally in Mexico City on the eve of the vote, more than 30,000 supporters came.

The Other Campaign's chief slogan was and is, "From below, and to the left," but its best expression may be, "Our dreams won't fit in your ballot boxes." Despite sympathy for López Obrador, many Marcos followers never believed elections mattered anyway. The Other Campaign's official stance on the last week's wrangling over vote totals is, "No comment," which is its sophisticated way of saying, "I told you so." Once Calderón is declared the official winner, the Marcos movement will swell with thousands of disillusioned defectors from the PRD.

Whoever becomes president of Mexico this year will face a deadlocked Congress that only cannonades of cash will move to action. He will face an impoverished people contemptuous of all politicians. Once the eventual winner of the election is sworn into office and draped in his tricolor sash on Dec. 1, other contenders—the PRI, television, Marcos and, most of all, cynicism—will have crawled away with Mexico's prize. The words of an American president will haunt his life. "If it weren't for the honor of the thing," Abe Lincoln once said, "I'd just as soon it happened to someone else."

The 2010s

At the age of sixty-two, Reavis explored the world of day laborers. Taking a variety of assignments from an agency, he describes various manual labor jobs and the people who take them in a series of stories in *Catching Out: The Secret World of Day Laborers* (Simon & Schuster, 2010). In this collection of vignettes of day labor life, Reavis navigates preconceptions, prejudices, and stereotypes that often eclipse clear vision and fill the world with hostilities—sometimes he navigates them brilliantly, at other times he is drawn into them. Nevertheless, Reavis makes clear that every honest writer must attempt such navigations and be aware of how race, ethnicity, age, gender, and all such aspects of identity are at play in every interaction.

from *Catching Out: The Secret World of Day Laborers*

CHAPTER 4: THE SQUARE PEG

The hall where I reported for work was one of those one-story, flat-roofed, red-brick affairs built circa 1959 by what must have been called the Small Business Administration School of Ranch Style Architecture. In its era the building's clean and efficient lines—nothing wasted, not an extra penny spent—made it "modern." By 2007, when I first passed through its double glass doors, it was simply ugly and old.

It was also out of place. It sat about four blocks west of downtown in what, fifty years before, had been a neighborhood of African American manual workers. Though a small-scale housing project remained—the source of many of the hall's workers—the neighborhood had been gentrified over the decades. Most of the neighborhood's residents, by 2007, were White college students and white-collar workers.

The building fit into its surroundings, or didn't, depending upon the hour. At five in the morning, it looked like any office building in any residential neighborhood, as if it housed an insurance agency or an optometry clinic. But by six, hard-bitten laborers were filing through is doors or loitering on its porch and driveway. At seven, the demographic began to shift as joggers huffed past in nylon gym suits, young White men and women for whom physical activity was a pleasure, not a curse. By nine, when most laborers who didn't "catch out" had gone home, students were on its sidewalks. Their backpacks carried CDs and books, not work gloves and breakfast biscuits.

Inside the building was one big room, about 15 feet by 30 feet, with offices and a restroom in smaller enclosures on its southern side. A dozen . . . sometimes two dozen men and a clutch of women sat scattered among thirty-six plastic lawn chairs. Sometimes a dozen more stood around the room, and usually, a half-dozen people were outside, smoking. All the while a television set at low volume displayed images from newscasts and quiz shows punctuated by commercials from personal injury lawyers and payday lenders.

At the west end of the room stood a counter, 12 feet long and nearly 5 feet tall, built of 4x8 Masonite sheets, painted blue, and topped with mock-mahogany Formica. When I entered each day, like everyone else, I went to the counter and signed my name on a list, putting an *N*, for "no," in a blank to indicate that I didn't have my own means of transportation.

On a swivel stool behind the counter sat Dolly, waiting for her telephone to ring. Sometimes it did ring. When it did, we could hear only mumbling. But afterward, if we were lucky, we'd hear a printer buzz as it printed a ticket.

One morning as I was waiting a college-age man came in, a new face in the hall. He was tall, but his flesh was soft and his skin very white. Auburn hair hung down to his shoulders. He wore a pastel T-shirt, cargo pants, and jogging shoes, plus a necklace on which hung a crystal and a five-pointed star.

Effervescent, he was talking to Stella, the office manager—a slender, narrow-faced White woman in her thirties—so loudly that the whole hall could hear.

"Most of my skills are office skills," he proclaimed. "I know Word and Excel, and with a little brushing up I could do PowerPoint as well. On my last internship in high school I was classified as an assistant file clerk at an insurance agency."

The guy was obviously in the wrong place, a square peg in a round hole, I told myself. He should have gone to Kelly Services or Manpower, firms that specialized in temporary jobs for white-collar workers.

But he told Stella that he had a car and that, though they hadn't given him enough work, he'd signed on and briefly reported to two competing halls.

To weed out bad apples and paperless aliens, Labor-4-U, like a lot of temporary agencies, required applicants to show two forms of government-issued identification, and their filters sometimes caught people.

Most applicants cleared the bar by providing Social Security cards and driver's licenses—Mr. Office Skills had both—or Social Security cards and an ID card issued by the state to people who don't drive.

The agency also required prospective hires to pass a twenty-minute multiple-choice test.

The test I'd taken, which, from what I heard, was the same for everyone, included questions like these:

◊ *Which of the following drugs have you taken in the past week?*
◊ *In the past year, how many times have you hit somebody?*
◊ *If someone threatens you, how important do you think it is to fight to defend yourself?*

A section of the test about workplace safety came with a ten-page booklet of text, within which were embedded answers to all of its questions.

Office Skills had no trouble passing the tests and was soon briefly seated among the rest of us. As a newbie, he had an advantage. If an agency is short of workers, or if its dispatchers aren't satisfied with some of the regulars, they preferentially assign new recruits to tickets, churning the workforce to improve its quality, they say. From that first day and for the rest of the week the agency kept Office Skills busy.

But when laborers fail to show for a repeat ticket, or turn down jobs, or simply can't handle the labor, dispatchers wordlessly put them on a second string, and Office Skills was benched pretty quickly. Why I did not know. I had been put on the B-team myself, I believe because I'd told Dolly that I didn't want to return to the culvert plant. Workers knew that business was unusually slow, or that they'd been benched, if they were still waiting for jobs when 7:30 came. Though some people hung around until 9:00 or 9:30 anybody who hadn't been dispatched by 8:00 was probably facing a jobless day.

One morning about two weeks after Office Skills signed on, I found myself in the hall mainly with women who—even though they tried their hardest and the hall's dispatchers did their best—were nearly always on the bench. Dispatchers were reluctant to assign them to tasks that were dirty or required prolonged exertion. The upshot was that when males were benched they were placed in competition with women for jobs.

One of the regulars among the hall's laboring women was Little Carrie. Blue-eyed and in her late fifties, she couldn't have weighed more than 95 pounds. Perhaps because we were close in age, or because both of us were white, she often took a seat next to me.

She rented a room a block from the hall. I occasionally ran into her on my way to report, and on weekends, I'd sometimes come upon her walking a fluffy, fifteen-pound, white dog on a rope, not a leash.

Little Carrie was chinless, and on the street, it was obvious that she walked with a stiff gait, due to arthritis, she said.

Sometimes, she had told me, she house-sat for a lady on the other side of town. The house-sitting job was an after-hours affair; she had to be in the house at night but was free to leave during the day. When she was house-sitting Carrie reported to an across-town labor hall, which usually assigned her to work in school and hospital cafeterias. Labor-4-U mainly sent her to office-cleaning jobs, and every now and then, to unloading trucks and opening and discarding boxes for retail stores.

Day labor, for Carrie, was a way to earn rent money, $250 a month, she said. She received $163 a month in food stamps, more than enough, she thought, and on Wednesday afternoons, if she wasn't at a day-labor job, she went to a nearby church to set tables for a fellowship supper, earning a meal and change. Twenty years earlier, before food stamps were issued via electronically readable plastic cards, she'd probably have sold her surplus to other workers in the hall. In those days people also sold counterfeit bus-fare passes. But information technology has its drawbacks and one of them, she told me, was that sometimes she still had food stamp credits when their expiration dates came.

That morning, while I was benched with Carrie, she reached into her purse, took out a tube of eyeliner and lipstick, even an eyebrow pencil, and tried to make herself "presentable." Chatting to a women next to her, she said that she had a daughter who lived in Europe, but that the two of them were so estranged that she hadn't heard from her in five years.

Turning toward me, she said that she'd suffered from allergies the day before and had taken two tablets that had kept her awake until 4:00 a.m. During the brief time she'd slept, she dreamed that while wearing jeans, she'd found $10 in a front pocket.

"I was rubbing myself right here, where the pocket would be, when I woke up," she said.

B-teams at day-labor halls, I thought, are for people who dream about $10 windfalls.

Sitting near us, as long as she could sit, and otherwise pacing in nervousness around the hall, was Gladys, a woman in her forties who was not much taller than Carrie but was of a much different kind. She wore rhinestone post earrings—Carrie had only a watch—and had a tattoo on each shoulder, though given her blackness, their designs were hard to discern.

Gladys's face reminded me of that of the late writer James Baldwin, but her hairdo was never unkempt—or un-thought-out—as his was. When she first appeared at the hall, her hair was in an Afro, perhaps an inch long. A month later, she practically skinned her head. After that, she adopted a Mohawk.

She had come to Labor-4-U from another hall, which, she complained, dispatched women only to restaurant and office jobs. Gladys wanted to earn a living just like the men—and even more, to work two tickets a day, one in the mornings, one at night. She claimed that she had been a long-haul trucker in an earlier stage of life, and also boasted that once, for a hall in Las Vegas, she had labored thirty-six hours non-stop. She said that she had come to Labor-4-U because she needed to earn a thousand dollars to pay for repair work on her car.

Her countenance was usually a frown. She spoke in a gruff voice, and despite the sign saying that workers should not crowd around the counter, Gladys was often there, pleading.

Desperation served her well. Within a week of her debut, she was strutting in steel-toe boots and a hard hat, not like the items the agency provided, but store-bought. The cost, I suppose, was negligible for her, since she paid no rent. On mornings when I arrived at the hall before five thirty, she was standing in its front yard, washing up at a hydrant. Gladys slept on a roll of blue foam, which she hid behind a bush on the eastern side of the hall.

It wasn't that she had anything against shelters, she said. The problem was that the city buses didn't start their routes early enough to allow her to be first on the sign-in sheet.

Within a couple of weeks of her first day, Gladys had developed a reputation at Labor-4-U. Dispatchers and managers liked her because she proved capable of handling any job, and the men only complained that she worked with too much brio, making them look lax.

Gladys was telling me about a ticket that she had gotten the night before when I heard Dolly call my name, followed by that of the Office Skills guy. It must have been about six thirty.

The job she had for us, Dolly said, was an eight-hour gig, "cleanup" at a construction site. Such jobs are common at day-labor halls, but their particulars varied widely. Sometimes construction cleanup was push-broom and mop work, indoors, dusty or muddy and dull, but hardly exhausting. Sometimes cleanup involved carrying scrap sheets of weighty plywood, short lengths of steel beam, or sacks of hardened cement, and that was a challenge for anyone.

Office Skills and I were assigned to a drugstore project in a suburb. We didn't know whether we'd be called upon to work indoors, outdoors, or both. He drove. His vehicle was a 2006 Buick in whose interior he'd tossed dozens of job application forms and empty bottles of springwater. As we rode, he played a CD whose music sounded to me like the chants of medieval monks. It was from a group called Nox Arcana, he said, telling me that the name came from Latin and meant something on the order of "Night Magic." He also told me that its creators saw themselves as providing a sound track for stories of Edgar Allan Poe.

That he would mention Poe gave me a feeling of dread. Not many men who know an author's name know how to tote plywood and cement.

Cleanup on construction jobs is customarily the responsibility not of subcontractors—carpentry, masonry, electrical, plumbing, roofing, or flooring crews—but of the GC, or general contractor, the person or firm with overall responsibility for a project. GCs never show up on time. Our ticket called for us to report at 7:00, but of course, no one was there but a crew of Mexican plasterers, already high in the air on scaffolds placed against the outside walls of the red-brick shell of the drugstore. Them, and a trucker from Texas.

We chatted with the trucker. He had come from a plant in Mississippi to deliver a half-dozen light poles, and like us, was waiting for the GC.

In the cab of his 18-wheeler was his traveling companion, a shaggy dog named Floosie. Ours was one of three unloading stops that the pair would make before picking up cargo for their return on what would be a six-day trip, the trucker said.

Gasoline and diesel prices were climbing, and the trucker told us that on this run, he was averaging 7.4 miles to a gallon. With heavier loads, he said, he got as little as 6 mpg. Prices didn't bother him, he claimed, because his company paid for fuel, about $1,500 per tank. He made payments only on his $130,000 rig.

Perhaps because he sized up Office Skills the same as I did, he asked why the young man wasn't in college.

"Oh, I tried that," Office Skills said, "down where my parents live. But the college I went to had a cybercafé. I spent all of my time playing video games." He had come to Labor-4-U "mainly to get away from my folks," and was living in a rooming house whose landlady, a middle-aged woman, had thus far given him room and board in exchange for chores.

Our chat lasted an hour and maybe a bit longer. Finally, a half-dozen Anglo electricians arrived and told us that the GC's second-in-command was on-site, in the GC's trailer on a corner of the lot.

Office Skills and I reported—to a fortyish man whose appearance almost made me laugh. He was of average height and a bit thin, but with a wide black mustache that drooped to his chin. He wore short pants and had spindly legs. His torso was swallowed in a pearl-button western shirt, and on his head sat a safety helmet in the form of a cowboy hat. From the waist down, he looked like a scoutmaster, from the waist up, like the sidekick to a sheriff in a Wild West serial.

Our job was outdoors, he said. Between the building and the two busy streets that bordered it was asphalt-clad parking space, and on its three sides, a band of dirt about twenty feet wide that landscapers were to sod with grass. Both the parking area and the band of soil were littered with the detritus of construction work: sections of discarded plastic pipe and steel electrical conduit, foam and fiberglass insulation, broken bricks, and the thin steel posts that in some structures are used as substitutes for pine studs. The curbing was here and there covered with runoff dirt, and at places, tradesmen had piled waste materials against it. The foreman pointed us to a shovel, a spade and a push broom, and we headed off to our task.

We had been scraping and sweeping the curbing for not more than twenty minutes when Office Space said that he had to go to his car, where he had left a tube of sunscreen lotion.

Not more than half an hour later he went back to apply it a second time.

Soon we were piling bricks in stacks that the GC's Bobcat—a gasoline-powered vehicle that's a cross between a forklift and a backhoe—would haul away. We were also carrying empty cement sacks and strands of steel wire to a Dumpster. From his seat on the Bobcat, the Cowboy Foreman was "rednecking" us, as the black workers say, keeping us under his eye, pointing out overlooked or unseen tasks, giving orders, measuring our worth.

He put us to carrying lengths of rebar to a spot just below his trailer-office. Office Skills was straining; for every trip he made, I made one and a half. When we'd finished toting the rebar, the Cowboy pointed to a mound of king-size cinder blocks, also on the would-be lawn. They were heavy—to me they felt like forty pounds—and I could carry just one at a time. But Office Skills didn't know how to carry. He'd grab a block and hold it below his waist, practically straddling it while walking.

He knew he wasn't up to par.

"I'm a total couch potato," he huffed as we passed on the block-carry detail. "I'm a gamer. I'm not competent at physical work."

Since we'd not started until about eight thirty, morning break seemed to come early at ten. Office Skills disappeared into the shell of the building on his way to his car on the site's lawn-less side. He had to get something to eat, a snack he had prepared, he said.

I was leaning against the outside wall of a corner of the building, where a watercooler sat. The Cowboy came up to me.

"I'm going to send your buddy home," he blustered. "He's not working and I won't put up with that."

Cowboy didn't give me time to comment.

"I've had 'em like him before, and every time, I send them home! I ain't afraid to do it, no way!" he snarled.

He may have continued this tirade for a while longer, but finally I got a chance to speak.

"You've got to do what you've got to do," I said with the deference appropriate to addressing one's boss. "But he's just a kid. Maybe he'll learn."

I think the Cowboy was fazed that I didn't feel complimented. One of the saddest things about the construction business is that usually among bosses, and sometimes even among workers, a macho work ethic prevails. If a worker can't lift, shove, carry, push, or bang with enough force or speed, a real man will stick out his chest and fire the weakling on the spot: That's what the ethos requires. It's as if readiness to fire someone is a test of a supervisor's manliness.

Machismo of that sort is heartless in purely male settings, but its most common victims are jobless women. A few days earlier, Dolly had sent four women to a cleanup job, only to have the foreman refuse to let them enter the site. Dolly filed a complaint with government authorities, but that didn't give the women a job for the day.

If Office Skills was a burr under his saddle, I told the Cowboy—stretching the truth a bit—he was the same for me, because I had been carrying more and moving faster to make up for the kid's weakness or sloth. But I'm man enough to take it, I was trying to say.

The Cowboy sighed, as if taking pity on me—for defending the kid, not for my labor. Then he took a drag on his cigarette and turned his head, looking around, as if in thought.

He spoke again. "Who is driving, you or him?"

When I explained, he hurled his cigarette to the ground, snuffed it with a heavy shuffle of his foot, and, I swear, spat to the side.

I reminded him that even if we left, he'd have to pay us for four hours, the minimum charge at Labor-4-U.

"Well, look," he said, as if nearly ashamed. "You warn him that I'm about to send his ass out of here."

I nodded and he went away.

When Office Skills returned from his car we filed in behind Cowboy to follow him to the back of the structure. As soon as he was gone again, I called Office Skills aside.

"Listen, the boss told me that he wants to fire you," I said.

The kid didn't comprehend. "What for?" he asked.

"Because he says you haven't been working."

"But I've been working," he whined.

The trash on the building's back side wasn't as plentiful as elsewhere, and the Cowboy was off riding his Bobcat somewhere. I began to pick up lumber near a spot where a crew of three masons was working. I carried the lumber a few feet and made a stack on the parking lot. Office Skills questioned our need to do that.

"Look," I told him, trying to teach him the ropes. "My job is moving stuff. I get paid for that. If I move stuff that I'm not supposed to move, they'll pay me for moving it back."

I was trying to tell him that we had to stay busy, whether our labor was useful or not. But he didn't understand. Instead, he walked over to the masons and asked which boards we needed to carry away. The result of the conversation was that I had to carry a half-dozen boards back to them.

I moved around the corner, still picking up trash, and Office Skills wandered off, for what purpose, I didn't know. When he returned, he asked me what time we'd break for lunch.

I told him, "Probably at noon."

He said that's what he figured, but that he'd asked the Cowboy, whose answer had been, "When I say so."

"Yeah, it's when he says so," I told him.

"But that's not fair," he said.

I guess the kid thought he was in high school where customs are rules.

I told him that in English we have a word, "shamming," which means to look busy, pretending to work even when doing nothing useful. To make the point, I caught one of the Mexican plasterers as he was passing by, and asked for the equivalent in Spanish: "*hacerse buey*," or "make like an ox." I explained to Office Skills that every worker knew, in one language or another, that shamming was a part of our jobs.

About noon the Cowboy reappeared, telling us that it was lunchtime. Office Skills and I crossed the street to a sandwich shop where he ordered vegetarian fare.

As we ate he told me that the day before he'd worked on a crew whose job was tying wire around cross points in rebar, in preparation for a cement crew. During the course of our conversation I learned that though he'd driven a crew of four others to the work site, he hadn't known that they were supposed to pay him a fare. Nobody had paid—and that meant, I was sure, that they despised the guy.

Perhaps twenty minutes after we returned to our chores Office Skills told me that bending to pick up trash made him dizzy, and that "I can't work under the sun. It just drains my energy away."

"Why don't you tell that to Dolly the next time she gives you a job?"

I asked, out of patience by then.

Fortunately, we were winding up the work at hand. Before two, we were done. The Cowboy had us stack our shovels and broom outside his trailer, then opened the door, sat down at a desk, and asked for the ticket—which I had in my shirt pocket. He filled it out and told us so long.

I glanced at what he'd written, five hours for Office Skills—an accurate figure—and seven for me. As an old hand on the day-labor range the sheriff's deputy knew how to inflict a little pain.

Gladys, and even Little Carrie, I believe—and any of the women at the hall—could have done our job more ably than Office Skills, and Gladys, more ably than me. But I think it's unlikely that the Cowboy would have welcomed them, and even if he didn't send them home, he'd have probably called a competing agency when he next needed a crew.

A couple of weeks later Office Skills drove up to the hall and asked a group of us who were standing outside where he might find another day-labor agency. He had been "terminated," he said, when he'd come in from a ticket the day before. "I guess I wasn't able to do the job," he said sheepishly.

"You should go to Manpower," I told him.

He said that he'd already applied.

Nobody else spoke to him.

He asked if any of us could loan him fifty dollars, which he claimed he needed by the end of the day "for rent." Maybe his landlady had soured on him just as the dispatchers had.

Day laborers aren't heartless. Two-dollar and five-dollar loans are an everyday affair. But fifty dollars is money that can only fall from the skies.

Nobody took up a collection for Office Skills, and perhaps more telling than that, nobody informed him—and I did not recall it at the moment—that only blocks away a plasma collection center was paying new donors fifty dollars a pint.

Reavis returns to radical politics, protest, police brutality—themes that run throughout his entire career—in this article published originally in the *Texas Observer,* September 2, 2011. Here, he brings to the fore the conflict between mainstream media and radical publications, a conflict that influences how history is written.

Fort Worth's Red Scare

On Monday, Sept. 4, 1933, for the first time in 10 years, Fort Worth celebrated Labor Day with a grand parade. The event was not marred, as its planners had feared it would be, by the unemployed rabble. Their leader, a Communist, had been jailed—and was dead before the festive procession began. A police band led a group of 2,000 down Main and Houston streets to the Tarrant County courthouse, followed by elected officials, including Texas Attorney General James Allred, soon to be governor.

Trundling behind the cops and the pols, according to the *Fort Worth Star-Telegram,* came the Union Band and groups of workers, from barbers and bricklayers to pressmen and painters.

Behind them came 250 to 300 uniformed members of the National Guard, the military force most frequently used to suppress strikers. The South Fort Worth Civic League and the Riverside Civic League led the fourth phalanx, which included delegations from luncheon clubs.

A "negro section"—two fraternal-organization bands and a bathing beauty float—brought up the rear. That afternoon, the whites held their own beauty pageant, crowning a "Queen of Labor" at a barbecue at Lake Worth.

News of this happy celebration ran on the front page of the *Star-*

Telegram, just above a story with a smaller headline, "'Reds' Watched By Police Here." The lead sentence read: "A squad of police patrolled city streets Monday to prevent any possible Communistic outbreak feared as the result of the death Saturday night of T.E. Barlow, 40, Communist leader."

Barlow had died at the City-Council Hospital a mere half-hour after his discharge from the Tarrant County Jail, unconscious and in the arms of deputies and a doctor.

Born in Ohio and raised in western Kentucky, Terrence Earl Barlow had learned the carpenter's trade from his socialist father and headed west at an early age. At 17, when he registered for the draft, he was employed as a carpenter at New Mexico's Chino copper mine, a mammoth enterprise that continues today. Only a black-and-white picture survives of him, but annotations on draft registration documents describe Barlow as of medium build with blue eyes and brown hair.

He was soon drafted, or perhaps joined the Army voluntarily; nobody knows which. In a commemorative piece written four years after Barlow's death for the *Labor Defender* magazine, Robert Warren, a truck driver and associate of the labor agitator, recalled Barlow's explanation for his time in uniform: "I was fooled, like every other man who fought."

After World War I, Barlow drifted into Texas. Jobless in 1932, he was earning his keep doing chores at Houston's Salvation Army barracks when he met members of the National Unemployed Council, an organization led by the Communist Party. The council was notorious for staging sometimes-rowdy demonstrations demanding cash relief and the enactment of unemployment insurance bills. Barlow's newfound associates sent him to the party's 1932 nominating convention in Chicago. When he returned he joined its ranks, even accepting a position as the Communist write-in candidate for lieutenant governor in Texas.

In early 1933, the party dispatched him to organize an Unemployed Council in Fort Worth, where, by official estimates, some 6,000 workers were idle. The local council, whose membership soon reached 800, held mass meetings and demonstrations at East Bluff Park, just north of the Tarrant County courthouse.

Barlow and the council first came to public attention in mid-June as a result of a classic act of Depression-era resistance—"an attempt to restore furniture to the home of an evicted worker," as a Communist newspaper, the *Southern Worker*, put it. Such actions bought time for tenants because "restoring" their furniture forced landlords to seek new eviction orders, a process that took days, weeks, or months.

Twice that month, Jack Daniel, 36, an unemployed refinery worker, and his wife and three children, had been evicted from their lodgings on Lagonda Avenue for non-payment of rent. Crowds from the council had restored their furniture, and in an effort to prevent a lockout, Daniel had removed and hidden the four-room home's front door.

On Monday, June 19, the Daniel family was evicted for the third time. Landlord Mary L. Holloman posted four shotgun-wielding guards on the home's front porch. That night, Daniel and a council member stood watch over his family's belongings on a parkway in front of the house, awaiting the arrival of picketers. A crowd, which fluctuated between 20 and 100, gathered outside Tuesday morning, and when it attempted to enter the house, a team of policemen, sheriff 's deputies and constables corralled 29 of its members, including Barlow.

Daniel wasn't arrested because he was house hunting at the time. Perhaps as a result of publicity over the restorations, the welfare department had intervened, offering to subsidize a first month's rent if the family would pick a new home.

Twenty-five of the council prisoners lingered in custody while bail was raised. "Some of us are better off in jail. We are at least getting food and a place to sleep," Barlow told a *Star-Telegram* reporter.

"Personally, I'd rather be on the outside," he added. "There might be another eviction somewhere, and I'd want to be there."

While he and others were still behind bars, somebody torched the vacant Lagonda house. Surprisingly, the affair ended on a less-than-tragic note for its principals; the Daniel family found new lodgings and the Lagonda property had been insured. "If I had imagined that there would be this much trouble, I'd have let that man stay there," Holloman said.

The council returned to public notice on the evening of Thursday, Aug. 31, when it rallied in Bluff Park to protest Gov. Miriam Ferguson's recent suspension of relief for the unemployed. In accord with a decision made at the meeting, Barlow and two companions, H. N. Macomb, 40, a barber, and E. E. Hardy, 27, an electrician, walked to a nearby Western Union office, where they telegrammed Ferguson protesting the cut. As they left the telegraph office, police arrested them on charges of unlawful assembly.

According to newspaper accounts and records of the grand jury inquiry into Barlow's death, any cash that prisoners brought into the city jail was held in the booking room. Once they had been assigned to cells, new inmates were subjected to a "trial" by an inmate-run kangaroo court, which usually "fined" them. At the sham court's stipulation, turnkeys withdrew monies to buy incidental items for the prisoners. The "court" assessed Barlow a 25-cent penalty and its judge, a murder suspect, signed a requisition for the procurement of coffee. When it had not arrived some two hours later, Barlow protested his sentence and demanded that his money be returned.

Charley Morgan, a 19-year-old laborer who, according to the *Star-Telegram*, was an amateur boxer, was the court's apparent bailiff. He threatened the unruly defendant and the two exchanged half a dozen blows. Barlow's eyes were blackened and his face bruised and bloodied. He "didn't seem to be hurt bad. I went into his cell and wiped the blood off his face with my handkerchief," Hardy later told the newspaper.

The following morning, Barlow, Hardy, and Macomb were formally charged after policemen testified that several people at the rally had talked of raiding a food warehouse. The court set bond at $1,500 for Barlow, $500 each for his companions. About noon the three were transferred to the county jail. An officer who oversaw their move later testified that "Barlow appeared perfectly rational when he received his personal effects at the sergeant's desk before the transfer to the county jail."

Charley Morgan, Barlow's assailant, was also discharged that day—to the streets. When officers went to serve him a grand jury summons, he could not be found. Three weeks later, in jail again, this time on an auto theft charge, he said, "As well as I remember, I hit only twice, in the left eye."

The afternoon he was transferred to county jail, Barlow played poker with other inmates, who observed that he seemed dazed and complained of a headache. About 4:30 p.m. the men were locked into their cells for the night. Barlow was quartered alone. Shortly afterward, several inmates heard a thump; seeing that Barlow had fallen from his bunk, they shouted for turnkeys, who summoned Burke Brewster, the jail's physician.

A four-page grand jury report on Barlow's demise was destroyed in a subsequent Tarrant County purge of historical records, and contemporary news accounts do not indicate what occurred between Brewster's arrival and Barlow's transfer to the hospital, perhaps two hours later. After pronouncing him dead, Brewster and two other physicians performed an autopsy.

A press summary of the post-mortem exam stated that Barlow had died of a blood clot resulting from a one-inch fracture of his right temple—an injury, the grand jury speculated, that could have been caused by Morgan's quick fists. The report also advanced the dubious finding that "Barlow's skull was one-sixteenth of an inch thick, which is one-half the thickness of the average white person's skull."

Barlow's followers never accepted the official account of his death.

Suspicious, the Unemployed Council and two of Barlow's brothers—one of whom described himself as a Socialist—paid for a private examination of the body. Afterward, Hardy and other firebrands voiced accusations that were given full play in the *Southern Worker*.

"The left shoulder was bruised with a cut on the upper forearm, the shoulder appearing to have been dislocated or broken. The back of the skull was crushed in. There was a small hole in the center of the forehead, which might have been made with an ice pick or a bullet.

"The left ankle was swollen and bruised as if it had been broken. The insteps and soles of the feet were beaten black. The toes of both feet were welded together in a sold mass of blisters, apparently having been burned with electricity, and or fire. The pores in the skin of the left leg had begun to ooze blood, as if they had been broken or twisted."

The Unemployed Council continued to rally over the weekend of Barlow's death, but on Monday no demonstration was held. Instead, most of the council's members stopped by the funeral home where Barlow's body lay. A reporter for the Star-Telegram who, according to the custom of the day, was not given a byline, wrote a story in a descriptive style that, sadly, is rare in today's press:

"It was Labor Day. A parade swept through the downtown streets as thousands of laborers formed a line of march to celebrate the re-employment of men long without work.

"In a building a few blocks away another long, almost unbroken line filed past a casket. This line, too, was composed principally of laborers.

"In the casket lay the body of a man who had championed the cause of the laborers, who milled about the building where his body reposed. Indirectly he had paid with his life for the work he did in their behalf.

"Attendants at the Shannon's mortuary, where the body is awaiting burial, estimated that well over 1,000 persons passed during the day before the casket. . . .

"Laborers, many of them in patched work clothes, removed frayed hats as they went to stand before Barlow's casket. Women, some carrying babies in their arms, came to pay tribute to the man whom they believed had tried to help them when their children were hungry and in want.

"Among the followers, sympathizers and the curious who came to view the body, there appeared time and again a woman, alone and dressed in white. Joining the line passing before the casket, she left the building only to return at intervals throughout the day and pass again before the body."

During a light rain, about 100 of Barlow's comrades buried him at Mount Olivet cemetery, his casket draped in a red flag with a blue hammer and sickle. Several well-wishers tossed work gloves onto the casket as it was lowered in the ground, and Hy Gordon of Houston, the Texas chairman of the Communist Party, delivered what the *Star-Telegram* called a benediction: "In the name of the party, fight for the creation of a workers government, where all will have plenty."

Mourners raised money to place a red granite tombstone at Barlow's gravesite with the inscription, "Gone But Not Forgotten."

That was true in 1933. Today, nobody knows his name.

Originally published in print in *The Independent* (online known as *Indy Week*), January 22, 2014, this article questions the identification of courts with justice, and deploys a kind of dry understated humor that functions as biting satire.

They Fought the Law

The Moral Monday court hearings are, of course, no pleasure for the accused, but they are also no doubt a headache for judges, bailiffs, court clerks, prosecutors and the like. But justice must be done, even when it resembles watching two seasons of reruns.

Two judges, Joy Hamilton and William Lawton, have been assigned to hear the cases of the 940 demonstrators—I am among them—who were arrested last summer. Considering that number, the judges likely will hear similar testimony and arguments for the rest of the year.

Earlier this month, about a dozen of us Moral Monday defendants who had been arrested on May 13 gathered in the Wake County Courthouse, joined by a half-dozen of the 120 Triangle-area attorneys who have volunteered to defend the demonstrators pro bono.

I was glad to get into the courtroom, not because I expected justice but because it was 11 degrees outdoors, and my ears were burning from the cold. Having to face the possibility of a fine, and maybe a short jail term, didn't bother me, because I am a tenured N.C. State professor and not much was at stake.

We were all slated to face Judge Hamilton, who, fortunately, is not a foreboding figure in a black robe. She's probably in her early 50s, and by her speech she could easily be a public school principal, even a guidance counselor.

All of us were originally charged with three offenses: display of a sign or placard, failure to disperse on command, and second-degree trespass. Saladin Muhammad, a 68-year-old African-American labor organizer from Rocky Mount, had been the first to draw a sentence. In October, Judge Hamilton found him guilty on all three counts. She fined him $100.

But in the intervening weeks, Moral Monday lawyers made shrewd references to Supreme Court cases and North Carolina law, and when our trial opened, the prosecutor, Lawrence Cameron, dismissed the placard and failure-to-disperse charges.

Although Chief Jeff Weaver, the prosecutor, and defense attorneys quickly concurred that nobody has the authority to capriciously oust visitors from the Legislature, Weaver and the sergeants at arms of the House and Senate testified that by singing, chanting and clapping, eight of us—six women and two men—had created an unlawful disturbance.

In prior trials the prosecution had alleged that by blocking doorways Moral Monday protesters had created a disturbance. Those of us arrested May 13 had gathered in front of the golden doors of the Senate at about 6 p.m. But the Senate wasn't in session and wouldn't begin its deliberations for an hour, by which we time we were all in custody.

The House did open at about 6 p.m., though its sergeant at arms had locked its front doors. But he blocked those doors, not us. He testified that House members were forced to enter the chamber by a set of rear entrances. Maybe that did create a disturbance: Is it still true that in North Carolina one doesn't send white men to enter through the back?

Under cross-examination, Weaver and the other order-keepers admitted that during our one-hour presence at the rotunda no member of the House or Senate, nor any employees of the Legislature, had asked police to silence us.

"My routine and my staff were disturbed more than anybody," one of law enforcers said.

The defenders argued that forcing order-keepers to do their jobs is not tantamount to creating an unlawful disturbance.

The case against us came down to simple terms: "This is an unlawful assembly," Chief Weaver had told us. We were supposed to leave.

We didn't.

The prosecution had us on videotape, start to finish. Using a bullhorn, Weaver warned that we had five minutes to comply, announced when we had two minutes to comply, and warned us again right before the arrests began. He paced in front of our group, each time delivering his announcement more than once. What he said wasn't clearly audible, either in real life or on tape, but we certainly noticed that he was addressing us.

When the prosecution rested—seven of the accused—everybody but me, took the stand. I didn't testify because my lawyer, Stewart Fisher of Durham, discouraged the idea, probably because he suspected I would have said something stupid. He was probably right.

But, one after another, the other seven testified. They said that they'd come to be heard, a couple of them, after they'd been rebuffed in prior attempts to contact their legislators. The sincerity of their voices was persuasive: they believed that Republican politicians might take public opposition into consideration. All seven defendants showed faith in the judicial and political system.

Each of them admitted to clapping, chanting, or singing, though the other man, Clayvon Everett, 66, said that he didn't sing very loudly. He voluntarily told the court that he'd been arrested before. "I couldn't believe that I had to march all over again for what I'd marched for as a teenager," he explained. He also testified that he hadn't been able to make out what Chief Weaver was saying. He was standing against the rotunda's wall, behind three or four rows of protesters who didn't go quiet when the bullhorn barked.

The six women who were charged—three white, three black—told the court that they could hear parts of Weaver's warning, "five minutes" or "two minutes" or, in one case, "premises," as in "leave the premises." Leslie Boyd, a woman in from the Asheville area, testified that she had come to protest in memory of her son who had a birth defect and died prematurely because he couldn't find an insurer willing to take him; nor could the family afford expensive tests. Her presentation so overpowered the courtroom that prosecutor Cameron didn't cross-examine her.

The video showed all of the women, and also a shadowy image of Everett, singing, chanting or clapping. I was pictured several times, always in the same posture. My hands were in the front pockets of my jeans; I was not clapping. I was chewing gum, not singing or chanting. I am 68.

I looked like a bemused old man.

My attorney allowed that maybe the video showed me mouthing three words to a song, "be all right." But it was clear, he argued, that I hadn't disturbed anybody.

The prosecution argued that I was "acting in concert" with the group and was therefore guilty of anything it did. That's what I believed, too. But in his summation, Fisher pointed out that the prosecution hadn't shown that I even knew any of the protesters and, in fact, I had met only one of them, nothing more.

Fisher had another card up his sleeve. During a lunch break, he noticed that I was wearing hearing aids. I wear them to teach classes and, now and again, for faculty meetings and funerals. However, I wasn't wearing hearing aids at the demonstration. Fisher argued that the prosecution had not shown that I could have heard, or did hear, Weaver's warnings.

When they closed their cases, all three defense attorneys argued for dismissals that Judge Hamilton refused to grant. I figured that we all were going to be convicted. When they can, all governments persecute their critics. Everybody knows that. Like the others, I believed that I was being tried for demonstrating, not for anything alleged in the charges against us. I felt it my duty to share their verdict—not because of some piety toward or fantasy about the workings of law or the Constitution—but to be faithful to an old adage known to convicts and cops: "Don't do the crime if you can't do the time." I was up for that.

When Hamilton began announcing her verdicts, I was the first to be named. She acquitted me. She also freed Everett, the other old-man defendant. However, she convicted the six women essentially of singing.

Reavis returns to familiar themes in this article: the criminal underworld of the Mexican mafia, aging, the banal cruelty of Texas's criminal justice bureaucracy and institutions, the shortfalls of philanthropy, and the perseverance of the underclasses. These themes emerge as Reavis describes the situation of his subject, Benito Alonso, the little-remembered man who smuggled guns into the Walls Unit in Huntsville, Texas, arming the notorious gangster, Fred Gómez Carrasco. (*Texas Observer,* February 2016)

No Place for Old Men

Benito Alonzo is a short, 140-pound, 80-year-old. His quiet-spoken manner, drooping jowls, and gray hair, trimmed in a buzz, give him the appearance of a benevolent grandfather, and indeed, he is a grandfather. In thick-framed black eyeglasses, he bears a resemblance to the defanged and aging Henry Kissinger. But Alonzo is neither a celebrity nor a statesman. He's a convict who has lately grown infirm.

He says he's been diagnosed with prostate cancer and he's afflicted with Hepatitis C. For several years he's been prescribed a drug called Lactulose, which Dr. Owen Murray, chief of medical affairs for the Texas penal system, says "we use for people whose livers are at the end of their lives." In November, the University of Texas Medical Branch in Galveston told Alonzo's son in a letter that during a recent medical examination it also found "evidence of cirrhosis," an often-fatal ailment.

I talked to Alonzo last December in the waiting room of the Polunsky Unit, near Livingston. That was not the way I wanted to see him: I had wanted to visit his cell, his pod, to observe how he passes his time—to see how he lives. But the Texas Department of Criminal Justice (TDCJ) doesn't allow reporters beyond its visiting rooms, and it forbids taking photographs inside the prisons. For a year I corresponded with Alonzo and a dozen other elderly inmates, querying them about their circumstances. Mail was the only connection we had. When I asked Alonzo, in Spanish, if he thought prison authorities could monitor our conversation in that language, he chuckled and said, "And in Japanese, Arabic or Russian." We conducted the rest of our chat in English.

Alonzo has been waiting since at least last March for the start of a 12-week course of the new liver drug that might keep him alive for years to come. He's been told that the treatment will cost $94,500. Were he back on the streets, Medicare would pick up the tab. But because federal courts have ruled that states must guarantee the safety and health of their inmates, Texas will have to pay. Alonzo frets that because of the expense, prison bureaucrats will stall the treatment until it's too late.

The state of Texas operates 109 prisons holding about 148,000 inmates. Some 27,000 of them are, like Alonzo, over the age of 50. They account for about 18 percent of the prison population, and are the fastest-growing demographic group among prisoners. By most estimates, they are also the most expensive to keep under lock and key. According to TDCJ spokesman Robert Hurst, the average cost of housing a Texas inmate is about $20,000 a year, but medical and end-of-life expenses hike that figure to some $30,000 for elderly inmates. In other jurisdictions the cost is even higher. A 2012 report from the ACLU calculates the average national expense for keeping a prisoner at $34,000 per year—and twice that much, $68,000, for inmates older than 50.

Both demographic factors and get-tough sentencing have transformed what were once mere penal institutions into hospitals, assisted living centers, and nursing homes, too. The University of Texas Medical Branch operates a freestanding hospital in Galveston for TDCJ, which also contracts with UTMB and the Texas Tech medical school to send prisoners to 146 community hospitals. Texas prisons now boast of "respiratory isolation rooms," "brace and limb services," and hospice facilities in which 90 Texas inmates were eased into eternity last year. More than 300 inmates in Texas prisons use wheelchairs, Dr. Murray says.

Alonzo's life has been one of alternating spans of heroin addiction and confinement. He served three separate stints in prison—for theft, burglary, and heroin possession—from 1958 to 1974. After his parole in 1974, allegedly under the influence of two of his brothers, Pedro and Adolfo, he delivered a pair of pistols to a warden's trustee who then smuggled them into Huntsville's Walls Unit. San Antonio gangster Fred Carrasco used those guns in an 11-day, hostage-taking standoff that culminated in a shootout. Alonzo is serving a life sentence for his connection to the incident.

He is not a humorless guy, and when I told him that he is the oldest convict among 5,500 men in "administrative segregation," as TDCJ terms solitary confinement, he seemed amused. Men in solitary are generally allowed a one-hour break each weekday in fenced, bathroom-sized, outdoor courtyards. Alonzo spends his exercise time "walking around in circles—like a psych patient," he says with a grin.

He's been in solitary since 1985 because he is what the prison system terms a "confirmed member" of a "Security Threat Group," in this case, the Mexican Mafia. His calm and good cheer may also be informed by a macho, gangland code. While thousands of convicts say that they are innocent of the charges that brought them to prison, guys like Alonzo don't whine. Doing so would violate the Mafia's code of manliness and spoil his image, which among convicts, is that of a respected elder.

But a younger "ad seg" prisoner, Jason J. Hernandez, a 42-year-old with a string of convictions for theft, sometimes complains on his behalf. Hernandez gripes, for example, that when ad seg prisoners are shackled for trips to medical facilities, their hands are also clapped into handcuffs and into a device known as a "black box." Black boxes make it difficult to raise one's hands and arms. Their purpose is to prevent assaults upon guards or fellow prisoners. But the upshot, Hernandez charges, is that prisoners whose mobility is limited cannot use handrails to get on or off of the "chain" buses that transport them. They must hop or crawl instead, and for elders, hopping poses a danger of falling. Alonzo must sometimes take more than one bus to travel for medical care to Galveston. (A spokesperson for TDCJ said correctional officers assist elderly inmates getting on and off buses.)

In one of the letters that Hernandez wrote me, he relays a story from "a senior," probably Alonzo: "He then told me that on one trip, an overweight man . . . was struggling into the chain bus. . . . His pants began to fall down to his knees. The prisoner asked the chain guards to please help him pull up his pants so that he wouldn't trip, because he'd just underwent surgery on his knees and couldn't bend down. The guards said, 'We're not going to lift his pants up for him.' The prisoner was stuck with his pants down in front of everyone."

Hernandez also says that staff shortages and negligence frequently imperil seniors. Convicts in solitary are moved every two weeks to prevent conspiracies, and Hernandez claims that during one of these cell switches in April he watched as two guards accompanied Alonzo, his hands cuffed tightly behind his back, to a 3-by-6-foot unventilated shower stall, one of a half-dozen located in a row, one tier below Hernandez's cell. The guards' apparent plan was to leave Alonzo there for a few minutes while they made the change. But the cell-switching was prolonged for more than half an hour, and the memory of a notorious incident a decade before sent Alonzo into a panic.

In 2003, an inmate at the McConnell Unit in Beeville died after spending two hours in a shower stall. An autopsy showed that the McConnell prisoner had been soaked in 190-degree waters that literally cooked his internal organs. Alonzo was an inmate at McConnell when that happened. Even though he was still dressed and water wasn't coming from the showerhead, Alonzo says, when the vaporous atmosphere of the shower-stall row made it hard for him to breathe he "started hollering and banging."

Prison spokesman Hurst says that TDCJ records don't show that anything of the kind happened, but according to Hernandez, when nobody rushed to Alonzo's aid he and inmates in neighboring cells began kicking their doors and hollering demands that the old man be taken out of the shower. Perhaps the guards, he says, were called to more pressing duties; the Texas prison system suffers from a shortage of some 3,500 correctional officers, and those on duty can't always promptly attend to matters. Hernandez alleges that by the time they came to his door to quiet the din, "I [had] blanked out and was ready to fight the team with all my might as hard as I could. . . . I tried to push the issue. I began to yell at the guards, 'What's up, bitch? What's up, you fucking pussies!'"

The racket and insults shook the guards to their senses, he says. Realizing that they'd forgotten about Alonzo, they promptly pulled him from the shower—and even apologized. They then moved him, for the next two weeks, into the cell next to Hernandez.

Though neither Hernandez nor Alonzo will say as much, Alonzo may be lucky that he's in solitary confinement. Prisons are stocked with aggressive young men who aren't called "offenders" for nothing. Old and infirm prisoners are generally too mellowed to be aggressive, but all too often, they are also incapable of defending themselves. While solitary has been shown to have deleterious effects on mental health, it does protect the weak from the strong, the prudent from the rowdy, and, presumably, the old from the young.

Years ago, the Texas Department of Corrections, as it was then called, segregated inmates strictly by race and more informally by age, but discrimination along both those lines fell in the wake of prison reforms. Today, TDCJ takes account of the dangers of aging largely by classifying inmates with mobility problems as eligible for assignment only to the lower bunks of its two-bunk cells. But the result, several elderly prisoners at the Michael Unit in East Texas wrote me, is a shortage of lower-level bunks—and some wind up "mis-housed" in solitary confinement.

The State of Texas does have a process for releasing old and infirm prisoners on humanitarian parole, but the record is underwhelming. A bureaucracy dating to 1987, the Texas Correctional Office on Offenders with Medical or Mental Impairments (its clunky acronym: TCOOMMI) was assigned to process medically recommended intensive supervision, or MRIS, paroles. MRIS is a way to move inmates, rendered harmless by their frailty or age, back into the civilian world.

TCOOMMI reports to the Texas Board of Pardons and Paroles on an inmate's health status, leaving the final parole decision to the board. In a February 2015 biennial report, TCOOMMI reported that of the 1,133 MRIS applications that had been submitted in fiscal year 2014, 318 had been found sufficiently meritorious for presentation to the parole board. Of those, the board had granted 67 releases—a mere 6 percent approval rate.

In a 2012 statement, TDCJ admitted that "the Parole Board's approval rates of MRIS cases remain low." But the board's performance hasn't shown signs of improvement. In the 2015 fiscal year, 445 prisoners older than 60 filed for medical paroles—but only 24 paroles were granted, all of them on the basis of infirmity, none on the basis of age. The roadblock is a provision of the law allowing the parole board to conclude that a prisoner constitutes a threat despite what doctors say.

The last years of Johnny R. Martinez, aka Juan Ramirez Martinez, provide a case in point. Martinez, short of stature and a bit chubby, was a small-time Austin hoodlum. He'd done prison time from 1962 to 1965 for aggravated robbery, from 1966 to 1968 for forging a check, and from 1971 to 1986 for possession of heroin. Each sentence had ended with a grant of parole. But in 1993, at the age of 52, he returned to prison after conviction for touching the genitals of two minors, both 11 and the grandchildren of his live-in girlfriend, Phyllis Ketcham. Though testimony from one of the children and secondhand reports from the mothers of both were aired in court, Martinez and Ketcham hotly denied his guilt.

Martinez was a diabetic. Ketcham had complained early in his sentence about the boots TDCJ issued him, saying that he was experiencing neuropathy, a common diabetic discomfort marked by numbness or pain in the soles of the feet. Around 2000, his vision began to fail, as it often does as diabetes advances.

Medical records provided to the *Observer* by Ketcham state that in 2002 he developed diabetic gangrene in his left foot and "was admitted on 07/25 to the hospital and taken to surgery that night for guillotine amputation of the foot." The fix didn't work. "The following Monday, 4 days later," the records state, "he was revised to a below the knee amputation." His medical records also note that by then, he was "legally blind." Later that year, the parole board rejected his first application for MRIS parole. Perhaps a one-legged blind man in a wheelchair can sexually assault children—but what are the odds?

In 2007, prison doctors again recommended Martinez for MRIS parole, again without success. Late that year he was placed on dialysis three days a week for "End State Renal Disease." An examination subsequently turned up cataracts and retinal detachment.

According to the medical records, on December 10, 2010, "when he was told by his fellow inmates that there is a blackened area that has developed over his right heel," Martinez reported for hospitalization again. His medical caretakers found a "foul smelling foot" with "wet and dry gangrene." Three days later, they amputated his right leg below the knee. At the time of discharge, Martinez, then 69, was being administered 16 oral medications and six insulin injections every day. His records show that he needed "total assist" with "dressing, toileting, and hygiene," but they don't indicate how much any of his care cost the state.

His declining health finally led to an MRIS parole—but not until June 2013, when he was taken to a private nursing home in Houston, blind, immobile, and with a new limitation, mental confusion. He died in the nursing facility last September, thoroughly tortured, if not by imprisonment, then by his decade-long medical decline.

Given the statistics on cases like Martinez and the reluctant disposition of the parole board, Benito Alonzo, who is still sighted and still ambulatory, likely wouldn't stand a chance of release under the beneficence of the MRIS program, even if he bothered to apply. He's also eligible for parole of the ordinary kind—and has been for the past 31 years. He's been denied parole 21 times, probably because his crime was notorious. Two women, both prison system employees, were killed along with Carrasco and a co-conspirator. Alonzo's crime was against the people of Texas, according to legal theory, but it's probably more important to his parole history that his was also a crime against TDCJ.

Benito Alonzo would today have a hard time exacting any revenge or harming anybody, and whether he lives or dies is of little concern except to a coterie of kin and perhaps a few in the circles of the . If he dies in prison, as we must currently expect, though he'd prefer to be interred in San Antonio, his corpse will be eligible for a casket and a grave at public expense, in the prison cemetery, of course.

Index

A

B

C

J

L

M

O

P

R

S

T

V

W

DICK J. REAVIS has authored six books, including *The Ashes of Waco: An Investigation* (1995) on the FBI / ATF siege of the Branch Davidians outside of Waco, Texas. Reavis has written hundreds of articles for Texas and national newspapers and magazines, including *The Texas Observer, San Antonio Express-News, Fort Worth Star-Telegram, Dallas Observer, San Antonio Light, Texas Parks & Wildlife, Soldier of Fortune, Salon.com,* and the *Wall Street Journal,* and he is a former staff writer and senior editor at *Texas Monthly.* Over his decades-long career, he has explored such diverse topics as motorcycle gangs, the Southern Civil Rights Movement, guerrillas, convicts, undocumented immigrants, and Mexican coal miners.

MICHAEL DEMSON is an Associate Professor of English at Sam Houston State University whose research explores the intersections of literature and radical political cultures. His recent publications include two collections of essays on Romantic literature, *Romantic Automata: Exhibitions, Figures, Organisms, Commemorating* (2020), and *Peterloo: Violence, Resilience, and Claim-making in the Romantic Era* (2019). He is also interested in popular radical graphic narratives, recently collaborating on an English translation of *Me, Mikko, and Annikki* (2019), a Finnish graphic novel by Tiitu Takalo. His own graphic novel, *Masks of Anarchy: From Percy Shelley to the Triangle Shirtwaist Factory Fire,* illustrated by Summer McClinton, was published in 2013. He has published widely in academic journals.

DICK J. REAVIS has authored six books, including *The Ashes of Waco: An Investigation* (1995) on the FBI / ATF siege of the Branch Davidians outside of Waco, Texas. Reavis has written hundreds of articles for Texas and national newspapers and magazines, including *The Texas Observer, San Antonio Express-News, Fort Worth Star-Telegram, Dallas Observer, San Antonio Light, Texas Parks & Wildlife, Soldier of Fortune, Salon.com,* and the *Wall Street Journal*, and he is a former staff writer and senior editor at *Texas Monthly*. Over his decades-long career, he has explored such diverse topics as motorcycle gangs, the Southern Civil Rights Movement, guerrillas, convicts, undocumented immigrants, and Mexican coal miners.

MICHAEL DEMSON is an Associate Professor of English at Sam Houston State University whose research explores the intersections of literature and radical political cultures. His recent publications include two collections of essays on Romantic literature, *Romantic Automata: Exhibitions, Figures, Organisms, Commemorating* (2020), and *Peterloo: Violence, Resilience, and Claim-making in the Romantic Era* (2019). He is also interested in popular radical graphic narratives, recently collaborating on an English translation of *Me, Mikko, and Annikki* (2019), a Finnish graphic novel by Tiitu Takalo. His own graphic novel, *Masks of Anarchy: From Percy Shelley to the Triangle Shirtwaist Factory Fire*, illustrated by Summer McClinton, was published in 2013. He has published widely in academic journals.

CPSIA information can be obtained
at www.ICGtesting.com
Printed in the USA
LVHW040054160922
728310LV00003B/8

9 781680 032260